THE

ORIGIN OF CIVILISATION

AND THE

PRIMITIVE CONDITION OF MAN

Classics in Anthropology

RODNEY NEEDHAM, editor

John Lubbock

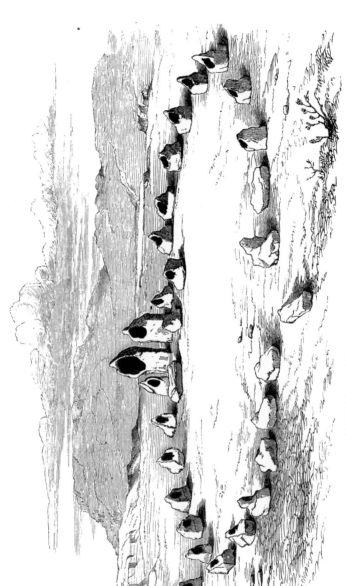

GROUP OF SACRED STONES IN THE DEKHAN.

Frontispiece.

JOHN LUBBOCK

THE

ORIGIN OF CIVILISATION

AND THE

PRIMITIVE CONDITION OF MAN

Edited and with an Introduction by

PETER RIVIÈRE

UNIVERSITY OF CHICAGO PRESS
Chicago and London

PETER RIVIÈRE is university lecturer
in social anthropology
and Fellow of Linare College,
Oxford University.

THE UNIVERSITY OF CHICAGO PRESS, CHICAGO 60637
THE UNIVERSITY OF CHICAGO PRESS, LTD., LONDON

©1978 by The University of Chicago
All rights reserved. Published 1978
Printed in the United States of America

82 81 80 79 78   54321

LIBRARY OF CONGRESS CATALOGING IN PULICATION DATA
Avebury, John Lubbock, Baron, 1834–1913.
The origin of civilisation and the primitive condition of man.
(Classics in anthropology)
Originally published in 1870
Includes bibliographical references and index.
1. Ethnology. 2. Man, Primitive. I. Title.
GN310.A93 1978   301.2   77-77486
ISBN O-226-49637-6

CONTENTS.

CONTENTS.

ILLUSTRATIONS.

DESCRIPTION OF THE PLATES.

DESCRIPTION OF THE FIGURES.

LIST OF THE PRINCIPAL WORKS QUOTED
IN THIS VOLUME.

Adelung. Mithridates.
Arago, Narrative of a Voyage round the World.
Asiatic Researches.
Astley, Collection of Voyages.
Atkinson, Oriental and Western Siberia.

Bachofen, Das Mutterrecht.
Bain, Mental and Moral Science.
Baker, Albert Nyanza.
    „   Nile Tributaries of Abyssinia.
Battel, The strange Adventures of, (Pinkerton's Voyages and Travels).
Beechey, Narrative of a Voyage to the Pacific.
Bosman, Description of Guinea (Pinkerton's Voyages and Travels).
Brett, Indian Tribes of Guiana.
Brooke, Lapland.
Bruce, Travels in Abyssinia.
Burchell, Travels in Southern Africa.
Burton, Lake Regions of Africa.
    „   First Footsteps in Africa.
    „   Abbeokuta and the Cameron Mountains.
    „   City of the Saints.

Caillié, Travels to Timbuctoo.
Callaway, Religious System of the Amazulu.
Campbell, Tales of the West Highlands.
Carver, Travels in North America.
Casalis, The Basutos.
Catlin, North American Indians.

Chapman, Travels in S. Africa.
Charlevoix, History of Paraguay.
Clarke, Travels.
Collins, English Colony in New S. Wales.
Cook, Voyage round the World. (In Hawkesworth's Voyages.)
    „   Second Voyage towards the South Pole.
    „   Third Voyage to the Pacific Ocean.
Cox, Manual of Mythology.
Crantz, History of Greenland.

Darwin, Animals and Plants under Domestication.
    „   Origin of Species.
    „   Researches in Geology and Natural History.
Davis, Dr. J. B., Thesaurus Craniorum.
Davis, The Chinese.
Davy, Account of Ceylon.
De Brosses, Du Culte des Dieux Fétiches.
Denham, Travels in Africa.
Dias, Diccionario da Lingua Tupy.
Dieffenbach, New Zealand.
Dobrizhoffer, History of the Abipones.
Drury, Adventures in Madagascar.
Dubois, Description of the People of India.
Dunn, The Oregon Territory.
Dulaure, Histoire Abregée des differentes Cultes.
D'Urville, Voyage au Pole Sud.
Earle, Residence in New Zealand.

Egede, Greenland.
Ellis, Three Visits to Madagascar.
    Polynesian Researches.
Erman, Travels in Siberia.
Erskine, Western Pacific.
Eyre, Discoveries in Central Australia.

Farrar, Origin of Language.
Fergusson, Tree and Serpent Worship.
Fitzroy, Voyage of the 'Adventure'
    and 'Beagle.'
Forbes Leslie, Early Races of Scotland.
Forster, Observations made during a
    Voyage round the World.
Franklin, Journey to the Shores of the
    Polar Sea.
Fraser, Travels in Koordistan and Me-
    sopotamia.
Freycinet, Voyage autour du Monde.

Gaius, Commentaries on Roman Law.
Gama, Descripcion Historica y Crono-
    logica de las Pedras de Mexico.
Gibbs, H.H., Romance of the Chevelere
    Assigne.
Girad-Teulon, La Mère chez certains
    Peuples de l'Antiquité.
Gladstone, Juventus Mundi.
Goguet, De l'Origine des Lois, des Arts,
    et des Sciences.
Graah, Voyage to Greenland.
Gray, Travels in Western Africa.
Grey, Sir G., Polynesian Mythology.
    ,,   Journal of two Expeditions
    of Discovery in North-West and
    Western Australia.

Hale, Ethnology of the United States
    Exploring Expedition.
Hallam, History of England.
Hanway, Travels in Persia.
Hayes, Open Polar Sea,
Hawkesworth, Voyages of Discovery in
    the Southern Hemisphere.
Hearne, Voyage to the Northern Ocean.
Herodotus.
Hill, Travels in Siberia.
Hooper, Tents of the Tuski.

Humboldt, Personal Researches.
Hunter, Comparative Dictionary of the
    Non-Aryan Languages of India and
    High Asia.
Hume, Essays.
   ,,   History of England.

Inman, Ancient Faiths in Ancient
    Names.

James, Expedition to the Rocky Moun-
    tains.
Journal of the Royal Institution.
Jukes, Voyage of the 'Fly.'

Kames, History of Man.
Kenrick, Phœnicia.
Keppel, Visit to the Indian Archipelago.
   ,,   Expedition to Borneo.
Klemm, Allgemeine Culturgeschichte
    der Menschheit.
   ,,   Werkzeuge und Waffen.
Koelle, Polyglotta Africana.
Kolben, History of the Cape of Good
    Hope.
Kolff, Voyage of the 'Dourga.'
Kotzebue, Voyage round the World.

Labat, Voyage aux Isles de l'Amérique.
Lafitau, Mœurs des Sauvages Améri-
    cains.
Laird, Expedition into the Interior of
    Africa.
Lander (R and J.), Niger Expedition.
Lang, Aborigines of Australia.
Latham, Descriptive Ethnology.
Lecky, History of Rationalism.
Lewin, Hill Tracts of Chittagong.
Lichtenstein, Travels in South Africa.
Lubbock, Prehistoric Times.
Lyon, Journal during the Voyage of
    Captain Parry.

McGillivray, Voyage of the 'Rattle-
    snake.'
M'Lennan, Primitive Marriage.
Maine, Ancient Law.
Marsden, History of Sumatra.

Mariner, Tonga Islands.
Martius, Von dem Rechtszustande unter den Ureinwohnern Brasiliens.
Merolla, Voyage to Congo (Pinkerton's Voyages and Travels).
Metz, Tribes of the Neilgherries.
Metlahkatlah, published by the Church Missionary Society.
Middendorf, Sibirische Reise.
Monboddo, Origin and Progress of Language.
Montesquieu, Esprit des Lois.
Moser, The Caucasus and its People.
Moor, Notices of the Indian Archipelago.
Mouhot, Travels in the Central Parts of Indo-China.
Müller (Max), Chips from a German Workshop.
    ,,   Lectures on Language, First Series.
    ,,   Lectures on Language, Second Series.
Müller (F. G.), Geschichte der Amerikanischen Urreligionen.

Nilsson, On the Stone Age.

Olaus Magnus.

Pallas, Voyages en différentes Provinces de l'Empire de Russie.
    ,,   Voyages entrepris dans les Gouvernements méridionaux de l'Empire.

Park, Travels.
Parkyns, Life in Abyssinia.
Perouse, Voyage autour du Monde.
Pliny, Natural History.
Prescott, History of Peru.
    ,,   History of Mexico.
Prichard, Natural History of Man.
Proceedings of the American Academy of Arts and Sciences.
Proceedings of the Boston Society of Natural History.
Proyart, History of Loango (Pinkerton's Voyages and Travels).

Raffles, History of Java.
Reade, Savage Africa.
Renan, Origin du Language.
Richardson, Journal of a Boat Journey
Robertson, History of America.

Scherzer, Voyage of the 'Novara.'
Schoolcraft, Indian Tribes.
Seemann, A Mission to Fiji.
Smith, A., Theory of Moral Sentiments, and Dissertation on the Origin of Languages.
    ,,   G. (Bishop of Victoria), Ten Weeks in Japan.
    ,,   I. History of Virginia.
    ,,   W., Voyage to Guinea.
Smithsonian Reports.
Snowden and Prall, Grammar of the Mpongwe Language. New York.
Speke, Discovery of the Source of the Nile.
Spiers, Life in Ancient India.
Spix and Martius, Travels in Brazil.
Sproat, Scenes and Studies of Savage Life.
Squiers, Serpent Symbol in America.
Stephens, South Australia.
Stevenson, Travels in South America.
Strahlenberg, Description of Russia, Siberia, and Great Tartary.
Systems of Land Tenure. Published by the Cobden Club.

Tacitus.
Tanner, Narrative of a Captivity among the North American Indians.
Taylor, New Zealand and its Inhabitants.
Tertre, History of the Caribby Islands.
Tindall, Grammar and Dictionary of the Namaqua (Hottentot) Language.
Transactions of the Americ. Antiq. Soc.
Transactions of the Ethnological Society.
Transactions of the R. S. of Victoria.
Tylor, Anahuac.
    ,,   Early History of Man.

Upham, History and Doctrine of Buddhism in Ceylon.

Vancouver, Voyage of Discovery.
Vogt, Lectures on Man.

Waitz, Anthropology.
Wallace, Travels in the Amazons and
   Rio Negro.
    ,,   Malay Archipelago.
Watson and Kaye, The People of
   India.
Wedgwood, Introduction to the Diction-
   ary of the English Language.

Whately (Archbishop of Dublin),
   Political Economy.
Whipple, Report on the Indian Tribes,
Wilkes, United States' Exploring Expe-
   dition.
Williams, Fiji and the Fijians
Wood, Natural History of Man.
Wrangel, Siberia and the Polar Sea.
Wright, Superstitions of England.

Yate, New Zealand.

Erratum.

Page 87, *for* Dulaure, **vol.** i. p 260 *read* vol. ii.

EDITOR'S INTRODUCTION

There must be few anthropologists today who have read Sir John Lubbock's *The Origin of Civilisation and the Primitive Condition of Man*,[1] and there are probably many who have never even heard of it or its author. Thus, in certain ways the appearance of this work in a series entitled Classics in Anthropology raises similar doubts to those expressed by Rodney Needham in his Introduction to Wake's *The Development of Marriage and Kinship*: "It is scarcely problematic whether a book may be described as a classic, meaning by this term a work of generally conceded excellence, when it made no memorable impact at the time of publication, exercised no discernible influence on the subsequent course of the discipline to which it was intended to contribute, and is now, seventy-seven years after its appearance, almost totally unknown."[2]

However, Needham was able to argue that Wake's work was neglected by his contemporaries because it was so far in advance of its time and anticipated ideas that were only to become common among social anthropologists many decades later.[3] On these grounds it was rightly claimed that Wake

1. London: Longmans, Green, and Co., 1870. Unless otherwise stated, citations to *Origin of Civilisation* given in parentheses in the text of this Introduction are to the present edition, which reproduces the original edition.

2. C. S. Wake, *The Development of Marriage and Kinship*, ed. R. Needham (Chicago: University of Chicago Press, 1967), p. v.

3. For an alternative view see Gay Weber, "Science and Society in Nineteenth-Century Anthropology," *History of Science* 12 (1974): 278.

and his work should be revived. With the present volume
the situation is rather different. It is true that one hundred
and eight years after its first appearance *The Origin of
Civilisation* is generally unknown and unread. Those ignorant
of it might defend their neglect of it on the grounds that its
contents are so hopelessly wrong that there can be no
justification in drawing a student's attention to them.[4] It
can also be argued that Lubbock failed to make any positive
or lasting contribution to the development of scientific
anthropology.[5]

On the other hand, Lubbock, unlike Wake, was a figure of
national, even international prominence. His was a household
name, for he was not simply an anthropologist but also a
natural scientist, politician, financier, and social reformer.
He was respected by his contemporaries in most fields of
life. Above all he was an extremely successful author. His
anthropological books, unlike those of Wake, sold as well as
any such books published in the last century. The second
edition of *The Origin of Civilisation* appeared in the same
year as the first (1870), and a steady demand for the book
resulted in five further revised editions, the seventh in 1912,
forty-two years after the first.[6] A similar story can be told of
Lubbock's other major anthropological work, *Prehistoric*

4. There are no good reasons in the history of ideas for ignoring ideas
just because they are wrong.

5. In lighthearted conversation George Stocking once suggested that
the development of anthropological thought could be seen as a prolonged
refutation of Lubbock's ideas; in other words, his contribution was, in a
sense, positive. It will be argued below that insofar as Lubbock was a
man of his time, Stocking's remark holds a grain of truth.

6. In *Nature* 90 (23 January 1913): 565–67, a reviewer of the seventh
edition commented unfavorably on Lubbock's failure to bring his work
up to date and noted the absence of any reference to Frazer, Wester-
marck, Crawley, or Hartland. However, he did write: "Lord Avebury's
work on primitive civilisation, first issued in 1870, now ranks as an
anthropological classic."

Times,[7] of which the first edition appeared in 1865 and the seventh in 1913. The important thing about Lubbock and his works is not their impact on scientific anthropology and its practitioners (past or present), but their enormous popularity with the wider reading public and the influence which, we must assume, his notions had on its anthropological ideas. For this reason alone, setting aside the eminence he had in his time, Lubbock's *The Origin of Civilisation* deserves a new edition and a close scrutiny.

Lubbock's ability to popularize, to express in straight forward and simple language the scientific problems of his time, is not in doubt. His contemporaries recognized this quality. Tylor wrote in a review of the second edition of *Prehistoric Times:* "On the present subject of prehistoric archaeology, . . . it is satisfactory that we have, in Sir John Lubbock's work, not only a good book of reference, but the best."[8] Of the first edition of this same work, another reviewer wrote: "It is a well written and well arranged work, characterised by parity of language and by its singular clearness and perspicuity."[9] With reference to *The Origin of Civilisation*, a reviewer commented that "the genius and indefatigable researches of Sir J. Lubbock have done more than, perhaps, any other man has accomplished to extend and to popularize the knowledge of primitive ethnology."[10]

7. *Prehistoric Times as Illustrated by Ancient Remains and the Manners and Customs of Modern Savages* (London & Edinburgh: Williams & Norgate, 1865).

8. E. B. Tylor, review of *Prehistoric Times* in *Nature* 1 (25 November 1869): 103–5.

9. Thomas Wright, "On the True Assignation of the Bronze Weapons, etc., Supposed to Indicate a Bronze Age in Western and Northern Europe," *Transactions of the Ethnological Society of London*, n.s., 4 (1866): 177.

10. H. B. T. [H. B. Tristram], *Contemporary Review* 15 (August–November 1870): 311–13.

Throughout this Introduction the names of the authors of unsigned or

Other reviewers referred to the work as "exceedingly readable"[11] and as "a comprehensive and able treatise";[12] they commented that his investigations were "extremely valuable" and that "even when they do no more than confirm the results of previous writers, [they] supply an exuberant amount of illustration of every degree of interest and novelty."[13]

It was this aspect of his work that the obituary writers also noticed. In *The Times* he was described as a great popularizer,[14] and in *Nature* it was said of him that he was "one of those gifted men who, without making any very profound advance in science, yet succeeded in making science acceptable and even welcome to the ordinary man. . . . Even his most strictly scientific monographs were written in an engaging manner, and none more so than his 'Origin of Civilisation.' "[15] In the *Dictionary of National Biography* it is reported of him that "as an expositor of science and an intellectual and moral mentor to the general public he had a vogue that is almost without parallel in modern times."

There was thus a general agreement on Lubbock's ability as a popularizer, and if any further evidence is needed, the present volume bears adequate witness. Yet, perhaps his greatest feat of popularization was to introduce and make generally known the division of prehistoric times into the four great ages of the Palaeolithic, Neolithic, Bronze, and Iron Ages.[16] However, there is a difference between accepting the

---

initialled publications have, wherever possible, been obtained from *The Wellesley Index to Victorian Periodicals, 1824–1900*, vols. 1 and 2.

11. S. Evans, *Nature* 3 (9 March 1871): 362–65.

12. *Athenaeum*, no. 2231 (30 July 1870), pp. 135–36.

13. *Westminster Review*, n.s., 38 (October 1870): 497–98.

14. *The Times*, 29 May 1913, pp. 9–10.

15. *Nature* 91 (5 June 1913): 350–51.

16. See Glyn E. Daniel, *A Hundred Years of Archaeology* (Duckworth: London, 1950), p. 79. Although Sir Arthur Keith ("Centenary of the Birth of Lord Avebury," *Man* 34 [1934]: 50) implies that the division

fact that Lubbock was a highly successful popularizer and explaining this success. The explanation must be sought at a number of different levels, but some reasons can be dealt with immediately and more summarily than others.

First, as we have just noted, Lubbock wrote in clear, concise, and readable English. Second, he was not above titillating his readers with shocking disclosures that he can hardly bring himself to reveal but which, he avers, his readers ought to know. Thus: "I have been careful to quote only from trustworthy authorities, but there are many things stated by them which I have not ventured to repeat; and there are other facts which even the travellers themselves were ashamed to publish."[17] And again: "From the very nature of the subjects dealt with in the present volume, I shall have to record many actions and ideas very abhorrent to us; so many in fact that if I pass them without comment or condemnation, it is because I am reluctant to fatigue the reader by wearisome iteration of disapproval. . . . Though I have endeavoured to avoid everything that was needlessly offensive, still it was impossible not to mention some facts which are very repugnant to our feelings."[18]

---

of the Stone Age into two periods was Lubbock's idea, Daniel points out that French archaeologists had already recognised two stone age periods, the *période de la pierre taillée* and the *période de la pierre polie*. Lubbock did no more than aptly christen and popularise ideas that were already current. Although it is a point that will be taken up again in sec. VIII, it is worth noting here that Sir Arthur Keith is one of the few people who claimed that Lubbock was more than a popularizer.

In passing it is also worth commenting on the fact that Lubbock declined ever to accept the existence of a Mesolithic period. While this position puts him in line with certain modern archaeological thinking in which the existence of a distinct Mesolithic period appears as an obstruction to the proper understanding of the development of lithic artifacts, it also reflects Lubbock's unwillingness to modify any of his ideas. This matter is also discussed in sec. VIII.

17. *Prehistoric Times*, p. 472.

18. *Origin of Civilisation*, pp. v–vi.

Third, Lubbock dealt, in an authoritative tone, with subjects that were central to some of the main social, religious,
and scientific issues of the day. These three factors, while
clearly important, do not by themselves explain Lubbock's
success. It is necessary to examine his works in greater detail
in order to show just what it was that he had to say and to
reveal the manner in which he said it that proved so acceptable to the general public. Before turning to this exercise,
there will be certain advantages in presenting a biographical
sketch of Sir John.

II

Unlike the case of some authors of the period, notably Wake
and to some extent McLennan,[19] whose works have been published in the present series, there is almost an excess of
material on Lubbock's life. The standard biography, Hutchinson's *Life of Sir John Lubbock, Lord Avebury*,[20] runs to over
600 pages in two volumes, and this work barely touches on
his anthropological interests and activities. For a life as full
as Lubbock's, no simple outline is possible, although space
forbids more; accordingly the following brief biographical
sketch is intended to give little more than a general idea of
the enormous range of his political, business, scientific, and

19. J. F. McLennan, *Primitive Marriage*, ed. Peter Rivière (1865;
University of Chicago Press, 1970). For an account of the difficulties experienced in tracing even the minimum amount of biographical information about C. S. Wake, see Rodney Needham, "Charles Staniland Wake,
1835–1910: A Biographical Record," in *Essays to the Memory of Professor
Sir Edward Evans-Pritchard*, ed. J. Beattie and R. G. Lienhardt (Oxford,
1975), pp. 354–87.

20. Horace G. Hutchinson, *Life of Sir John Lubbock, Lord Avebury*,
2 vols. (Macmillan & Co.: London, 1914). Unless otherwise stated the
biographic information contained in this section is drawn from Hutchinson's work. The essential primary sources on Lubbock's life are the
Avebury Papers in the British Museum, his diaries and other material
in the possession of his family, and papers at the Royal Society.

other concerns, and to indicate some of the events in his life that are important to our present purpose."[21]

John Lubbock was born on April 30, 1834, the eldest son of Sir John William Lubbock, the third Baronet, who had some fame as a scientist and astronomer. Lubbock's formal education was relatively brief and ceased when, at the age of 14, he left Eton to enter the family banking business in the City of London. His lack of formal education in no way hindered his meteoric scientific career, although it might be blamed for a certain naiveté and shallowness in some of his arguments.[22] There seems little doubt that the really important event in Lubbock's formative years was the chance that brought Charles Darwin to live at Down in Kent, near the Lubbock family house. Lubbock and Darwin formed a close friendship, and even if he was not exactly "nurtured in the cradle of Evolution," as Sir Arthur Keith was later to write,[23] Lubbock was very much present during the stormy infancy of biological evolutionism.[24]

21. "He was a banker, statesman, social reformer, economist, sociologist, antiquarian, folk-lorist, anthropologist, geologist, psychologist, educationist, zoologist, entomologist, botanist, statistician, numismatist and naturalist" (Keith, "Centenary of the Birth of Lord Avebury," p. 49).

22. For example, his discussion of the origin of morals in chapter 7, *Origin of Civilisation*, where he fails to refer to any of the traditional philosophical debates on this topic.

23. Sir Arthur Keith, "Anthropology," in *The Life-Work of Lord Avebury*, ed. Adrian Grant Duff (Watts & Co.: London, 1924), chapter 4, p. 68.

24. "The theory of evolution had so few adherents that Huxley wrote: 'I do not call to mind among the biologists more than Asa Gray, who fought the battle so splendidly in the United States, Hooker who was no less vigorous here, Sir John Lubbock, and myself. Wallace was far away in the Malay Archipelago'" (Grant Duff, *Life-Work of Lord Avebury*, p. 17 n.).

Lubbock was (of course!) present at the famous meeting between Huxley and Bishop Wilberforce in Oxford at the 1860 meetings of the British Association.

Under Darwin's guidance Lubbock's first original scientific work was published when he was nineteen. By then he had already been a member of the Royal Institution for four years, and a year later, in 1855, he was elected to the Geological Society with none other than Charles Lyell as his sponsor. Three years after that, at the astonishingly young age of twenty-three, he was elected a Fellow of the Royal Society.[25] By this time he was acquainted with virtually all the leading figures in British scientific and intellectual life: Darwin, Lyell, Huxley, Hooker, Wallace, Kingsley, Prestwich, Evans, Bush, Tyndall, Galton, Spencer, and Tylor.[26] From then on Lubbock knew virtually everyone and went everywhere, and his voluminous correspondence in the British Museum reveals that he was at some time or another in contact with almost every well-known scientific figure of the age.

His scientific interests did not distract him from his business. In 1856 he invented a system to improve the handling of checks drawn on country banks, and in 1863 he was appointed Secretary to the London Bankers. In this same year he first became president of the Ethnological Society of London and had the first indication of his future involvement in politics by receiving an invitation, declined probably on his father's insistence, to stand as the Liberal parliamentary candidate for the City of London. The year 1865 was a particularly busy one for Lubbock. His father died and he succeeded to the title; he was elected to the senate of London University; he stood as Liberal parliamentary candidate for the constituency of West Kent (with J. S. Mill as a member of his elec-

25. As John Burrow puts it: "Lubbock was born, as it were, with an F.R.S. in his mouth" (*Evolution and Society* [Cambridge University Press, 1970], p. 228).

26. "It was during this time that I made the acquaintance of . . . Sir John Lubbock . . . who . . . had attracted the friendship of most of the men of the day who were destined to become famous in science" (Francis Galton, *Memories of my Life* [Methuen & Co.: London, 1908], p. 177).

tion committee) but lost; and *Prehistoric Times* was published. A direct relation between these last two events was later claimed, for it was said that "The majority against him ... was larger than it would otherwise have been in consequence of the opinions on the Antiquity of Man expressed in his *Prehistoric Times*."[27]

In 1868 he sat on the Royal Commission on monetary reform, was appointed a public school commissioner, and stood for and lost West Kent once again. In 1869 he was elected the first president of the Metaphysical Society, and 1870 saw the publication of *The Origin of Civilisation*, his appointment to the Royal Commission of scientific education, and his election as the Liberal member of Parliament for Maidstone, a seat which he was to hold until 1880. The following year, 1871, he became the first president of the Anthropological Institute, the body that was formed from the amalgamation of the Ethnological Society and the Anthropological Society.[28] In this same year he introduced and passed through Parliament

27. Hutchinson (*Life of Sir John Lubbock*, 1: 74). This provides an interesting parallel with the experience of McLennan, who is said to have lost half his briefs consequent upon the appearance of *Primitive Marriage*, also in 1865 (see McLennan, *Primitive Marriage*, p. xi).

28. For an excellent account of the background and circumstances of the formation of the Anthropological Institute see George Stocking, "What's in a Name? The Origins of the Royal Anthropological Institute," *Man* 7 (1971): 369–90.

That Sir John was asked to be the first president of the reunified Institute was, perhaps, not simply the result of Huxley's being unacceptable to the anthropologists. Lubbock appears to have been an extremely diplomatic individual. His daughter, Mrs. Adrian Grant Duff, wrote of him that he was "often chosen by his friends or colleagues to deal with a recalcitrant member, or one whose manners had caused offence, and he was usually successful, for he would say: 'You are always so nice to me that, if only you would treat so-and-so in the same way, I am sure that all would go well' " (*Life-Work of Lord Avebury*, p. 19).

This view of Lubbock is supported both by Sir Arthur Keith ("Centenary of the Birth of Lord Avebury," p. 50) and Sir C. Hercules Read ("Obituary of Lord Avebury," *Man* 13 [1913]: 97–98).

the Bank Holiday Act, which allowed an additional public holiday on the first Monday in August.[29] From 1872 to 1880 he was vice-chancellor of London University, and during this period he became a trustee of the British Museum (1878) and president of the Institute of Bankers (1879). He received honorary degrees from Oxford (1875), Dublin (1879), and Cambridge (1883). He was made president of the British Association for 1881, the year of the association's fiftieth anniversary.[30]

In the 1880 parliamentary elections Sir John lost his seat at Maidstone, but he was immediately invited to stand as the Liberal candidate for London University. This seat he won and held until 1900, when he received his peerage and went "upstairs." As a parliamentarian he was much concerned with acts to protect ancient monuments and regulate working hours, getting a bill through Parliament to limit the working week to 74 hours. He was keen on parliamentary reform and played an active role in the Proportional Representation Society. In 1889 he was elected to the newly formed London County Council, and the year after became its chairman. He delivered the first Huxley Memorial Lecture in 1900,[31] and the same year was created Lord Avebury, a title that reflected not simply his academic interest in prehistoric times but his practical efforts to preserve their remains.[32]

Sir John's period of greatest political involvement, approximately 1870–1900, saw a relative waning of his archaeological

29. August Bank Holiday now falls on the last Monday in August. For a while this holiday was jocularly known as St. Lubbock's Day.

30. His presidential address on the occasion of the Association's anniversary meeting was published as *Fifty Years of Science, Being the Address Delivered at York to the British Association, August 1881* (Macmillan & Co.: London, 1882).

31. "Huxley's Life and Work," in *Essays and Addresses 1900–1903* (Macmillan & Co.: London, 1903).

32. In the case of Avebury Ring, through buying the land on which the monument stands.

and anthropological interests, but a flowering of his other scientific concerns. This is evidenced by a series of publications including *The Origin and Metamorphosis of Insects* (1873), *British Wild Flowers Considered in Relation to Insects* (1875), *Ants, Bees and Wasps* (1882),[33] *Flowers, Fruits and Leaves* (1886), and *Contribution to our Knowledge of Seedlings* (1892). These works, for the most part and unlike his anthropological writings, involved original research of the most time-consuming sort. Even so this did not diminish his interests in other causes, such as the "deserving working classes," and from lectures to workingmen's clubs he produced a booklet on his one hundred best books.[34] He also published three short collections of essays, *The Pleasures of Life*, part 1 (1887) and part 2 (1889), and *The Use of Life* (1894). These volumes had the most enormous success, selling together more than half-a-million copies and being translated into forty languages, including Arabic, Hindi, Marathi, Gujerati, and Japanese.[35] These works are of some interest to us since they clearly indicate how divorced Sir John was from the everyday life and circumstances of the majority of his countrymen. The topics he chose included the duty of happiness, the happiness of duty, the pleasures of travel, the pleasures of home, ambition,

33. On August 19, 1882, there appeared in *Punch* (p. 82) a cartoon of Sir John Lubbock, in which he is represented as a bee surrounded by flowers. The caption reads:
> How doth the Banking Busy Bee
> Improve his shining Hours
> By studying on Bank Holidays
> Strange Insects and Wild Flowers!

34. *The 100 Best Books in the World of Literature, as Selected by Sir John Lubbock* (London: Harmsworth Brothers, 1899). All the books were available as a set. With cloth binding, the set cost £9; with half Persian Morocco, £12; and with full Morocco, £18. The Queen had a set in half Morocco. Easy terms, that is, hire purchase, were available.

35. His biographer lamented, "It is regretted that Lord Avebury is better known from *The Pleasures of Life* than *Prehistoric Times* or *The Origin of Civilisation*" (Hutchinson, *Life of Sir John Lubbock*, 1: 239).

wealth, the beauties of nature, labour and rest, and many similar subjects, To the modern reader, Sir John's views are sanctimonious, pompous, and patronising in the extreme, and exhibit almost every prejudice and ignorance of a liberal-minded but securely privileged Victorian.[36]

After the receipt of his peerage, Lord Avebury continued to be as busy as ever. During the last decade of his life he had a renewed interest in anthropology and archaeology. As well as bringing out new editions of both his earlier works, *Prehistoric Times* and *The Origin of Civilisation*, he prepared a new volume, *On Marriage, Totemism and Religion: An Answer to Critics*.[37] In 1908, at the age of nearly 75, he was elected president of the Society of Antiquaries and delivered a presidential address.[38] On February 22, 1913, still a trustee of the British Museum, he went to see the newly discovered Piltdown remains and recorded in his diary: "I was able to go to the British Museum. We had the wonderful Sussex skull exhibited—the most Simian of any yet found."[39] Just over two months later, on May 28, 1913, he died in his eightieth year.

This brief summary of his activities ignores his extensive programs of public lectures, his attendance at innumerable

36. A satirical rejoinder was made by Frank Govett in a similar sort of volume entitled *The Pains of Life* (London: Swan Sonnenschein, 1889). Govett wrote essays on the same topics as Lubbock, but from an opposing point of view. He complained that "The active sense of dissatisfaction, effecting all progress, is retarded . . . by such works as 'The Pleasures of Life,' by Sir John Lubbock, which seeks to induce a contentment with the *status quo* by the enumeration of advantages, wrongly estimated, or beyond the reach of the vast majority of mankind" (p. 173). He rightly points out that the great majority of Lubbock's fellow countrymen do not have their own homes and are never able to travel for pleasure or to view the beauties of nature.

37. Longmans, Green and Co.: London, 1911.

38. *Address of Lord Avebury, P.C., F.R.S., President of the Society of Antiquaries of London, Delivered at the Anniversary Meeting, April 30, 1908* (London: Society of Antiquaries, 1908).

39. Quoted by Hutchinson, *Life of Sir John Lubbock*, 2:316.

conferences, his involvements in various charitable organizations, his journeys abroad to visit museums and archaeological sites and excavations, and his tours in Great Britain and Europe, which resulted in a number of works in which he attempted to relate the scenery to the underlying geological formations.[40] It would take up too much space to list the honors, commercial, political, and academic, that he received, or to give the names of all the societies to which he belonged or was elected, and for many of which he at sometime acted as an officer. Nor has anything been said in this briefest of biographical sketches about his intense family life. In the end the truly remarkable thing about Lubbock was his apparently boundless energy, and it is difficult to see how he found time for half the things he did. In an age of energetic men, it would appear that even his contemporaries were impressed by his energy, and Lord Roseberry wrote to him: "not content with presiding over all London wholesale, and half London in detail [this was the period when Lubbock was M.P. for London University and chairman of the L.C.C.], you have written (I suppose with your unoccupied toes) two articles . . . this month."[41] Lubbock's daughter claimed that he never allowed a minute to be wasted; he wore elastic-sided boots, on the ground that a language could be learnt in a lifetime of lacing up shoes, and he corrected proofs at the theater during the intermissions.[42]

What were Lubbock's own ambitions? According to Dar-

40. For example, *The Scenery of Switzerland and the Causes to Which It Is Due* (London: Macmillan & Co., 1896); and *The Scenery of England and the Causes to Which It Is Due* (London: Macmillan & Co., 1902). Although it is not necessarily an indicator of the volume's merit, the copy of *The Scenery of Switzerland* held by the Radcliffe Science Library in Oxford still had its pages unopened when examined in 1976. It was left in its undisturbed state.

41. Quoted by Sir Bernard Mallet, in Grant Duff, *Life-Work of Lord Avebury*, p. 58.

42. Grant Duff, *Life-Work of Lord Avebury*, p. 23.

win, Lubbock had told him that he wanted to be president
of the Royal Society, Lord Mayor of London, and the Chan-
cellor of the Exchequer, to which Darwin remarked that he
could have been any one of them if he had given up the other
two.[43] While we need not take this anecdote at face value, it
does underline the range of Lubbock's interests, and it raises
the question of Lubbock's competence in his different fields of
endeavor and the quality of what he did. Apparently critics
said of him that "bankers considered him a great scientist and
men of science a great banker,"[44] but his obituary writer in
The Times more fairly remarked that "his personality enabled
him to achieve a larger measure of success in a greater range
of labours than has been attained by most of those who have
devoted themselves to the class of work he made his own."[45]
There seems no reason to doubt that he was a competent
businessman and a conscientious member of Parliament who
had a genuine desire for social reform and the improvement of
the laboring classes. As a scientist his position is more am-
biguous. He might well be regarded as one of the first great
academic entrepreneurs, and this aspect of his career is reflected in the words of an obituary writer who stated that
"without being a great researcher, Lord Avebury took a very
prominent part in encouraging the research of others."[46] The
same writer singled out *The Origin of Civilisation* as Lubbock's most stimulating work, and it is probably true to say
that despite his numerous contributions to botany, entomol-
ogy, and biology (the value of which we must leave for others
better qualified to assess, although we may note that his
works on these subjects appear to have been no less popular

43. Mallet, in Grant Duff, *Life-Work of Lord Avebury*, p. 63.
44. Hutchinson, *Life of Sir John Lubbock*, 1:xii.
45. Obituary, *The Times*, 29 May 1913, pp. 9–10.
46. Obituary, *Proceedings of the Royal Society*, series B 87 (1913–14):
i–iii.

than his anthropological writings; for example, *Ants, Bees and Wasps* went into eighteen printings, the most recent appearing in 1929), it is for his archaeological and anthropological work that those who know him best remember him. It is to the more detailed consideration of Lubbock as anthropologist that we must now turn.

III

Lubbock came to anthropology through archaeology, a subject which, through its close ties with geology and paleontology, was intimately associated with the whole disputatious question of evolution and specifically with the age of the world and the antiquity of man. It had been in geology that the first battles had been fought. On one side in this argument were the "catastrophic diluvialists," who accepted Ussher's date of 4004 B.C. for the creation of the world and who maintained that observable geological formations were the result of one or more catastrophic events of which Noah's flood was the most recent. On the other side were the "fluvialists," who claimed that ancient rocks and geological formations were the result of the same processes as were currently observable. For example, Charles Lyell in *The Principles of Geology* (1830) had argued that geological strata could only be interpreted correctly by assuming that the agencies that had formed them had proceeded in a uniform way and at a uniform rate to similar, observable present-day agencies. It need hardly be said that this position, which became known as "uniformitarianism," had considerable implications for the age of the world. The success of the uniformitarians by the mid-century (at least, among many scientific thinkers) had demolished Ussher's time scale and had created a chronological depth in which both biological evolution and the great antiquity of man became possibilities. Furthermore the acceptance of

uniformitarianism was an essential prerequisite for the development of a scientific archaeology based on stratigraphy.
The human remains and artifacts found buried beneath deep,
undisturbed deposits must have been there at least as long as
the deposits, and their presence in conjunction with the remains of extinct animals could only mean that the humans
and the animals had once coexisted. While this may seem very
obvious to us, there was great resistance to the concept, since
its acceptance required from many a fundamental reappraisal
of their conventional world view and of the biblical authority
on which it was based. Besides, it was not simply a matter of
accepting a greater antiquity for man, but of recognising that
their European forefathers had lived in a savage condition not
greatly unlike that observable in contemporary Africa,
America, and Australia. By the late 1850s, however, the evidence from numerous excavations had become overwhelming,
and many who had previously doubted became converted.

Lubbock was right at the center of all this during the 1850s.
We have noted in the last section his early friendship with
those who were directly responsible for the scientific advances
made at the time, and in particular with those involved in
archaeological excavations. In 1854 he made his first trip to
France to inspect archaeological sites, and in the following
year, at the age of 21, he himself excavated from the Thames
gravel at Taplow the skull of a musk ox, for which he was
much praised by Lyell, Darwin, and others.

His early articles, some of which were later to form chapters of *Prehistoric Times*, were purely archaeological in
nature. These are mainly popularizations, and effective ones,
of recent archaeological work and deal with such topics as
Danish shell-mounds, Swiss lake-dwellings, cavemen, and
North American archaeology. However, it is the first three
chapters of *Prehistoric Times* by which Lubbock left his mark
on archaeology. It is in these chapters, dealing with the bronze

and stone ages, that Lubbock introduced to the British public
the division of the prehistorical world into the four great ages:
palaeolithic, neolithic, bronze, and iron.

In passing, two further chapters from *Prehistoric Times*,
those entitled "The Antiquity of Man" and which originally
had formed the basis of lectures at the British Institution, are
worthy of mention. They constitute a masterpiece of popularization on a difficult and controversial subject that was not
simply of scientific but also of moral, emotional, and cosmo-
logical significance. Lubbock presents the geological, archaeological, and paleontological evidence for man's great antiquity with conciseness, clarity, and authority. We have already referred to the view that Lubbock lost the 1865 election
because of his statements about the antiquity of man in *Prehistoric Times*. At the same time Bagehot wrote to Lubbock
saying that it would be a long time before the ideas contained
in that work were accepted.[47] But on this, Bagehot was
wrong, and one wonders to what degree Lubbock's own writings were responsible for breaking down the opposition to the
ideas contained therein.

The archaeological information that Lubbock retailed was
not simply basically correct for its time, but in a very general
way was to provide a framework of knowledge that, although
it has undergone much detailed modification, still holds good
today. The concepts of stratigraphical formation, uniform
processes, and evolution are part of both our scientific and
conventional wisdom, and Lubbock must be hailed as one of
their first and most influential disseminators.

However, from our immediate point of view, *Prehistoric
Times* has another importance, since it marks Lubbock's
move to more anthropological concerns.[48] Three chapters of

47. Hutchinson, *Life of Sir John Lubbock*, 1: 89–90.
48. This does not mean that his interest in archaeological matters
waned; it did not. His activities in the field during the following few

Prehistoric Times are devoted to "modern savages," and it
was out of these chapters that his *Origin of Civilisation* grew,
although as a contemporary reviewer remarked, the latter is
a "substantially new book."[49] Accordingly the examination of
Lubbock's anthropological ideas will include those contained
in *Prehistoric Times* as well as *The Origin of Civilisation*. Indeed it might be difficult to do otherwise, since some ideas
implicit in *The Origin of Civilisation* are more clearly expressed in *Prehistoric Times*.

The easiest and best way to approach Lubbock's anthropological work is through the reasons he gives for it and the
conclusions he draws from it. On these points he is himself
quite explicit.

IV

The opening words of *The Origin of Civilisation* are

> The study of the lower races of men, apart from the direct im-
> portance which it possesses in an empire like ours, is of great
> interest from three points of view. In the first place, the condition
> and habits of existing savages resemble in many ways, though not
> in all, those of our own ancestors in a period now long gone by; in
> the second, they illustrate much of what is passing among ourselves,
> many customs which have evidently no relation to present circum-
> stances, and even some ideas which are rooted in our minds, as

years included, for example: "On Mr. Bateman's Researches in Ancient
British Tumuli," *Transactions of the Ethnological Society of London*
(*Trans. E.S.L.*), n.s., 3 (1865): 307–21; "On the True Assignation of the
Bronze Weapons, etc., Found in Northern and Western Europe," *Trans.
E.S.L.*, n.s., 5 (1867): 105–14; "On the Flint Implements Recently Dis-
covered at Pressigny-le-Grand," *Trans. E.S.L.*, n.s., 5 (1867): 221–27
(with Japetus Steenstrup).

He also edited a translation (he was not the translator, as Glyn Daniel
states in *A Hundred Years of Archaeology*, p. 42) of Sven Nilsson's *The
Primitive Inhabitants of Scandinavia* (London: Longmans, Green & Co.,
1868). He was president at the third session of the International Congress of Prehistoric Archaeologists at Norwich in 1868.

49. George Rolleston, *Academy* 11 (22 October 1870): 11.

fossils are imbedded in the soil; and thirdly, we can even, by means of them penetrate some of that mist which separates the present from the future.

Leaving aside for the moment Lubbock's allusion to the role of anthropology in the empire, the other three reasons for studying savages can best be understood when they are taken in conjunction with the conclusions to which they lead. The conclusions are

> That existing savages are not the descendants of civilised ancestors.
> That the primitive condition of man was one of utter barbarism.
> That from this condition several races have independently raised themselves. [P. 323]

These conclusions make it clear that the reason for studying savage races is to provide further ammunition for the evolutionists in their heated dispute with the degenerationists. The former, with whom Lubbock sided, argued that the history of man was one of steady improvement, while the latter claimed that past and present savage tribes were examples of disgraced peoples who had fallen from God's favor.[50] That *The*

50. There is not space in this short Introduction to examine the argument that raged round this topic into the 1870s. However, some idea of it can be obtained from the following excerpts from an interchange concerning *The Origin of Civilisation*.

An anonymous reviewer (*Christian Advocate and Review* 4 [1870]: 922–33), taking a strong pro-Scripture and degenerationist position, dismisses Lubbock's extended time scale for lack of any proof and takes grave exception to any suggestion of an ape ancestry for man: "He [Lubbock] concludes that the first being 'worthy to be called a man, was in advance of the condition of some animal progenitor.' As this evidently tends to the ancestral ape notion of Lord Monboddo, in the last century, or the gorilla speculation of Professor Huxley, in the present day, we may at once dismiss it as . . . requiring no pains to refute." The reviewer in his turn concludes that "should science ever enable us to determine with more certainty than at present the duration of the four ages of drift, stone, bronze, and iron, we may be quite sure that the supremacy of the Bible will not one whit be shaken thereby."

Another reviewer, Sebastian Evans (*Nature* 3 [1871]: 362–65), lays

Origin of Civilisation is a contribution to this argument is clear enough, but if any more proof were required, it is abundantly provided by the appendix to the volume. This, the substance of papers presented by Lubbock before the British Association at Dundee in 1867 and Exeter in 1869, is a direct reply to the two most ardent supporters of the degenerationist position, Dr. Whately, archbishop of Dublin, and the Duke of Argyll.[51]

Even if the relationship between the reasons for the book and its purpose are so transparent, it is worth examining the arguments in some detail in order to demonstrate the premises, some overt, some covert, on which they are based. To a great extent this exercise has to be performed piecemeal since *The Origin of Civilisation* is singularly lacking in any analytical framework. With the exception of the chapters on religion,

---

about the reviewer quoted above. "Now that Sir John Lubbock's work on the 'Origin of Civilisation' has reached a second edition, it is perhaps only natural that those who make it their business to warn the public against the encroachments of Science should raise an alarm against the first. In a recent number of the *Christian Advocate & Review* appears, accordingly, an article specially devoted to the demolition of Sir John's theories, and the vindication of human degeneracy. With the felicitous instinct of clerical antagonism, the Advocate and Reviewer makes his fiercest onslaught precisely where his opponent happens to be least vulnerable and lays about him with all the fine, fervid imbecility distinctive of his particular clique."

51. Richard Whately, *Introductory Lectures on Political Economy*, 4th ed. (London: John W. Parker & Son, 1855). See lectures 4 ("Man Considered as a Social Being"), 5 ("Origin of Civilized Society"), and 6 ("Beginning of Advances in Civilization"). The reader might also wish to refer to Whately's "On the Origin of Civilisation," in *Miscellaneous Lectures and Reviews* (London: Parker, Son, and Bourn, 1861), lecture 2, pp. 26–59.

For the Duke of Argyll's writings on this subject, see "Recent Speculations on Primeval Man," in *Good Words for 1868* (London: Strahan & Co., 1868), pp. 155–59, 249–53, 279–86, 385–92.

Although it is a matter for speculation, it seems likely that Lubbock chose the title of his work to parallel Darwin's, rather than respond to Whately's.

which form the core of the work, there are no preformulated evolutionary stages, of the sort that typify the studies of such evolutionists as Bachofen, McLennan, and Morgan, into which the ethnographic data may be fitted. Indeed contemporary reviewers noted this: one refers to the book's "somewhat loose arrangement";[52] another states, "Without any intention of disputing Sir J. Lubbock's three propositions (which need not imply a full reception of them), it seems to us that exception may be taken to the premises as not of themselves bearing out the conclusions in support of which they are advanced. . . . Romans of the time of Cato, Tasmanians, Bushmen, ancient Germans, Classic Greeks, Jews, and Samoiedes, are all irregularly and indiscriminately adduced"; and this critic went on to say, with reference to the evolution of religion, that "to prove this systematic development we should have preferred to see some more systematic collection of instances."[53]

To a large extent these criticisms are well founded, and on first reading of *The Origin of Civilisation* one is left with an impression of a jumble of ethnographic snippets. However, increasing familiarity with the work does reveal, if not order, at least certain consistent themes in Lubbock's presentation of the material.

In the first place, we can of course identify the concept of evolution, which can almost be regarded as the motive force in his anthropological writings. This is not surprising in view of the biographical details given in section II above, but it does make Lubbock distinct from many of his contemporaries whose social evolutionism was untainted by biological evolutionism.[54] However, it is worth looking at Lubbock's evolu-

52. [St. George Mivart], *Quarterly Review* 137 (July 1874): 40–77.

53. H.B.T. [Henry Baker Tristram], *Contemporary Review* 15 (August-November 1870): 311–13.

54. I do not wish to deal here with the point of view put forward by George Stocking (J. C. Prichard, *Researches into the Physical History of*

tionism in some detail, since it helps to explain the stand that he took on certain points. A start on this can be made by going back to consider in greater detail the three interests that the study of savages had for Lubbock.

In relation to the conclusions reached, it can be seen that the three interests refer to the past, present, and future of man.

The first interest, the study of modern savages as a means of illuminating the nature of one's own extinct ancestors, receives relatively little emphasis in *The Origin of Civilisation*, but it forms a fundamental part of *Prehistoric Times*, as is indicated by the remainder of the title, *as Illustrated by Ancient Remains and the Manners and Customs of Modern Savages*. Lubbock's interest in anthropology arose directly out of his archaeological studies and his employment of a method that has become known as the use of "ethnographic parallels." Lubbock is perfectly explicit about the nature of the method, and using a palaeontological analogy, he writes:

> Many mammalia which are extinct in Europe have representatives still living in other countries. Our fossil pachyderms, for instance, would be almost unintelligible but for the species which still inhabit some parts of Asia and Africa; the secondary marsupials are illustrated by the existing representatives in Australia and South

---

Man, ed. George W. Stocking [Chicago: University of Chicago Press, 1973], Editor's Introduction) and supported by Gay Weber ("Science and Society") that the first half of the nineteenth century was not characterized by a hiatus in the development of anthropological thought. Stocking and Weber argue that during this period anthropological thought continued to develop, but that it went through a stage of close alliance with the biological sciences. While it is acceptable to suppose that these sciences may have been influential in the development of some evolutionist anthropologists' thought, it would be wrong to say that all of them were so influenced. For example, there is no evidence to show that McLennan had any knowledge of the biological sciences.

It might be noted that a contemporary reviewer (George Rolleston, *Academy* 11] 22 October 1870]: p. 11) drew attention to the fact that Tylor approached the ethnographic material as a historian, Lubbock as a naturalist.

America; and in the same manner if we wish clearly to understand the antiquities of Europe, we must compare them with the rude implements and weapons in other parts of the world. In fact, the Van Diemaner and South American are to the antiquary, what the opossum and the sloth are to the geologist.[55]

The problem of ethnographic parallels or, as Glyn Daniel has called it, "the comparative ethnographic fallacy,"[56] is a perennial one for archaeologists and prehistorians,[57] but does not call for extended discussion here. However, it may be pointed out that while it may be legitimate to deduce the nature and function of some archaeological find from the knowledge of a technique or artifact from an observable society, there are very definite limits on what can be safely deduced. To accept, as Lubbock did, that a rough identity between the material culture of a prehistoric people and some existing society involves, even implies, a corresponding identity between all aspects of their culture, social and family organization, values, laws, morals, and so on, is to tumble head first into the fallacy. It also necessarily rests on the assumption of total cultural consistency. This leads to the sort of problem that Lubbock found himself confronted with in the case of the Sandwich Islanders. Their relationship terminology, which fails to discriminate between kin except on a generational basis, indicates the existence of a very primitive type of social organization, but at the same time the society has advanced economic and political institutions. The difficulty can only be resolved by resorting to special pleading: "There are, I think, reasons in the social habits of these islanders which go far to explain the persistence of this archaic nomenclature. From the mildness of the climate and the abundance of food, children soon become independent; the prevalence of large houses, used as mere dormitories, and

55. *Prehistoric Times*, p. 336.

56. Daniel, *A Hundred Years of Archaeology*, p. 186.

57. See B. Orme, "Twentieth-century Prehistorians and the Idea of Ethnographic Parallels," *Man* 9 (1974): 199–212.

the curious prejudice against eating in common, must also
have greatly tended to retard the development of special
family feelings."[58]

A second difficulty in the use of ethnographic parallels lies
in the fact that while the method is intended to illuminate the
archaeological record, when the general framework of understanding is an evolutionary one, both sources of evidence, the
archaeological and the ethnographic, tend to be used to inter-
pret each other, and the method becomes tautological. Thus
the evolutionary stages through which it is assumed that
societies inevitably advance can be observed both in the
archaeological data and among existing savages. That the
archaeological record may then be used to order the ethnographic material is only too clearly portrayed by the use of
such terms as "stone-age peoples" to refer to living societies.

The method of ethnographic parallels is not given much
prominence in *The Origin of Civilisation*. However, there is an
implicit parallel drawn between the existing conditions of
savage life and the conditions under which the prehistoric ancestors of civilized man lived. It was through this parallel that
Lubbock was able to reach his conclusions both about the
original abject condition of man and the fact that man had
evolved from this condition. Both these arguments were essential if the evolutionist position was to be substantiated,
and that of the degenerationists finally refuted. But the
method of ethnographic parallels is not of itself enough, since
it was inadequate to deal with or to explain the similarities
and differences among peoples in widely separated regions of
the earth. The problem could be formulated in terms of independent invention versus diffusion, but either answer could be
used to support the evolutionist's position.

Most late nineteenth-century anthropologists favored independent invention, but they certainly did not ignore or dis-

58. *Origin of Civilisation*, p. 64.

miss the possibility of diffusion.[59] The important point to which they all subscribed was the unity of the human race, and either position could be used as evidence for this premise. If the existence of similar customs in different parts of the world was explained in terms of independent invention, then the similarities were evidence of mankind's unity. On the other hand, if the similarities were understood to result from diffusion, of people or ideas, this could also be taken as evidence of man's unity. In the case of the migration of people, the unity of mankind is given; in the case of the borrowing of ideas, the very ability of one people to adopt ideas from another was taken as evidence of their basic unity. However, for Lubbock and his evolutionist colleagues, while it was necessary to accept the similarities, it was equally essential to stress the differences, for it was the difference between savage and civilized men that they were concerned to demonstrate.

There is an interesting section in *Prehistoric Times* on this point, and it is worth looking at for what it reveals about Lubbock's thinking on this matter. Discussing the differences between savage peoples, he writes:

> The civilisation, moreover, of the Stone age differs not only in degree, but also in kind, varying according to climate, vegetation, food, etc; from which it becomes evident—at least to all those who believe in the unity of the human race—that the present habits of savage races are not to be regarded as depending directly on those which characterised the first men, but on the contrary as arising from external conditions, influenced indeed to a certain extent by national character, which however is after all but the result of external conditions acting on previous generations. [P. 446)

The explanation of human differences, both physical and cultural, by environmental determinism was nothing new, and the effect, for example, of climate as an explanation of

59. For a discussion of the oscillation between diffusionist and evolutionist modes of explanation see George Stocking's Introduction to Prichard's *Researches into the Physical History of Man.*

human variability can be traced back to classic times. However, as can be seen in the above quotation, evolution added
a new slant to this form of explanation. Lubbock becomes
even more explicit on this point in the following pages as his
argument slides from an examination of the differences between savage races to a discussion of those between savage
races and civilized peoples.

The ground for the differences between savages and civilized peoples has been prepared by the demonstration of the
differences between savage races. It follows from this that
there must equally be differences between savages and civilized peoples, and Lubbock starts his argument about the
nature of these differences with a mind open enough to raise
the following possibility: "where such notions [of moral recti-
tude] do exist, they differ widely, as we have seen, from our
own; and it would open up too large a question to enquire
whether in all cases, our standard is the correct one" (p. 459).
But he then proceeds to document the inferiority of savage
races: savages are cruel because they are less sensitive to pain,
they are excessively stupid, and they lack religious conceptions. He then goes even further than this to suggest that in
his primordial state man was even inferior to certain animals
from whom he copied ideas and objects.

> The chimpanzee builds himself a house or shelter almost equal to
> that of some savages. Our earliest ancestors therefore may have had
> this art; but even if not, when they became hunters, and as we find
> to be the case with all hunting tribes, supplemented the inefficiency
> of their weapons by a wonderful acquaintance with the manners
> and customs of the animals on which they preyed, they could not
> fail to observe, and perhaps to copy, the houses which various spe-
> cies of animals construct for themselves. [P. 474]

But, Lubbock continues, early man could only live as animals do while he was confined to the tropics, and when he
started to move into other, harsher environments, it became
necessary for him to invent artifacts in order to survive.

Lubbock then quotes Wallace at length not only in support of the presumed unity of the human race but also on the degree to which man had freed himself from the control of nature. Man by his technical inventiveness is no longer subordinate to the laws of nature; that is to say, natural selection no longer exercises the same control on the physical constituency of man, since he can protect himself from environmental determinants. But as his body was freed from these influences, so man's mind came under the force of natural selection and thus evolved to the high state in which it is found among civilized peoples. Man gradually escapes from "natural selection" and replaces it with "man's selection," thus ensuring a wonderful future for humanity.

Even if this theory of natural selection is not acceptable, Lubbock continues, there is further evidence to support the claim of man's improving conditions. Increasing civilization results in increasing happiness because "if any animal increases in numbers it must be because the conditions are becoming more favourable to it, in other words, because it is happier and more comfortable" (p. 482). He then produces figures to show that the population density in areas occupied by savage races is lower than that in urban Europe. As further proof, it is claimed that under civilization food is more abundant, while savage men can "scarcely find a scanty and precarious subsistence" (p. 483). The sufferings of savages are contrasted with the blessings of civilization, many of which have been brought about by the growth of science. The future improvement in the condition of man will arise from the joint efforts of science and religion, which for too long have been separate institutions. Although science might not make men more virtuous (Lubbock quotes Lord Brougham in support of the opposite contention), it will make men more innocent. As evidence for this he points to the very low percentage of convicted persons in England and Wales who are literate.

Education will teach people that sinning does not lead to happiness.

The conclusions to this are best left in Lubbock's own words:

> The most sanguine hopes for the future are justified by the whole experience of the past. It is surely unreasonable to suppose that a process [that is, natural selection] which has been going on for so many thousand years, should have now suddenly ceased. . . . The great principle of natural selection, which in animals affects the body and seems to have little influence on the mind; in man affects the mind and has little influence on the body. In the first it tends mainly to the preservation of life; in the second to the improvement of the mind and consequently to the increase of happiness. . . . the evils under which we suffer nearly all may be attributed to ignorance or sin. That ignorance will be diminished by the progress of science is of course self-evident, that the same will be the case with sin, seems little less so. Thus, then, both theory and experience point to the same conclusion. The future happiness of our race, which poets hardly ventured to hope for, science boldly predicts. Utopia, which we have long looked upon as synonymous with an evident impossibility, which we have ungratefully regarded as "too good to be true," turns out on the contrary to be the necessary consequence of natural laws, and once more we find that the simple truth exceeds the most brilliant flights of the imagination. [P. 490–92]

Nowhere in *The Origin of Civilisation* does Lubbock express himself with such vehement optimism about the future of mankind. There he restricts himself to saying that "if the past history of man has been one of deterioration, we have but a groundless expectation of future improvement: on the other hand, if the past has been one of progress, we may fairly hope that the future will be so also" (p. 323).

It should now be clear from Lubbock's own words why he thought that the study of the lower races of men could "penetrate some of that mist which separates the present from the future." It is evolution governed by the process of natural selection that permits the extrapolation of past improvement into future progress. We can now quickly dispose of Lubbock's second reason for studying savages, to help in the

identification of "survivals," the extant residues from earlier
stages of evolution still lingering in modern society. Once
again it is in the relationship between science and religion
that Lubbock most clearly expresses his views. For example:

> we know that a belief in witchcraft was all but universal until re-
> cently even in our own country. This dark superstition has indeed
> flourished for centuries in Christian countries, and has only been
> expelled at length by the light of science. It still survives wherever
> science has not penetrated.
>
> The immense service which Science has thus rendered the cause
> of religion and of humanity, has not hitherto received the recogni-
> tion which it deserves. Science is still regarded by many excellent,
> but narrow-minded, persons as hostile to religious truth, while in
> fact she is only opposed to religious error. No doubt her influence
> has always been exercised in opposition to those who present con-
> tradictory assertions under the excuse of mystery, and to all but
> the highest conceptions of Divine power. The time, however, is ap-
> proaching when it will be generally perceived that so far from science
> being opposed to religion, true religion is, without science, impos-
> sible; and if we consider the various aspects of Christianity as
> understood by different nations, we can hardly fail to perceive that
> the dignity, and therefore the truth, of their religious beliefs is in
> direct relation to the knowledge of science and of the great physical
> laws by which our universe is governed. [Pp. 255–56]

However, unlike Tylor, Lubbock was not an ardent hunter
of survivals, and in his works one only finds trivial examples.
In *The Origin of Civilisation* he comments on the binding of
Chinese women's feet, which in his opinion "is less mischievous than the compression of the waist as practised in
Europe," or on the fact that "we ourselves still confuse affinity and consanguinity" (pp. 48, 113). In general Lubbock reserved his reformist zeal for his political life.

The three reasons that Lubbock advances for the study of
savage races form a coherent pattern when seen as an aspect
of his evolutionist standpoint. First, the ethnographic material
can be used in conjunction with archaeological evidence to
demonstrate that evolution has occurred; second, as man becomes increasingly master of his own fate, such study can be

used to identify "survivals" which science can then eliminate; and third, the natural progression revealed by the ethnographic record divines man's glorious future, in which the ignorance of the lower races will have been abolished. Taken together, these reasons for studying savage peoples furnish, for Lubbock, conclusive proof of the evolutionist argument.

From this general view of Lubbock's evolutionist position, with its euphoric ideas on the advantages of science and the future of man that must have been so congenial to many of his contemporary readers, we can now turn to examine certain strands in his argument in some greater detail.

V

We have already touched several times on the subject of religion, and from the extensive quotation just given, it is clear that Lubbock, while unwilling to dismiss religion as false, clearly did not accept biblical writings as literal and historical accounts. Despite the fact that he routinely conducted family prayers, there is no evidence to suggest that he was a deeply religious man, and the writer in the *Dictionary of National Biography* ambiguously states: "At an early period of his life, he moved away from orthodoxy and dogma, but his nature was in the highest degree reverent. He did not dissociate himself from the observances of religion, and both in speech and in print he refrained from anything controversial or aggressive."

This last comment may be true insofar as it applies to Christianity, but Lubbock was exceptional among the evolutionist anthropologists in denying the lower races any religious conceptions. In *Prehistoric Times* Lubbock claimed very firmly that many, if not all, savage tribes lacked religious conceptions. He argues that "It has been asserted over and over again that there is no race of men so degraded as to be entirely without a religion—without some idea of a deity. So far from this being true, the very reverse is the case. Many, we might almost say all, of the most savage races are, according to the nearly universal testimony of travellers, in this condition" (pp. 467–68).

Tylor was critical of this view but conceded that the difference between Lubbock and himself was nominal rather than real, since the matter depended on what definition of religion was adopted. Tylor was inclined to admit the absence of religion as a theoretical possibility but found that no cases existed.[60] In *The Origin of Civilisation* Lubbock notes this criticism and agrees that to some extent the presence or absence of religious concepts depends on the definition of religion employed. Even so, he uncompromisingly holds to his original view and argues that if the definition of religious feeling is to be reduced to the sensation of fear coupled with the idea of other beings more powerful than man, then indeed religion is universal and general, but it is not confined to man. "The bay of a dog to the moon is as much an act of worship as some ceremonies which have been so described by travellers," he claims (p. 121). He further asserts that it is "very difficult to suppose people so backward as to be unable to count their own fingers should be sufficiently advanced in their intellectual conceptions as to have any system of belief worthy of the name" (p. 125).

Even if Lubbock declined to acknowledge the universality of religious conceptions, it was still necessary for him to make certain definitional statements about the nature of religion and its development, for this is the topic that forms the core of *The Origin of Civilisation*, occupying 150 out of a total of 350 pages. It is also the only part of his work in which any form of evolutionary framework is properly developed. His investigation is founded on an assumption that we have al-

60. *Nature* 1 (25 November 1869): 103–5.

ready considered, and in this case takes this form: "races in a
similar stage of mental development, however distinct the
regions they inhabit, have very similar religious conceptions"
(p. 115). Lubbock is then faced with a double problem: to
identify the nature of the earliest religious feeling that has
grown out of its absence, and to be able to link this earliest
form to its most developed form. He resolves these difficulties
in two ways. First,

> Religion, as understood by the lower savage races, differs essen-
> tially from ours; nay, it is not only different, but even opposite.
> Thus their deities are evil, not good. . . . In fact, the so-called
> religion of the lower races bears somewhat the same relation to
> religion in its higher forms that astrology does to astronomy, or
> alchemy to chemistry. Astronomy is derived from astrology, yet
> their spirit is in entire opposition; and we shall find the same differ-
> ence between the religions of backward and of advanced races.
> [P. 116]

By this argument Lubbock is able to identify in man a
potential for religious feeling while at the same time keeping
distinct the actual forms to which this feeling gives rise.

Second, it is necessary to detail the development of religious conceptions, and Lubbock claims that this is a process
of increasing respect for the deity. On the basis of "the estimate in which the Deity is held" (p. 119), Lubbock identifies
seven great stages in the development of religious thought.
These are (1) *atheism*, in which the existence of a deity is not
denied but there exist no clear ideas on the subject; (2)
fetichism, in which man assumes he can force the deity to
comply with his wishes; (3) *nature-worship* or *totemism*, in
which natural objects are worshipped; (4) *shamanism*, in
which the deities are more powerful than men and of a different nature; (5) *idolatry* or *anthropomorphism*, in which the
deities, although more powerful than men, have the same
form and remain part of nature rather than being its creators.
In a sixth, unnamed level, the deity is a supernatural being

who created nature. In the seventh and final stage, morality becomes associated with religion. With this framework organized, Lubbock scours the ethnography and allots races to their appropriate levels.

The evolutionary framework for the development of religious conceptions that Lubbock proposed was not exceptional; it was no better or worse than the series of evolutionary stages advanced for other social phenomena by various of his contemporaries. However, what is exceptional is Lubbock's stand concerning the existence of savage races without religious conceptions. He never altered his position on this; his claim did not remain simply unamended in the final editions of both *Prehistoric Times* and *The Origin of Civilisation*, but was strenuously reasserted in *Marriage, Totemism and Religion* despite increasing criticism from all quarters. The Very Reverend James Carmichael, dean of Montreal, for example, wrote that Sir John Lubbock, as the chief contestant of universal religiousness, had ignored the increasing amount of evidence that indicated the opposite, and had overcome the objections by shifting his definition. Thus, Carmichael continued, "Sir John Lubbock repairs his damaged argument, working with the implements of the most bigoted member of an old-fashioned missionary society." He further upbraids Lubbock in these words:

> When one considers the influence that Sir John Lubbock's *Prehistoric Times* has had on the reading public, and the shock that his statements as to the utter irreligiousness of certain tribes gave many of his readers, one feels inclined to question his authority as a teacher, when his quotations are submitted to the simple test of verification. One wonders how such a man as Sir John Lubbock could gather into the compass of a few concluding pages of a really great work such a tissue of misguiding information.

Carmichael feels that this cannot have been done intentionally to mislead, but rather that Lubbock has read selectively,

choosing passages that support his pet theory; and he concludes:

> If Sir John Lubbock, in the hurry of a busy life, has not fallen under
> this common temptation, then one knows not how to explain the
> extraordinary fact that one of the keenest minds in the English
> scientific world has so persistently left undone what he ought to have
> done, and done what he ought not to have done, as he gave to the
> public quotations from other writers.[61]

An explanation of Lubbock's exceptional position on this
topic among the liberal and humanitarian thinkers of the last
century is more or less contained in Carmichael's words. It
seems likely that Lubbock was forced into this position on
the question of the universality of religion because of his commitment to a pet theory, the theory of evolution. We have
earlier noted that in *Prehistoric Times*, on matters of material
culture, Lubbock is not above drawing parallels between the
artifacts of savages and those of animals, even implying that
the former might have adopted them from the latter. Clearly
the question of religious conceptions and their origin posed
more serious problems, since it could hardly be claimed that
these existed in animals (and even less that man had borrowed
them from animals), although Lubbock comes close to it
when drawing a parallel between the baying of dogs and the
ceremonies of savages. Given this, Lubbock, in order to maintain a consistent argument about the evolution of man from
animals, was committed by his theoretical predisposition to
depriving the lowest races of religious conceptions. The
existence of savages lacking religious feeling was in keeping

61. James Carmichael, "Sir John Lubbock and the Religion of Savages," *Popular Science Monthly* 48 (December 1895): 220–8. Lubbock
ignores Carmichael in *Marriage, Totemism and Religion: An Answer to
Critics* although an example of Lubbock's misuse of the facts in *The
Origin of Civilisation* and later repeated in *Marriage, Totemism and Religion* has recently come to light. See C. N. Starcke, *The Primitive Family
in Its Origin and Development*, ed. Rodney Needham (Chicago: University of Chicago Press, 1976), Editor's Introduction, pp. xvii–xix.

with and further proof of the unbroken evolutionary development of man from animals. It is noticeable that Lubbock avoids any discussion of whence and when the human potential for religious ideas arose. It is enough that this potential, even in its least developed form ("vague ideas as to the existence of evil spirits"), as it occurs among the Australian aborigines (p. 158), can be recognized, for then its progress can be traced as it grows hand-in-hand with the mental development of mankind. This mental development was seen as being of a similar nature to the maturation of the individual from infancy to adulthood. This notion, which involved the assumed childlike nature of savages, was not new to the nineteenth century, but it provided the evolutionist anthropologists with an invaluable explanatory model. We will now turn to Lubbock's use of this assumption.

VI

The use by Victorian anthropologists of the analogy between children and savages is general, and it proved a useful formula by which the notion of the unity of mankind and the distance between civilized man and savage could be jointly maintained.[62] Wake used the analogy explicitly in this way in an article entitled "The Psychological Unity of Mankind." He accepted the assumption of the period that the species and the individual member of the species evolved in a similar way, and on the basis of this argued that if it could be shown that the races of man evolved in the same way as the individual, then man was a single species. He claimed that "a comparison may be made between the intellectual phenomena presented by the several great divisions of the human race, and those exhibited by man in the gradual evolution of his mental

62. There is not space here to examine the exact nature of this analogy, but it certainly involves more than mere "similarity."

faculties." He then proceeded to draw up stages in the development of the individual man and identify them with the five great divisions of mankind. The result was an evolutionary framework with the following stages: selfish/aborigines; wilful/Amerindians; emotional/Negroes; empirical/Asiatic; and rational/Caucasian.[63]

Lubbock did not employ an evolutionary framework of this sort, but the assumption about the childlike nature of savages is central to his whole argument and is quite explicitly expressed. We first find this formula in *Prehistoric Times* where he goes so far as to write: "Savages have often been likened to children, but so far as intelligence is concerned, a child of four years is far superior; although if we take for comparison a child belonging to a civilized race at a sufficiently early age, the parallel is fair enough" (pp. 462–63). In that volume Lubbock also compares savages with children because of their common failure to appreciate properly the passage of time (p. 460), to pronounce correctly certain sounds (p. 464), and their common tendency to behave with thoughtlessness and impulsiveness (p. 465). Lubbock sums up by saying that "savages have the character of children with the passions and strength of men" (p. 465).

A clearer enunciation of his position in regard to this question is to be found in the appendix to *The Origin of Civilisation* and is best given in Lubbock's own words:

> The close resemblance existing in ideas, language, habits, and character between savages and children, though generally admitted, has usually been disposed of in a passing sentence, and regarded rather as a curious accident than as an important truth. . . . The opinion is rapidly gaining ground among naturalists, that the development of the individual is an epitome of that of the species, a conclusion which, if fully borne out, will evidently prove most instructive. . . . Regarded from this point of view, the similarity exist-

63. C. S. Wake, "The Psychological Unity of Mankind," *Memoirs Read before the Anthropological Society of London* 3 (1870): 134–47.

ing between savages and children assumes a singular importance
and becomes almost conclusive as regards the question [evolution
versus degeneration] now at issue. [Pp. 360–61]

This "important truth" is accepted unquestioningly by
Lubbock, and in the main body of the text he makes extensive
use of it to explain various features of savage life. A few examples will suffice: "The mind of the savage, like that of the
child, is easily fatigued" (p. 4) explains the savage's inability
to concentrate for long. Food prohibitions among savages are
explained by the following: "To us the idea [that people
acquire the qualities of what they eat] seems absurd. Not so
children. I have myself heard a little girl say to her brother,
'If you eat so much goose you will be quite silly' " (p. 13). In
the discussion on the origin of moral feeling, the example of
children is given as evidence of the existence of the innate
feeling of right and wrong (there is a parallel here with the
assumed religious potential of all races), although they are
not naturally aware of what exactly is right or wrong (p. 274).
Or finally, when considering the origin of language, Lubbock
claims that "the words most frequently required, and especially those used by children, are generally represented by the
simplest and easiest sounds, merely because they are the
simplest" (p. 283).

Thus the assumed similarity between savage and child,
together with the slightly more complex idea that the development of the individual parallels the evolution of the species, fitted in well with Lubbock's Darwinian position, and
provided, as far as Lubbock was concerned, conclusive proof
that the evolutionists were right and the degenerationists
wrong. However, we can take this identification of child and
savage a step further and show that this idea was not simply
consistent with Lubbock's evolutionist stance but coincided
with a more general view of the world. It is worth considering
this point, since it seems to throw some light on the popu-

larity of his writings and the claim made earlier that Lubbock was decidedly a man of his times.

In discussing the growth of religious beliefs and the gradual replacement of old gods and superstitions by new gods, Lubbock writes: "gradually the worship of the latter [the old deities] sinks in the social scale, and becomes confined to the ignorant and the young. Thus a belief in witchcraft still flourishes among our agricultural labourers and the lowest classes in our great cities, and the deities of our ancestors survive in the nursery tales of our children" (p. 118).[64] Later he quotes the inability of a Scottish Highlander to express himself properly as a further example of the "difficulty which an undeveloped mind finds in raising itself to any elevated conception" (p. 232).

One can draw from these passages the conclusion that in Lubbock's thinking there is a parallel on the one hand among savages, children, and the uneducated working classes, and on the other among civilized peoples, adults, and the educated classes. This hierarchical ordering of the world readily fits with Lubbock's concern for the uneducated working classes and his utopian belief that a better society will result from the efforts of education and science. It is also consistent with his claim that the knowledge of savage races is of "peculiar importance to an Empire such as ours" (p. viii). He casts imperialism in the role of a beneficent father who will bring the blessings of civilization to his childlike savage subjects.[65]

64. The view that the lower classes of Europe were as degraded as savages was general at the time. See Weber, "Science and Society," p. 277.

65. As a parliamentarian Lubbock does not seem to have shown the same interest in savages as he did in the welfare of the working classes. At times he seems to have taken a rather callous line with regard to savage peoples, suggesting that on the principle of the survival of the fittest they will anyhow die out. See *The Origin of Civilisation*, p. 322.

There seems little evidence for Sir Bernard Mallet's claim that imperialism did not appeal to Lubbock (*Life-Work of Lord Avebury*, p. 59).

There is at first glance a curious omission from this series of associations, the relationship between men and women. In fact, however, its absence accords well with the position and status of women, at least ideally, in upper and upper-middle-class Victorian England, and provides further evidence in support of the contention that Lubbock was a true representative of his time and station. Lubbock does not simply regard the inferior position of women, their subjection and harsh treatment, "which is almost universal among savages [and] one of the deepest stains upon their character,"[66] as evidence of uncivilized society, but even equates the development of civilization with the improvement in the status of women, referring to this as one of civilization's great advantages.[67] In other words the domination of women by men is an aspect of savage society but not of civilized society,[68] and this can well account for the absence of this relationship from Lubbock's hierarchical world view.

VII

An examination of *The Origin of Civilisation* reveals a number of other assumptions that play an essential role in Lubbock's approach to the ethnographic material and which can also be identified as reflecting his place in Victorian society. These assumptions center on the nature of family ties and the sanctity of property, and deserve consideration since they lead Lubbock into certain difficulties with his scientific views.

The fundamental assumption that Lubbock makes about family relationships is clearly put forth at the very beginning

66. *Prehistoric Times*, p. 462.

67. *Origin of Civilisation*, p. 50

68. Lubbock seems well aware that this ideal is not lived up to when he writes of "the remarkable subordination of the wife to the husband, which is so characteristic of marriage, and so curiously inconsistent with all our avowed ideas" (*Origin of Civilisation*, p. 90).

of his chapter "Marriage and Relationship," where he writes:

> Nothing, perhaps, gives a more instructive insight into the true
> condition of savages than their ideas on the subject of relationship
> and marriage; nor can the great advantages of civilisation be more
> conclusively proved than by the improvement which it has effected
> in the relation between the sexes.
>
> Marriage, and the relationship of a child to its father and mother,
> seem to us so natural and obvious, that we are apt to look on them
> as aboriginal and general to the human race. This, however, is very
> far from being the case. The lowest races have no institution of
> marriage; true love is almost unknown among them; and marriage,
> in its lowest phases, is by no means a matter of affection and com-
> panionship. [P. 50]

Lubbock then proceeds to document his claim that there is
a lack of any close relationship between the sexes among savages, and traces the development of marriage from its crude
origins, when "marriage, in the proper sense of the term, cannot be said to exist at all, still for the sake of convenience, we
may term it a condition of communal marriage" (p. 60), to
its Victorian form of permanent monogamy. At the same time
he refers to the development of relationships recognised within the family: "Again, our family system, which regards a
child as equally related to his father and his mother, seems
so natural that we experience a feeling of surprise on meeting
with any other system. Yet we shall find, I think, reason for
concluding that a man was first regarded as merely related to
his family; then to his mother but not to his father; then to
his father and not to his mother; and only at last to both
father and mother" (p. 52).

From this we can see that Lubbock accepts in principle the
broad evolutionary outline proposed by such writers as
Bachofen and McLennan: an evolution that involved not
simply a development from communal marriage to monogamy
but also from matriliny to patriliny. Lubbock, however, is
critical of certain aspects of these two writers' evolutionary
frameworks. He dismisses the matriarchal aspect of Bachofen's

scheme on the grounds that there are few if any historical records of women ever having exercised supreme power and that such a situation is even more unlikely in savage society, where "the position of women is one of complete subjection, and it seems to me perfectly clear that the idea of marriage is founded on the rights, not of the woman, but of the man" (p. 68). This is a view perfectly consistent with that outlined in section VI.

Lubbock's criticisms of McLennan are more detailed, but once again we can see that they are based on his presuppositions about the nature of marital and family relationships. Lubbock disagrees with McLennan both about the importance of polyandry and endogamy as normal stages in the evolution of society (Lubbock accepted their occurrence but regarded them as exceptional) and about the order of the stages. In particular Lubbock claimed that communal marriage gave way to individual marriage as a result of marriage by capture. His argument runs as follows: under the communal system no man had individual rights to any particular woman of the tribe, all women being held in common. However, this ruling did not apply to women captured in war. The tribe had no particular right to such a woman, and the man who captured her kept possession of her. Thus:

> These captives then would naturally become the wives in our sense of the term.
>
> Several causes would tend to increase the importance of the separate, and decrease that of communal marriage. The impulse which it would give to, and receive back from, the development of the affections; the convenience with reference to domestic arrangements, the natural wishes of the wife herself, and last, not least, the inferior energy of the children sprung from 'in and in' marriages, would all tend to increase the importance of individual marriage. [P. 94]

Here Lubbock uses an argument based on the assumption that private property (the individual wife) will result in the growth of familial and marital affection, with natural selec-

tion, it will be noticed, acting to further the movement toward the monogamous family. There is this same appeal to
property when Lubbock comes to explain the movement from
matriliny to patriliny.

> When, however, marriage became more respected, and the family
> affections stronger, it is easy to see that the rule under which a
> man's property went to his sister's children, would become un-
> popular, both with the father, who would naturally wish his children
> to inherit his property, and equally so with the children themselves.
> [Pp. 108–9]

He then stresses this point in these words:

> The recognition of paternal responsibility grew up, I believe, gradu-
> ally and from force of circumstances, aided by the impulses of
> natural affection. On the other hand, the adoption of relationship
> through the father's line, instead of through the mother's, was
> probably effected by the natural wish which every one would feel
> that his property should go to his own children. [Pp. 109–10]

Later we find Lubbock yet again affirming the relationship
between the notion of property and the presence of the family. In his final chapter, "Laws," Lubbock dismisses the view
that, since it is nothing more than an extension of the family,
monarchy was the earliest form of government, with the
sovereign taking the place of the father, on the grounds that
early family life was too disorganized to act as a model for a
unique lawgiver, and that the origin of law as law, rather than
the tyrannous rules, precedents, and customs that savages
have to obey, rightly belongs at more advanced levels of
civilization. However, while accepting with other writers the
likelihood that the first law related to property in land (pp.
308–9), Lubbock sees the notion of property arising from the
fact of possession. When the latter becomes a matter of public
concern and its regulation formalized, the concept of property
is born (p. 318). So we can see here the consistency in Lubbock's argument: among savages neither the family nor the
idea of law is present, and the appearance of both can be cor-
related with the rise of the notion of property. The view of

the family as the property-owning corporate group is exactly what one might expect from someone of Lubbock's background, and here we can see how this view has colored his approach to the ethnography.

However, there is another aspect to this same argument, and it leads Lubbock into certain difficulties that he fails to resolve, even if he appreciates them. The difficulties lie mainly in his discussion of the origin of character and morals (chapter VII). This chapter begins with some comments on the contradictory nature of the descriptions of the character of savages, but concludes that "On the whole, however, I think we may assume that life and property are far less secure in savage than in civilised communities" (p. 260). But rather than discuss the relative character of different races, Lubbock turns his attention to their respective moral conditions. He first quotes some remarks of Wallace, who argued that while civilized communities have advanced much further in terms of intellectual achievement, the same progress has not been made with morals. Wallace argues that man has the potential for obeying moral laws through a natural impulse to do so, and that such a perfect state is nearly achieved among those at low levels of civilization. On the other hand he claims that " 'the mass of our populations have not at all advanced beyond the savage code of morals, and have in many cases sunk below it' " (p. 261).

Lubbock refutes this, stating that the opposite is true and that man has "made more progress in moral than in either material or intellectual advancement; for while even the lowest savages have many material and intellectual attainments, they are, it seems to me, almost entirely wanting in moral feeling" (p. 261). Given Lubbock's pronouncements on the glorious achievements of science quoted earlier, this position at first sight seems surprising. But his argument develops thus: Wallace and other observers who have reported on the

high moral tone of savage life have been misled by appearances, and what has been recorded could equally well have
been observed among

> rooks and bees, and most other gregarious animals. . . . Moreover,
> in small communities almost all the members are related to one
> another, and family affection puts on the appearance of virtue. But
> though parental and filial affection possesses a very moral aspect,
> they have a totally different origin and a distinct character.
>
> We do not generally attribute moral feelings to quadrupeds and
> birds, yet there is perhaps no stronger feeling than that of the
> mother for her offspring. She will submit to any sacrifices for their
> welfare, and fight against almost any odds for their protection. No
> follower of Mr. Darwin will be surprised at this; because for gen-
> eration after generation, those mothers in whom this feeling was
> most strong have had the best chance of rearing their young. It is
> not, however, moral feeling in the strict sense of the term; and she
> would indeed be a cold-hearted mother who cherished and pro-
> tected her infant only because it was right to do so. [P. 263]

From this Lubbock is able to conclude that savage men,
like animals, are deficient in moral feeling and "that moral
feelings deepen with the gradual growth of race" (p. 270).[69]
The origin of moral feelings is associated by Lubbock with
the development of religious ideas; a development that, as we
have already seen, culminates in an association of religion and
morality. Man then began to recognize his deities as beneficent beings who

> would naturally be supposed to regard with approbation all that
> tended to benefit their worshippers, and to condemn all actions of
> the opposite character. This step was an immense benefit to man-
> kind, since that dread of the unseen powers which had previously
> been wasted on the production of mere ceremonies and sacrifices,
> at once invested the moral feelings with a sacredness, and conse-
> quently with a force, which they had not until then possessed. [P.
> 273]

The conclusion drawn from this is that authority is the
origin of moral feeling. This claim is perfectly in accord with
Lubbock's hierarchical views which we examined in section

69. See also, "The Moral Condition of Savages" (privately printed,
1870).

VI. The preordained superiority of God over man, parent over child, upper class over lower, European over savage, is, for Lubbock, a moral relationship involving authority, beneficence, and patronage.

Here it is that we can see how Lubbock's double commitment leads him into difficulties. It is his attempt simultaneously to maintain that savage men are like but different from civilized men, and like but different from animals. He has to juggle between his acceptance of mankind's unity and his evolutionist position that denies a break between men and animals. His acceptance of a distinction between family affection as an innate quality shared with animals and moral feeling as a separate quality that develops with society highlights the problem. He could have avoided the difficulty if, like Tylor, he had accepted that all societies had morals and that they had grown out of family affections.[70] As it is, he needs must deny the lowest races morals because animals cannot have them, and then explain their apparent high morality by resorting to innate feelings that are also observable in animals. By taking this stand he fails to remain consistent with his stated views about the nature of family life and organization in savage societies. For example, only a few pages before his reliance on family affection, in particular, maternal feelings, to explain away the apparently high moral plane of savage life, he cites, in support of his contention of the low character of savages, missionaries from Tahiti who reckoned that "not less than two-thirds of the children were murdered by their parents" (p. 260). In chapter VIII, "Language," we find Lubbock claiming that the lack of terms of endearment from many primitive people's vocabularies indicates the low moral state and poor family life among such peoples (p. 291).

70. For Tylor, "morality, like charity, begins at home" ("Primitive Society," *Contemporary Review* 21 (April 1873): 718.) In the second part of this article (22 [June 1873]: 53–72) there are some interesting functionalist remarks about revenge acting to maintain social solidarity.

Lubbock shifts uneasily between his two commitments, and
nowhere is this clearer than in his treatment of the development of the family. The Victorian monogamous family as a
moral, property owning unit was the result of a long process
of evolution from a state in which neither marital nor parental
ties were recognized. Specifically, the family has developed
as a result of the gradual recognition of authority (which gave
rise to morals) and of the notion of property. In the absence
of these, society was little better than an animal community,
but since savages and civilized men shared a common humanity, the former had the potential for progress. Unfortunately,
the facts could not always be made to fit this model, so that
the two components that formed it, the animality and the
humanity of savage man, had often to be separated and used
in different contexts. It is this, perhaps, that represents the
most serious flaw in Lubbock's argument.

In 1929 J. G. Myers claimed that Lubbock managed to
keep his various interests well separated from one another. He
wrote, "the anthropologist influenced but little the entomologist or the politician. Thus he took no academic anthropological theories with him into Parliament."[71] While consideration
of Lubbock as a biologist has been left out, the whole thrust
of the argument in this introduction has been exactly the opposite of Myers' assertion. We have tried to show that Lubbock was very much a man of his time and place and that the
ideas and prejudices of that period are very well portrayed
in Lubbock's understanding and interpretation of man and
society.

VIII

There are two further and connected aspects of Lubbock's
career and character which we have referred to in passing but

71. J. G. Myers, "Lubbock as an Entomologist and Comparative
Psychologist," in *Ants, Bees, and Wasps* (London: Kegan Paul, Trench,
Trubner & Co., 1929).

which now deserve to be treated in greater detail. These are his claim to the originality of his work, and his refusal to move from any position that he had adopted.

In the *D.N.B.* Lubbock is given credit for innovations in the fields of botany and animal behavior, and a recent reassessment of his activities in these subjects supports this view and stresses the originality of his techniques and methods.[72] Elsewhere the situation is not so certain. We have already noted Sir Arthur Keith's claim that Lubbock was more than a popularizer, and we suggested at the same place that this is barely true of his archaeological work. In sections VI and VII we have isolated from his anthropological works certain features of his thought as typical of his social milieu. These notions were not new to the period, nor was his use of them in the explanation of social phenomena original. Such ideas as the right of the naturally superior to dominate the naturally inferior have a history stretching back over two thousand years, and Lubbock simply gave a contemporary tone to them. It is true that his application of biological evolutionism to the elucidation of social evolution was new, but we have just shown that the adoption of this method proved more of a handicap than an advantage to him, and on the whole his evolutionary framework is more confused and confusing than are those of most of his contemporaries.

Even so Lubbock had views on his own originality and seems to have been rather sensitive about the subject. Certainly he was quick to draw the attention of those who used ideas that Lubbock regarded as his own and who had failed to attribute them to him. Thus as early as 1865 in a footnote to the Preface of *Prehistoric Times*, Lubbock calls the reader's notice to the fact that Lyell in his *Antiquity of Man* had used whole sentences verbatim from an article by Lubbock without

72. George Ballester, "The Science of Animal Behaviour in Late Nineteenth-Century Britain with Special Reference to Its Application to Human Society (Thesis, Oxford University, in preparation).

mentioning their source. Lubbock's professed reason for pointing this out is to clear himself of any future accusation of plagiarism, but the impression the note leaves is that it is he who is making the accusation (p. x).

Another example of him defending his originality occurred in 1901, when he wrote to Frazer complaining that the distinction between magic and religion that occurred in *The Golden Bough* was first posited by himself in *The Origin of Civilisation*.[73] Frazer accepted this and promised to rectify the matter in the third edition of *The Golden Bough*, which he duly did in these terms:

> Lord Avebury has courteously pointed out to me that the fundamental difference between magic and religion was dwelt on by him many years ago. See his *Origin of Civilisation* (London, 1870), pp. 116, 164 *sq.*, and the Preface to the sixth edition of that work (London, 1902), p. vi. I am glad to find myself in agreement with Lord Avebury on this subject, and only regret that in preparing my second edition I was unaware that the view here taken has the support of his high authority.[74]

However, if we turn back to Lubbock's statements on this point we find nothing like the certainty that one might suppose from Frazer's words. In 1870 Lubbock barely used the notion of magic. The term does not appear in the index, and it is not one of his stages of religious development, although it appears to be the motive force in many, particularly that of fetishism. It is not until the preface of the sixth edition of 1902 that Lubbock clarifies his thoughts on the subject. There he contrasts magic, which acts directly on nature, with religion, which deals with the relations between men and spirits or deities. Fetishism is opposed to religion in being the attempt to control or dominate spirits rather than submit to them (p. vi). But even if we give Lubbock the benefit of the

73. Hutchinson, *Life of Sir John Lubbock*, 2: 146–48, 188–89.

74. J. G. Frazer, *The Golden Bough* (London: Macmillan & Co., 1911), 1: 225 n.

doubt and accept that in 1870 he clearly saw the opposition between magic and religion (though he failed to state it clearly), it is ridiculous for him to claim to have been the first to note this distinction, which had been a fundamental part of conventional European wisdom for centuries. Finally, of course, the similarities and differences that Frazer drew between magic, science, and religion are very much more systematic than anything proposed by Lubbock.

These claims on Lubbock's part to be the originator of certain ideas can be taken as an aspect of his refusal to accept, or of his denial of the existence of, any modifications to his original ideas. An example already given was his refusal to incorporate the mesolithic into his four-age scheme of prehistory. It is best illustrated by the fact that he was still publishing at the end of his life new editions of *Prehistoric Times* (forty eight years after the first edition) and *The Origins of Civilization* (forty two years after the first edition) with little or no amendment to his original views. In his Preface to the sixth edition of *The Origin of Civilization* he is quite explicit on this point:

> During the thirty years which have elapsed since the first edition of this book was published, many valuable works have appeared on the subject, and much light has been thrown on the manners and customs, the ideas and beliefs of various races of men.
>
> While, however, the additional evidence is of great interest, and adds much to our knowledge of the subject, I see no reason to change in any essential respects the opinions originally expressed. [1902 ed., p. v]

Lubbock could not have been more certain that he was right. He was willing to dispute the facts with such eminent ethnographers as Fison and Howitt,[75] and he chose to ignore

75. Sir John Lubbock, "On the Customs of Marriage and Systems of Relationship among the Australians," *Journal of the Anthropological Institute* 14 (1885): 292–300. Some of the argument in this article is later repeated in *Marriage, Totemism and Religion*.

the writings of the new wave of anthropologists, and this it must be remembered was the age of Durkheim, Mauss, Doas, and Rivers, to name but a few. His last major publication, *Marriage, Totemism and Religion*, is aptly subtitled *An Answer to Critics*, and in it he reiterated all his old opinions. In chapter 1 of that work he attempts to substantiate his claim that there was a human condition in which communal marriage was practised. In chapter 2 he demonstrates once again that his theory of the origin of marriage, based on the idea of the captured woman as private property, is right. On the question of totemism, in chapter 3, Lubbock reaffirms his explanation of its origin in the practice of calling first individuals and then families after a particular animal as a sort of nickname. In chapter 4 he is concerned to demonstrate that witchcraft and magic are not religious phenomena, and this forms a prolegomenon to the final two chapters, in which the claim is once again upheld that there exist savage peoples without religion. Nothing has changed.

It may have been noticeable to the reader that no attempt has been made in this Introduction to assess the importance of Lubbock in modern anthropology. The reason for this is that it is extremely difficult to identify within modern anthropology a single one of his ideas or explanations—which we shall not say survived intact, because that would be asking too much—but which has even given rise to a tradition of anthropological thought. Lubbock's ideas died with him, and it is arguable that they only lived as long as they did as a result of his careful nurturing. It is ironic that that inevitable natural law failed to operate in the realm of his ideas; they did not evolve, so that by the last decade of his life they were like prehistoric monsters that had survived beyond their time. Despite this, Lubbock's works are important. His conviction about his rightness and his originality means that his writ-

ings form an invaluably precise documentation of one strand
in the development of anthropological thought. It may not be
a strand that has remained acceptable to professional anthropologists, but the acknowledged popularity and readability of
his books with their tone of great authority mark Lubbock as
one of the creators of the representation of the "savage" that
is not uncommon in the Western world today.

IX

A number of things has been left to one side in the preparation of this Introduction. No attempt has been made to offer
a complete bibliography even of Lubbock's anthropological
writings, although reference to most of the major works will
be found in the footnotes. It has not been our attention to
examine minutely his relationship to and private thoughts
about his contemporaries in anthropology, although given the
abundance of his correspondence and private papers, such an
exercise would have been feasible, and indeed there is room
for a full-length biography of this eminent Victorian. Instead
we have concentrated on Lubbock's public image as portrayed in his published works. That these sources do not give
a complete picture hardly needs saying, but for our present
purpose they are adequate, for through them we can place
Lubbock and *The Origin of Civilisation* in the development of
anthropology.

This new edition of *The Origin of Civilisation* is a reproduction of the original 1870 edition. No changes to the text have
been made, and the index, bibliography, and footnotes have
also been left in their original form, since they will prove adequate for most readers' needs and help retain some of the
character of the period.

The actual copy used for reproduction was the property of
Henry Balfour, first curator of the Pitt Rivers Museum,

Oxford. The copy appears to have belonged originally to Japetus Steenstrup, to whom Lubbock presented it and with whom Lubbock had published an article on flint implements in 1867 (see note 48). I am extremely grateful to the current curator of the Pitt Rivers Museum, Mr. B. A. L. Cranstone, for permission to use this copy from the Balfour Library. The drawing of Sir John Lubbock which is included as a frontispiece respresents him in approximately 1880. It is reproduced here by kind permission of the Hon. Editor of *Man*. Lubbock's signature, which appears beneath the portrait, was taken from a letter to Henry Balfour, dated December 21, 1886.

PETER RIVIÈRE

PREFACE.

———◦◦◦———

IN my work on 'Prehistoric Times' I have devoted several chapters to the description of modern savages, because the weapons and implements now used by the lower races of men throw much light on the signification and use of those discovered in ancient tumuli, or in the drift gravels ; and because a knowledge of modern savages and their modes of life enables us more accurately to picture, and more vividly to conceive, the manners and customs of our ancestors in bygone ages.

In the present volume, which is founded on a course of lectures delivered at the Royal Institution in the spring of 1868, I propose more particularly to describe the social and mental condition of savages, their art, their systems of marriage and of relationship, their religions, language, moral character, and laws. Subsequently I shall hope to publish those portions of my lectures which have reference to their houses, dress, boats, arms, implements, &c. From the very nature of the subjects dealt with in the present volume, I shall

have to record many actions and ideas very abhorrent
to us; so many in fact that if I pass them without
comment or condemnation, it is because I am reluctant to fatigue the reader by a wearisome iteration
of disapproval.   In the chapters on Marriage and
Religion more especially, though I have endeavoured to
avoid everything that was needlessly offensive, still it
was impossible not to mention some facts which are
very repugnant to our feelings.   Yet were I to express
my sentiments in some cases, my silence in others might
be held to imply indifference, if not approval.

Montesquieu[1] commences with an apology that
portion of his great work which is devoted to Religion.
As, he says, 'on peut juger parmi les ténèbres celles
qui sont les moins épaisses, et parmi les abîmes ceux
qui sont les moins profonds, ainsi l'on peut chercher
entre les religions fausses celles qui sont les plus con-
formes au bien de la société ; celles qui, quoiqu'elles
n'aient pas l'effet de mener les hommes aux félicités de
l'autre vie, peuvent le plus contribuer à leur bonheur
dans celle-ci. Je n'examinerai donc les diverses religions
du monde que par rapport au bien que l'on en tire dans
l'état civil, soit que je parle de celle qui a sa racine
dans le ciel, ou bien de celles qui ont la leur sur la
terre.' The difficulty which I have felt has taken a
different form, but I deem it necessary to say these

---

[1] 'Esprit des Lois,' liv. xxiv. ch. 1.

few words of explanation, lest I should be supposed to approve that which I do not expressly condemn.

Klemm, in his 'Allgemeine Culturgeschichte der Menschen,' and recently Mr. Wood, in a more popular manner ('Natural History of Man'), have described the various races of man consecutively; a system which has its advantages, but which does not well bring out the general stages of progress in civilisation.

Various other works, amongst which I must specially mention Müller's 'Geschichte der Americanischen Urreligionen,' 'M'Lennan's Primitive Marriage,' and Bachofen's 'Das Mutterrecht,' deal with particular portions of the subject. Maine's interesting work on 'Ancient Law,' again, considers man in a more advanced stage than that which is the special subject of my work.

The plan pursued by Tylor in his remarkable work on the 'Early History of Mankind,' more nearly resembles that which I have sketched out for myself, but the subject is one which no two minds would view in the same manner, and is so vast that I am sure my friend will not regard me as intruding on a field which he has done so much to make his own.

Nor must I omit to mention Lord Kames' 'History of Man,' and Montesquieu's 'Esprit des Lois,' both of them works of great interest, although written at a time when our knowledge of savage races was even more imperfect than it is now.

Yet the materials for such a work as the present are immense, and are daily increasing. Those interested in the subject become every year more and more numerous; and while none of my readers can be more sensible of my deficiencies than I am myself, yet after ten years of study, I have been anxious to publish this portion of my work, in the hope that it may contribute something towards the progress of a science which is in itself of the deepest interest, and which has a peculiar importance to an Empire such as ours, comprising races in every stage of civilisation yet attained by man.

HIGH ELMS, DOWN, KENT:
February, 1870.

THE ORIGIN OF CIVILISATION.

&c.

CHAPTER I.

INTRODUCTION.

THE study of the lower races of men, apart from the
direct importance which it possesses in an empire like
ours, is of great interest from three points of view. In the
first place, the condition and habits of existing savages
resemble in many ways, though not in all, those of our
own ancestors in a period now long gone by; in the
second, they illustrate much of what is passing among ourselves, many customs which have evidently no relation to
present circumstances, and even some ideas which are
rooted in our minds, as fossils are imbedded in the soil;
and thirdly, we can even, by means of them, penetrate
some of that mist which separates the present from the
future.

Well, therefore, has it been observed by Maine, in his
excellent work on 'Ancient Law,' that, ' even if they gave
more trouble than they do, no pains would be wasted
in ascertaining the germs out of which has assuredly
been unfolded every form of moral restraint which con-
trols our actions and shapes our conduct at the present

moment.   The rudiments of the social state, so far as they
are known to us at all, are known through testimony of three
sorts—accounts by contemporary observers of civilisations
less advanced than their own, the records which particular
races have preserved concerning their primitive history,
and ancient law.   The first kind of evidence is the best
we could have expected.   As societies do not advance con-
currently, but at different rates of progress, there have
been epochs at which men trained to habits of methodical
observation have really been in a position to watch and
describe the infancy of mankind.'[1]   He refers particularly to
Tacitus, whom he praises for having 'made the most of such
an opportunity;' adding, however, 'but the " Germany,"
unlike most celebrated classical books, has not induced
others to follow the excellent example set by its author,
and the amount of this sort of testimony which we possess
is exceedingly small.'

   This is very far, however, from being the case; at all
epochs some ' men trained to habits of methodical observation have really been in a position to watch and describe
the infancy of mankind,' and the testimony of our modern
travellers is of the same sort as that for which we are indebted to Tacitus.   It is, indeed, much to be regretted that
Mr. Maine, in his admirable work, did not more extensively
avail himself of this source of information, for an acquaintance with the laws and customs of modern savages would
have enabled him greatly to strengthen his arguments
on some points, while it would certainly have modified his
views on others.   Thus he lays it down as an obvious
proposition that 'the organisation of primitive societies
would have been confounded, if men had called themselves
relatives of their mother's relatives,' while I shall pre-

---

[1] Maine's Ancient Law, p. 120.

sently show that, as indeed Mr. McLennan has already pointed out, relationship through females is a common custom of savage communities all over the world.

But though our information with reference to the social and moral condition of the lower races of man is much more considerable than Mr. Maine supposed, it is certainly very far from being satisfactory either in extent or in accuracy. Travellers naturally find it far easier to describe the houses, boats, food, dress, weapons, and implements of savages, than to understand their thoughts and feelings. The whole mental condition of a savage is so different from ours, that it is often very difficult to follow what is passing in his mind, or to understand the motives by which he is influenced. Many things appear natural and almost self-evident to him, which produce a very different impression on us. ' What !' said a negro to Burton, ' am I to starve, while my sister has children whom she can sell?'

Though savages always have a reason, such as it is, for what they do and what they believe, their reasons often are very absurd. Moreover, the difficulty of ascertaining what is passing in their minds is of course much enhanced by the difficulty of communicating with them. This has produced many laughable mistakes. Thus, when Labillardière enquired of the Friendly Islanders the word for 1,000,000, they seem to have thought the question absurd, and gave him one which apparently has no meaning; when he asked for 10,000,000, they said ' looole,' which I will leave unexplained; for 100,000,000 ' laounoua,' that is to say, ' nonsense ; ' while for the higher numbers they gave him certain coarse expressions, which he has gravely published in his table of numerals.

A mistake made by Dampier led to more serious results. He had met some Australians, and apprehending an attack, he says :—' I discharged my gun to scare them, but avoided shooting any of them; till finding the young man in great danger from them, and myself in some, and that though the gun had a little frightened them at first, yet *they had soon learnt to despise it*, tossing up their hands, and crying, " pooh, pooh, pooh ; " and coming on afresh with a great noise, I thought it high time to charge again, and shoot one of them, which I did. The rest, seeing him fall, made a stand again, and my young man took the opportunity to disengage himself, and come off to me ; my other man also was with me, who had done nothing all this while, having come out unarmed ; and I returned back with my men, designing to attempt the natives no farther, being very sorry for what had happened already.'[1] Pooh, pooh, however, or puff, puff, is the name which savages, like children, naturally apply to guns.

Another source of error is that savages are often reluctant to contradict what is said to them. Thus Mr. Oldfield,[2] speaking of the Australians, tells us :—' I have found this habit of non-contradiction to stand very much in my way when making enquiries of them; for, as my knowledge of their language was only sufficient to enable me to seek information on some points by putting suggestive questions, in which they immediately concurred, I was frequently driven nearly to my wits' end to arrive at the truth. A native once brought me in some specimens of a species of eucalyptus, and being desirous of ascertaining the habit of the plant, I asked, " A tall tree ?" to which his ready answer was in the affirmative. Not feeling quite satisfied, I again demanded, " A low bush ? " to which " yes " was also the response.'

Again, the mind of the savage, like that of the child, is easily fatigued, and he will then give random answers to

---

[1] Pinkerton's Voyages, vol. xi. p. 473.   [2] Trans. Ethn. Soc. N.S. vol. iii. p. 255.

spare himself the trouble of thought. Speaking of the Ahts (N.W. America), Mr. Sproat [1] says :—'The native mind, to an educated man, seems generally to be asleep; and, if you suddenly ask a novel question, you have to repeat it while the mind of the savage is awaking, and to speak with emphasis until he has quite got your meaning. This may partly arise from the questioner's imperfect knowledge of the language; still, I think, not entirely, as the savage may be observed occasionally to become forgetful, when voluntarily communicating information. On his attention being fully aroused, he often shows much quickness in reply and ingenuity in argument. But a short conversation wearies him, particularly if questions are asked that require efforts of thought or memory on his part. The mind of the savage then appears to rock to and fro out of mere weakness, and he tells lies and talks nonsense.'

' I frequently enquired of the negroes,' says Park, ' what became of the sun during the night, and whether we should see the same sun, or a different one, in the morning; but I found that they considered the question as very childish. The subject appeared to them as placed beyond the reach of human investigation; they had never indulged a conjecture, nor formed any hypothesis, about the matter.' [2]

Such ideas are, in fact, entirely beyond the mental range of the lower savages, whose extreme mental inferiority we have much difficulty in realising.

Speaking of the wild men in the interior of Borneo, Mr. Dalton says that [3] they are found living ' absolutely in a state of nature, who neither cultivate the ground, nor live

[1] Scenes and Studies of Savage Life, p. 120.
[2] Park's Travels, vol. i. p. 265.
[3] Moor's Notices of the Indian Army, p. 49. See also Keppel's Expedition to Borneo, vol. ii. p. x.

in huts; who neither eat rice nor salt, and who do not
associate with each other, but rove about some woods, like
wild beasts; the sexes meet in the jungle, or the man
carries away a woman from some campong. When the
children are old enough to shift for themselves, they
usually separate, neither one afterwards thinking of the
other: at night they sleep under some large tree, the
branches of which hang low. On these they fasten the
children in a kind of swing ; around the tree they make a
fire to keep off the wild beasts and snakes,—they cover
themselves with a piece of bark, and in this also they wrap
their children ; it is soft and warm, but will not keep out
the rain. The poor creatures are looked on and treated
by the other Dyaks as wild beasts.'

Lichtenstein thus describes a Bushman :—' One of our
present guests, who appeared about fifty years of age,
who had grey hair and a bristly beard, whose forehead,
nose, cheeks, and chin were all smeared over with black
grease, having only a white circle round the eye washed
clean with the tears occasioned by smoking—this man had
the true physiognomy of the small blue ape of Caffraria.
What gives the more verity to such a comparison was
the vivacity of his eyes, and the flexibility of his eyebrows,
which he worked up and down with every change of
countenance. Even his nostrils and the corners of his
mouth, nay his very ears, moved involuntarily, expressing his hasty transitions from eager desire to watch-
ful distrust. There was not, on the contrary, a single
feature in his countenance that evinced a consciousness of
mental powers, or anything that denoted emotions of the
mind of a milder species than what belong to man in his
mere animal nature. When a piece of meat was given him,
and half rising he stretched out a distrustful arm to take
it, he snatched it hastily, and stuck it immediately into

the fire, peering around with his little keen eyes, as if fearing lest some one should take it away again :—all this was done with such looks and gestures, that anyone must have been ready to swear he had taken the example of them entirely from an ape. He soon took the meat from the embers, wiped it hastily with his right hand upon his left arm, and tore out large half-raw bits with his teeth, which I could see going entire down his meagre throat.'[1]

Under these circumstances it cannot be wondered that we have most contradictory accounts as to the character and mental condition of savages. Nevertheless, by comparing together the accounts of different travellers, we can to a great extent avoid these sources of error; and we are very much aided in this by the remarkable similarity between different races. So striking indeed is this, that different races in similar stages of development often present more features of resemblance to one another than the same race does to itself, in different stages of its history.

Some ideas, indeed, which seem to us at first inexplicable and fantastic are yet very widely distributed. Thus among many races a woman is absolutely forbidden to speak to her son-in-law. Franklin[2] tells us that among the American Indians of the far North, ' it is considered extremely improper for a mother-in-law to speak or even look at him ; and when she has a communication to make to him, it is the etiquette that she should turn her back upon him, and address him only through the medium of a third person.'

Further south among the Omahaws, ' neither the father-in-law nor mother-in-law will hold any direct communica-

[1] Lichtenstein, vol. ii. p. 224.
[2] Journey to the Shores of the Polar Sea, vol. i. p. 137.

tion with their son-in-law; nor will he, on any occasion, or under any consideration, converse immediately with them, although no ill will exists between them; they will not, on any account, mention each other's name in company, nor look in each other's faces; any conversation that passes between them is conducted through the medium of some other person.'[1]

Harmon says that among the Indians east of the Rocky Mountains the same rule prevails. Lafitau,[2] indeed, makes the same statements as regards the North American Indians generally. We find it among the Crees and Dacotahs and again in Florida. Rochefort mentions it among the Caribs, and in South America it recurs among the Arawaks.

In Asia among the Mongols and Calmucks a woman must not speak to her father-in-law nor sit down in his presence. Among the Ostiaks[3] of Siberia, 'une fille mariée évite autant qu'il lui est possible la présence du père de son mari, tant qu'elle n'a pas d'enfant; et le mari, pendant ce tems, n'ose pas paroître devant la mère de sa femme. S'ils se rencontrent par hasard, le mari lui tourne le dos, et la femme se couvre le visage. On ne donne point de nom aux filles Ostiakes; lorsqu'elles sont mariées, les hommes les nomment Imi, femmes. Les femmes, par respect pour leurs maris, ne les appellent pas par leur nom; elles se servent du mot de Tahé, hommes.'

In China, according to Duhalde, the father-in-law, after the wedding day, 'never sees the face of his daughter-in-law again, he never visits her,' and if they chance to meet

---

[1] James's Expedition to the Rocky Mountains, vol. i. p. 232.

[2] Mœurs des Sauvages Américains, vol. i. p. 576.

[3] Pallas, vol. iv. pp. 71, 577. He makes the same statement with reference to the Samoyedes. loc. cit. p. 99.

he hides himself.[1] A similar custom prevails in Borneo and in the Fiji Islands. In Australia Eyre states that a man must not pronounce the name of his father-in-law, his mother-in-law, or his son-in-law.

In Central Africa Caillié [1] observes that, 'From this moment the lover is not to see the father and mother of his future bride: he takes the greatest care to avoid them, and if by chance they perceive him they cover their faces, as if all ties of friendship were broken. I tried in vain to discover the origin of this whimsical custom; the only answer I could obtain was, "It is our way." The custom extends beyond the relations; if the lover is of a different camp, he avoids all the inhabitants of the lady's camp, except a few intimate friends whom he is permitted to visit. A little tent is generally set up for him, under which he remains all day, and if he is obliged to come out, or to cross the camp, he covers his face. He is not allowed to see his intended during the day, but, when everybody is at rest, he creeps into her tent and remains with her till daybreak.' While among the Bushmen in the far South, Chapman recounts exactly the same thing, yet none of these observers had any idea how general the custom is.

Mr. Tyler, who has some very interesting remarks on these customs in his 'Early History of Man,' observes that 'it is hard even to guess what state of things can have brought them into existence,' nor, so far as I am aware, has anyone else attempted to explain them. In the Chapter on Marriage I shall, however, point out the manner in which I conceive that they have arisen.

Another curious custom is that known in Bearn under

[1] Astley's Collection of Voyages, vol. iv. p. 91.
[2] Caillié's Travels to Timbuctoo, vol. i. p. 94.

the name of La Couvade. Probably every Englishman
who had not studied other races would assume, as a matter of course, that on the birth of a child the mother would
everywhere be put to bed and nursed.   But this is not the
case.   In many races the father, and not the mother, is
doctored when a baby is born.

Yet though this custom seems so ludicrous to us, it is
very widely distributed. Commencing with South America,
Dobritzhoffer tells us that ' No sooner do you hear that
a woman has borne a child, than you see the husband
lying in bed, huddled up with mats and skins, lest some
ruder breath of air should touch him, fasting, kept in
private, and for a number of days abstaining religiously
from certain viands ; you would swear it was he who had
had the child. . . . I had read about this in old times,
and laughed at it, never thinking I could believe such
madness, and I used to suspect that this barbarian custom
was related more in jest than in earnest ; but at last I
saw it with my own eyes among the Abipones.'

In Brazil among the Coroados, Martius tells us that ' As
soon as the woman is evidently pregnant, or has been delivered, the man withdraws.   A strict regimen is observed
before the birth ; the man and the woman refrain for a
time from the flesh of certain animals and live chiefly on
fish and fruits.' [1]

Further north, in Guiana, Mr. Brett[2] observes that some
of the men of the Acawoio and Caribi nations, when
they have reason to expect an increase of their families,
consider themselves bound to abstain from certain kinds
of meat, lest the expected child should, in some very
mysterious way, be injured by their partaking of it.   The
Acouri (or Agouti) is thus tabooed, lest, like that little

[1] Spix and Martius's Travels in Brazil, vol. ii. p. 247.
[2] Brett's Indian Tribes of Guiana, p. 355.

animal, the child should be meagre ;— the *Haimara*, also, lest it should be blind—the outer coating of the eye of that fish suggesting film or cataract; the *Labba*, lest the infant's mouth should protrude like the labba's, or lest it be spotted like the labba, which spots would ultimately become ulcers. The *Marudi* is also forbidden, lest the infant be still-born, the screeching of that bird being considered ominous of death.' And again :—' On the birth of a child, the ancient Indian etiquette requires the father to take to his hammock, where he remains some days as if he were sick, and receives the congratulations and condolence of his friends. An instance of this custom came under my own observation; where the man, in robust health and excellent condition, without a single bodily ailment, was lying in his hammock in the most provoking manner; and carefully and respectfully attended by the women, while the mother of the new-born infant was cooking—none apparently regarding her!' [1]

Similar statements have been made by various other travellers, including De Tertre, Giliz, Biet, Fermin, and in fact almost all who have written on the natives of South America.

In Greenland, after a woman is confined, the ' husband must forbear working for some weeks, neither must they drive any trade during that time; ' [2] in Kamskatka, for some time before the birth of a baby, the husband must do no hard work. Similar notions occur among the Chinese of West Yunnan, among the Dyaks of Borneo, in the north of Spain, in Corsica, and in the south of France where it is called ' faire la Couvade.' While, however, I regard this curious custom as of much ethnological interest, I cannot agree with Mr. Tyler in regarding it as evidence that the races by whom it is practised belong to

---

[1] Brett, *loc. cit.* p. 101.   [2] Egede's Greenland, p. 196.

one variety of the human species.[1]   On the contrary, I
believe that it originated independently, in several distinct parts of the world.

It is of course evident that a custom so ancient, and so
widely spread, must have its origin in some idea which
satisfies the savage mind.   Several have been suggested.
Professor Max Müller,[2] in his 'Chips from a German
Workshop,' says :—' It is clear that the poor husband was
at first tyrannized over by his female relations, and afterwards frightened into superstition.   He then began to
make a martyr of himself till he made himself really ill,
or took to his bed in self-defence.   Strange and absurd as
the Couvade appears at first sight, there is something in
it with which, we believe, most mothers-in-law can sym-
pathise.'   Lafitau [3] regards it as arising from a dim re-
collection of original sin, rejecting the Carib and Abipon
explanation, which I have little doubt is the correct one,
that they do it because they believe that if the father
engaged in any rough work, or was careless in his diet
' cela feroit mal à l'enfant, et que cet enfant participeroit
a tous les défauts naturels des animaux dont le père auroit
mangé.'

This idea, namely, that a person imbibes the characteristics of an animal which he eats, is very widely distributed.
Thus the Malays at Singapore give a large price for the
flesh of the tiger, not because they like it, but because
they believe that the man who eats tiger ' acquires the
sagacity as well as the courage of that animal.'[4]   In
ancient times those who wished for children used to eat
frogs, because that animal lays so many eggs.' [5]

[1] *Loc. cit.* p. 296.
[2] Chips from a German Workshop, vol. ii. p. 281.
[3] Mœurs des Sauvages Américains,
vol. i. p. 259.

[4] Keppel's Visit to the Indian
Archipelago, p. 13.
[5] Inman's Ancient Faiths in
Ancient Names, p. 383.

'The Dyaks of Borneo have a prejudice against the flesh of deer, which the men may not eat, but which is allowed to women and children. The reason given for this is, that if the warriors eat the flesh of deer, they become as faint-hearted as that animal.'[1]

The Caribs will not eat the flesh of pigs or of tortoises, lest their eyes should become as small as those of these animals.[2] The Dacotahs eat the liver of the dog, in order to possess the sagacity and bravery of that animal.[3] The Arabs also impute the passionate and revengeful character of their countrymen to the use of camel's flesh.[4]

Tyler mentions[5] that ' an English merchant in Shanghai, at the time of the Taeping attack, met his Chinese servant carrying home a heart, and asked him what he had got there. He said it was the heart of a rebel, and that he was going to take it home and eat it to make him brave.' The New Zealanders, after baptising an infant, used to make it swallow pebbles, so that its heart might be hard and incapable of pity.[6]

Even cannibalism is sometimes due to this idea, and the New Zealanders eat their most formidable enemies partly for this reason. It is from the same kind of idea that ' eyebright,' because the flower somewhat resembles an eye, was supposed to be good for ocular complaints.

To us the idea seems absurd. Not so to children. I have myself heard a little girl say to her brother, ' If you eat so much goose you will be quite silly; ' and there are perhaps few children to whom the induction would not seem perfectly legitimate.

[1] Keppel's Expedition to Borneo, vol. i. p. 231.

[2] Müller's Geschichte der Americanischen Urreligionen, p. 221.

[3] Schoolcraft's Indian Tribes, vol. ii. p. 80.

[4] Astley's Collection of Voyages, vol. ii. p. 143.

[5] Early History of Man, p. 131.

[6] Yate's New Zealand, p. 82.

From the same notion the Esquimaux, ' to render barren women fertile or teeming, take old pieces of the soles of our shoes to hang about them; for, as they take our nation to be more fertile, and of a stronger disposition of body than theirs, they fancy the virtue of our body communicates itself to our clothing.' [1]

In fact savages do not act without reason any more than we do, though their reasons may often be bad ones and seem to us singularly absurd. Thus they have a great dread of having their portraits taken. The better the likeness, the worse they think for the sitter; so much life could not be put into the copy except at the expense of the original. Once when a good deal annoyed by some Indians, Kane got rid of them instantly by threatening to draw them if they remained. Catlin tells an amusing, but melancholy anecdote, in reference to this feeling. On one occasion he was drawing a chief named Mahtocheega, in profile. This when observed excited much commotion among the Indians : ' Why was half his face left out ? ' they asked; ' Mahtocheega was never ashamed to look a white in the face.' Mahtocheega himself does not seem to have taken any offence, but Shonka, ' the Dog,' took advantage of the idea to taunt him. ' The Englishman knows,' he said, ' that you are but half a man; he has painted but one-half of your face, and knows that the rest is good for nothing.' This view of the case led to a fight, in which poor Mahtocheega was shot; and as ill-luck would have it, the bullet by which he was killed tore away just that part of the face which had been omitted in the drawing.

This was very unfortunate for Mr. Catlin, who had great difficulty in making his escape, and lived some months

[1] Egede's Greenland, p. 198.

after in fear for his life; nor was the matter settled until both Shonka and his brother had been killed in revenge for the death of Mahtocheega.

Franklin also mentions that the North American Indians ' prize pictures very highly, and esteem any they can get, however badly executed, as efficient charms.' [1]

The natives of Bornou had a similar horror of being ' written;' they said ' that they did not like it; that the Sheik did not like it; that it was a sin; and I am quite sure, from the impression, that we had much better never have produced the book at all.'[2] In his Travels in Lapland Sir A. de C. Brooke says :—' I could clearly perceive[3] that many of them imagined the magical art to be connected with what I was doing, and on this account showed signs of uneasiness, till reassured by some of the merchants. An instance of this happened one morning, when a Laplander knocked at the door of my chamber, and entered it, as they usually did, without further ceremony. Having come to Alten to Hammerfest on some business, curiosity had induced him, previously to his return, to pay the Englishman a visit. After a dram he seemed quite at his ease; and producing my pencil, I proceeded, as he stood, to sketch his portrait. His countenance now immediately changed, and taking up his cap, he was on the point of making an abrupt exit, without my being able to conjecture the cause. As he spoke only his own tongue, I was obliged to have recourse to assistance; when I found that his alarm was occasioned by my employment, which he at once comprehended, but suspected that, by obtaining a likeness of him, I should acquire over him a certain power and influence that might be prejudicial. He there-

[1] Voyage to the Polar Seas, vol. ii. p. 6.
[2] Denham's Travels in Africa, vol. i. p. 275.
[3] Brooke's Lapland, p. 354.

fore refused to allow it, and expressed a wish, before any
other steps were taken, to return to Alton, and ask the
permission of his master.' Mr. Ellis mentions the existence of a similar feeling in Madagascar.[1]

We can hardly wonder that writing should seem to
savages even more magical than drawing. Carver, for
instance, allowed the North American Indians to open
a book as often as and wherever they pleased, and then
told them the number of leaves. 'The only way they
could account,' he says, 'for my knowledge, was by concluding that the book was a spirit, and whispered me
answers to whatever I demanded of it.'[2] Further south
the Minatarrees, seeing Catlin intent over a copy of the
'New York Commercial Advertiser,' were much puzzled,
but at length came to the conclusion that it was a medi-
cine-cloth for sore eyes. One of them eventually bought
it for a high price.[3]

This use of writing as a medicine prevails largely in
Africa, where the priests or wizards write a prayer on a
piece of board, wash it off and make the patient drink it.
Caillié,[4] met with a man who had a great reputation for
sanctity, and who made his living by writing prayers on a
board, washing them off, and then selling the water, which
was sprinkled over various objects, and supposed to improve or protect them.

Mungo Park on one occasion profited by this idea. 'A
Bambarran having,' he says, 'heard that I was a Christian,
immediately thought of procuring a saphie; and for this
purpose brought out his *walha* or writing-board, assuring me that he would dress me a supper of rice, if I would
write him a saphie to protect him from wicked men. The

[1] Three Visits to Madagascar, p. 358.   [3] American Indians, vol. ii. p. 92.
[2] Travels, p. 255.   [4] Travels, vol. i. p. 262.

proposal was of too great consequence to me to be refused : I therefore wrote the board full from top to bottom on both sides; and my landlord, to be certain of having the whole force of the charm, washed the writing from the board into a calabash with a little water, and having said a few prayers over it, drank this powerful draught; after which, lest a single word should escape, he licked the board until it was quite dry.'[1]

In Africa, the prayers written as medicine or as amulets are generally taken from the Koran. It is admitted that they are no protection from firearms, but this does not the least weaken the faith in them, because, as guns were not invented in Mahomet's time, he naturally provided no specific against them.[2]

Among the Kirghiz also, Atkinson tells us that the Mullas sell similar amulets, ' at the rate of a sheep for each scrap of paper.'[3]

The science of medicine indeed, like that of astronomy, and like religion, takes among savages very much the character of witchcraft. Ignorant as they are of the processes by which life is maintained, of anatomy and of physiology, the true nature of disease does not occur to them. Many savage races do not believe in natural death, and if a man, however old, dies without being wounded, conclude that he must have been the victim of magic.

Thus then, when a savage is ill, he naturally attributes his sufferings to some enemy within him, or to some foreign object, and the result is a peculiar system of treatment which is very curious both for its simplicity and universality.

' It is remarkable in the Abiponian (Paraguay) phy-

[1] Park's Travels, vol. i. pp. 357. See also p. 56.

[2] Astley's Collection of Voyages, vol. ii. p. 35.

[3] Siberia, p. 310.

sicians,' says Father Dobrizhoffer,[1] 'that they cure every
kind of disease with one and the same medicine. Let us examine this method of healing. They apply their lips to the
part affected, and suck it, spitting after every suction.   At
intervals they draw up their breath from the very bottom
of their breast and blow upon that part of the body which
is in pain.   That blowing and sucking are alternately repeated . . . This method of healing is in use amongst all
the savages of Paraguay and Brazil that I am acquainted
with, and, according to Father Jean Grillet, amongst the
Galibe Indians. . . . The Abipones, still more irrational,
expect sucking and blowing to rid the body of whatever
causes pain or inconvenience.   This belief is constantly
fostered by the jugglers with fresh artifices.   For when
they prepare to suck the sick man, they secretly put thorns,
beetles, worms, &c. into their mouths, and spitting them
out, after having sucked for some time, say to him, pointing to the worm or thorn, " See here the cause of your
disorder."   At this sight the sick man revives, when he
thinks the enemy that has tormented him is at length
expelled.'

   At first one might almost be disposed to think that some
one had been amusing himself at the expense of the
worthy father, but we shall find the very same mode of
treatment among other races.   Martius tells us that the
cures of the Guaycurus (Brazil) ' are very simple, and
consist principally in fumigating or in sucking the part
affected, on which the Payé spits into a pit, as if he
would give back the evil principle which he has sucked
out, to the earth and bury it.'[2]   Father Bagert mentions
that the Californian sorcerers suck and blow upon those
who are ill, and finally show them some small object,
which they assure them has been extracted, and which
was the cause of the pain.   Wilkes thus describes a scene

[1] History of the Abipones, vol. ii. p. 249.
[2] Travels in Brazil, vol. ii. p. 77.

at Wallawalla on the Columbia River :—'The doctor, who was a woman, bending over the body, began to suck his neck and chest in different parts, in order more effectually to extract the bad spirit. She would every now and then seem to obtain some of the disease and then faint away. On the next morning she was still found sucking the boy's chest. . . . So powerful was the influence operated on the boy that he indeed seemed better. . . . The last time Mr. Drayton visited the doctress, she exhibited a stone, about the size of a goose's egg, saying that she had taken the disease of the boy out of him.'[1]

Among the Prairie Indians also, all diseases are treated alike, being referred to one cause, viz. the presence of an evil spirit, which must be expelled. This the medicine-man 'attempts, in the first place, by certain incantations and ceremonies, intended to secure the aid of the spirit or spirits he worships, and then, by all kinds of frightful noises and gestures, and sucking over the seat of pain with his mouth.'[2] Speaking of the Hudson's Bay Indians, Hearne says :—'Here it is necessary to remark, that they use no medicine either for internal or external complaints, but perform all their cures by charms. In ordinary cases, sucking the part affected, blowing and singing.'[3]

Again, in the extreme north, Crantz tells us that among the Esquimaux old women are accustomed 'to extract from a swollen leg a parcel of hair or scraps of leather ; they do it by sucking with their mouth, which they had before crammed full of such stuff.'[4] Passing now to the Lap-landers, we are told that if anyone among them is ill, a wizard sucks his forehead and blows in his face, thinking thus to cure him.

[1] United States Exploring Expedition, vol. iv. p. 400.
[2] Schoolcraft's Indian Tribes, vol. i. p. 250.
[3] Voyage to the Northern Ocean, p. 189.
[4] History of Greenland, vol. i. p. 214.

In South Africa, Chapman thus describes a similar custom : a man having been injured, he says, 'our friend sucked at the wound, and then . . . extracted from his mouth a lump of some substance which was supposed to be the disease.'[1]

In Australia, we are told by ex-Governor Eyre in his interesting work, that, 'as all internal pains are attributed to witchcraft, sorcerers possess the power of relieving or curing them. Sometimes the mouth is applied to the surface where the pain is seated, the blood is sucked out, and a bunch of green leaves applied to the part ; besides the blood, which is derived from the gums of the sorcerer, a bone is sometimes put out of the mouth, and declared to have been procured from the diseased part; on other occasions the disease is drawn out in an invisible form, and burnt in the fire, or thrown into the water.'[2]

Another curious remedy practised by the Australians is to tie a line round the forehead or neck of the patient, while some kind friend rubs her lips with the other end of the string, until they bleed freely ; this blood is supposed to come from the patient, passing along the string.[3]

Thus then we find all over the world this primitive cure by sucking out the evil, which perhaps even with ourselves lingers among nurses and children in the universal nursery remedy of 'Kiss it and make it well.'

A dislike of twins is widely distributed. In the Island of Bali[4] (near Java), the natives 'have the singular idea, when a woman is brought to bed of twins, that it is an unlucky omen, and immediately on its being known, the woman, with her husband and children, is obliged to go and live on the sea-shore, or among the tombs, for the

---

[1] Travels in Africa, vol. ii. p. 45.
[2] Discoveries in Central Australia vol. ii. p. 360. See also Oldfield's Trans. Ethn. Soc. N.S. vol. iii. p. 243.
[3] English Colony in New South Wales, pp. 363, 382.
[4] Moor's Notices of the Indian Archipelago, p. 96.

space of a month to purify themselves, after which they may return into the village upon a suitable sacrifice being made. Thus an evidence of fertility is considered by them unfortunate, and the poor woman and her new-born babes are exposed to all the inclemency of the weather out of doors, just at the time when they need the most attention.' This idea is, however, far from being peculiar to that island.

Among the Khasias of Hindostan[1] 'in the case of twins being born, one used frequently to be killed: it is considered unlucky, and also degrading, to have twins, as they consider that it assimilates them with the lower animals.'

Among the Ainos of Japan,[2] when twins are born, one is always destroyed. At Arebo in Guinea, Smith and Bosman[3] tell us that when twins are born, both they and the mother are killed. 'In Nguru, one of the sister provinces to Unyanyembé, twins are ordered to be killed and thrown into the water the moment they are born, lest droughts and famines or floods should oppress the land. Should anyone attempt to conceal twins, the whole family would be murdered.'[4]

The American Indians,[5] also, on the birth of twins killed one; perhaps merely under the idea that one strong child was better than two weak ones.

This is not however, I think, the general cause of the prejudice against twins. I should rather see it in the curious idea that one man would only have one child; so that twins imply infidelity of an aggravated character. Thus in the introduction to the curious old Chevalier Assigne, or Knight of the Swan :—

[1] Steel, Trans. Ethn. Soc. N.S. vol. vii. p. 308.

[2] Bickmore, Proc. Bost. Soc. of Nat. His., 1867.

[3] Voyage to Guinea, p. 233. Pinkerton, vol. xv. p. 526. Elsewhere in Guinea twins are welcomed.

[4] Speke's Discovery of the Source of the Nile, pp. 541, 542.

[5] Lafitau, vol. i. p. 592.

The king and queen are sitting on the wall together :

> The kynge loked adowne, and byholde under,
> And seygh a pore womman, at the yate sytte,
> Withe two chylderen her byfore, were borne at a byrthe ;
> And he turned hym thenne, and teres lette he falle.
> Sythen sykede he on hyghe, and to the qwene sayde,
> Se ye the yonder pore womman.   Now that she is pyned
> With twynlenges two, and that dare I my hedde wedde.
> The qwene nykked him with nay, and seyde it is not to leve :
> Oon manne for oon chylde, and two wymmen for tweyne ;
> Or ellis hit were unsemelye thynge, as me wolde thenke,
> But eche chylde hadde a fader, how manye so ther were.[1]

Since reading this I have found that the very same idea occurs in Guinea.[2]

Some curious ideas prevalent among savages arise from the fact that as their own actions are due to life, so they attribute life even to inanimate objects.   Even Plato assumed that every thing which moves itself must have a soul, and hence that the world must have a soul. Hearne tells us that the North American Indians prefer a hook that has caught a big fish to a handful that have never been tried.   And that they never put two nets together for fear they should be jealous.[3]

The Bushmen thought Chapman's big waggon was the mother of his smaller ones; they 'despise an arrow that has once failed of its mark ; and on the contrary, consider one that has hit as of double value. They will, therefore, rather make new arrows, how much time and trouble soever it may cost them, than collect those that have missed, and use them again.' [4]

The natives of Tahiti sowed some iron nails given them by Captain Cook, hoping thus to obtain young ones.   They

---

[1] The Romance of the Chevelere Assigne, edited by H. H. Gibbs, Esq. Trubners, 1868.

[2] Astley's Collection of Voyages, vol. iii. p. 83.   At p. 358 in the same vol., we find a curious variation of this idea among the Hottentots.

[3] *Loc. cit.*, p. 330.

[4] Lichtenstein's Travels in South Africa, vol. ii. p. 271.

also believe that 'not only all animals, but trees, fruit, and even stones, have souls, which at death or upon being consumed, or broken, ascend to the divinity, with whom they first mix, and afterwards pass into the mansion allotted to each.'

The Tongans were of opinion that ' if an animal dies,[1] its soul immediately goes to Bolotoo; if a stone or any other substance is broken, immortality is equally its reward; nay, artificial bodies have equal good luck with men, and hogs, and yams. If an axe or a chisel is worn out or broken up, away flies its soul for the service of the gods. If a house is taken down, or any way destroyed, its immortal part will find a situation on the plains of Bolotoo.'

Lichtenstein relates that the king of the Coussa Kaffirs having broken off a piece of the anchor of a stranded ship, died soon afterwards; upon which all the Kaffirs made a point of saluting the anchor very respectfully whenever they passed near it, regarding it as a vindictive being.

Some similar accident probably gave rise to the ancient Mohawk notion that some great misfortune would happen if anyone spoke on Saratoga Lake. A strong-minded English woman on one occasion while being ferried over insisted on talking, and, as she got over safely, rallied her boatman on his superstition; but I think he had the best of it after all, for he at once replied, ' The Great Spirit is merciful, and knows that a white woman cannot hold her tongue.' [2]

The forms of salutation among savages are sometimes very curious, and their modes of showing their feelings quite unlike ours. Kissing appears to us to be the natural language of affection. ' It is certain,' said Steele, ' that nature was its author, and it began with the first

---

[1] Mariner's Tonga Islands, vol. ii. p. 137.
[2] Burton's Abbeokuta, vol. i. p. 198.

courtship : ' but this seems to be quite a mistake ; in fact
it was unknown to the Australians, the New Zealanders,
the Papouans, and the Esquimaux ; the West African
negroes, we are told, do not like it, otherwise I should
have thought that when once discovered, it would have
been universally popular.

The Polynesians and the Malays always sit down when
speaking to a superior ; a Chinaman puts on his hat instead
of taking it off. Cook asserts that the people of Mallicollo
show their admiration by hissing, and the same is the case,
according to Casalis, among the Kaffirs.[1] In some of the
Pacific Islands, and some parts of Africa, it is considered
respectful to turn your back to a superior. The Todas
of the Neilgherry Hills are said to show respect by 'raising the open right hand to the brow, resting the thumb
on the nose ; ' and it has been asserted that in one tribe
of Esquimaux it is customary to pull a person's nose as
a compliment, though it is but right to say that Dr. Rae
thinks there was some mistake on the point ; on the other
hand, Dr. Blackmore mentions that ' the sign of the Arapa-
hoes, and from which they derive their name,' consists in
seizing the nose with the thumb and forefinger.[2]

It is asserted that in China, a coffin is regarded as an
appropriate present for an aged relative, especially if he
be in bad health.

---

[1] The Basutos ; by the Rev. E. Casalis, p. 234.
[2] Trans. Ethn. Soc., 1869, p. 310.

ANCIENT SKETCH OF A MAMMOTH.

CHAPTER II.

THE earliest traces of art yet discovered belong to the Stone Age,—to a time so early that the Reindeer was abundant in the south of France, and that probably, though on this point there is some doubt, even the mammoth had not entirely disappeared. These works of art are sometimes sculptures, if one may say so, and sometimes drawings or etchings made on bone or horn with the point of a flint.

They are of peculiar interest, both as being the earliest works of art known to us,—older than any Egyptian statues, or any of the Assyrian monuments, and also because, though so ancient, they show really considerable skill. There is, for instance, a certain spirit about the subjoined group of reindeer (fig. 1), copied from a specimen in the collection of the Marquis de Vibraye. The mammoth (Pl. I.) represented on the opposite page, though less artistic, is perhaps even more interesting. It is scratched on a piece of mammoth's tusk, and was found in the cave of La Madelaine in the Dordogne.

It is somewhat remarkable that while even in the Stone Period we find very fair drawings of animals, yet in the latest part of the Stone Age, and throughout that of Bronze, they are almost entirely wanting, and the ornamentation is confined to various combinations of straight and curved lines and geometrical patterns. This, I believe, will eventually be found to imply a difference of race between the population of Western Europe at these

Fig. 1.

GROUP OF REINDEER.

different periods. Thus at present the Esquimaux (see figs. 2–4) are very fair draughtsmen, while the Polynesians, though much more advanced in many ways, and though very skilful in ornamenting both themselves and their weapons, have very little idea indeed of representing animals or plants. Their tattooings, for instance, and the patterns on their weapons, are, like the ornaments of the Bronze Age, almost invariably of a geometrical character. Representations of animals and plants are not, indeed, entirely wanting; but, whether attempted in drawing or in sculpture, they are always rude and grotesque. With the Esquimaux the very reverse is the case; among them we find none of those graceful spirals, and other geometrical patterns, so characteristic of Polynesia; but, on the other hand, their weapons are often covered with

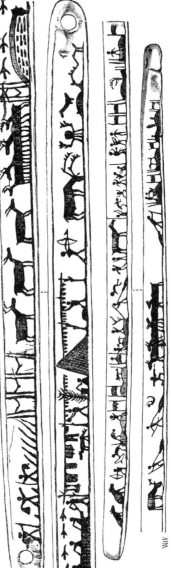

Figs. 2–4.

ETCHINGS ON ESQUIMAUX WEAPONS.

representations of animals and hunting scenes. Thus
Beechey,[1] describing the weapons of the Esquimaux at
Hotham's Inlet, says :—

'On the outside of this and other instruments there were
etched a variety of figures of men, beasts, birds, &c., with
a truth and character which showed the art to be common
among them. The reindeer were generally in herds; in
one picture they were pursued by a man in a stooping
posture, in snow-shoes; in another he had approached
nearer to his game, and was in the act of drawing his
bow. A third represented the manner of taking seals
with an inflated skin of the same animal as a decoy; it
was placed upon the ice, and not far from it was a man
lying upon his belly, with a harpoon ready to strike the
animal when it should make its appearance. Another was
dragging a seal home upon a small sledge; and several
baidars were employed harpooning whales which had been
previously shot with arrows; and thus, by comparing one
with another, a little history was obtained which gave us
a better insight into their habits than could be elicited
from any signs or intimations.' Some of these drawings
are represented in figs. 2–4, which are taken from specimens presented by Captain Beechey to the Ashmolean
Museum at Oxford.

Hooper[2] also mentions drawings among the Tuski, especially 'a sealskin tanned and bleached perfectly white,
ornamented all over in painting and staining with figures
of men, boats, animals, and delineations of whale-fishing,
&c.—a valuable curiosity.'

In the same way we may, I think, fairly hope eventually
to obtain from the ancient drawings of the bone caves a
better insight into the habits of our predecessors in

[1] Narrative of a Voyage to the Pacific, vol. i. p. 251.
[2] Tents of the Tuski, p. 65.

Western Europe; to ascertain, for instance, whether their reindeer were domesticated or wild. As yet, however, mere representations of animals have been met with, and nothing has been found to supplement in any way the evidence derivable from the implements, &c.

But though we thus find art—simple, indeed, but by no means contemptible—in very ancient times, and among very savage tribes, there are also other races who are singularly deficient in it.

Thus, though some Australians are capable of making rude drawings of animals, &c., others on the contrary, as Oldfield [1] tells us, ' seem quite unable to realise the most vivid artistic representations. On being shown a large coloured engraving of an aboriginal New Hollander, one declared it to be a ship, another a kangaroo, and so on; not one of a dozen identifying the portrait as having any connection with himself. A rude drawing, with all the lesser parts much exaggerated, they can realise. Thus, to give them an idea of a man, the head must be drawn disproportionately large.'

Dr. Collingwood,[2] speaking of the Kibalans of Formosa, to whom he showed a copy of the ' Illustrated London News,' tells us that he found it ' impossible to interest them by pointing out the most striking illustrations, which they did not appear to comprehend.'

Denham, in his ' Travels in Central Africa,' says that Bookhaloom, a man otherwise of considerable intelligence, though he readily recognised figures, could not understand a landscape. ' I could not,' he says, ' make him understand the intention of the print of the sand wind in the desert, which is really so well described by Captain Lyon's drawing; he would look at it upside down; and

[1] Trans. Ethn. Soc. N.S. vol. iii. p. 227.
[2] *Ibid.* vol. vi. p. 139.

when I twice reversed it for him, he exclaimed, " Why!
why! it is all the same." A camel or a human figure
was all I could make him understand, and at these he
was all agitation and delight—" Gieb! gieb! Wonderful! wonderful!" The eyes first took his attention, then
the other features ; at the sight of the sword he exclaimed,
" Allah! Allah!" and, on discovering the guns, instantly
exclaimed, " Where is the powder? " " ' [1]

So also the Kaffir has great difficulty in understanding
drawings, and perspective is altogether beyond him.
Central and Southern Africa seems, indeed, to be very
backward in matters of art. Still the negroes are not
altogether deficient in the idea. Their idols cannot be
called indeed works of art, but they often not only represent men, but give some of the African characteristics
with grotesque fidelity.

The Kaffirs also can carve fair representations of
animals and plants, and are fond of doing so. The handles
of their spoons are often shaped into unmistakeable like-
nesses of giraffes, ostriches, and other animals.

As to the Bushmen, we have rather different accounts.
It has been stated by some that they have no idea of perspective nor how a curved surface can possibly be represented on a flat piece of paper; while, on the contrary,
other travellers assert that they readily recognise drawings
of animals or flowers. The Chinese, although so advanced
in many ways, are, we know, very deficient in the idea of
perspective.

Probably, no race of men in the Stone Age had attained the art of communicating facts by means of letters,
nor even by the far ruder system of picture-writing; nor
does anything, perhaps, surprise the savage more than to

[1] Denham, Travels in Africa, vol. i. p. 167.

find that Europeans can communicate with one another by means of a few black scratches on a piece of paper.

Even the Peruvians had no better means of recording events than the Quippu or Quipu, which was a cord about two feet long, to which a number of different coloured threads were attached in the form of a fringe. These threads were tied into knots, whence the name Quippu meaning a knot. These knots served as cyphers, and the various threads had also conventional meanings attached to them and indicated by the various colours. This singular and apparently very cumbersome mode of assisting the memory reappears in China and in Africa. Thus, ' As to [1] the original of the Chinese characters, before the commencement of the monarchy, little cords with sliding knots, each of which had its particular signification, were used in transacting business. These are represented in two tables by the *Chinese*, called *Ho-tû*, and *Lo-shu*. The first colonies who inhabited *Se-chwen* had no other literature besides some arithmetical sets of counters made with little knotted cords, in imitation of a string of round beads ; with which they calculated and made up all their accounts in commerce.' Again, in West Africa, we are told that the people of Ardrah [2] ' can neither write nor read. They use small cords tied, the knots of which have their signification. These are also used by several savage nations in America.' It seems not impossible that tying a knot in a pocket-handkerchief may be the direct lineal representative of this ancient and widely extended mode of assisting the memory.

The so-called picture-writing is, however, a great advance. Yet from representations of hunts in general such as those of the Esquimaux (see figs. 2–4), it is indeed but a

---

[1] Astley's Collection of Voyages, vol. iv. p. 194.

[2] *Ibid.* vol. iii. p. 71.

step to record pictorially some particular hunt. Again, the
Esquimaux almost always places his mark on his arrows,
but I am not aware that any Polynesian ever conceived the
idea of doing so. Thus we get among the Esquimaux a
double commencement, as it were, for the representation
of ideas by means of signs.

This art of pictorial writing was still more advanced
among the Red Skins.

Thus Carver tells us that on one occasion his Chipéway
guide fearing that the Naudowessies, a hostile tribe, might
accidentally fall in with and attack them, ' peeled the bark
from a large tree near the entrance of a river, and with
wood-coal mixed with bear's grease, their usual substitute
for ink, made in an uncouth but expressive manner the
figure of the town of the Ottagaumies. He then formed
to the left a man dressed in skins, by which he intended
to represent a Naudowessie with a line drawn from his
mouth to that of a deer, the symbol of the Chipéways.
After this he depicted still farther to the left a canoe as
proceeding up the river, in which he placed a man sitting
with a hat on; this figure was designed to represent an
Englishman, or myself, and my Frenchman was drawn
with a handkerchief tied round his head, and rowing the
canoe; to these he added several other significant emblems, among which the pipe of peace appeared painted
on the prow of the canoe. The meaning he intended to
convey to the Naudowessies, and which I doubt not appeared perfectly intelligible to them, was that one of the
Chipéway chiefs had received a speech from some Naudowessie chiefs at the town of the Ottagaumies, desiring him
to conduct the Englishman, who had lately been among
them, up the Chipéway river; and that they thereby required, that the Chipéway, notwithstanding he was an
avowed enemy, should not be molested by them on his

FIG. 5.

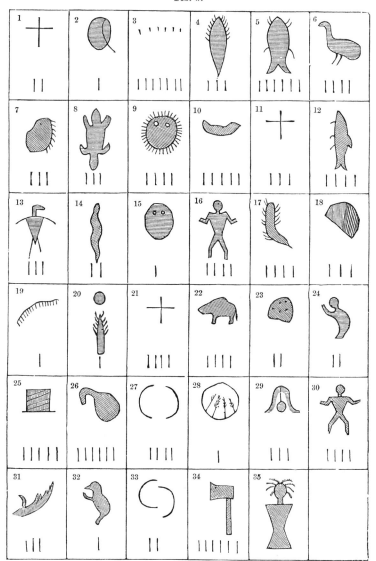

INDIAN CENSUS ROLL.

passage, as he had the care of a person whom they esteemed as one of their nation.' [1]

An excellent account of the Red Skin pictorial art is given by Schoolcraft in his 'History of the Indian Tribes in the United States.'

Fig. 5 represents the census-roll of an Indian band at Mille Lac, in the territory of Minnesota, sent in to the United States agent by Nago-nabe, a Chippewa Indian, during the progress of the annuity payments in 1849. The Indians generally denote themselves by their ' totem ' or family sign, but in this case, as they all had the same totem, he had designated each family by a sign denoting the common name of the Chief. Thus number 5 denotes a Catfish, and the six strokes indicate that the Catfish's family consisted of six individuals; 8 is a beaver skin, 9 a sun, 13 an eagle, 14 a snake, 22 a buffalo, 34, an axe, 35 the priest, and so on.

Fig. 6 is the record of a noted chief of the St. Mary's band, called Shin-ga-ba-was-sin, or the Image-stone, who died on Lake Superior in 1828. He was of the totem of the crane, as indicated by the figure. The six strokes on the right, and the three on the left, are marks of honour. The latter represent three important general treaties of peace in which he had taken part at various times.[2] Among the former marks are included his presence under Tecumseh, at the battle of Moraviantown, where he lost a brother.

Fig. 7 represents the adjedatig or tomb-board of Wabo-jeeg, a celebrated war-chief, who died on Lake Superior, about 1793. He was of the family or clan of the reindeer. This fact is symbolized by the figure of the deer. The reverse position denotes death. His own personal name, which was the White Fisher, is not noticed. The

[1] Carver's Travels, p. 418.   [2] Schoolcraft, Indian Tribes, vol. i. p. 357.

seven marks on the left denote that he had led seven
war parties. The three perpendicular lines below the
totem represent three wounds received in battle. The
figure of a moose's head relates to a desperate conflict

FIG. 6.   FIG. 7.

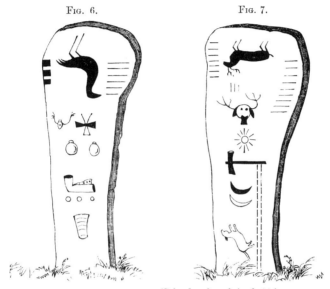

INDIAN GRAVE POSTS. (Schoolcraft, vol. i. pl. 50.)

with an enraged animal of this kind. Fig. 8 is copied
from a bark letter which was found above St. Anthony's
Falls, in 1820. 'It consisted of white birch bark, and
the figures had been carefully drawn. No. 1 denotes
the flag of the Union : No. 2 the cantonment, then recently established at Cold Spring, on the western side of
the cliffs, above the influx of the St. Peters : No. 4 is the
symbol of the commanding officer (Colonel H. Leavenworth), under whose authority a mission of peace had been
sent into the Chippewa country : No. 11 is the symbol of
Chakope, or the Six, the leading Sioux chief, under whose
orders the party moved : No. 8 is the second chief, called

Wabedatunka, or the Black Dog. The symbol of his name is No. 10; he has fourteen lodges. No. 7 is a chief,

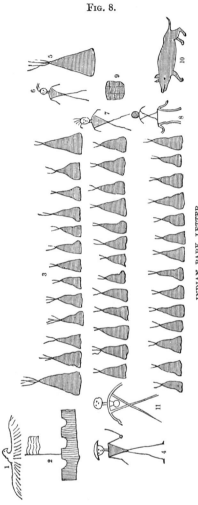

FIG. 8.

INDIAN BARK LETTER.

subordinate to Chakope, with thirteen lodges, and a bale of goods (No. 9) which was devoted, by the government, to the objects of the peace. The name of No. 6, whose wigwam is No. 5, with thirteen subordinate lodges, was not given.'[1]

This was intended to imply that a party of Sioux headed by Chakope and accompanied, or at least countenanced by Colonel Leavenworth, had come to this spot in the hope of meeting the Chippewa hunters and concluding a peace. The Chippewa chief Babesacundabee, who found this letter, read off its meaning without doubt or hesitation.

On one occasion a party of explorers with two Indian guides, saw one morning, just as they were about to start, a pole stuck in the direction they were

[1] Schoolcraft's Indian Tribes, vol. i. pp. 352, 353.

going, and holding at the top a piece of bark, covered with drawings, which were intended for the information of any other Indians who might pass that way. This is represented in fig. 9.

No. 1 represents the subaltern officer in command of the party. He is drawn with a sword to denote his rank. No. 2 denotes the secretary. He is represented as holding a book, the Indians having understood him to be an attorney. No 3 represents the geologist, appropriately indicated by a hammer. Nos. 4 and 5 are attachés; No. 6 the interpreter. The group of figures marked 9 repre-

FIG. 9.

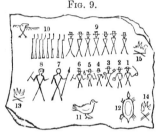

INDIAN BARK LETTER.

sents seven infantry soldiers, each of whom, as shown in group No. 10, was armed with a musket. No 15 denotes that they had a separate fire, and constituted a separate mess. Figs. 7 and 8 represent the two Chippewa guides. These are the only human figures drawn without the distinguishing symbol of a hat. This was the characteristic seized on by them, and generally employed by the Indians, to distinguish the *Red* from the *White* race. Figs. 11 and 12 represent a prairie hen and a green tortoise, which constituted the sum of the preceding day's chase, and were eaten at the encampment. The inclination of the pole was designed to show the course pursued; and there were three hacks in it below the scroll of bark, to indicate the estimated length of this part of the journey, com-

puting from water to water.   The following figure (fig. 10)
gives the biography of Wingemund, a noted chief of
the Delawares. 1 shows that it belonged to the oldest
branch of the tribe, which use the tortoise on their
symbol. 2 is his totem or symbol; 3 is the sun, and
the ten strokes represent ten war parties in which he
was engaged.   Those figures on the left represent the
captives which he made in each of his excursions, the

FIG. 10.

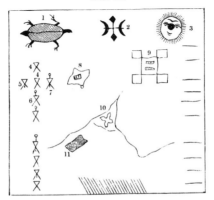

INDIAN BARK LETTER.

men being distinguished from the women, and the captives being denoted by having heads, while a man without his head is of course a dead man.   The central
figures represent three forts which he attacked; 8 one
on lake Erie, 9 that of Detroit, and 10 Fort Pitt at the
junction of the Alleghany and the Monongahela.   The
sloping strokes denote the number of his followers.[1]

Fig. 11 represents a petition presented to the President
of the United States for the right to certain Lakes (8) in
the neighbourhood of Lake Superior (10).

No 1 represents Oshcabawis the leader, who is of the

[1] Schoolcraft, vol. i. p. 353.

Fig. 11.

INDIAN PETITION.

Crane clan. The eyes of his followers are all connected with his to symbolise unity of views, and their hearts to denote unity of feeling. No 2 is Wai-mit-tig-oazh, whose totem is a Marten : No 3 is Ogemageezhig, also a Marten ; 4 is another Marten, Muk-o-mis-ud-ains, the little Tortoise : 5 is O-mush-kose, the little Elk, belonging however to the Bear totem : 6 belongs to the Manfish totem ; and 7 to the Catfish. The eye of the leader has a line directed forwards to the President, and another backwards to the Lakes (8).

In some places of Western Europe, rock sculptures have been discovered, to which we cannot yet safely ascribe any meaning, but on which perhaps the more complete study of the picture-writing of modern savages may eventually throw some light.

We will now pass to art as applied to the purposes of personal decoration. Savages are passionately fond of ornaments. In some of the very lowest races, indeed, the women are almost undecorated, but that is only because the men keep all the ornaments themselves. As a general rule we may say that Southerners ornament themselves, Northerners their clothes. In fact all savage races who leave much of their skin uncovered, delight in painting themselves in the most brilliant colours they can obtain. Black, white, red, and yellow are the favourite, or, rather, perhaps, the commonest colours. Although perfectly naked, the Australians of Botany Bay were by no means without ornaments. They painted themselves with red ochre, white clay, and charcoal ; the red was laid on in broad patches, the white generally in stripes, or on the face in spots, often with a circle round each eye ; [1] through the septum of the nose they wore a bone, as thick as a man's finger and five or six inches long. This was of

[1] Hawkesworth's Voyages, vol. iii. p. 635.

course very awkward, as it prevented them from breathing freely through the nose, but they submitted cheerfully to the inconvenience for the sake of appearance.

They had also necklaces made of shells, neatly cut and strung together; earrings, bracelets of small cord; and strings of plaited human hair, which they wound round their waists. Some also had gorgets of large shells hanging from the neck across the breast. On all these things they placed a high value.

Spix and Martius[1] thus describe the ornaments of a Coroado woman. 'On the cheek she had a circle, and over that two strokes; under the nose several marks resembling an M; from the corners of the mouth to the middle of the cheek were two parallel lines, and below them on both sides many straight stripes; below and between her breasts there were some connected segments of circles, and down her arms the figure of a snake was depicted. This beauty wore no ornaments, except a necklace of monkeys' teeth.'

The savage also wears necklaces and rings, bracelets and anklets, armlets and leglets—even, if I may say so, bodylets. Round their bodies, round their necks, round their arms and legs, their fingers, and even their toes, they wear ornaments of all kinds. From their number and weight these must sometimes be very inconvenient. Lichtenstein saw the wife of a Beetuan chief wearing no less than seventy-two brass rings.

Nor are they particular as to the material: copper, brass, or iron, leather, or ivory, stones, shells, glass, bits of wood, seeds, or teeth—nothing comes amiss. In South East Island, one of the Louisiade Archipelago, M'Gillivray even saw several bracelets made each of a lower human jaw, crossed by a collar-bone; and other travellers have

---

[1] Travels in Brazil, vol. ii. p. 224.

seen brass curtain rings, the brass plates for keyholes, the lids of sardine cases, and other such incongruous objects, worn with much gravity and pride.

The Felatah ladies in Central Africa spend several hours a day over their toilet. In fact they begin over-night by carefully wrapping their fingers and toes in henna leaves, so that by morning they are a beautiful purple. The teeth are stained alternately blue, yellow, and purple, one here and there being left of its natural colour, as a contrast. About the eyelids they are very particular; they pencil them with sulphuret of antimony. The hair is coloured carefully with indigo. Studs and other jewellery are worn in great profusion.[1]

Not content with hanging things round their necks, arms, ankles, and in fact wherever nature has enabled them to do so, savages also cut holes in themselves for the purpose.

The Esquimaux from Mackenzie River westward make two openings in their cheeks, one on each side, which they gradually enlarge, and in which they wear an ornament of stone resembling in form a large stud, and which may therefore be called a cheek stud.

Throughout a great part of Western America, and again in Africa, we also find the custom of wearing a piece of wood through the central part of the lower lip. A small hole is made in the lip during infancy, and it is then extended by degrees until it is sometimes as much as two inches long.

Some races extend the lobe of the ear until it reaches the shoulder; others file the teeth in various manners.

Dr. J. B. Davis has a Dyak skull in which the six front teeth have each been carefully pierced with a small hole, into which a pin with a spherical brass head has been

---

[1] Laird, Expedition into the Interior of Africa, vol. ii. p. 94.

driven. In this way, the upper lip being raised, the shining knob on each tooth would be displayed.[1] Some of the African tribes also chip their teeth in various manners, each community having a fashion of its own.

Ornamentation of the skin is almost universal among the lower races of men. In some cases every individual follows his own fancy; in others each clan has a special pattern. Thus, speaking of Abbeokuta, Captain Burton[2] says :—' There was a vast variety of tattoos and ornamentation, rendering them a serious difficulty to strangers. The skin patterns were of every variety, from the diminutive prick to the great gash and the large boil-like lumps. They affected various figures—tortoises, alligators, and the favourite lizard, stars, concentric circles, lozenges, right lines, welts, gouts of gore, marble or button-like knobs of flesh, and elevated scars, resembling scalds, which are opened for the introduction of fetish medicines, and to expel evil influences. In this country every tribe, sub-tribe, and even family, has its blazon,[3] whose infinite diversifications may be compared with the lines and ordinaries of European heraldry.'

In South Africa the Nyambanas are characterised by a row of pimples or warts, about the size of a pea, and extending from the upper part of the forehead to the tip of the nose. Among the Bachapin Kaffirs, those who have distinguished themselves in battle are allowed the privilege of marking their thigh with a long scar, which is rendered indelible and of a bluish colour by rubbing ashes into the fresh wound.

The tribal mark of the Bunns[4] (Africa) consists of three

[1] Thesaurus Craniorum, p. 289.
[2] Abbeokuta, vol. i. p. 104.
[3] Ogubonna's family, for instance, have three small squares of blue tattoo upon each cheek, combined with the three Egba cuts.
[4] Trans. Ethn. Soc. vol. v. p. 86.

slashes from the crown of the head, down the face, towards the mouth; the ridges of flesh stand out in bold relief. This painful operation is performed by cutting the skin, and taking out a strip of flesh; palm oil and wood ashes are then rubbed into the wound, thus causing a thick ridge.

The Bornouese in Central Africa have twenty cuts or lines on each side of the face, which are drawn from the corners of the mouth towards the angles of the lower jaw and cheekbone. They have also one cut in the centre of the forehead, six on each arm, six on each leg, four on each breast, and nine on each side, just above the hips. This makes 91 large cuts, and the process is said to be extremely painful on account of the heat and flies.[1]

The women of Brumer Island, on the south coast of New Guinea, were tattooed on the face, arms, and front of the body, but generally not on the back, in vertical stripes less than an inch apart, and connected by zigzag markings. On the face these are more complicated, and on the forearm and wrist they were frequently so elaborate as to resemble lace-work.[2] The men were more rarely tattooed, and then only with a few lines or stars on the right breast. Sometimes, however, the markings consisted of a double series of large stars and dots stretching from the shoulder to the pit of the stomach.

The inhabitants of Tanna have on their arms and chests elevated scars, representing plants, flowers, stars, and various other figures. 'The inhabitants of Tazovan, or Formosa, by a very painful operation, impress on their naked skins various figures of trees, flowers, and animals. The great men in Guinea have their skin flowered like damask; and in Decan, the women likewise have flowers cut into their flesh on the forehead, the arms, and the

---

[1] Denham, vol. iii. p. 175.

[2] McGillivray's Voyage of the Rattlesnake, vol. i. p. 262.

breast, and the elevated scars are painted in colours, and exhibit the appearance of flowered damask.'[1]

In the Tonga Islands 'the men are tattooed from the middle of the thigh to above the hips. The women are only tattooed on the arms and fingers, and there very slightly.'[2] In the Fiji Islands, on the contrary, the women are more tattooed than the men. When tastefully executed, tattooing has been regarded by many travellers as a real ornament. Thus Laird says that some of the tattooing in West Africa 'in the absence of clothing gives a finish to the skin.'[3]

In the Gambier Islands, Beechey says,[4] 'tattooing is so universally practised, that it is rare to meet a man without it; and it is carried to such an extent that the figure is sometimes covered with small checkered lines from the neck to the ancles, though the breast is generally exempt, or only ornamented with a single device. In some, generally elderly men, the face is covered below the eyes, in which case the lines or net-work are more open than on other parts of the body, probably on account of the pain of the operation, and terminate at the upper part in a straight line from ear to ear, passing over the bridge of the nose. With these exceptions, to which we may add the fashion, with some few, of blue lines, resembling stockings, from the middle of the thigh to the ankle, the effect is becoming, and in a great measure destroys the appearance of nakedness. The patterns which most improve the shape, and which appear to me peculiar to this group, are those which extend from the armpits to the hips, and are drawn forward with a curve which seems to contract the waist, and at a short distance gives the figure

[1] Forster's Observations made during a Voyage round the World, p. 588.
[2] Cook's Voyage towards the South Pole, vol. i. p. 218.
[3] Narrative of an Expedition into the Interior of Africa, vol. i. p. 291.
[4] Beechey, vol. i. p. 138.

an elegance and outline, not unlike that of the figures seen on the walls of the Egyptian tombs.'

Fig. 12 represents a Caroline Islander, after Freycinet, and gives an idea of the tattooing, though it cannot

Fig. 12.

CAROLINE ISLANDER.

be taken as representing the form or features characteristic of those islanders.

The tattooing of the Sandwich Islanders is less orna-

mental, the devices being, according to Arago, ' unmeaning
and whimsical, without taste, and in general badly executed.'[1] Perhaps, however, the most beautiful of all was
that of the New Zealanders (see figs. 13 and 14), who were
generally tattooed in curved or spiral lines. The process
is extremely painful, particularly on the lips ; but to shrink
from it, or even to show any signs of suffering while under
the operation, would be thought very unmanly. The

Fig. 13.   Fig. 14.

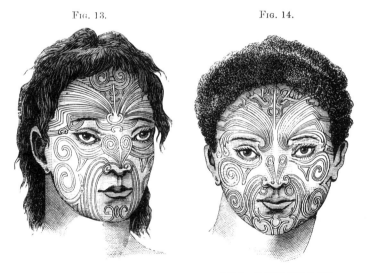

HEAD OF NEW ZEALANDER.   HEAD OF NEW ZEALANDER.

natives used the ' Moko ' or pattern of their tattooing as a
kind of signature. The women have their lips tattooed
with horizontal lines. To have red lips is thought to be a
great reproach.

Many similar cases might be given in which savages
ornament themselves, as they suppose, in a manner which
must be very painful. Perhaps none is more remarkable

[1] Arago's Letters, Pt. II. p. 147.

than the practice which we find in several parts of the world of modifying the human form by means of tight bandages. The small size of the Chinese ladies' feet is a well-known case, but is less mischievous than the compression of the waist as practised in Europe. Some of the American tribes even modified the form of the head. One would have supposed that any such compression would have exercised a very prejudicial effect on the intellect, but as far as the existing evidence goes, it does not appear to do so.

The Fijians give a great deal of time and attention to their hair, as is shown in Pl. II. Most of the chiefs have a special hairdresser, to whom they sometimes devote several hours a day. Their heads of hair are often more than three feet in circumference, and Mr. Williams measured one which was nearly five feet round. This forces them to sleep on narrow wooden pillows or neck-rests, which must be very uncomfortable. They also dye the hair. Black is the natural and favourite colour, but some prefer white, flaxen, or bright red.

'On one head,' says Mr. Williams,[1] 'all the hair is of a uniform height; but one-third in front is ashy or sandy, and the rest black, a sharply defined separation dividing the two colours. Not a few are so ingeniously grotesque as to appear as if done purposely to excite laughter. One has a large knot of fiery hair on his crown, all the rest of his head being bald. Another has the most of his hair cut away, leaving three or four rows of small clusters, as if his head were planted with small paint-brushes. A third has his head bare except where a large patch projects over each temple. One, two, or three cords of twisted hair often fall from the right temple, a foot or eighteen inches long. Some men wear a number of these braids so as to

[1] Fiji and the Fijians, vol. i. p. 158.

FIJIAN MODES OF DRESSING THE HAIR.

Plate II.

form a curtain at the back of the neck, reaching from one ear to the other. A mode that requires great care, has the hair wrought into distinct locks radiating from the head. Each lock is a perfect cone about seven inches long, having the base outwards; so that the surface of the hair is marked out into a great number of small circles, the ends being turned in in each lock, towards the centre of the cone.'

CHAPTER III.

MARRIAGE AND RELATIONSHIP.

NOTHING, perhaps, gives a more instructive insight into the true condition of savages than their ideas on the subject of relationship and marriage; nor can the great advantages of civilisation be more conclusively proved than by the improvement which it has effected in the relation between the two sexes.

Marriage, and the relationship of a child to its father and mother, seem to us so natural and obvious, that we are apt to look on them as aboriginal and general to the human race. This, however, is very far from being the case. The lowest races have no institution of marriage; true love is almost unknown among them; and marriage, in its lowest phases, is by no means a matter of affection and companionship.

The Hottentots, says Kolben,[1] 'are so cold and indifferent to one another that you would think there was no such thing as love between them.' Among the Koussa Caffirs, Lichtenstein asserts that there is 'no feeling of love in marriage.'[2] In North America, the Tinné Indians had no word for 'dear' or 'beloved;' and the Algonquin language is stated to have contained no verb meaning 'to love;' so that when the Bible was translated by the missionaries into that language it was necessary to invent a word for the purpose.

[1] Kolben's Hist. of the Cape of Good Hope, vol. i. p. 162.

[2] Travels in South Africa, vol. i. p. 261.

In Yariba,[1] says Lander (Central Africa), 'marriage is celebrated by the natives as unconcernedly as possible · a man thinks as little of taking a wife as of cutting an ear of corn—affection is altogether out of the question.' The King of Boussa,[2] he tells us in another place, 'when he is not engaged in public affairs, usually employs all his leisure hours in superintending the occupations of his household, and making his own clothes. The Midiki (queen) and he have distinct establishments, divided fortunes, and separate interests; indeed, they appear to have nothing in common with each other, and yet we have never seen so friendly a couple since leaving our native country.' Among the Mandingoes marriage is merely a form of regulated slavery. Husband and wife 'never laugh or joke together.' 'I asked Baba,' says Caillié, 'why he did not sometimes make merry with his wives. He replied that if he did he should not be able to manage them, for they would laugh at him when he ordered them to do anything.'[3]

In India the Hill tribes of Chittagong, says Captain Lewin, regard marriage 'as a mere animal and convenient connection;' as the 'means of getting their dinner cooked. They have no idea of tenderness, nor of chivalrous devotion.'[4]

Among the Guyacurus of Paraguay 'the bonds of matrimony are so very slight, that when the parties do not like each other, they separate without any further ceremony. In other respects they do not appear to have the most distant notions of that bashfulness so natural to the rest of mankind.'[5] The Guaranis seem to have been in a very similar condition.[6]

[1] R. and J. Lander's Niger Expedition, vol. i. p. 161.
[2] *Ibid.* vol. ii. p. 106. See also p. 197.
[3] Travels, vol. i. p. 350.
[4] Hill Tracts of Chittagong, p. 116.
[5] Charlevoix, Hist. of Paraguay, vol. i. p. 91.
[6] *Loc. cit.* p. 352.

Among the Samoyedes [1] of Siberia the husbands show little affection for their wives, and, according to Pallas, ' daignent à-peine leur dire une parole de douceur.'

In Australia ' little real affection exists between husbands and wives, and young men value a wife principally for her services as a slave; in fact, when asked why they are anxious to obtain wives, their usual reply is, that they may get wood, water, and food for them, and carry whatever property they possess.' [2] The position of women in Australia seems indeed to be wretched in the extreme. They are treated with the utmost brutality, beaten and speared in the limbs on the most trivial provocation. Few women, says Eyre, ' will be found, upon examination, to be free from frightful scars upon the head, or the marks of spear wounds about the body. I have seen a young woman who, from the number of these marks, appeared to have been almost riddled with spear wounds. If at all good-looking their position is, if possible, even worse than otherwise.'

Again, our family system, which regards a child as equally related to his father and his mother, seems so natural that we experience a feeling of surprise on meeting with any other system. Yet we shall find, I think, reason for concluding that a man was first regarded as merely related to his family; then to his mother but not to his father; then to his father and not to his mother; and only at last to both father and mother. Even among the Romans, the word ' familia ' meant ' slaves,' and a man's wife and children only formed a part of his family inasmuch as they were his slaves; so that a son who was emancipated—that is to say, made free—had no share in the inheritance, having ceased to belong to the family. We shall, however, be better able to understand this part

[1] Pallas's Voyages, vol. iv. p. 94.　　[2] Eyre's Discoveries, vol. ii. p. 321.

of the question when we have considered the various phases which marriage presents; for it is by no means of an uniform character, but takes almost every possible form. In some cases nothing of the sort appears to exist at all; in others it is essentially temporary, and exists only till the birth of the child, when both man and woman are free to mate themselves afresh. In others, the man buys the woman, who becomes as much his property as his horse or his dog.

In Sumatra there were formerly three perfectly distinct kinds of marriage: the 'Jugur,' in which the man purchased the woman; the 'Ambel-anak,' in which the woman purchased the man; and the 'Semando,' in which they joined on terms of equality. In the mode of marriage by Ambel-anak, says Marsden,[1] 'the father of a virgin makes choice of some young man for her husband, generally from an inferior family, which renounces all further right to, or interest in, him; and he is taken into the house of his father-in-law, who kills a buffalo on the occasion, and receives twenty dollars from his son's relations. After this, the buruk baik' nia (the good and bad of him) is invested in the wife's family. If he murders or robs, they pay the bañgun, or the fine. If he is murdered, they receive the bañgun. They are liable to any debts he may contract in marriage; those prior to it remaining with his parents. He lives in the family, in a state between that of a son and a debtor. He partakes as a son of what the house affords, but has no property in himself. His rice plantation, the produce of his pepper garden, with everything that he can gain or earn, belongs to the family. He is liable to be divorced at their pleasure, and though he has children, must leave all, and return naked as he came.'

[1] Marsden's Hist. of Sumatra, p. 262.

'The Semando [1] is a regular treaty between the parties, on the footing of equality. The adat paid to the girl's friends has usually been twelve dollars. The agreement stipulates that all effects, gains, or earnings are to be equally the property of both; and, in case of divorce by mutual consent, the stock, debts, and credits are to be equally divided. If the man only insists on the divorce, he gives the woman her half of the effects, and loses the twelve dollars he has paid. If the woman only claims the divorce, she forfeits her right to the proportion of the effects, but is entitled to keep her tikar, bantal, and dandan (paraphernalia), and her relations are liable to pay back the twelve dollars; but it is seldom demanded. This mode, doubtless the most conformable to our ideas of conjugal right and felicity, is that which the chiefs of the Rejang country have formally consented to establish throughout their jurisdiction, and to their orders the influence of the Malayan priests will contribute to give efficacy.'

The Jugur marriage need not be particularly described.

The Hassaniyeh Arabs have a very curious form of marriage, which may be called 'three-quarter' marriage; that is to say, the woman is legally married for three days out of four, remaining perfectly free for the fourth.

In Ceylon there were two kinds of marriage—the Deega marriage, and the Beena marriage. In the former the woman went to her husband's hut; in the latter the man transferred himself to that of the woman. Moreover, according to Davy, marriages in Ceylon were provisional for the first fortnight, at the expiration of which they were either annulled or confirmed. [2]

Among the Reddies [3] of Southern India a very singular

---

[1] Marsden's Hist. of Sumatra, p.263.   [3] Shortt, Trans. Ethn. Soc. New
[2] Davy's Ceylon, p. 286.   Series, vol. vii. p. 194.

custom prevails :—'A young woman of sixteen or twenty years of age may be married to a boy of five or six years! She, however, lives with some other adult male—perhaps a maternal uncle or cousin—but is not allowed to form a connection with the father's relatives; occasionally it may be the boy-husband's father himself—that is, the woman's father-in-law! Should there be children from these liaisons, they are fathered on the boy-husband. When the boy grows up the wife is either old or past child-bearing, when he in his turn takes up with some other " boy's " wife in a manner precisely similar to his own, and procreates children for the boy-husband.'

Polyandry, or the marriage of one woman to several men at once, is more common than is generally supposed, though much less so than polygamy, which is almost universally permitted among the lower races of men. One reason—though I do not say the only one—for this is obvious when pointed out. Long after our children are weaned milk remains an important and necessary part of their food. We supply this want with cow's milk; but among people who have not domesticated animals this cannot, of course, be done, and consequently the children are not weaned until they are two, three, or even four years old. During all this period the husband and wife generally remain apart, and consequently, unless a man has several wives, he is often left without any at all. Thus in Fiji ' the relatives of a woman take it as a public insult if any child should be born before the customary three or four years have elapsed, and they consider themselves in duty bound to avenge it in an equally public manner.' [1]

It seems to us natural and proper that husband and

---

[1] A Mission to Fiji, p. 191.

wife should enjoy as much as possible the society of one another; but, among the Turkomans, according to Fraser, for six months or a year, or even sometimes two years, after a marriage, the husband was only allowed to visit his wife by stealth.

Klemm states that the same is the case among the Circassians until the first child is born. Among the Fijians husbands and wives do not usually spend the night together. In Chittagong (India), although, 'according to European ideas, the standard of morality among the Kyoungtha is low,' yet husband and wife are on no account permitted to sleep together until seven days after marriage.[1]

Burckhardt[2] states, that in Arabia, after the wedding, if it can be called so, the bride returns to her mother's tent, but again runs away in the evening, and repeats these flights several times, till she finally returns to her tent. She does not go to live in her husband's tent for some months, perhaps not even till a full year, from the wedding-day.

Lafitau informs us that among the North American Indians the husband only visits the wife as it were by stealth:—'ils n'osent aller dans les cabanes particuliers où habitent leurs épouses, que durant l'obscurité de la nuit . . . . ce serait une action extraordinaire de s'y présenter le jour.'[3]

In Futa, one of the West African kingdoms, it is said that no husband is allowed to see his wife's face until he has been three years married.

In Sparta, and in Crete, according to Xenophon and Strabo, married people were for some time after the wedding only allowed to see one another as it were clan-

---

[1] Lewin's Hill Tracts of Chittagong, p. 51.

[2] Burckhardt's Notes, vol. vi. p. 269,

quoted in M'Lennan's Primitive Marriage, p. 302.

[3] *Loc. cit.* vol. i. p. 576

destinely; and a similar custom is said to have existed among the Lycians. So far as I am aware, no satisfactory explanation of this custom has yet been given. I shall, however, presently venture to suggest one.

There are many cases in which savages have no such thing as any ceremony of marriage. I have said nothing, says Metz, 'about the marriage ceremonies of the Badagas (Hindostan), because they can scarcely be said to have any.' The Kurumbas, another tribe of the Neilgherry Hills, 'have no marriage ceremony.'[1] According to Colonel Dalton,[2] the Keriahs of Central India 'have no word for marriage in their own language, and the only ceremony used appears to be little more than a sort of public recognition of the fact.' So also the Spanish missionaries found no word for marriage, nor any marriage ceremony, among the Indians of California.[3] Farther north, among the Kutchin Indians, 'there is no ceremony observed at marriage or birth.'[4]

The marital rite, says Schoolcraft, 'among our tribes' (*i.e.* the Redskins of the United States) 'is nothing more than the personal consent of the parties, without requiring any concurrent act of a priesthood, a magistracy, or witnesses; the act is assumed by the parties, without the necessity of any extraneous sanction.'[5]

According to Brett, there is no marriage ceremony among the Arawaks of South America.[6] Martius makes the same assertion with reference to the Brazilian tribes generally,[7] and the same is the case with some of the Australian tribes.[8]

There is, says Bruce, 'no such thing as marriage in Abyssinia, unless that which is contracted by mutual con-

[1] Trans. Ethn. Soc. vol. vii. p. 276.
[2] *Ibid.* vol. vi. p. 25.
[3] Bagaert, Smithsonian Report, 1863, p. 368.
[4] Smithsonian Report, 1866, p. 326.
[5] Indian Tribes, p. 248, 132.
[6] Guiana, p. 101.
[7] *Loc. cit.* p. 51.
[8] Eyre's Discoveries, vol. ii. p. 319

sent, without other form, subsisting only till dissolved by
dissent of one or other, and to be renewed or repeated as
often as it is agreeable to both parties, who, when they
please, live together again as man and wife, after having
been divorced, had children by others, or whether they
have been married, or had children with others or not.
I remember to have once been at Koscam in presence of
the Iteghe (the queen), when, in the circle, there was a
woman of great quality, and seven men who had all been
her husbands, none of whom was the happy spouse at that
time.' [1]   And yet 'there is no country in the world where
there are so many churches.' [2] Among the Bedouin Arabs
there is a marriage ceremony in the case of a girl, but
the re-marriage of a widow is not thought sufficiently
important to deserve one.   Speke says, 'there are no such
things as marriages in Uganda.' [3]

Of the Mandingoes (West Africa), Caillié [4] says that
husband and wife are not united by any ceremony ; and
Hutton [5] makes the same statement as regards the Ashan-
tees.   In Congo and Angola [6] 'they use no peculiar ceremonies in marriage, nor scarce trouble themselves for
consent of friends.'   La Vaillant says that there are no
marriage ceremonies among the Hottentots ; [7] and the
Bushmen, according to Mr. Wood, had in their language
no means of distinguishing an unmarried from a married
girl. [8]

Yet we must not assume that marriage is necessarily
and always lightly regarded, where it is unaccompanied by
ceremonial.   Thus 'marriage in this island (Tahiti), as
appeared to us,' says Cook, 'is nothing more than an

[1] Bruce's Travels, vol. iv. p. 487.
[2] Ibid. vol. v. p. 1.
[3] Journal, p. 361.
[4] Loc. cit. vol. i. p. 350.
[5] Klemm, Cultur d. Menschen, vol.
iii. p. 280.

[6] Astley's Coll. of Voyages, vol. iii.
p. 221, 227.
[7] Voyages, vol. ii. p. 58.
[8] Natural History of Man, vol. i.
p. 269.

agreement between the man and woman, with which the priest has no concern. Where it is contracted it appears to be pretty well kept, though sometimes the parties separate by mutual consent, and in that case a divorce takes place with as little trouble as the marriage. But though the priesthood has laid the people under no tax for a nuptial benediction, there are two operations which it has appropriated, and from which it derives considerable advantages. One is tattooing, and the other circumcision.'[1] Yet he elsewhere informs us that married women in Tahiti are as faithful to their husbands as in any other part of the world.

We must bear in mind that there is a great distinction between what may be called 'lax' and 'brittle' marriages. In some countries the marriage tie may be broken with the greatest ease, and yet, as long as it lasts, is strictly respected; while in other countries the very reverse is the case.

Perhaps on the whole any marriage ceremony is better than none at all, but some races have practices at marriage which are extremely objectionable. Some, also, are very curious, and no doubt symbolical. Thus, among the Canadian Indians, Carver[2] says that when the chief has pronounced the pair to be married, 'the bridegroom turns round, and, bending his body, takes his wife on his back, in which manner he carries her, amidst the exclamations of the spectators, to his tent.' Bruce, in Abyssinia, observed an identical custom. When the ceremony is over, he says, 'the bridegroom takes his lady on his shoulders, and carries her off to his house. If it be at a distance he does the same thing, but only goes entirely round about the bride's house.'[3]

[1] Cook's Voyage round the World. Hawkesworth's Voyages, vol. ii. p. 240. For Caroline Islands, see Klemm, *loc. cit.* vol. iv. p. 299.   [2] Travels, p. 374.   [3] Vol. vii. p. 67.

In China, when the bridal procession reaches the bride-groom's house, the bride is carried into the house by a matron, and 'lifted over a pan of charcoal at the door.'[1]

We shall presently see that these are no isolated cases, nor is the act of lifting the bride over the bridegroom's threshold an act without a meaning. I shall presently mention many allied customs, to the importance and significance of which our attention has recently been called by Mr. M'Lennan, in his masterly work on 'Primitive Marriage.'

I will now attempt to trace up the custom of marriage in its gradual development. In the Andaman Islands,[2] Sir Edward Belcher states that the custom is for the man and woman to remain together until the child is weaned, when they separate as a matter of course, and each seeks a new partner. The Bushmen of South Africa are stated to be entirely without marriage. Among the Nairs (India), as Buchanan tells us, ' no one knows his father, and every man looks on his sister's children as his heirs.' The Tee-hurs of Oude 'live together almost indiscriminately in large communities, and even when two people are re-garded as married the tie is but nominal.'[3] Although in this state of things marriage, in the proper sense of the term, cannot be said to exist at all, still, for the sake of convenience, we may term it a condition of communal marriage; and among the numerous cases in which more or less isolated races of men have made considerable pro-gress in some directions, while remaining very backward in others, there is perhaps hardly any more remarkable case than the backwardness (until lately) of the Sand-wich Islanders in their social relations, as manifested

[1] Davis. The Chinese, vol. i. p. 285.
[2] Trans. Ethn. Soc. vol. v. p. 45.
[3] The People of India, by J. F.

Watson, and J. W. Kaye, published by the Indian Government, vol. ii. pl. 85.

in their language. This is shown in the following table, thus :—

Hawaian.	*English.*

Kupuna signifies
{
Great grandfather
Great great uncle
Great grandmother
Great grand aunt
Grandfather
Granduncle
Grandmother
Grandaunt
Grandfather
Granduncle
Grandmother
Grandaunt.
}

Makua kana   =
{
Father
Father's brother
Father's brother-in-law
Mother's brother
Mother's brother-in-law
Grandfather's brother's son.
}

Makua waheena =
{
Mother
Mother's sister
Mother's sister-in-law
Father's sister
Father's sister-in-law.
}

Kaikee kana   =
{
Son
Sister's son
Brother's son
Brother's son's son
Brother's daughter's son
Sister's son's son
Sister's daughter's son
Mother's sister's son's son
Mother's brother's son's son.
}

Hunona   =
{
Brother's son's wife
Brother's daughter's husband
Sister's son's wife
Sister's daughter's husband.
}

Waheena   =   { Wife
                  Wife's sister
                  Brother's wife
                  Wife's brother's wife
                  Father's brother's son's wife
                  Father's sister's son's wife
                  Mother's sister's son's wife
                  Mother's brother's son's wife.

Kana   =   { Husband
                  Husband's brother
                  Sister's husband.

Punalua   =   Wife's sister's husband (brother-in-law).
Kaikoaka   =   Wife's brother.

The key of this Hawaian or Sandwich Island [1] system is the idea conveyed in the word waheena (woman). Thus—

Waheena   =   { Wife
                  Wife's sister
                  Brother's wife
                  Wife's brother's wife.

All these are equally related to each husband. Hence the word—

Kaikee = Child, also signifies the brother's wife's child;

and no doubt the wife's sister's child, and the wife's brother's wife's child. So, also, as the sister is wife to the brother-in-law (though not to her brother), and as the brother-in-law is husband to his brother's wife, he is consequently a father to his brother's children. Hence 'Kaikee' also means 'sister's son' and 'brother's son.' In fact 'Kaikee' and 'Waheena' correspond to our words 'child' and 'woman,' and there are apparently no words

---

[1] Morgan, Proceedings of the American Association, 1868.

answering to 'son,' 'daughter,' 'wife,' or 'husband.' That this does not arise from poverty of language is evident, because the same system discriminates between other relationships which we do not distinguish.

Perhaps the contrast is most clearly shown in the terms for brother-in-law and sister-in-law.

Thus, when a woman is speaking—

Sister-in-law = husband's brother's wife = punalua
Sister-in-law = husband's sister = kaikoaka.
But brother-in-law whether sister's husband or husband's brother } = kana, *i.e.* husband.

When, on the contrary, a man is speaking—

Sister-in-law = wife's sister = waheena, *i.e.* wife
Sister-in-law = brother's wife = waheena, *i.e.* wife.

And so—

Brother-in-law = wife's brother = kaikoaka
Brother-in-law = wife's sister's husband = punalua.

Thus a woman has husbands and sisters-in-law, but no brothers-in-law; a man, on the contrary, has wives and brothers-in-law, but no sisters-in-law. The same idea runs through all other relationships : cousins, for instance, are called brothers and sisters.

So again, while the Romans distinguished between the

Father's brother = patruus, and the mother's brother = avunculus
Father's sister = amita, and the mother's sister = matertera ;

the first two in Hawaian are makua kana, which also signifies father ; and the last two are makua waheena, which also means mother.

Thus the idea of marriage does not, in fact, enter into

the Hawaian system of relationship. Uncleship, auntship, cousinship, are ignored; and we have only—

> Grandparents
> Parents
> Brothers and sisters
> Children and
> Grandchildren.

Here it is clear that the child is related to the group. It is not specially related either to its father or its mother, who stand in the same relation as mere uncles and aunts; so that every child has several fathers and several mothers.

There are, I think, reasons in the social habits of these islanders which go far to explain the persistence of this archaic nomenclature. From the mildness of the climate and the abundance of food, children soon become independent; the prevalence of large houses, used as mere dormitories, and the curious prejudice against eating in common, must also have greatly tended to retard the development of special family feelings. Yet the system of nomenclature above mentioned did not correspond with the actual state of society as found by Captain Cook and other early voyagers.

Among the Todas of the Neilgherry Hills, however, when a man marries a girl she becomes the wife of all his brothers as they successively reach manhood; and they also become the husbands of all her sisters as they become old enough to marry. In this case ‘ the first-born child is fathered upon the eldest brother, the next-born on the second, and so on throughout the series. Notwithstanding this unnatural system, the Todas, it must be confessed, exhibit much fondness and attachment towards their offspring; more so than their practice of mixed intercourse would seem to foster.’ [1]

[1] Shortt. Tran . Ethn. Soc. N.S. vol. vii. p. 240.

In the Tottiyars of India, also, we have a case in which it is actually recorded that 'brothers, uncles, and nephews hold their wives in common.'[1] So also, according to Nicolaus,[2] the Galactophagi had communal marriage, 'where they called all old men fathers, young men sons, and those of equal age brothers.' 'Among the Sioux and some other North American tribes the custom is to buy the eldest of the chief's daughters, then the others all belong to him, and are taken to wife at such times as the husband sees fit.'[3] Such social conditions as these tend to explain the frequency of adoption among the lower races of men, and the fact that it is often considered to be as close a connection as real parentage. Among the Esquimaux, Captain Lyon tells us that 'this curious connection binds the parties as firmly together as the ties of blood; and an adopted son, if senior to one by nature, is the heir to all the family riches.'[4]

In Central Africa, Denham states that 'the practice of adopting children is very prevalent among the Felatahs; and though they have sons and daughters of their own, the adopted child generally becomes heir to the whole property.'[5]

'It is a custom,' says Mariner,[6] 'in the Tonga Islands for women to be what they call mothers to children or grownup young persons who are not their own, for the purpose of providing them, or seeing that they are provided, with all the conveniences of life;' this is often done even if the natural mother be still living, in which case the adopted mother 'is regarded the same as the natural mother.'

[1] Dubois' Description of the People of India, p. 3.

[2] Bachofen, Das Mutterrecht, p. 21.

[3] Ethn. Journal, 1869, p. 286.

[4] Journal, p. 353.

[5] Denham's Travels in Africa, vol. iv. p. 131.

[6] Mariner's Tonga Islands, vol. ii. p. 98.

Among the Romans, also, adoption was an important feature, and was effected by the symbol of a mock birth, without which it was not regarded as complete. This custom seems to have continued down to the time of Nerva, who, in adopting Trajan, transferred the ceremony from the marriage-bed to the temple of Jupiter.[1] Diodorus[2] gives a very curious account of the same custom as it existed among the Greeks, mentioning that Juno adopted Hercules by going through a ceremony of mock birth.

In other cases the symbol of adoption represented not the birth, but the milk-tie. Thus, in Circassia, the woman offered her breast to the person she was adopting. In Abyssinia, Parkyn tells us that 'if a man wishes to be adopted as the son of one of superior station or influence, he takes his hand, and, sucking one of his fingers, declares himself to be his " child by adoption ;" and his new father is bound to assist him as far as he can.'[3]

The same idea underlies perhaps the curious Esquimaux habit of licking anything which is presented to them, apparently in token of ownership.[4]

Dieffenbach[5] also mentions the practice of licking a present in New Zealand; here, however, it is the donor who does so. In the Tonga Islands, Captain Cook tells us that the natives ' have a singular custom of putting everything you give them to their heads, by way of thanks as we conjectured.'[6]

Assuming then that the communal marriage system shown in the preceding pages to prevail, or have prevailed, so widely among races in a low stage of civilisation, represents the primitive and earliest social condition of man, we

[1] Das Mutterrecht, p. 254.
[2] IV. 39. See Appendix.
[3] Parkyn's Abyssinia, p. 198.
[4] Franklin's Journeys, 1819–22, vol. i.
p. 34.
[5] New Zealand, vol. ii. p. 104.
[6] Voyage towards the South Pole, vol. i. p. 221.

now come to consider the various ways in which it may
have been broken up and replaced by individual marriage.

Montesquieu lays it down, almost as an axiom, that
' l'obligation naturelle qu'a le père de nourrir ses enfants
a fait établir le mariage, qui déclare celui qui doit remplir
cette obligation.' [1] Elsewhere he states that ' il est arrivé
dans tous les pays et dans tous les temps que la religion
s'est mêlée des mariages.' [2] How far these assertions are
from the truth will be conclusively shown in the following
pages.

Bachofen [3] and M'Lennan,[4] the two most recent authors
who have studied this subject, both agree that the primitive condition of man, socially, was one of pure Hetairism,[5]
when marriage did not exist; or as we may perhaps for
convenience call it, Communal marriage, where every man
and woman in a small community were regarded as equally
married to one another.

Bachofen considers that after awhile the women, shocked
and scandalised by such a state of things, revolted against
it, and established a system of marriage with female
supremacy, the husband being subject to the wife, property and descent being considered to go in the female
line, and women enjoying the principal share of political
power.   The first period he calls that of ' Hetairism ; '
the second of ' Mutterrecht, or motherright.'

In the third stage he considers that the ethereal influence of the father prevailed over the more material idea
of motherhood.   Men claimed preeminence, property and
descent were traced in the male line, sun worship superseded moon worship, and many other changes in social
organisation took place,—mainly because it came to be
recognised that the creative influence of the father was more

[1] Esprit des Lois, vol. ii. p. 186.
[2] Loc. cit. p. 299.
[3] Das Mutterrecht.
[4] Primitive Marriage.
[5] Ibid. xviii. xix.

important than the material tie of motherhood. The father in fact was the author of life, the mother a mere nurse.

Thus, he regards the first stage as lawless, the second as material, the third as spiritual. I believe, however, that communities in which women have exercised the supreme power are rare and exceptional, if indeed they ever existed at all. We do not find in history, as a matter of fact, that women do assert their rights, and savage women would, I think, be peculiarly unlikely to uphold their dignity in the manner supposed. On the contrary, among the lowest races of men, as, for instance, in Australia, the position of the women is one of complete subjection, and it seems to me perfectly clear that the idea of marriage is founded on the rights, not of the woman, but of the man, being an illustration of

> the good old plan,
> That he should take who has the power,
> And he should keep who can.

Among low races the wife is indeed literally the property of the husband; as Petruchio says of Catherine:

> I will be master of what is mine own.
> She is my goods, my chattels; she is my house,
> My household stuff, my field, my barn,
> My horse, my ox, my ass, my anything.

So thoroughly is this the case that, as I have already mentioned a Roman's 'family' originally, and indeed throughout classical times, meant his slaves, and the children only formed part of the family because they were his slaves; so that if a father freed his son, the latter ceased to be one of the family, and had no part in the inheritance. Nay, even at the present day, in some parts of Africa, a man's property goes, not to his children, as such, but to his slaves.

Hearne tells us, that among the Hudson's Bay Indians 'it has ever been the custom for the men to wrestle for any woman to whom they are attached; and, of course, the strongest party always carries off the prize. A weak man, unless he be a good hunter and well beloved, is seldom permitted to keep a wife that a stronger man thinks worth his notice. . . . This custom prevails throughout all their tribes, and causes a great spirit of emulation among their youth, who are upon all occasions, from their childhood, trying their strength and skill in wrestling.'[1] Franklin also says that the Copper Indians hold women in the same low estimation as the Chipe-wyans do, 'looking upon them as a kind of property, which the stronger may take from the weaker;'[2] and Richard-son[3] 'more than once saw a stronger man assert his right to take the wife of a weaker countryman. Anyone may challenge another to wrestle, and, if he overcomes, may carry off the wife as the prize.' Yet the women never dream of protesting against this, which, indeed, seems to them perfectly natural. The theory therefore of Dr. Bachofen, and the sequence of social customs suggested by him, although supported with much learning, cannot, I think, be regarded as correct.[4]

M'Lennan, like Bachofen, starts with a stage of hetairism or communal marriage. The next stage was, in his opinion, that form of polyandry in which brothers had their wives in common; afterwards came that of the *levirate*, i.e. the system under which, when an elder brother died, his second brother married the widow, and so on with the others in succession. Thence he considers that some tribes branched off into endogamy, others into

[1] Hearne, p. 104.
[2] Journey to the Shores of the Polar Seas, vol. viii. p. 43.
[3] Richardson's Boat Journey, vol. ii.

p. 24.
[4] See for instance Lewin's Hill Tracts of Chittagong, pp. 47, 77, 80, 3, 98, 101.

exogamy;[1] that is to say, some forbade marriage out of,
others within, the tribe. If either of these two systems
was older than the other, he considers that exogamy
must have been the most ancient. Exogamy was based
on infanticide,[2] and led to the practice of marriage by
capture.[3]

In a further stage the idea of female descent, producing
as it would a division in the tribe, obviated the necessity
of capture as a reality and reduced it to a symbol.

In support of this view Mr. M'Lennan has certainly
brought forward many striking facts; but, while admitting
that it probably represents the succession of events in
some cases, I cannot but think that these are exceptional.
Fully admitting the prevalence of infanticide among
savages, it will, I think, be found that among the lowest
races, boys were killed as frequently as girls. Eyre expressly states that this was the case in Australia.[4] In
fact the distinction between the sexes implies an amount
of forethought, and prudence, which the lower races of
men do not possess.

For reasons to be given shortly, I believe that communal marriage was gradually superseded by individual
marriage founded on capture, and that this led firstly to
exogamy and then to female infanticide; thus reversing
M'Lennan's order of sequence. Endogamy and regulated
polyandry, though frequent, I regard as exceptional, and
as not entering into the normal progress of development.

Like M'Lennan and Bachofen, I believe that our present
social relations have arisen from an initial stage of
hetairism or communal marriage. It is obvious, however, that even under communal marriage, a warrior who
had captured a beautiful girl in some marauding expe-

---

[1] *Loc. cit.* p. 145.
[2] *Loc. cit.* p. 138.
[3] *Loc. cit.* p. 140.
[4] Discoveries, &c., vol. ii. p. 324.

dition would claim a peculiar right to her, and, when possible, would act custom at defiance. We have already seen that there are other cases of the existence of marriage under two forms side by side in one country; and there is, therefore, no real difficulty in assuming the co-existence of communal and individual marriage. It is true that under a communal marriage system no man could appropriate a girl entirely to himself without infringing the rights of the whole tribe. Such an act would naturally be looked on with jealousy, and only regarded as justifiable under peculiar circumstances. A war-captive, however, was in a peculiar position : the tribe had no right to her; her capturer might have killed her if he chose; if he preferred to keep her alive he was at liberty to do so; he did as he liked, and the tribe was no sufferer.

M'Lennan,[1] indeed, says that 'it is impossible to believe that the mere lawlessness of savages should be consecrated into a legal symbol, or to assign a reason—could this be believed—why a similar symbol should not appear in transferences of other kinds of property.' The symbol of capture, however, was not one of lawlessness, but, on the other hand, of—according to the ideas of the time—lawful possession. It did not refer to those from whom the captive was taken, but was intended to bar the rights of the tribe into which she was introduced. Individual marriage was, in fact, an infringement of communal rights; the man retaining to himself, or the man and woman mutually appropriating to one another, that which should have belonged to the whole tribe. Thus, among the Andamaners, any woman who attempted to resist the marital privileges claimed by any member of the tribe was liable to severe punishment.[2]

Nor is it, I think, difficult to understand why the symbol

[1] *Loc. cit.* p. 44.   [2] See Trans. Ethn. Soc. N. S. vol. ii. p. 35.

of capture does not appear in transferences of other kinds of property. Every generation requires fresh wives; the actual capture, or at any rate the symbol, needed therefore repetition. This, however, does not apply to land; when once the idea of landed property arose, the same land descended from owner to owner. In other kinds of property again, there is an important, though different kind of, distinction. A man made his own bow and arrows, his own hut, his own arms; hence the necessity of capture did not exist, and the symbol would not arise.

M'Lennan supposes that savages were driven by female infanticide, and the consequent absence or paucity of women, into exogamy and marriage by capture. I shall presently give my reasons for rejecting this explanation.

He also considers that marriage by capture followed, and arose from, that remarkable custom, namely, of marrying always out of the tribe, for which he has proposed the appropriate name of exogamy. On the contrary, I believe that exogamy arose from marriage by capture, not marriage by capture from exogamy: that capture, and capture alone, could give a man the right to monopolise a woman, to the exclusion of his fellow-clansmen; and that hence, even after all necessity for actual capture had long ceased, the symbol remained; capture having, by long habit, come to be received as a necessary preliminary to marriage.

That marriage by capture has not arisen from female modesty is, I think, evident, not only because we have no reason to suppose that such a feeling prevails specially among the lower races of man, but also, firstly, because it cannot explain the mock resistance of the relatives, and secondly, because the very question to be solved is why it has become so generally the custom to win the female not by persuasion but by force.

M'Lennan's view throws no light on the remarkable

ceremonies of expiation for marriage, to which I shall presently call attention.

I will, however, first proceed to show how widely 'capture,' either actual or symbolical, enters into the idea of marriage. Mr. M'Lennan was, I believe, the first to appreciate its importance. I have taken some of the following evidence from his valuable work, adding, however, several additional cases.

It requires strong evidence, which, indeed, exists in abundance, to satisfy us that the origin of marriage is independent of all sacred and social considerations; that it had nothing to do with mutual affection or consent; that it was invalidated by any appearance of consent; and that it is tobe symbolised not by any demonstration of warm affection on the one side, and tender devotion on the other, but by brutal violence and unwilling submission.

Yet, as already mentioned, the evidence is overwhelming. So completely did the Caribs supply themselves with wives from the neighbouring races, and so little communication did they hold with them, that the men and women actually spoke different languages. So again in Australia (Pl. III.) the men, says Oldfield, ' are in excess of the other sex, and, consequently, many men of every tribe are unprovided with that especial necessary to their comfortable subsistence, a wife; who is a slave in the strictest sense of the word, being a beast of burden, a provider of food, and a ready object on which to vent those passions that the men do not dare to vent on each other. Hence, for those coveting such a luxury, arises the necessity of stealing the women of some other tribe; and, in their expeditions to effect so laudable a design, they will cheerfully undergo privations and dangers equal to those they incur when in search of blood-revenge. When, on such an errand, they discover an unprotected female, their pro-

ceedings are not of the most gentle nature. Stunning
her by a blow from the dowak (to make her love them,
perhaps), they drag her by the hair to the nearest thicket
to await her recovery. When she comes to her senses
they force her to accompany them ; and as at worst it is
but the exchange of one brutal lord for another, she generally enters into the spirit of the affair, and takes as much
pains to escape as though it were a matter of her own free
choice.' [1]

The following is the manner in which the natives about
Sydney used to procure wives :—' The poor wretch is
stolen upon in the absence of her protectors. Being first
stupified with blows, inflicted with clubs or wooden swords,
on the head, back, and shoulders, every one of which is
followed by a stream of blood, she is then dragged through
the woods by one arm, with a perseverance and violence
that it might be supposed would displace it from its socket.
The lover, or rather the ravisher, is regardless of the stones
or broken pieces of trees which may lie in his route, being
anxious only to convey his prize in safety to his own party,
when a scene ensues too shocking to relate. This outrage
is not resented by the relations of the female, who only
retaliate by a similar outrage when they find an opportunity. This is so constantly the practice among them
that even the children make it a play-game or exercise.' [2]

In Bali,[3] one of the islands between Java and New
Guinea, also it is stated to be the practice that girls are
' stolen away by their brutal lovers, who sometimes surprise them alone, or overpower them by the way, and
carry them off with dishevelled hair and tattered garments to the woods. When brought back from thence,
and reconciliation is effected with enraged friends, the

---

[1] Trans. Ethn. Soc. vol. iii. p. 250.   [3] Notices of the Indian Archipelago,
[2] Collins's English Colony in New   p. 90.
South Wales, p. 362.

Plate III.

AUSTRALIAN ABORIGINAL MARRIAGE CEREMONY.

poor female becomes the slave of her rough lover, by a certain compensation-price being paid to her relatives.'

So deeply rooted is the feeling of a connection between force and marriage, that we find the former used as a form long after all necessity for it had ceased; and it is very interesting to trace, as Mr. M'Lennan has done, the gradual stages through which a stern reality softens down into a mere symbol.

It is easy to see that if we assume the case of a country in which there are four certain neighbouring tribes, who have the custom of exogamy, and who trace pedigrees through the mother, and not through the father—a custom which, as we shall presently see, is so common that it may be said to be the usual one among the lower races—after a certain time the result would be that each tribe would consist of four septs or clans, representing the four original tribes, and hence we should find communities in which each tribe is divided into clans, and a man must always marry a woman of a different clan. But as communities become larger and more civilised, the actual 'capture' became inconvenient, and at last impossible.

Gradually therefore it came to be more and more a mock ceremony, forming, however, a necessary part of the marriage ceremony. Of this many cases might be given.

Speaking of the Khonds of Orissa, Major-General Campbell says that on one occasion he 'heard loud cries proceeding from a village close at hand; fearing some quarrel, I rode to the spot, and there I saw a man bearing away upon his back something enveloped in an ample covering of scarlet cloth; he was surrounded by twenty or thirty young fellows, and by them protected from the desperate attacks made upon him by a party of young women. On seeking an explanation of this novel scene,

I was told that the man had just been married, and his precious burden was his blooming bride, whom he was conveying to his own village. Her youthful friends (as it appears is the custom) were seeking to regain possession of her, and hurled stones and bamboos at the head of the devoted bridegroom, until he reached the confines of his own village.' [1]

Sir W. Elliot also mentions that not only amongst the Khonds, but also in ' several other tribes of Central India, the bridegroom seizes his bride by force, either affected or real ; ' [2] and the same was customary among the Badagas of the Neilgherry Hills. [3]

Dalton mentions that among the Kols of Central India, when the price of a girl has been arranged, ' the bridegroom and a large party of his friends of both sexes enter with much singing and dancing, and *sham fighting* in the village of the bride, where they meet the bride's party, and are hospitably entertained. ' [4]

M. Bourien [5] thus describes the marriage ceremony among the wild tribes of the Malay Peninsula :—' When all are assembled, and all ready, the bride and bridegroom are led by one of the old men of the tribe, towards a circle more or less great, according to the presumed strength of the intended pair ; the girl runs round first, and the young man pursues a short distance behind ; if he succeed in reaching her and retaining her, she becomes his wife ; if not, he loses all claim to her. At other times, a larger field is appointed for the trial, and they pursue one another in the forest. The race, according to the words of the chronicle, " is not to the swift nor

[1] Quoted in M'Lennan's Primitive Marriage, p. 28.

[2] Trans. Ethn. Soc. 1869, p. 125.

[3] Metz. The tribes of the Neilgherries, p. 74. See also Lewin's Hill Tracts of Chittagong, p. 36, 80.

[4] Trans. Ethn. Soc. vol. vi. p. 24. See also p. 27, and the Tribes of India, vol. i. p. 15.

[5] Trans. Ethn. Soc. 1865, p. 81.

the battle to the strong," but to the young man who has had the good fortune to please the intended bride.'

Among the Kalmucks, Dr. Hell tells us that after the price of the girl has been duly agreed on, when the bridegroom comes with his friends to carry off his bride, 'a sham resistance is always made by the people of her camp, in spite of which she fails not to be borne away on a richly caparisoned horse, with loud shouts and feu de joie.'[1]

Dr. Clarke[2] gives a charmingly romantic account of the ceremony. 'The girl,' he says 'is first mounted, who rides off in full speed. Her lover pursues; if he overtakes her, she becomes his wife, and the marriage is consummated on the spot; after this she returns with him to his tent. But it sometimes happens that the woman does not wish to marry the person by whom she is pursued; in this case, she will not suffer him to overtake her. We were assured that no instance occurs of a Kalmuck girl being thus caught, unless she have a partiality to the pursued. If she dislikes him, she rides, to use the language of English sportsmen, " neck or nought, " until she has completely effected her escape, or until her pursuer's horse becomes exhausted, leaving her at liberty to return, and to be afterwards chased by some more favoured admirer.'

'Among the Tunguses and Kamchadales,' says Ernan,[3] 'a matrimonial engagement is not definitively arranged and concluded until the suitor has got the better of his beloved by force, and has torn her clothes.' Attacks on women are not allowed to be avenged by blood, unless they take place within the yourt or house. The man is not regarded as to blame, if the woman 'has ventured to

[1] M'Lennan's Primitive Marriage, p. 30.
[2] Travels, vol. i. p. 332.
[3] Travels in Siberia, vol. ii. p. 442. See also Kames' History of Man, vol. ii. p. 58.

leave her natural place, the sacred and protecting hearth.'
Pallas observes that in his time, marriage by capture
prevailed also among the Samoyedes.[1]

Among the Mongols[2] when a marriage is arranged,
the girl 'flies to some relations to hide herself. The
bridegroom coming to demand his wife, the father-in-law
says, " My daughter is yours ; go, take her wherever you
can find her." Having thus obtained his warrant, he,
with his friends, runs about searching ; and having found
her, seizes her as his property, and carries her home as it
were by force.

In the Korea when a man marries, he mounts on
horseback, attended by his friends, and, having ridden
about the town, stops at the bride's door, where he is
received by her relations, who then carry her to his house,
and the ceremony is complete.'[3]

Among the Esquimaux of Cape York (Smith Sound)
according to Dr. Hayes,[4] there is no marriage ceremony
further than that the boy is required to carry off his
bride by main force ; for, even among these blubber-eating
people, the woman only saves her modesty by a sham
resistance, although she knows years beforehand that
her destiny is sealed, and that she is to become the wife
of the man from whose embraces, when the nuptial day
comes, she is obliged by the inexorable law of public
opinion to free herself if possible, by kicking and scream-
ing with might and main, until she is safely landed in
the hut of her future lord, when she gives up the combat
very cheerfully and takes possession of her new abode.

In Greenland, according to Egede, ' when a young man
likes a maiden he commonly proposes it to their parents

[1] Vol. iv. p. 97. See also Astley's
Collection of Voyages, vol. iv. p. 575.
[2] Astley, vol. iv. p. 77.
[3] *Ibid.* p. 342.
[4] Open Polar Sea, p. 432.

and relations on both sides; and after he has obtained
their consent, he gets two or more old women to fetch the
bride (and if he is a stout fellow he will fetch her himself).
They go to the place where the young woman is, and carry
her away by force.' [1]

We have already seen (p. 69) that marriage by capture
exists in full force among the Northern Redskins.

The aborigines of the Amazon Valley, says Wallace,[2]
' have no particular ceremony at their marriages, except
that of always carrying away the girl by force, or making
a show of doing so, even when she and her parents are
quite willing.'

M. Bardel, in the notes to D'Urville's Voyage, mentions
that among the Indians round Conception in South
America, after a man has agreed on the price of a girl
with her parents, he surprises her, and carries her off to
the woods for a few days, after which the happy couple
return home.[3]

In Tierra del Fuego, as Admiral Fitzroy tells us,[4] as
soon ' as a youth is able to maintain a wife by his exer-
tions in fishing or birdcatching, he obtains the consent of her relations, and . . . . having built or stolen
a canoe for himself, he watches for an opportunity, and
carries off his bride. If she is unwilling she hides herself in the woods until her admirer is heartily tired of
looking for her, and gives up the pursuit, but this seldom
happens.'

Williams mentions, as prevailing among the Fijians,
the custom ' of seizing upon a woman by apparent or
actual force, in order to make her a wife. On reaching
the home of her abductor, should she not approve of the

[1] History of Greenland, p. 143.

[2] Travels in the Amazons, p. 497.

[3] Vol. iii. p. 277, and 22.

[4] Voyage of the Adventure and
Beagle, vol. ii. p. 182.

match, she runs to some one who can protect her; if, however, she is satisfied, the matter is settled forthwith; a feast is given to her friends the next morning, and the couple are thenceforward considered as man and wife.' [1]

Earle [2] gives the following account of marriage in New Zealand, which he regards as ' most extraordinary,' while in reality it is, as we now see, nothing of the sort : ' The New Zealand method of courtship and matrimony is,' he says, ' most extraordinary ; so much so that an observer could never imagine any affection existed between the parties. A man sees a woman whom he fancies he should like for a wife ; he asks the consent of her father, or, if an orphan, of her nearest relation ; which, if he obtains, he carries his "intended" off by force, she resisting with all her strength ; and, as the New Zealand girls are generally pretty robust, sometimes a dreadful struggle takes place ; both are soon stripped to the skin ; and it is sometimes the work of hours to remove the fair prize a hundred yards. If she breaks away she instantly flies from her antagonist, and he has his labour to commence again. We may suppose that if the lady feels any wish to be united to her would-be spouse she will not make too violent an opposition ; but it sometimes happens that she secures her retreat into her father's house, and the lover loses all chance of ever obtaining her ; whereas, if he can manage to carry her in triumph into his own, she immediately becomes his wife.'

Even after a marriage, it is customary in New Zealand to have a mock scuffle. Mr. Yate [3] gives a good illustration. There was, he says, ' a little opposition to the wedding, but not till it was over, as is always the custom here. The bride's mother came to me the preceding afternoon,

---

[1] Fiji and the Fijians, vol. i. p. 174.　　[3] Yate's New Zealand, p. 96.
[2] Residence in New Zealand, p. 244.

and said she was well pleased in her heart that her daughter was going to be married to Pahau; but that she must be angry about it with her mouth in the presence of her tribe, lest the natives should come and take away all her possessions, and destroy her crops. This is customary on all occasions. If a chief meets with an accident he is stripped, as a mark of respect; if he marries a wife he has to lose all his property; and this is done out of respect— not from disrespect, as it was once printed, inadvertently, in an official publication. A chief would think himself slighted if his food and garments were not taken away from him upon many occasions. To prevent this Manga, the old mother, acted with policy. As I was returning, therefore, from the church with the bridegroom and bride, she met the procession and began to assail us all furiously. She put on a most terrific countenance, threw her garments about, and tore her hair like a fury; then said to me, "Ah, you white missionary, you are worse than the devil: you first make a slave-lad your son by redeeming him from his master, and then marry him to my daughter, who is a lady. I will tear your eyes out! I will tear your eyes out!" The old woman, suiting the action to the word, feigned a scratch at my face, at the same time saying in an under tone that it was "all mouth" and that she did not mean what she said. I told her I should stop her mouth with a blanket. "Ha, ha, ha!" she replied; "that was all I wanted: I only wanted to get a blanket, and therefore I made this noise." The whole affair went off after this remarkably well; all seemed to enjoy themselves; and everyone was satisfied.' It is evident, however, that Yate did not thoroughly understand the meaning of the scene.

Among the Ahitas of the Philippine Islands, when a man wishes to marry a girl, her parents send her before sunrise into the woods. She has an hour's start, after which the lover goes to seek her. If he finds her and brings her back before sunset, the marriage is acknowledged; if not, he must abandon all claim to her.

In the West African kingdom of Futa,[1] after all other preliminaries are arranged, 'one difficulty yet remains, viz., how the young man shall get his wife home; for the women-cousins and relations take on mightily, and guard the door of the house to prevent her being carried away. At last, by the bridegroom's presents and generosity, their grief is assuaged. He then provides a friend, well-mounted, to carry her off; but as soon as she is on horseback the women renew their lamentations, and rush in to dismount her. However, the man is generally successful, and rides off with his prize to the house prepared for her.'

Gray mentions that a Mandingo (West Africa) wishing to marry a young girl at Kayaye, applied to her mother, who 'consented to his obtaining her in any way he could. Accordingly, when the poor girl was employed preparing some rice for supper, she was seized by her intended husband, assisted by three or four of his companions, and carried off by force. She made much resistance, by biting, scratching, kicking, and roaring most bitterly. Many, both men and women, some of them her own relations, who witnessed the affair, only laughed at the farce, and consoled her by saying that she would soon be reconciled to her situation.' Evidently therefore this was not, as Gray seems to have supposed, a mere act of lawless violence, but a recognised custom, which called for no interference on the part of spectators.

Denham,[3] describing a marriage at Sockna (North

---

[1] Astley's Collection of Voyages, p. 56.
vol. ii. p. 240.
[2] Gray's Travels in Western Africa,

[3] *Loc. cit.* vol. i. p. 39.

Africa), says that the bride is taken on a camel to the bridegroom's house, 'upon which it is necessary for her to appear greatly surprised, and refuse to dismount; the women scream, the men shout, and she is at length persuaded to enter.'

In Circassia weddings are accompanied by a feast, 'in the midst of which the bridegroom has to rush in, and, with the help of a few daring young men, carry off the lady by force; and by this process she becomes the lawful wife.' [1] According to Spencer, another important part of the ceremony consists in the bridegroom drawing his dagger and cutting open the bride's corset.

As regards Europe, Plutarch [2] tells us that in Sparta the bridegroom usually carried off his bride by force, evidently, however, of a friendly character. The Romans, also, had a very similar custom. In North Friesland, 'a young fellow called the bride-lifter lifts the bride and her two bridesmaids upon the waggon in which the married couple are to travel to their home.' [3] M'Lennan states that in some parts of France, down to the seventeenth century, it was customary for the bride to feign reluctance to enter the bridegroom's house.

In Poland, Lithuania, Russia, and parts of Prussia, according to Seignior Gaya,[4] young men used to carry off their sweethearts by force, and then apply to the parents for their consent.

Lord Kames,[5] in his 'Sketches of the History of Man,' mentions that the following marriage ceremony was, in his day, or at least had till shortly before, been customary among the Welsh :—'On the morning of the wedding-day the bridegroom, accompanied with his friends on horse-

---

[1] Moser, The Caucasus and its People, p. 31; quoted by M'Lennan, loc. cit. p. 36.

[2] See also Herodotus, vi. 65.

[3] M'Lennan, loc. cit. p. 33.

[4] Marriage Ceremonies, p. 35. See also Olaus Magnus, vol. xiv. chapter 9.

[5] History of Man, vol. ii. p. 59.

back, demands the bride. Her friends, who are likewise
on horseback, give a positive refusal, on which a mock
scuffle ensues. The bride, mounted behind her nearest
kinsman, is carried off, and is pursued by the bridegroom
and his friends, with loud shouts. It is not uncommon
on such an occasion to see 200 or 300 sturdy Cambro-
Britons riding at full speed, crossing and jostling, to the
no small amusement of the spectators. When they have
fatigued themselves and their horses, the bridegroom is
suffered to overtake his bride. He leads her away in
triumph, and the scene is concluded with feasting and
festivity.'

Thus, then, we see that marriage by capture, either as
a stern reality or as an important ceremony, prevails in
Australia and among the Malays, in Hindostan, Central
Asia, Siberia, and Kamskatka; among the Esquimaux,
the Northern Redskins, the Aborigines of Brazil, in Chile
and Tierra del Fuego, in the Pacific Islands, both among
the Polynesians and the Fijians, in the Philippines, among
the Arabs and Negroes, in Circassia, and, until recently,
throughout a great part of Europe.

I have already referred to the custom of lifting the bride
over the doorstep, which we find in such different and
distant races as the Romans, Redskins of Canada, the
Chinese, and the Abyssinians. Hence, also, perhaps our
honeymoon, during which the bridegroom keeps his bride
away from her relatives and friends; hence even, perhaps,
as Mr. M'Lennan supposes, the slipper is in mock anger
thrown after the departing bride and bridegroom.

The curious custom which forbids the father and
mother-in-law to speak to their son-in-law, and *vice versâ*,
which I have already shown (p. 7) to be very widely
distributed, but for which no satisfactory explanation has
yet been given, seems to me a natural consequence of

marriage by capture. When the capture was a reality, the indignation of the parents would also be real; when it became a mere symbol, the parental anger would be symbolised also, and would be continued even after its origin was forgotten.

The separation of husband and wife, to which also I have referred (p. 56), may also arise from the same custom. It is very remarkable indeed, how persistent are all customs and ceremonies connected with marriage. Thus our 'bride cake,' which so invariably accompanies a wedding, and *which should always be cut by the bride*, may be traced back to the old Roman form of marriage by 'confarreatio' or eating together. So also among the Iroquois, bride and bridegroom used to partake together of a cake of 'sagamité,'[1] which the bride offered to her husband. The Fiji Islanders[2] have a very similar custom. Again among the Tipperahs, one of the Hill tribes of Chittagong, the bride prepares some drink, 'sits on her lover's knee, drinks half, and gives him the other half; they afterwards crook together their little fingers.'[3] In one form or another a similar custom is found among most of the Hill tribes of India.

Mr. M'Lennan conceives that marriage by capture arose from the custom of exogamy, that is to say, from the custom which forbad marriage within the tribe. Exogamy, again, he considers to have arisen from the practice of female infanticide. I have already indicated the reasons which prevent me from accepting this explanation, and which induce me to regard exogamy as arising from marriage by capture, not marriage by capture from exogamy. Mr. M'Lennan's theory seems to me quite

[1] Lafitau, vol. i. p. 566, 571.
[2] Fiji and the Fijians, vol. i. p. 170.
[3] Lewin's Hill Tracts of Chittagong, pp. 71, 80

inconsistent with the existence of tribes which have marriage by capture and yet are endogamous. The Bedouins, for instance, have unmistakeably marriage by capture, and yet the man has a right to marry his cousin, if only he be willing to give the price demanded for her.[1]

Mr. M'Lennan, indeed, feels the difficulty which would be presented by such cases, the existence of which he seems, however, to doubt; adding, that if the symbol of capture be ever found in the marriage ceremonies of an endogamous tribe, we may be sure that it is a relic of an early time at which the tribe was organised on another principle than that of exogamy.[2]

That marriage by capture has not arisen merely from female coyness is I think evident, as already mentioned, firstly, because it does not account for the resistance of the relatives, and secondly, because the very question to be solved is why it has become so generally the custom to win the wife by force rather than by persuasion.

The explanation which I have suggested derives additional probability from the evidence of a general feeling that marriage was an act for which some compensation was due to those whose rights were invaded.

The nature of the ceremonies by which this was effected makes me reluctant to enter into this part of the subject at length; and I will here therefore merely indicate in general terms the character of the evidence.

I will firstly refer to certain details given by Dulaure [3] in his chapter on the worship of Venus, of which he regards these customs merely as one illustration, although they have, I cannot but think, a signification deeper than, and different from, that which he attributes to them.

We must remember that the better known savage races

---

[1] See Klemm, Allg. Culturg. d. Menschen, vol. iv. p. 146.

[2] *Loc. cit.* p. 53.

[3] Hist. Abregée des diff. Cultes.

have, in most cases, now arrived at the stage in which paternal rights are recognised, and hence that fathers can and do sell their daughters into matrimony. The price of a wife is of course regulated by the circumstances of the tribe, and every, or nearly every, industrious young man is enabled to buy one for himself. As long, however, as communal marriage rights were in force this would be almost impossible. That special marriage was an infringement of these communal rights, for which some compensation was due, seems to me the true explanation of the offerings which virgins were so generally compelled to make before being permitted to marry.

In many cases the exclusive possession of a wife could only be legally acquired by a temporary recognition of the preexisting communal rights. Thus, in Babylonia, according to Herodotus,[1] every woman was compelled to offer herself once in the temple of Venus, and only after doing so was she considered free to marry. The same was, according to Strabo, the law in Armenia.[2] In some parts of Cyprus also, among the Nasamones,[3] and other Æthiopian tribes, he tells us there was a very similar custom, and Dulaure asserts that it existed also at Carthage, and in several parts of Greece. The account which Herodotus gives of the Lydians, though not so clear, seems to indicate a similar law.

The customs of the Thracians, as described by Herodotus,[4] point to a similar feeling. Among races somewhat more advanced, the symbol supersedes the reality of this detestable custom, and St. Augustine found it necessary to protest against that which prevailed, even at his time, in Italy.[5]

Diodorus Siculus mentions that in the Balearic Islands,

[1] Clio, 199.
[2] Strabo, lib. 2.
[3] Melpomene, 172.
[4] Terpsichore, v. 6.
[5] Dulaure, *loc. cit.* vol. i. p. 160.

Majorca, Minorca, and Ivica, the bride was for one night considered as the common property of all the guests present; after which she belonged exclusively to her husband.

In India, according to Grosse,[1] and particularly in the valleys of the Ganges, virgins were compelled before marriage to present themselves in the temples dedicated to Juggernaut, and the same is said to have been customary in Pondicherry and at Goa.[2]

Among the Sonthals, one of the aboriginal Indian tribes, the marriages take place once a year, mostly in January. 'For six days all the candidates for matrimony live together in promiscuous concubinage;' after which only are the separate couples regarded as having established their right to marry.[3]

Carver mentions[4] that while among the Naudowessies, he 'observed that they paid uncommon respect to one of their women, and found that she was entitled to it on account of a transaction that, in Europe, would have rendered her infamous.' She invited forty of the principal warriors to her tent, provided them with a feast, and treated them in every respect as husbands. On enquiry he was informed that this was an old custom, but had fallen into abeyance, and 'scarcely once in an age any of the females are hardy enough to make this feast, notwithstanding a husband of the first rank awaits as a sure reward the successful giver of it.'

Speaking of the Greenland Esquimaux, Egede expressly states that 'those are reputed the best and noblest tempered who, without any pain or reluctancy, will lend their friends their wives.'[5]

---

[1] Histoire Abregée des Cultes, vol. i. p. 431.

[2] *Ibid.*, vol. ii. p. 108.

[3] The People of India, by J. F. Watson and J. W. Kaye, vol. i. p. 2.

[4] Travels in North America, p. 245.

[5] History of Greenland, p. 142.

The same feeling, probably, gave rise to the curious custom existing, according to Strabo,[1] among the (Parthian) Tapyrians, that when a man had had two or three children by one wife, he was obliged to leave her, so that she might marry some one else.   There is some reason to suppose that a similar custom once prevailed among the Romans; thus Cato, who was proverbially austere in his morals, did not think it right permanently to retain his wife Martia, whom his friend Hortensius wished to marry. This he accordingly permitted, and Martia lived with Hortensius until his death, when she returned to her first husband.   The high character of Cato is sufficient proof that he would not have permitted this, if he had regarded it as wrong; and Plutarch expressly states that the custom of lending wives existed among the Romans. Akin to this feeling is that which induces so many savage tribes[2] to provide their guests with temporary wives. To omit this would be regarded as quite inhospitable. The practice, moreover, seems to recognise the existence of a right inherent in every member of the community, and to visitors as temporary members; which, in the case of the latter, could not be abrogated by arrangements made before their arrival, and, consequently, without their concurrence.   The prevalence of this custom brings home to us forcibly the difference existing between the savage and the civilised modes of regarding the relation of the sexes to one another.

Perhaps the most striking case of all is that afforded by some of the Brazilian tribes.   The captives taken by them in war used to be kept for some time and fatted up; after which they were killed and eaten.   Yet even here, during

[1] Strabo, ii. 515, 520.

[2] For instance, the Esquimaux, North and South American Indians, Polyne-sians, Eastern and Western Negroes, Arabs, Abyssinians, Caffirs, Mongols, Tutski, &c.

the time that they had to live, the poor wretches were always provided with a temporary wife.[1]

This view also throws some light on the remarkable subordination of the wife to the husband, which is so characteristic of marriage, and so curiously inconsistent with all our avowed ideas; nay, it also tends to explain those curious cases in which Hetairæ were held in greater estimation than those women who were, as we should consider properly and respectably, married to a single husband.[1] The former were originally fellow-countrywomen and relations; the latter captives and slaves. And even when this ceased to be the case, the idea would long survive the circumstances which gave rise to it.

We know that in Athens courtesans were highly respected. 'The daily conversations they listened to,' says Lord Kames,[3] ' on philosophy, politics, poetry, enlightened their understanding and improved their taste. Their houses became agreeable schools, where everyone might be instructed in his own art. Socrates and Pericles met frequently at the house of Aspasia, for from her they acquired delicacy of taste, and, in return, procured to her public respect and reputation. Greece at that time was governed by orators, over whom some celebrated courtesans had great influence, and by that means entered deep into the government.'

So also it was an essential of the model Platonic Republic that, ' among the guardians, at least, the sexual arrangements should be under public regulation, and the monopoly of one woman by one man forbidden.' [4]

In the famous Indian city of Vesali ' marriage was forbidden, and high rank attached to the lady who held office

[1] Lafitau, Mœurs des Sauv. Amer. vol. ii. p. 294.
[2] Bachofen, Das Mutterrecht, p. xix. p. 125. Burton's Lake Regions of Africa, vol. i. p. 198.
[3] History of Man, vol. ii. p. 50.
[4] Bain's Mental and Moral Science.

as Chief of the Courtesans.' When the Holy Buddha (Sak-yamuni), in his old age, visited Vesali, 'he was lodged in a garden belonging to the chief of the courtesans, and received a visit from this grand lady, who drove out to see him, attended by her suite in stately carriages. Having approached and bowed down, she took her seat on one side of him and listened to a discourse on Dharma. . . . . On entering the town she met the rulers of Vesali, gorgeously apparelled; but their equipages made way for her. They asked her to resign to them the honour of entertaining Sakyamuni; but she refused, and the great man himself, when solicited by the rulers in person, also refused to break his engagement with the lady.' [1]

Until recently the courtesans were the only educated women in India.[2] Even now many of the great Hindoo temples have bands of courtesans attached to them, who ' follow their trade without public shame. It is a strange anomaly that, while a courtesan, born of, or adopted into, a courtesan family, is not held to pursue a shameless vocation, other women who have fallen from good repute are esteemed disgraceful.' [3] There is in reality, however, nothing anomalous in this. The former continue the old custom of the country, under solemn religious sanction; the latter, on the contrary, have given way to lawless inclinations, have outraged public feelings, have probably broken their marriage vows, and brought disgrace on their families. In Ancient Egypt, again, it would appear that illegitimate children were under certain circumstances preferred over those born in wedlock.[4]

When the special wife was a stranger and a slave, while

[1] Mrs. Spier's Life in Ancient India, p. 281.
[2] Dubois' People of India, pp. 217, 402.
[3] The People of India, by J. F. Watson and J.W. Kaye, vol. iii. p. 165.
[4] Bachofen, Das Mutterrecht, p. 125.

the communal wife was a relative and a freewoman, such feelings would naturally arise, and would, in some cases, long survive the social condition to which they owed their origin.

I now pass to the curious custom, for which M'Lennan has proposed the convenient term 'exogamy' — that, namely, of necessarily marrying out of the tribe. Tylor, who called particular attention to this custom in his interesting work on 'The Early History of Man,' which was published in the very same year as M'Lennan's 'Primitive Marriage,' thought that 'the evils of marrying near relatives might be the main ground of this series of restrictions.' Morgan also considers exogamy as 'explainable, and only explainable, as a reformatory movement to break up the intermarriage of blood relations,' and which could only be effected by exogamy, because all in the tribe were regarded as related. In fact, however, exogamy afforded little protection against the marriage of relatives, and, wherever it was systematised, it permitted marriage even between half brothers and sisters, either on the father's or mother's side. Where an objection to the intermarriage of relatives existed, exogamy was unnecessary; where it did not exist, exogamy could not arise.

M'Lennan says, 'I believe this restriction on marriage to be connected with the practice in early times of female infanticide, which, rendering women scarce, led at once to polyandry within the tribe, and the capturing of women from without.'[1] He has not alluded to the natural preponderance of men over women. Thus, throughout Europe, the proportion of boys to girls is as 106 to 100.[2] Here, therefore, even without infanticide, we see that there is

---

[1] *Loc. cit.* p. 138.   [2] Wait's Anthropology, p. 111.

no exact balance between the sexes. In many savage races, in various parts of the world, it has been observed the men are much more numerous, but it is difficult to ascertain how far this is due to an original difference, and how far to other causes.

It is conceivable that the difference between endogamous and exogamous tribes may be due to the different proportion of the sexes : those races tending to become exogamous where boys prevail; those, on the other hand, endogamous where the reverse is the case.[1] I am not, however, aware that we have any statistics which enable us to determine this point, nor do I believe that it is the true explanation of the custom.

Infanticide is, no doubt, very prevalent among savages. As long, indeed, as men were few in number, enemies were scarce and game was tame. Under these circumstances, there was no temptation to infanticide. There were some things which women could do better than men, some occupations which pride and laziness, or both, induced them to leave to the women. As soon, however, as in any country population became even slightly more dense, neighbours became a nuisance. They invaded the hunting grounds, and disturbed the game. Hence, if for no other reason, wars would arise. Once begun, they would continually break out again and again, under one pretence or another. Men for slaves, women for wives, and the thirst for glory, made a weak tribe always a temptation to a strong one. Under these circumstances, female children became a source of weakness in several ways. They ate, and did not hunt. They weakened their mothers when young, and, when grown-up, were a temptation to surrounding tribes. Hence female infanticide is very prevalent, and easily accounted for.

[1] See Das Mutterrecht, p. 109.

Yet I cannot regard it as the true cause of exogamy. On the other hand, we must remember that under the communal system the women of the tribe were all common property. No one could appropriate one of them to himself, without infringing on the general rights of the tribe. Women taken in war were, on the contrary, in a different position. The tribe, as a tribe, had no right to them, and men surely would reserve to themselves exclusively their own prizes. These captives then would naturally become the wives in our sense of the term.

Several causes would tend to increase the importance of the separate, and decrease that of communal marriage. The impulse which it would give to, and receive back from, the development of the affections; the convenience with reference to domestic arrangements, the natural wishes of the wife herself, and last, not least, the inferior energy of the children sprung from 'in and in' marriages, would all tend to increase the importance of individual marriage.

Even were there no other cause, the advantage of crossing, so well known to breeders of stock, would soon give a marked preponderance to those races by whom exogamy was largely practised, and hence we need not be surprised to find exogamy very prevalent among the lower races of man.

When this state of things had gone on for some time, usage, as M'Lennan well observes, would 'establish a prejudice among the tribes observing it — a prejudice strong as a principle of religion, as every prejudice relating to marriage is apt to be—against marrying women of their own stock.' [1]

We should not, perhaps, have à priori expected to find among savages any such remarkable restriction, yet

[1] Loc. cit. p. 140.

it is very widely distributed; and from this point of view we can, I think, clearly see how it arose.

In Australia, where the same family names are common almost over the whole continent, no man may marry a woman whose family name is the same as his own, and who belongs therefore to the same tribe.[1] 'No man,' says Mr. Lang, 'can marry a woman of the same clan, though the parties be no way related according to our ideas.'[2]

In Eastern Africa, Burton[3] says that 'some clans of the Somal will not marry one of the same, or even of a consanguineous family;' and the Bakalari have the same rule.[4]

Du Chaillu,[5] speaking of Western Equatorial Africa, says, 'the law of marriages among the tribes I have visited is peculiar; each tribe is divided into clans; the children in most of the tribes belong to the clan of the mother, and these cannot by any possible laws marry among themselves, however removed in degree they may have been connected: it is considered an abomination among them. But there exists no objection to possessing a father's or brother's wife. I could not but be struck with the healthful influence of such regulations against blood marriages among them.'

In India the Warali tribes are divided into sections, and no man may marry a woman belonging to his own section. In the Magar tribes these sections are called Thums, and the same rule prevails. Col. Dalton tells us that 'the Hos, Moondahs, and Oraons are divided into clans or keelis, and may not take to wife a girl of the

---

[1] Eyre's Discoveries in Australia, vol. ii. p. 329. Grey's Journal, p. 242.
[2] The Aborigines of Australia, p. 10.
[3] First Footsteps, p. 120.
[4] Trans. Ethn. Soc. N. S. vol. i. p. 321.
[5] *Ibid.* p. 307.

same keeli.' Again the Garrows are divided into 'Maharis,' and a man may not marry a girl of his own 'Mahari.'

The Munnieporees and other tribes inhabiting the hills round Munniepore—the Koupooees, Mows, Murams, and Murrings—as M'Lennan points out on the authority of M'Culloch, 'are each and all divided into four families : Koomrul, Looang, Angom, and Ningthaja. A member of any of these families may marry a member of any other, but the intermarriage of members of the same family is strictly prohibited.' The Todas, says Metz,[2] 'are divided into five distinct classes, known by the names Peiky, Pekkan, Kuttan, Kennae, and Tody; of which the first is regarded as the most aristocratic. These classes do not even intermarry with each other, and can therefore never lose their distinctive characteristics.'

The Khonds, says General Campbell, 'regard it as degrading to bestow their daughters in marriage on men of their own tribe; and consider it more manly to seek their wives in a distant country.'[3] Major M'Pherson also tells us that they consider marriage between people of the same tribe as wicked, and punishable with death. The Kalmucks, according to De Hell, are divided into hordes, and no man can marry a woman of the same horde. The bride, says Bergman, is always chosen from another stock; 'among the Dubets, for instance, from the Torgot stock, and among the Torgots from the Dubet stock.'

The same custom prevails among the Circassians and the Samoyeds.[4] The Ostiaks regard it as a crime to

---

[1] Account of the Valley of Munniepore, 1859, pp. 49–69.
[2] Tribes of the Neilgherry Hills, p.21.
[3] M'Lennan, p. 95.
[4] Pallas, vol. iv. p. 96.

marry a woman of the same family or even of the same name.[1]

When a Jakut (Siberia) wishes to marry, he must, says Middendorf,[2] choose a girl from another clan. No one is permitted to marry a woman from his own clan. In China, says Davis,[3] ' marriage between all persons of the same surname being unlawful, this rule must of course include all descendants of the male branch for ever; and as, in so vast a population, there are not a great many more than one hundred surnames throughout the empire, the embarrassments that arise from so strict a law must be considerable.'

Amongst the Tinné Indians of North-west America, ' a Chit-sangh cannot, by their rules,[4] marry a Chit-sangh, although the rule is set at naught occasionally; but when it does take place the persons are ridiculed and laughed at. The man is said to have married his sister, even though she may be from another tribe, and there be not the slightest connection by blood between them. The same way with the other two divisions. The children are of the same colour as their mother. They receive caste from their mother; if a male Chit-sangh marry a Nah-tsingh woman, the children are Nah-tsingh, and if a male Nah-tsingh marry a Chit-sangh woman, the children are Chit-sangh, so that the divisions are always changing. As the fathers die out the country inhabited by the Chit-sangh becomes occupied by the Nah-tsingh, and so *vice versâ*. They are continually changing countries, as it were.'

Among the Kenaiyers (N. W. America), ' it was the custom that the men of one stock should choose their wives from another, and the · offspring belonged to the

[1] Pallas, vol. iv. p. 69.
[2] Sibirische Reise, p. 72.
[3] The Chinese, vol. i. p. 282.

[4] Notes on the Tinneh. Hardisty, Smithsonian Report, 1866, p. 315.

race of the mother. This custom has fallen into disuse,
and marriages in the same tribe occur; but the old people
say that mortality among the Kenaiyer has arisen from
the neglect of the ancient usage. A man's nearest heirs
in this tribe are his sister's children.'[1] The Tsimsheean
Indians of British Columbia[2] are similarly divided into
tribes, and totems or ' crests, which are common to all the
tribes. The crests are the whale, the porpoise, the eagle,
the coon, the wolf, and the frog. In connection with
these crests, several very important points of Indian
character and law are seen. The relationship existing
between persons of the same crest is nearer than that
between members of the same tribe, which is seen in this
that members of the same tribe may marry, but those of
the same crest are not allowed to do so under any circumstances; that is, a whale may not marry a whale, but a
whale may marry a frog, &c.'

Indeed, as regards the Northern Redskins generally, it
is stated[3] in the Archæologia Americana that ' every
nation was divided into a number of clans, varying in the
several nations from three to eight or ten, the members of
which respectively were dispersed indiscriminately throughout the whole nation. It has been fully ascertained that
the inviolable regulations by which these clans were per-
petuated amongst the southern nations were, first, that no
man could marry in his own clan; secondly, that every
child should belong to his or her mother's clan.'

The Indians of Guiana[4] ' are divided into families, each
of which has a distinct name, as the *Siwidi, Karuafudi,
Onisidi*, &c. Unlike our families, these all descend in the
female line, and no individual of either sex is allowed to

---

[1] Richardson's Boat Journey, vol. i.
p. 406. See also Smithsonian Report,
1866, p. 326.
[2] Metlahkatlah, published by the
Church Missionary Soc. 1869, p. 6.
[3] M'Lennan, p. 121. Lafitau, vol. i.
p. 558. Tanner's Narrative, p. 313.
[4] Brett's Indian Tribes of Guiana,
p. 98.

marry another of the same family name.   Thus, a woman
of the Siwidi family bears the same name as her mother,
but neither her father nor her husband can be of that
family.   Her children and the children of her daughters
will also be called Siwidi, but both her sons and daughters
are prohibited from an alliance with any individual bearing the same name; though they may marry into the
family of their father, if they choose.   These customs are
strictly observed, and any breach of them would be considered as wicked.'

Lastly, the Brazilian races, according to Martius, differ
greatly in their marriage regulations.   In some of the very
scattered tribes, who live in small families far remote from
one another, the nearest relatives often intermarry.   In more
populous districts, on the contrary, the tribes are divided
into families, and a strict system of exogamy prevails.[1]

Thus, then, we see that this remarkable custom of
exogamy prevails throughout Western and Eastern Africa,
in Circassia, Hindostan, Tartary, Siberia, China, and
Australia, as well as in North and South America.

The relations existing between husband and wife in the
lower races of Man, as indicated in the preceding pages,
are sufficient to remove all surprise at the prevalence of
polygamy.   There are, however, other causes, not less
powerful, though perhaps less prominent, to which much
influence must be ascribed.   Thus in all tropical regions
girls become marriageable very young; their beauty is
acquired early, and soon fades, while men, on the contrary, retain their full powers much longer.   Hence
when love depends, not on similarity of tastes pursuits or
opinions, but entirely on external attractions, we cannot
wonder that every man who is able to do so, provides
himself with a succession of favourites, even when the first

[1] *Loc. cit.* p. 63.

wife remains not only nominally the head, but really his confidant and adviser. Another cause has no doubt exercised great influence. Milk is necessary for children, and in the absence of domestic animals it consequently follows that they are not weaned until they are several years old. The effect of this on the social relations has been already referred to (*antè*, p. 55).

Polyandry, on the contrary, is far less common, though more frequent than is generally supposed. M'Lennan and Morgan, indeed, both regard it as a phase through which human progress has necessarily passed. If, however, we define it as the condition in which one woman is married to several men, but (as distinguished from communal marriage) to them exclusively, then I am rather disposed to regard it as an exceptional phenomenon, arising from the paucity of females.

M'Lennan, indeed,[1] gives a long list of tribes which he regards as polyandrous, namely, those of Thibet, Cashmeer, and the Himalayan regions, the Todas, Coorgs, Nairs, and various other races in India, in Ceylon, in New Zealand[2] and one or two other Pacific islands, in the Aleutian Archipelago, among the Koryaks, the Saporogian Cossacks, on the Orinoco, in parts of Africa, and in Lancerota. To these he adds the ancient Britons, some of the Median cantons, the Picts, and the Getes, while traces of it occurred among the ancient Germans. To these I may add that of some families among the Iroquois. On the other hand, several of the above cases are, I think, merely instances of communal marriage. Indeed, it is evident that where our information is incomplete, it must often be far from easy to distinguish between communal marriage and true polyandry.

If we examine the above instances, some of them will,

---

[1] *Loc. cit.* p. 180.   [2] Lafitau, *loc. cit.* vol. i. p. 555.

I think, prove untenable. The passage referred to in Tacitus[1] does not appear to me to justify us in regarding the Germans as having been polyandrous.

Erman is correctly referred to by M'Lennan, as mentioning the existence of 'lawful polyandry in the Aleutian Islands.' He does not, however, give his authority for the statement. The account he gives of the Koryaks by no means, I think, proves that polyandry occurs among them. The case of the Kalmucks, to judge from the account given by Clarke,[2] is certainly one in which brothers, but brothers only, have a wife in common.

For Polynesia, M'Lennan relies on the Legend of Rupe, as told by Sir G. Grey.[3] Here, however, it is merely stated that two brothers named Ihuatamai and Ihuwareware, having found Hinauri, when she was thrown by the surf on the coast at Wairarawa, 'looked upon her with pleasure, and took her as a wife between them both.' This seems to me rather a case of communal marriage than of polyandry, especially when the rest of the legend is borne in mind. Neither does the evidence as regards Africa seem to me at all satisfactory. Reade, in the passage referred to by Mr. M'Lennan, merely says that 'the sisters of the king may negotiate with whom and with as many as they please for the contribution of royal heirs; provided always that the man is strong, good-looking, and of a decent position in life: conditions which these ladies cannot, I am sure, find very harsh.'[4] This implies lax morality, but is not even an indication of regular polyandry.

Polyandry is no doubt very widely distributed over India, Thibet, and Ceylon. In the latter island the joint husbands are always brothers.[5] But, on the whole, lawful polyandry (as opposed to mere laxness of morality)

[1] Germ. xx.
[2] Travels, vol. i. p. 241.
[3] Polynesian Mythology, p. 81.
[4] Reade's Savage Africa, p. 43.
[5] Davy's Ceylon, p. 286.

seems to be an exceptional system, generally intended to avoid the evils arising from monogamy where the number of women is less than that of men.

Passing on now to the custom of endogamy, M'Lennan remarks that 'the separate endogamous tribes are nearly as numerous, and they are in some respects as rude, as the separate exogamous tribes.'[1]

So far as my knowledge goes, on the contrary, endogamy is much less prevalent than exogamy, and it seems to me to have arisen from a feeling of race-pride, and a disdain of surrounding tribes which were either really or hypothetically in a lower condition.

Thus among the Ahts of N. W. America, as mentioned by Sproat, ' though the different tribes of the Aht nation are frequently at war with one another, women are not captured from other tribes for marriage, but only to be kept as slaves. The idea of slavery connected with capture is so common, that a free-born Aht would hesitate to marry a woman taken in war, whatever her rank had been in her own tribe.'[2]

Some of the Indian races, as the Kocchs and the Hos, are forbidden to marry excepting within the tribe. The latter at least, however, are not truly endogamous, for, as already mentioned, they are divided into 'keelis,' or clans, and ' may not take to wife a girl of their own keeli.'[3] Thus they are in fact exogamous, and it is possible that some of the other cases of endogamy might, if we were better acquainted with them, present the same duplex phenomenon.

Among the Yerkalas[4] of Southern India 'a custom prevails by which the first two daughters of a family may be

[1] Loc. cit. p. 145.
[2] Sproat, Scenes and Studies of Savage Life, p. 98.
[3] Antè, p. 95.
[4] Shortt. Trans. Ethn. Soc. N. S. vol. vii. p. 187.

claimed by the maternal uncle as wives for his sons. The value of a wife is fixed at twenty pagodas. The maternal uncle's right to the first two daughters is valued at eight out of twenty pagodas, and is carried out thus :—if he urges his preferential claim, and marries his own sons to his nieces, he pays for each only twelve pagodas; and, similarly, if he, from not having sons, or any other cause, forego his claim, he receives eight pagodas of the twenty paid to the girls' parents by anybody else who may marry them.'

The Doingnaks, a branch of the Chukmas, appear also to have been endogamous, and Captain Lewin mentions that they ' abandoned the parent stem during the chief-ship of Jaunbux Khan about 1782. The reason of this split was a disagreement on the subject of marriages. The chief passed an order that the Doingnak should intermarry with the tribe in general. This was contrary to ancient custom, and caused discontent and eventually a break in the tribe.'[1] This is one of the very few cases where we have evidence of a change in this respect. The Kalangs of Java, who have some claim to be regarded as the aborigines of the island, are also endogamous, and when a man asks a girl in marriage he must prove his descent from their peculiar stock.[2]

The Mantchu Tartars forbid marriages between those whose family names are different.[3] In Guam brothers and sisters used to intermarry, and it is even stated that such unions were preferred as being most natural and proper.[4] Endogamy would seem to have prevailed in the Sandwich Islands,[5] and in New Zealand, where, as Yate mentions, ' great opposition is made to anyone taking,

[1] Lewin's Hill Tracts of Chittagong, p. 65.
[2] Raffles' History of Java, vol. i. p. 328.
[3] M'Lennan, loc. cit. p. 146.
[4] Arago's Letters. Freycinet's Voyage, vol. ii. p. 17.
[5] Ibid. p. 94.

except for some political purpose, a wife from another tribe; so that such intermarriages seldom occur.' [1]

The idea of relationship as existing amongst us, founded on marriage, and implying equal connection of a child to its father and mother, seems so natural and obvious that there are, perhaps, many to whom the possibility of any other has not occurred. The facts already recorded will, however, have prepared us for the existence of peculiar ideas as to relationship. The strength of the foster-feeling—the milk-tie—among the Scotch Highlanders, is a familiar instance of a mode of regarding relationship very different from that prevalent amongst us.

We have also seen that, under the custom of communal marriage, a child was regarded as related to the tribe, but not specially to any particular father or mother. It is evident that under communal marriage—and little less so wherever men had many wives—the tie between father and son must have been very slight. Obviously, however, there are causes in operation which always tend to strengthen the connection between the parent and off-spring, and especially between the mother and her child. Among agricultural tribes, and under settled forms of government, the chiefs often have very large harems, and their importance even is measured by the number of their wives, as in other cases by that of their cows or horses.

This state of things is in many ways very prejudicial. It checks, of course, the natural affection and friendly intercourse between man and wife. The King of Ashantee, for instance, always has 3,333 wives; but no man can love so many women, nor can so many women cherish any personal affection for one man.

Even among hunting races, though men were unable to maintain so many wives, still, as changes are of frequent occurrence, the tie between a mother and child is much stronger than that which binds a child to its father. Hence we find that among many of the lower races relationship through females is the prevalent custom, and we are thus able to understand the curious practice that a man's heirs are not his own, but his sister's children.

Montesquieu [1] regarded relationship through females as intended to prevent the accumulation of landed property in few hands—an explanation manifestly inapplicable to many, nay the majority, of cases in which the custom exists, and the explanation above suggested is, I have no doubt, the correct one.

Thus, when a rich man dies in Guinea, his property, excepting the armour, descended to the sister's son, expressly, according to Smith, on the ground that he must certainly be a relative.[2]   Battel mentions that the town of Longo (Loango) ' is governed by four chiefs, which are sons of the king's sisters; for the king's sons never come to be kings.' [3] Quatremère mentions that ' Chez les Nubiens, dit Abou Selah, lorsqu'un roi vient à mourir et qu'il laisse un fils et un neveu du côté de sa sœur, celui-ci monte sur le trône de préférence à l'héritier naturel.'[4]

In Central Africa, Caillié [5] says that ' the sovereignty remains always in the same family, but the son never succeeds his father; they choose in preference a son of the king's sister, conceiving that by this method the sovereign power is more sure to be transmitted to one of the blood royal; a precaution which shows how little faith is put in the virtue of the women of this country.'

In Northern Africa we find the same custom among the Berbers ; [6] and Burton mentions it as existing in the East.

[1] Esprit des Lois, vol. i. p. 70.

[2] Smith's Voyage to Guinea, p. 143. See also Pinkerton's Voyages, vol. xv. p. 417, 421, 528. Astley's Collection of Voyages, vol. ii. p. 63, 256.

[3] Pinkerton's Voyages, vol. xvi. p. 331.

[4] Mém. géogr. sur l'Égypte et sur quelques contrées voisines. Paris, 1811. Quoted in Bachofen's Mutterrecht, p. 108.

[5] Caillié's Travels, vol. i. p. 153.

[6] La Mère, chez certains peuples de l'Antiquité, p. 45.

Even Herodotus [1] had observed a case in point. ' The Lycians,' he says, 'have one custom peculiar to themselves, in which they differ from all other nations; for they take their name from their mothers, and not from their fathers; so that if anyone asks another who he is, he will describe himself by his mother's side, and reckon up his maternal ancestry in the female line.' Polybius makes the same statement as regards the Locrians; and on Etruscan tombs descent is stated in the female line. In India the Kasias, the Kocch, and the Nairs have the system of female kinship. Buchanan [2] tells us that among the Buntar in Tulava a man's property does not descend to his own children, but to those of his sister. Sir W. Elliot states that the people of Malabar, ' notwithstanding the same diversity of caste as in other provinces, all agree in one remarkable usage—that of transmitting property through females only.' [3] He adds, on the authority of Lieutenant Conner, that the same is the case in Travancore, among all the castes except the Ponans and the Namburi Brahmans.

As Latham states, ' no Nair son knows his own father, and, *vice versâ*, no Nair father knows his own son. What becomes of the property of the husband? It descends to the children of his sisters.' [4]

Among the Limboos (India), a tribe near Darjeeling,[5] the boys become the property of the father on his paying the mother a small sum of money, when the child is named, and enters his father's tribe: girls remain with the mother, and belong to her tribe.'

Marsden tells us,[6] that among the Battas of Sumatra,

[1] Clio, 173.
[2] Vol. iii. p. 16.
[3] Trans. Ethn. Soc. 1869, p. 119.
[4] Descriptive Ethnology, vol. ii. p. 463.
[5] Campbell, Trans. Ethn. Soc. N. S. vol. vii. p. 155.
[6] Marsden's History of Sumatra, p. 376.

'the succession to the chiefships does not go, in the first instance, to the son of the deceased, but to the nephew by a sister; and that the same extraordinary rule, with respect to the property in general, prevails also amongst the Malays of that part of the island, and even in the neighbourhood of Padang. The authorities for this are various and unconnected with each other, but not sufficiently circumstantial to induce me to admit it as a generally established practice.'

Among the Kenaiyers of Cook's Inlet, Sir John Richardson tells us that a man's property descends not to his own children, but to those of his sister.[1] The same is the case with the Kutchin.[2]

Carver[3] mentions that among the Hudson's Bay Indians the children 'are always distinguished by the name of the mother; and if a woman marries several husbands, and has issue by each of them, they are all called after her. The reason they give for this is, that as their offspring are indebted to the father for their souls, the invisible part of their essence, and to the mother for their corporeal and apparent part, it is more rational that they should be distinguished by the name of the latter, from whom they indubitably derive their being, than by that of the father, to which a doubt might sometimes arise whether they are justly entitled.' A similar rule prevailed in Haiti and Mexico.[4]

As regards Polynesia, Mariner states that in the Friendly or Tonga Islands 'nobility descends by the female line, for when the mother is not a noble, the children are not nobles.'[5] It would seem, however, from another passage, that these islanders were passing the stage of relation-

---

[1] Boat Journey, vol. i. p. 406.
[2] Smithsonian Report, 1866, p. 326.
[3] Carver, p. 378. See also p. 259.
[4] Müller, Americanischen Urreligionen, p. 167, 539.
[5] Tonga Islands, vol. ii. pp. 89, 91.

ship through females to that through males. The existence of inheritance through females is clearly indicated in
the Fijian custom known as Vasu.

So also in Western Australia, 'children, of either sex,
always take the family name of their mother.'[1]

Tacitus,[2] speaking of the Germans, says 'children are
regarded with equal affection by their maternal uncles
as by their fathers; some even consider this as the more
sacred bond of consanguinity, and prefer it in the re-
quisition of hostages.' He adds, ' a person's own children,
however, are his heirs and successors; no wills are made.'
From this it would appear as if female inheritance had
been recently and not universally abandoned.

Among the ancient Jews, Abraham married his half-
sister, Nahor married his brother's daughter, and Amram
his father's sister; this was permitted because they were
not regarded as relations. Tamar also evidently might
have married Amnon, though they were both children
of David: ' Speak unto the king,' she said, ' for he will
not withhold me from thee;' for, as their mothers were
not the same, they were no relations in the eye of the law.

Solon also permitted marriage with sisters on the
father's side, but not on the mother's.

Here, therefore, we have abundant evidence of the
second stage, in which the child is related to the mother,
and not to the father; whence a man's heir is his sister's
child, who is his nephew,—not his own child, who is in
some cases regarded as no relation to him at all.

When, however, marriage became more respected, and
the family affections stronger, it is easy to see that the
rule under which a man's property went to his sister's
children, would become unpopular, both with the father,

---

[1] Eyre, *loc. cit.* p. 330.   [2] De Mor. Germ. xx.

who would naturally wish his children to inherit his property, and equally so with the children themselves.

M. Girard Teulon, indeed, to whom we are indebted for a very interesting memoir on this subject,[1] regards the first recognition of his parental relationship as an act of noble self-devotion on the part of some great genius in ancient times.

'Le premier,' he says, 'qui consentit à se reconnaître père fut un homme de génie et de cœur, un des grands bienfaiteurs de l'humanité. Prouve en effet que l'enfant t'appartient. Es-tu sûr qu'il est un autre toi-même, ton fruit? que tu l'as enfanté? ou bien, à l'aide d'une généreuse et volontaire crédulité, marches-tu, noble inventeur, à la conquête d'un but supérieur?'[2]

Bachofen also, while characterising the change from male to female relationship as the 'wichtigsten Wendepunkt in der Geschichte des Geschlechts-verhältnisses,' explains it, as I cannot but think, in an altogether erroneous manner. He regards it as a liberation of the spirit from the deceptive appearances of nature, an elevation of human existence above the laws of mere matter, as a recognition that the creative power is the most important, and, in short, as a subordination of the material to the spiritual part of our nature. By this step, he says, 'Man durchbricht die Banden des Tellurismus und erhebt seinen Blick zu den höhern Regionen des Kosmos.'[3]

This seems to me, I confess, a very curious notion, and one with which I cannot at all agree. The recognition of paternal responsibility grew up, I believe, gradually and from the force of circumstances, aided by the impulses of natural affection. On the other hand, the adoption of relationship through the father's line, instead of through

---

[1] La Mère chez certains peuples de l'Antiquité.

[2] *Loc. cit.* p. 32.

[3] Bachofen, Das Mutterrecht, p. xxvii.

the mother's, was probably effected by the natural wish which every one would feel that his property should go to his own children. It is true that we have scarcely any actual records of this change, but as it is easy to see how it might have been brought about, and difficult to suppose that the opposite step can ever have been made ; as moreover we find relationship through the father very general, not to say universal, in civilised races, while the opposite system is very common among savages, it is evident that this change must frequently have been effected.

Taking all these facts then into consideration, whenever we find relationship through females only, I think we may safely look upon it as the relic of an ancient barbarism.

As soon as the change was made, the father would take the place held previously by the mother, and he, instead of she, would be regarded as the parent. Hence on the birth of a child, the father would naturally be very careful what he did, and what he ate, for fear the child should be injured. Thus, I believe, arises the curious custom to which I referred in my first chapter.

Relationship to the father at first excludes that to the mother, and from having been regarded as no relation to the former, children came to be looked on as none to the latter.

In South America, where it is customary to treat captives well in every respect, for a certain time, giving them clothes, food, a wife, &c., and then to kill and eat them, any children they may have are killed and eaten also.[1] In North America, as we have seen, the system of relationship through females prevails among the rude races of the North. Further south, as Lafitau long ago pointed out, we find a curious, and so to say intermediate, system among the Iroquois and Hurons, to whom, as Mr. Morgan has shown,

---

[1] Lafitau, vol. ii. p. 307.

we may add the Tamils of India.[1]—A man's brother's children are reckoned as his children, but his sister's children are his nephews and nieces, while a woman's brother's children are her nephews and nieces, and her sister's children are her children.[2]

The curious system thus indicated is shown more fully in the following table, extracted from Mr. Morgan's very interesting memoir:[3]—

Red Skin.

Hanih	=	Father, and also Father's brother Father's father's brother's son, and so on.
Noyeh	=	Mother, and also Mother's sister Mother's mother's sister's daughter, and so on.
Haje	=	Brother (elder), and also Father's brother's son Mother's sister's son, and so on.
Harakwuk	=	Son Brother's son (male speaking) Sister's son (female speaking).

Tamil.

Takkappan	=	Father, and also Father's brother Father's father's brother's son, and so on Mother's sister's husband.
Tay	=	Mother, and also Mother's sister Father's brother' wife Mother's mother's sister's daughter, and so on.
Tamaiyan	=	Brother elder, and also Father's brother's son Mother's sister's son, and so on.
Makan	=	Son Brother's son (male speaking) Sister's son (female speaking).

---

[1] Proc. American Academy of Arts and Sciences, 1866, p. 456.

[2] Lafitau, vol. i. p. 552.

[3] *Loc. cit.* p. 456.

That these names really imply ideas as to relationship, and have not arisen from mere poverty of language, is shown by the fact that in other respects their nomenclature is even richer than ours. Thus they have different words for an elder brother and a younger brother; an elder sister and a younger sister; so again the names for a brother's son, a brother's daughter, a sister's son, and a sister's daughter, depend on whether the person speaking is a man or a woman. Thus they distinguish relationships which we correctly regard as equivalent, and confound others which are really distinct. Moreover, as the languages of distinct and distant races, such as the Iroquois of America and the Tamil of Southern India, agree in so many points, we cannot dismiss these peculiarities as mere accidents, but must regard them as founded on similar, though peculiar, views on the subject of relationship.

That in the case of the Iroquois this system arose from that of relationship through females, and did not degenerate from ours, is evident; because in it, though a man's sister's children are his nephews and nieces, his sister's grandchildren are also his grandchildren; indicating the existence of a period when his sister's children were his children, and, consequently, when relationship was traced in the female line. A man's brother's children are his children, because his brother's wives are also his wives.

How completely the idea of relationship through the father, when once recognised, might replace that through the mother, we may see in the very curious trial of Orestes. Agamemnon, having been murdered by his wife Clytemnestra, was avenged by their son Orestes, who killed his mother for the murder of his father. For this act he was prosecuted before the tribunal of the gods by the Erinnyes, whose function it was to punish those who shed the blood of relatives. In his defence, Orestes asks them why they did not punish Clytemnestra for the murder of Agamemnon; and when they reply that marriage does not constitute blood relationship,—'She was not the kindred of the man whom she slew,'—he pleads that by the same rule they cannot touch *him*, because a man is a relation to his father, but not to his mother. This view, which seems to us so unnatural, was supported by Apollo and Minerva, and being adopted by the majority of the gods, led to the acquittal of Orestes.

Hence we see that the views prevalent on relationship—views by which the whole social organisation is so profoundly affected—are by no means the same among different races, nor uniform at the same historical period. We ourselves still confuse affinity and consanguinity; but into this part of the question it is not my intention to enter: the evidence brought forward in the preceding pages is, however, I think sufficient to show that children were not in the earliest times regarded as related equally to their father and their mother, but that the natural progress of ideas is, first, that a child is related to his tribe generally; secondly, to his mother, and not to his father; thirdly, to his father, and not to his mother; lastly, and lastly only, that he is related to both.

CHAPTER IV.

RELIGION.

THE religion of savages, though of peculiar interest, is in many respects, perhaps, the most difficult part of my whole subject. I shall endeavour to avoid, as far as possible, anything which might justly give pain to any of my readers. Many ideas, however, which have been, or are, prevalent on religious matters are so utterly opposed to our own that it is impossible to discuss the subject without mentioning some things which are very repugnant to our feelings. Yet, while savages show us a melancholy spectacle of gross superstitions and ferocious forms of worship, the religious mind cannot but feel a peculiar satisfaction in tracing up the gradual evolution of more correct ideas and of nobler creeds.

M. Arbrousset quotes the following touching remarks made to him by Sekesa, a very respectable Kaffir : [1] 'Your tidings,' he said, 'are what I want; and I was seeking before I knew you, as you shall hear and judge for yourselves. Twelve years ago I went to feed my flocks. The weather was hazy. I sat down upon a rock and asked myself sorrowful questions; yes, sorrowful, because I was unable to answer them. "Who has touched the stars with his hands? On what pillars do they rest?" I asked myself. "The waters are never weary: they know no other law than to flow, without ceasing, from morning till

---

[1] The Basutos. Casalis, p. 239.

night, and from night till morning; but where do they
stop? and who makes them flow thus? The clouds also
come and go, and burst in water over the earth. Whence
come they? Who sends them? The diviners certainly
do not give us rain, for how could they do it? and why
do I not see them with my own eyes when they go up to
heaven to fetch it? I cannot see the wind, but what is
it? Who brings it, makes it blow, and roar and terrify
us? Do I know how the corn sprouts? Yesterday there
was not a blade in my field; to-day I returned to the
field and found some. Who can have given to the earth
the wisdom and the power to produce it?" Then I buried
my face in both my hands.'

This, however, was an exceptional case. As a general
rule savages do not set themselves to think out such questions, but adopt the ideas which suggest themselves most
naturally; so that, as I shall attempt to show, races in a
similar stage of mental development, however distinct
their origin may be, and however distant the regions they
inhabit, have very similar religious conceptions. Most of
those who have endeavoured to account for the various
superstitions of savage races have done so by crediting
them with a much more elaborate system of ideas than
they in reality possess. Thus Lafitau supposes that fire was
worshipped because it so well represents ' cette suprême
intelligence dégagée de la nature, dont la puissance est
toujours active.' [1]   Again, with reference to idols, he observes [2] that ' La dépendance que nous avons de l'imagination et des sens, ne nous permettant pas de voir Dieu
autrement qu'en Enigme, comme parle saint Paul, a causé
une espêce de nécessité de nous le montrer sous des images
sensibles, les-quelles fussent autant de symboles, qui nous

---

[1] Mœurs des Sauvages Américains, vol. i. p. 152.   [2] Loc. cit. p. 121.

élevassent jusqu'à lui, comme le portrait nous remet dans l'idée de celui dont il est la peinture.' Plutarch, again, supposed that the crocodile was worshipped by Egypt because, having no tongue, it was a type of the Deity who made laws for nature by his mere will ! Explanations, however, such as these are radically wrong.

I have felt doubtful whether this chapter should not be entitled 'the superstitions' rather than 'the religion' of savages ; but have preferred the latter, partly because many of the superstitious ideas pass gradually into nobler conceptions, and partly from a reluctance to condemn any honest belief, however absurd and imperfect it may be.   It must, however, be admitted that religion, as understood by the lower savage races, differs essentially from ours ; nay, it is not only different, but even opposite. Thus their deities are evil, not good ; they may be forced into compliance with the wishes of man ; they require bloody, and rejoice in human, sacrifices ; they are mortal, not immortal ; a part of, not the author of nature ; they are to be approached by dances rather than by prayers ; and often approve what we call vice, rather than what we esteem as virtue.

In fact, the so-called religion of the lower races bears somewhat the same relation to religion in its higher forms that astrology does to astronomy, or alchemy to chemistry. Astronomy is derived from astrology, yet their spirit is in entire opposition ; and we shall find the same difference between the religions of backward and of advanced races. We regard the Deity as good ; they look upon him as evil ; we submit ourselves to him ; they endeavour to obtain the control of him ; we feel the necessity of accounting for the blessings by which we are surrounded ; they think the blessings come of themselves, and attribute all evil to the interference of malignant beings.

These characteristics are not exceptional and rare. On the contrary I shall attempt to show that, though the religions of the lower races have received different names, they agree in their general characteristics, and are but phases of one sequence, having the same origin, and passing through similar, if not identical, stages. This will explain the great similarities which occur in the most distinct and distant races, which have puzzled many ethnologists, and in some cases led them to utterly untenable theories. Thus even Robertson, though in many respects he held very correct views as to the religious condition of savages, remarks that sun-worship prevailed among the Natchez and the Persians, and observes,[1] 'this surprising coincidence in sentiment between two nations in such different states of improvement is one of the many singular and unaccountable circumstances which occur in the history of human affairs.'

Although however we find the most remarkable coincidences between the religions of distinct races, one of the peculiar difficulties in the study of religion arises from the fact that, while each nation has generally but one language, we may almost say that in religious matters, *quot homines tot sententiæ*; no two men having exactly the same views, however much they may wish to agree.

Many travellers have pointed out this difficulty. Thus Captain Cook, speaking of the South Sea Islanders, says: 'Of the religion [2] of these people we were not able to acquire any clear and consistent knowledge; we found it like the religion of most other countries—involved in mystery and perplexed with apparent inconsistencies.' Many also of those to whom we are indebted for information on the subject, fully expecting to find among savages

---

[1] History of America, book iv. p. 127.   [2] Hawkesworth's Voyages, vol. ii. p 237.

ideas like our own, obscured only by errors and superstitions, have put leading questions, and thus got misleading answers. We constantly hear, for instance, of a Devil, but in fact no spiritual being in the mythology of any savage race possesses the characteristics of Satan. Again, it is often very difficult to determine in what sense an object is worshipped. A mountain, or a river, for instance, may be held sacred either as an actual Deity or merely as his abode; and in the same way a statue may be actually worshipped as a god, or merely reverenced as representing the Divinity.

To a great extent, moreover, these difficulties arise from the fact that when Man, either by natural progress or the influence of a more advanced race, rises to the conception of a higher religion, he still retains his old beliefs, which long linger on, side by side with, and yet in utter opposition to, the higher creed. The new and more powerful Spirit is an addition to the old Pantheon, and diminishes the importance of the older deities; gradually the worship of the latter sinks in the social scale, and becomes confined to the ignorant and the young. Thus a belief in witchcraft still flourishes among our agricultural labourers and the lowest classes in our great cities, and the deities of our ancestors survive in the nursery tales of our children. We must therefore expect to find in each race traces— nay, more than traces, of lower religions. Even if this were not the case we should still be met by the difficulty that there are few really sharp lines in religious systems. It might be supposed that a belief in the immortality of the soul, or in the efficacy of sacrifices, would give us good lines of division; but it is not so: these and many other ideas rise gradually, and even often appear at first in a form very different from that which they ultimately assume.

Hitherto it has been usual to classify religions according to the nature of the object worshipped. Fetichism, for instance, being the worship of inanimate objects, Sabæism that of the heavenly bodies. The true test, however, seems to me to be the estimate in which the Deity is held. The first great stages in religious thought may, I think, be regarded as—

Atheism ; understanding by this term not a denial of the existence of a Deity, but an absence of any definite ideas on the subject.

Fetichism ; the stage in which man supposes he can force the Deity to comply with his desires.

Nature-worship, or *Totemism ;* in which natural objects, trees, lakes, stones, animals, &c. are worshipped.

Shamanism ; in which the superior deities are far more powerful than man, and of a different nature. Their place of abode also is far away, and accessible only to Shamans.

Idolatry, or Anthropomorphism ; in which the gods take still more completely the nature of men, being, however, more powerful. They are still amenable to persuasion ; they are a part of nature, and not creators. They are represented by images or idols.

In the next stage the Deity is regarded as the author, not merely a part, of nature. He becomes for the first time a really supernatural being.

The last stage to which I will refer is that in which morality is associated with religion.

Since the above was written my attention was called by De Brosse's 'Culte des Dieux Fetiches' to a passage in Sanchoniatho, quoted by Eusebius. From his description of the first thirteen generations of men I extract the following passages :—

Generation 1.—The 'first men consecrated the plants

shooting out of the earth, and judged them gods, and worshipped them, upon whom they themselves lived.'

Gen. 2.—The second generation of men 'were called Genus and Genea, and dwelt in Phœnicia ; but when great droughts came, they stretched their hands up to heaven towards the sun, for him they thought the only Lord of Heaven.'

Gen. 3.—Afterwards other mortal issue was begotten, whose names were Phōs, Pur, and Phlox (i.e. Light, Fire, and Flame). These found out the way of generating fire by the rubbing of pieces of wood against each other, and taught men the use thereof.

Gen. 4.—The fourth generation consists of giants.

Gen. 5.—With reference to the fifth he mentions the existence of communal marriage, and that Usous ' consecrated *two pillars* to Fire and Wind, and bowed down to them, and poured out to them the blood of such wild beasts as had been caught in hunting.'

Gen. 6.—Hunting and fishing are invented ; which seems rather inconsistent with the preceding statement.

Gen. 7.—Chrysor, whom he affirms to be Vulcan, discovered iron and the art of forging. ' Wherefore he also was worshipped after his death for a god, and they called him Diamichius (or Zeus Michius).'

Gen. 8.—Pottery was discovered.

Gen. 9.—Now comes Agrus, 'who had a much-worshipped statue, and a temple carried about by one or more yoke of oxen in Phœnicia.

Gen. 10.—Villages were formed, and men kept flocks.

Gen. 11.—Salt was discovered.

Gen. 12.—Taautus or Hermes discovered letters. The Cabiri belong to this generation.

Thus then we find mentioned in order the worship of plants, heavenly bodies, pillars, and men ; later still comes

Idolatry coupled with Temples.   It will be observed that he makes no special mention of Shamanism, and that he regards the worship of plants as aboriginal.

The opinion that religion is general and universal has been entertained by many high authorities.   Yet it is opposed to the evidence of numerous trustworthy observers. Sailors, traders, and philosophers, Roman Catholic priests and Protestant missionaries, in ancient and in modern times, in every part of the globe, have concurred in stating that there are races of men altogether devoid of religion. The case is the stronger because in several instances the fact has greatly surprised him who records it, and has been entirely in opposition to all his preconceived views.   On the other hand, it must be confessed that in some cases travellers denied the existence of a religion merely because the tenets were unlike ours.   The question as to the general existence of religion among men is, indeed, to a great extent a matter of definition.   If the mere sensation of fear, and the recognition that there are probably other beings more powerful than man, are sufficient alone to constitute a religion, then we must, I think, admit that religion is general to the human race.   But when a child dreads the darkness, and shrinks from a lightless room, we never regard that as an evidence of religion.   Moreover, if this definition be adopted, we cannot longer regard religion as peculiar to man.   We must admit that the feeling of a dog or a horse towards its master is of the same character ; and the baying of a dog to the moon is as much an act of worship as some ceremonies which have been so described by travellers.

In 'Prehistoric Times,'[1] I have quoted the following writers as witnesses to the existence of tribes without

[1] Prehistoric Times, 2nd edition, p. 564.

religion. For some of the Esquimaux tribes, Captain Ross;[1] for some of the Canadians, Hearne; for the Californians, Baegert, who lived among them seventeen years, and La Perouse; for many of the Brazilian tribes, Spix and Martius, Bates and Wallace; for Paraguay, Dobritzhoffer; for some of the Polynesians, Williams' Missionary Enterprises, the Voyage of the Novara, and Dieffenbach; for Damood Island (north of Australia), Jukes (Voyage of the Fly); for the Pellew Islands, Wilson; for the Aru Islands, Wallace; for the Andamaners, Mouatt; for certain tribes of Hindostan, Hooker and Shortt; for some of the eastern African nations, Burton and Grant; for the Bachapin Kaffirs, Burchell; and for the Hottentots, Le Vaillant. I will here only give a few instances.

'It is evident,' says M. Bik,[2] 'that the Arafuras of Vorkay (one of the Southern Arus) possess no religion whatever. . . . Of the immortality of the soul they have not the least conception. To all my enquiries on this subject they answered, "No Arafura has ever returned to us after death, therefore we know nothing of a future state, and this is the first time we have heard of it." Their idea was, Mati, Mati sudah (When you are dead there is an end of you). Neither have they any notion of the creation of the world. They only answered " None of us are aware of this; we have never heard anything about it, and therefore do not know who has done it all." To convince myself more fully respecting their want of knowledge of a Supreme Being, I demanded of them on whom they called for help in their need, when, far from their homes, engaged in the trepang fishery, their vessels were overtaken by violent tempests, and no human power could save them, their wives and children, from destruction. The

[1] See also Franklin's Journey to the Polar Sea, vol. ii. p. 265.

[2] Quoted in Kolff's Voyages of the Dourga, p. 159.

eldest among them, after having consulted the others, answered that they know not on whom they could call for assistance, but begged me, if I knew, to be so good as to inform them.'

'The wilder Bedouins,'[1] says Burton, 'will enquire where Allah is to be found : when asked the object of the question, they reply, " If the Eesa could but catch him they would spear him upon the spot,—who but he lays waste their homes and kills their cattle and wives ? " Yet, conjoined to this truly savage incapability of conceiving the idea of a Supreme Being, they believe in the most ridiculous exaggerations : many will not affront a common pilgrim, for fear of being killed by a glance or a word.'

Burton also considers that atheism is 'the natural condition of the savage and uninstructed mind, the night of spiritual existence, which disappears before the dawn of a belief in things unseen. A Creator is to creation what the cause of any event in life is to its effect ; those familiar to the sequence will hardly credit its absence from the minds of others.'[2]

Among the Koossa Kaffirs, Lichtenstein[3] affirms that 'there is no appearance of any religious worship whatever.'

'It might be the proper time now,' says Father Baegert, 'to speak of the form of government and the religion of the Californians previous to their conversion to Christianity ; but neither the one nor the other existed among them. They had no magistrates, no police, and no laws ; idols, temples, religious worship or ceremonies, were unknown to them, and they neither believed in the true and only God, nor adored false deities. . . . I made diligent enquiries, among those with whom I lived, to ascertain

[1] First Footsteps in East Africa, p. 52.

[2] Abbeokuta, vol. i. p. 179.

[3] Lichtenstein, vol. i. p. 253.

whether they had any conception of God, a future life and their own souls, but I never could discover the slightest trace of such a knowledge. Their language has no words for " God " and " soul." ' [1]

Although, as Captain John Smith [2] quaintly put it, there was ' in Virginia no place discovered to be so savage in which they had not a religion, Deere, and bows and arrows,' still the ruder tribes in the far North, according to the testimony of Hearne, who knew them intimately, had no religion.

Several tribes, says Robertson, [3] ' have been discovered in America, which have no idea whatever of a Supreme Being, and no rites of religious worship. Inattentive to that magnificent spectacle of beauty and order presented to their view, unaccustomed to reflect either upon what they themselves are, or to enquire who is the author of their existence, men, in their savage state, pass their days like the animals round them, without knowledge or veneration of any superior power. Some rude tribes have not in their language any name for the Deity, nor have the most accurate observers been able to discover any practice or institution which seemed to imply that they recognised his authority, or were solicitous to obtain his favour.'

In the face of such a crowd of witnesses it may at first sight seem extraordinary that there can still be any difference of opinion on the subject. This, however, arises partly from the fact that the term ' Religion ' has not always been used in the same sense, and partly from a belief that, as has no doubt happened in several cases, travellers may, from ignorance of the language, or from shortness of residence, have overlooked a religion which really existed.

[1] Baegert. Smithsonian Trans., 1863–4, p. 390.

[2] Voyages in Virginia, p. 138.

[3] History of America, book iv. p. 122.

For instance, the first describers of Tahiti asserted that the natives had no religion, which subsequently proved to be a complete mistake; and several other similar cases might be quoted. As regards the lowest races of men, however, it seems to me, even *à priori*, very difficult to suppose that a people so backward as to be unable to count their own fingers should be sufficiently advanced in their intellectual conceptions as to have any system of belief worthy of the name of a religion.

We shall, however, obtain a clearer view of the question if we consider the superstitions of those races which have a rudimentary religion, and endeavour to trace these ideas up into a more developed condition.

Here again we shall perhaps be met by the doubt whether travellers have correctly understood the accounts given to them. In many cases, however, when the narrator had lived for months, or years, among those whom he was describing, we need certainly feel no suspicion, and in others we shall obtain a satisfactory result by comparing together the statements of different observers and using them as a check one upon the other.

The religious theories of savages are certainly not the result of deep thought, nor must they be regarded as constituting any elaborate or continuous theory. A Zulu candidly said to Mr. Callaway,[1] 'Our knowledge does not urge us to search out the roots of it; we do not try to see them; if anyone thinks ever so little, he soon gives it up, and passes on to what he sees with his eyes; and he does not understand the real state of even what he sees.' Dulaure truly observes, that the savage 'aime mieux soumettre sa raison, souvent révoltée, à ce que ses institutions ont de plus absurde, que se livrer à l'examen, parceque ce travail est toujours pénible pour celui qui ne s'y

---

[1] The Religious System of the Amazulu, p. 22.

est point exercé.' With this statement I entirely concur, and I believe that through all the various religious systems of the lower races may be traced a natural and unconscious process of development.

Dreams are intimately associated with the lower forms of religion. To the savage they have a reality and an importance which we can scarcely appreciate. During sleep the spirit seems to desert the body; and as in dreams we visit other localities and even other worlds, living as it were a separate and different life, the two phenomena are not unnaturally regarded as the complements of one another. Hence the savage considers the events in his dreams to be as real as those of his waking hours, and hence he naturally feels that he has a spirit which can quit the body. 'Dreams,' says Burton, 'according to the Yorubans and to many of our fetichists, are not an irregular action and partial activity of the brain, but so many revelations brought by the manes of the departed.'[2]   So strong was the North American faith in dreams that on one occasion, when an Indian dreamt he was taken captive, he induced his friends to make a mock attack on him, to bind him and treat him as a captive, actually submitting to a considerable amount of torture, in the hope thus to fulfil his dream.[3] The Greenlanders[4] also believe in the reality of dreams, and think that at night they go hunting, visiting, courting, and so on.   It is of course obvious that the body takes no part in these nocturnal adventures, and hence it is natural to conclude that they have a spirit which can quit the body.

In Madagascar[5] 'the people throughout the whole island pay a religious regard to dreams, and imagine that their

---

[1] Histoire des Cultes,' vol. i. p. 22.
[2] Abbeokuta, vol. i. p. 204.
[3] Lafitau, *loc. cit.* vol. i. p. 366.
[4] Crantz, *loc. cit.* vol. i. p. 200.
[5] The Adventures of Robert Drury, p. 171.   See also pp. 176, 272.

good demons (for I cannot tell what other name to give their inferior deities, which, as they say, attend on their owleys,) tell them in their dreams what ought to be done, or warn them of what ought to be avoided.'

Lastly, when they dream of their departed friends or relatives, savages firmly believe themselves to be visited by their spirits, and hence believe, not indeed in the immortality of the soul, but in its survival of the body. Thus the Manganjas, South Africa, expressly ground their belief in a future life on the fact that their friends visit them in their sleep. Again, savages are rarely ill; their sufferings generally arise from wounds; their deaths are generally violent. As an external injury received in war causes pain, so when they suffer internally they attribute it to some internal enemy. Hence whence the Australian, perhaps after too heavy a meal, has his slumbers disturbed, he never doubts the reality of what is passing, but considers that he is attacked by some being whom his companions cannot see.

This is well illustrated in the following passage from the 'United States Exploring Expedition:'[1] 'Sometimes, when the Australians are asleep, Koin makes his appearance, seizes upon one of them and carries him off. The person seized endeavours in vain to cry out, being almost strangled. At daylight, however, he disappears, and the man finds himself conveyed safely to his own fireside. From this it would appear that the demon is here a sort of personification of the night-mare—a visitation to which the natives, from their habits of gorging themselves to the utmost when they obtain a supply of food, must be very subject.'

Speaking of the North-Western Americans, Mr. Sproat

---

[1] *Loc. cit.* vol. vi. p. 110.

says : [1] 'The apparition of ghosts is especially an occasion
on which the services of the sorcerers, the old women, and
all the friends of the ghost-seer are in great request.
Owing to the quantity of indigestible food eaten by the
natives, they often dream that they are visited by ghosts.
After a supper of blubber, followed by one of the long
talks about departed friends, which take place round the
fire, some nervous and timid person may fancy, in the
night time, that he sees a ghost.'

In some cases the belief that man possesses a spirit
seems to have been suggested by the shadow. Thus,
among the Fijians,[2] 'some speak of man as having two
spirits. His shadow is called "the dark spirit," which
they say goes to Hades. The other is his likeness reflected
in water or a looking-glass, and is supposed to stay near
the place in which a man dies. Probably this doctrine of
shadows has to do with the notion of inanimate objects
having spirits. I once placed a good-looking native
suddenly before a mirror. He stood delighted. " Now,"
said he softly, " I can see into the world of spirits."

The North American Indians also consider a man's
shadow as his soul or life. ' I have,' says Tanner, ' heard
them reproach a sick person for what they considered im-
prudent exposure in convalescence, telling him that his
shadow was not well settled down in him.' [3]

The natives of Benin ' call a man's shadow his passadoor,
or conductor, and believe it will witness if he lived well or
ill. If well, he is raised to great happiness and dignity in
the place before mentioned; if ill, he is to perish with
hunger and poverty.' [4] They are indeed a most super-

[1] Scenes and Studies of Savage Life,
p. 172.

[2] Williams' Fiji and the Fijians,
vol. i. p. 241.

[3] Tanner's Captivity, p. 291.

[4] Astley's Collection of Voyages, vol.
iii. p. 99. Pinkerton, vol. xvi. p. 531.
See also Callaway On the Religious
System of the Amazulu, p. 91.

stitious race; and Lander mentions a case in which an echo was taken for the voice of a Fetish.[1]

Thunder, also, was often regarded either as an actual deity, or as a heavenly voice. 'One night,' says Tanner, 'Picheto (a North American chief) becoming much alarmed at the violence of the storm, got up and offered some tobacco to the thunder, entreating it to stop.'[2]

I have already mentioned that savages almost always regard spirits as evil beings. We can, I think, easily understand why this should be. Amongst the very lowest races every other man—amongst those slightly more advanced, every man of a different tribe, is regarded as naturally, and almost necessarily hostile. A stranger is synonymous with an enemy, and a spirit is but a member of an invisible tribe.

The Hottentots, according to Thunberg, have very vague ideas about a good Deity. 'They have much clearer notions about an evil spirit, whom they fear, believing him to be the occasion of sickness, death, thunder, and every calamity that befalls them.'[3] The Bechuanas attribute all evil to an invisible god, whom they call Murimo, and 'never hesitate to show their indignation at any ill experienced, or any wish unaccomplished, by the most bitter curses. They have no religious worship, and could never be persuaded by the missionaries that this was a thing displeasing to God.'[4]

The Abipones of South America, so well described by Dobritzhoffer, had some vague notions of an evil spirit, but none of a good one.[5] The Coroados[6] of Brazil 'acknow-

[1] Niger Expedition, vol. iii. p. 242.

[2] Tanner's Narrative of a Captivity among the Indians, p. 136.

[3] Thunberg. Pinkerton's Voyages, vol. xv. p. 142. Astley, *loc. cit.* p. 366.

[4] Lichtenstein, vol. ii. p. 332.

[5] Dobritzhoffer, *loc. cit.* vol. ii. pp. 35, 64.

[6] Spix and Martius, vol. ii. p. 243.

ledge no cause of good, or no God, but only an evil principle, which . . . . leads him astray, vexes him, brings
him into difficulty and danger, and even kills him.'

In Virginia and Florida the evil spirit was worshipped
and not the good, because the former might be propitiated,
while the latter was sure to do all the good he could.[1]
So also the 'Cemis' of the West Indian Islands were
regarded as evil, and 'reputed to be the authors of every
calamity that affects the human race.'[2]   The Redskin,
says Carver,[3] 'lives in continual apprehension of the
unkind attacks of spirits, and to avert them has recourse
to charms, to the fantastic ceremonies of his priest, or the
powerful influence of his manitous.   Fear has of course a
greater share in his devotions than gratitude, and he pays
more attention to deprecating the wrath of the evil than
securing the favour of the good beings.'   The Tatars of
Katschiutzi also considered the evil spirit to be more
powerful than the good.[4]   The West Coast Negroes, according to Artus,[5] represent their deities as 'black and mischievous, delighting to torment them various ways.'
They said 'that the Europeans' God was very good, who
gave them such blessings, and treated them like his
children. Others asked, murmuring, why God was not as
kind to them ?   Why did not he supply them with woollen
and linen cloth, iron, brass, and such things, as well as
the Dutch ?   The Dutch answered, that God had not
neglected them, since he had sent them gold, palm-wine,
fruits, corn, oxen, goats, hens, and many other things
necessary to life, as tokens of his bounty.   But there was
no persuading them these things came from God.   They

---

[1] Müller's Americanischen Urreligionen, p. 151.
[2] Robertson's America, book iv.
p. 124.

[3] Travels, p. 388.
[4] Pallas, vol. iii. p. 433.
[5] Astley's Collection of Voyages, vol.
ii. p. 664.

said the earth, and not God, gave them gold, which was dug out of its bowels : that the earth yielded them maize and rice; and that not without the help of their own labour; that for fruits they were obliged to the Portuguese, who had planted the trees; that their cattle brought them young ones, and the sea furnished them with fish; that, however, in all these their own industry and labour was required, without which they must starve; so that they could not see how they were obliged to God for any of those benefits.'

When Burton spoke to the Eastern Negroes about the Deity, they eagerly asked where he was to be found, in order that they might kill him; for they said, 'Who but he lays waste our homes, and kills our wives and cattle?'

The following expression of Eesa feelings, overheard by Burton, gives a dreadful illustration of this idea. An old woman, belonging to that Arab tribe, having a toothache, offered up the following prayer : 'Oh, Allah, may thy teeth ache like mine! Oh, Allah, may thy gums be as sore as mine!' Can this be called 'religion'? Surely in spirit it is the very reverse.

In New Zealand[1] each disease was regarded as being caused by a particular god; thus 'Tonga was the god who caused headache and sickness : he took up his abode in the forehead. Moko-Tiki, a lizard god, was the source of all pains in the breast; Tu-tangata-kino was the god of the stomach; Titi-hai occasioned pains in the ankles and feet; Rongomai and Tuparitapu were the gods of consumption; Koro-kio presided over childbirth.'

'Sickness,' says Yate,[2] 'is brought on by the "Atua," who, when he is angry, comes to them in the form of a lizard, enters their inside, and preys upon their vitals till they

[1] Taylor's New Zealand and its Inhabitants, p. 34.
[2] Yate's New Zealand, p. 141.

die. Hence they use incantations over the sick, with the expectation of either propitiating the angry deity or of driving him away ; for the latter of which purposes they make use of the most threatening and outrageous language.' The Stiens of Cambodia believe ' in an evil genius, and attribute all disease to him. If anyone be suffering from illness, they say it is the demon tormenting him ; and, with this idea, make, night and day, an insupportable noise around the patient.'[1]

The Koussa Kaffirs,[2] says Lichtenstein, ascribe all their diseases ' to one of three causes : either to being enchanted by an enemy ; to the anger of certain beings, whose abode appears to be in the rivers ; or to the power of evil spirits.' Among the Kols of Nagpore, as Colonel E. T. Dalton tells us, ' all disease in men and in cattle is attributed to one or two causes, the wrath of some evil spirit who has to be appeased, or the spell of some witch or sorcerer ;'[3] the Circassians and some of the Chinese have also the same belief.[4]

Hence it is that mad people are in many countries looked on with so much reverence, since they are looked on as the special abode of some Deity. Savages who believe that diseases are owing to magic, naturally conclude that death is so too. Far from having realised to themselves the idea of a future life, they have not even learnt that death is the natural end of this. We find a very general conviction among savages that there is no such thing as natural death, and that when a man dies without being wounded, he must be the victim of magic.

Thus, Mr. Lang,[5] speaking of the Australians, says, that whenever a native dies, ' no matter how evident it may be

[1] Mouhot's Travels in the Central Parts of Indo-China, vol. i. p. 250.

[2] Lichtenstein, vol. ii. p. 255.

[3] Trans. Ethn. Soc. N.S. 1868, p. 30 ; 1870, p. 21.

[4] Klemm, Aleg. Cult. d. Menschen. vol. iv. p. 36.

[5] Lecture on the Aborigines of Australia, p. 14. See also Oldfield, Trans. Ethn. Soc. N.S. vol. iii. p. 236.

that death has been the result of natural causes, it is at once set down that the defunct was bewitched by the sorcerers of some neighbouring tribe.'   Among the natives of Southern Africa no one is supposed to die naturally.[1] The Bechuanas, says Philip, 'and all the Kaffir tribes, have no idea of any man dying except from hunger, violence, or witchcraft. If a man die even at the age of ninety, if he do not die of hunger or by violence, his death is imputed to sorcery or to witchcraft, and blood is required to expiate or avenge it.'[2]   So also Battel tells us that 'none on any account dieth, but that some other has bewitched them to death.'[3]   Dobritzhoffer[4] tells us that, 'If an Abipon die from being pierced with many wounds, or from having his bones broken, or his strength exhausted by extreme old age, his countrymen all deny that wounds or weakness occasioned his death, and anxiously try to discover by which of the jugglers, and for what reason, he was killed.' Stevenson[5] states that in South America, 'The Indians never believe that death is owing to natural causes, but that it is the effect of sorcery and witchcraft. Thus on the death of an individual one or more diviners are consulted, who generally name the enchanter, and are so implicitly believed, that the unfortunate object of their caprice or malice is certain to fall a sacrifice.' Wallace[6] found the same idea among the tribes of the Amazons; Muller[7] mentions it as prevalent among the Dacotahs; Hearne[8] among the Hudson's Bay Indians.

But though spirits are naturally much to be dreaded on various accounts, it by no means follows that they should be

---

[1] Chapman's Travels in Africa, vol. i. p. 47.

[2] Philip's South Africa, vol. i. p. 118.

[3] Adventures of Andrew Battel, Pinkerton, vol. xvi. p. 334. See also Astley, vol. ii. p. 300.

[4] *Loc. cit.* vol. ii. p. 84.

[5] Travels in South America, vol. i. p. 60.

[6] *Loc. cit.* p. 500.

[7] Amer. Urreligionen, p. 82.

[8] *Loc. cit.* p. 338.

conceived as necessarily wiser or more powerful than men.
Of this our table-turners and spirit-rappers give a modern
illustration. The natives of the Nicobar Islands were in
the habit of putting up scarecrows to frighten the ' Eewees '
away from their villages.[1]   The inhabitants of Kamt-
schatka, according to Kotzebue,[2] insult their deities if
their wishes are unfulfilled. They even feel a contempt
for them. If Kutka, they say, had not been so stupid,
would he have made inaccessible rocks, and too rapid
rivers ?[3]   The Lapps, according to Klemm, made idols
for their deities, and placed each in a separate box, on
which they indicated the name of the deity, so that
each might know its own box.[4]

Vancouver[5] mentions that the inhabitants of Owhyhee
were seriously offended with their deity for permitting
the death of a popular young chief named Whokaa. Yate
observes[6] that the New Zealanders, attributing certain
diseases to the attacks of the Atua, endeavour either to
propitiate or drive him away; in the latter case ' they
make use of the most threatening and outrageous language;
sometimes telling their deity that they will kill and eat
him.'

The negro of Guinea beats his Fetish if his wishes are
not complied with, and hides him in his waist-cloth if
about to do anything of which he is ashamed, so that the
Fetish may not be able to see what is going on.[7]

During a storm the Bechuanas cursed the deity for
sending thunder;[8] and the Namaquas shot poisoned

[1] Voyage of the Novara, vol. ii. p.
66.

[2] *Loc. cit.* vol. ii. p. 13.

[3] Klemm, Cult. d. Menschen, vol. ii.
p. 318.

[4] *Loc. cit.* vol. iii. p. 81.

[5] Voyage of Discovery, vol. iii. p. 14.

[6] Account of New Zealand, p. 141.
D'Urville's Voyage de l'Astrolabe, vol.
iii. pp. 245, 440, 470.

[7] Astley's Collection of Voyages, vol.
ii. p. 668.

[8] Chapman's Travels in Africa, vol.
i. p. 45.

arrows at storms to drive them away.[1] When the Basuto (Kaffir) is on a marauding expedition, he 'gives utterance to those cries and hisses in which cattle drivers indulge when they drive a herd before them; thinking in this manner to persuade the poor divinities (of the country they are attacking) that he is bringing cattle to their worshippers, instead of coming to take it from them.'[2]

According to Thomson,[3] the natives of Cambodia assumed that the Deity did not understand foreign languages. Franklin[4] says that the Cree Indians treat their Deity, whom they call Kepoochikawn, 'with considerable familiarity, interlarding their most solemn speeches with expostulations and threats of neglect if he fails in complying with their requests.'

The North Australian native[5] will not go near graves 'at night by himself; but when they are obliged to pass them they carry a fire-stick to keep off the spirit of darkness.'

The Kyoungtha of Chittagong are Buddhists. Their village temples contain a small stand of bells and an image of Boodh, which the villagers generally worship morning and evening, 'first ringing the bells to let him know that they are there.'[6] The Sinto temples of the Sun Goddess in Japan also contain a bell, 'intended to arouse the goddess and to awaken her attention to the prayers of her worshippers.'[7]

According to the Brahmans,[8] 'two things are indispensably necessary to the sacrificer in performing the ceremony: several lighted lamps, and a bell.'

The Tartars of the Altai picture to themselves the Deity

[1] Wood's Natural History of Man, vol. i. p. 307.
[2] Casalis' Basutos, p. 253.
[3] Trans. Ethn. Soc. vol. vi. p. 250.
[4] Visit to the Polar Seas, vol. iv. p. 146.
[5] Keppel's Visit to the Indian Archipelago, vol. ii. p. 182.
[6] Lewin's Hill Tracts of Chittagong, p. 39.
[7] Smith's Ten Weeks in Japan, p. 49.
[8] Dubois, The People of India, p. 400.

as an old man, with a long beard, and dressed in the uniform of a Russian officer of Dragoons.[1]

Even the Greeks and Romans believed stories very
derogatory not only to the moral character, but to the
intellect and power, of their deities. Thus they were
liable to defeat from mortals: Mars, though the God of
War, was wounded by Diomede and fled away howling
with pain. They had little or no power over the elements,
they had no foreknowledge, and were both morally and
mentally often represented as inferior to men. Even Homer
does not seem to have embraced the idea of Omnipotence.[2]
In fact, it may truly be said that the savage has a much
greater respect for his chief than for his god.[3]

This low estimate of spirits is shown in a very striking
manner by the behaviour of savages during eclipses. All
over the world we find races of men who believe that the sun
and moon are alive, and who consider that during eclipses
they are either quarrelling with each other or attacked by
the evil spirits of the air. Hence it naturally follows,
although to us it seems absurd, that the savage endeavours
to assist the sun or moon. The Greenlanders [4] regard the
sun and moon as sister and brother; the former being the
female, and being constantly pursued by the latter. During
an eclipse they think the moon 'goes about among the
houses to pilfer their skins and eatables, and even to kill
those people that have not duly observed the rules of
abstinence. At such times they hide away everything,
and the men carry chests and kettles on the top of the
house, and rattle and beat upon them to frighten away
the moon, and make him return to his place. At an
eclipse of the sun the women pinch the dogs by the ears;

---

[1] Klemm, Cult. d. Mens. vol. iii. p. 86.

[2] Gladstone's Juventus Mundi, pp. 198, 228.

[3] See Burton's Abbeokuta, vol. i. p. 180, Dubois, *loc. cit.* pp. 304, 430.

[4] Crantz, vol. i. p. 232.

if they cry, 'tis a sure sign that the end of the world is not yet come,' The Caribs, says Lafitau, accounted for eclipses by supposing either that the moon was ill, or that she was attacked by enemies; these they endeavoured to drive away by dances, by cries, and by the sacred rattle.[1] The Chiquito Indians,[2] according to Dobritzhoffer, think that the sun and moon during eclipses are 'cruelly torn by dogs, with which they think that the air abounds, when they see their light fail; attributing their blood-red colour to the bites of these animals. Accordingly, to defend their dear planets from those aërial mastiffs, they send a shower of arrows up into the sky, amid loud vociferations, at the time of the eclipse.' When the Guaycurus, says Charlevoix, 'think themselves threatened with a storm, they sally out of their towns, the men armed with their mancanas, and the women and children howling with all their might; for they believe that, by so doing, they put to flight the devil that intended to excite it.'[3] The ancient Peruvians, also, used to beat their dogs during eclipses, in order, apparently, that by their howlings they might frighten away the evil spirits.[4] The Chinese of Kiatka thought that eclipses were caused by the evil spirit placing his hand on the moon, in whose defence they immediately made as much noise as possible.[5] The Stiens of Cambodia,[6] like the Cambodians themselves, account for eclipses by the hypothesis 'that some being has swallowed up the sun and the moon; and, in order to deliver them, they made a frightful noise, beat the tam-tam, uttered savage cries, and shot arrows into the air, until the sun reappeared.'

[1] Lafitau, vol. i. pp. 248, 252. Tertre, History of the Caribby Islands, p. 272.
[2] *Loc. cit.* vol. ii. p. 84.
[3] History of Paraguay, vol. i. p. 92. See also p. 203.
[4] Martius, *loc. cit.* p. 32.
[5] Pallas, vol. iv. p. 220.
[6] Mouhot's Travels in Indo-China, vol. i. p. 253.

During an eclipse the Sumatrans [1] also 'make a loud noise with sounding instruments, to prevent one luminary from devouring the other, as the Chinese, to frighten away the dragon; a superstition that has its source in the ancient systems of astronomy (particularly the Hindu), where the nodes of the moon are identified with the dragon's head and tail. They tell of a man in the moon who is continually employed in spinning cotton, but that every night a rat gnaws his thread, and obliges him to begin his work afresh.'

'In Eastern Africa,' Speke [2] mentions that on one occasion, 'as there was a partial eclipse of the moon, all the Wanguana marched up and down from Rumanika's to Nnanagi's huts, singing and beating our tin cooking-pots to frighten off the spirit of the sun from consuming entirely the chief object of reverence, the moon.' Lander [3] mentions that at Boussa, in Central Africa, an eclipse was attributed to an attack made by the sun on the moon. During the whole time the eclipse lasted the natives made as much noise as possible, 'in the hope of being able to frighten away the sun to his proper sphere, and leave the moon to enlighten the world as at other times.'

One of the difficulties in arriving at any clear conception of the religious system of the lower races arises from a confusion between a belief in ghosts and that in an immortal spirit. Yet the two are essentially distinct; and the spirit is not necessarily regarded as immortal because it does not perish with the body. The negroes, for instance, says one of our keenest observers, Captain Burton, 'believe in a ghost, but not in spirit; in a present immaterial, but not in a future.' [4]

---

[1] Marsden's History of Sumatra, p. 194.

[2] Speke, p. 243.

[3] R. and I. Lander's Niger Expedition, vol. ii. pp. 180, 183.

[4] Trans. Ethn. Soc. N.S. vol. i. p. 323.

Counting on nothing after the present life, there is for them no hope beyond the grave. They wail and sorrow with a burden of despair. 'Amekwisha'—'he is finished' —is the East African's last word concerning parent or friend. 'All is done for ever,' sing the West Africans. The least allusion to loss of life makes their black skins pale. 'Ah,' they exclaim, 'it is bad to die; to leave house and home, wife and children; no more to wear soft cloth, nor eat meat, nor smoke tobacco.'[1]

The Hudson's Bay Indians, according to Hearne,[2] a good observer and one who had ample means of judging, had no idea of any life after death.

In other cases, the spirit is supposed to survive the body for a certain time, and to linger about its old abode.

Ask the negro, says M. Du Chaillu,[3] 'where is the spirit of his great-grandfather, he says he does not know; it is done. Ask him about the spirit of his father or brother who died yesterday, then he is full of fear and terror; he believes it to be generally near the place where the body has been buried, and among many tribes the village is removed immediately after the death of one of the inhabitants.' The same belief prevails among the Amazulu Kaffirs, as has been well shown by Mr. Callaway.[4] They believe that the spirits of their deceased fathers and brothers still live, because they appear in dreams; by inverse reasoning, however, grandfathers are generally regarded as having ceased to exist.

Bosman mentions that on the Guinea Coast, when 'any considerable person dies, they perplex one another with horrid fears, proceeding from an opinion that he appears for several nights successively near his late dwelling.'[5]

[1] Burton, Trans. Ethn. Soc., vol. i. p. 323.
[2] Loc. cit. p. 344.
[3] Trans. Ethn. Soc. N.S. vol. i. p. 309.
[4] The Religious System of the Amazulu, 1869.
[5] Bosman, loc. cit. p. 402.

Thus it seems that the power of a ghost after death bears some relation to that which the man possessed when alive. Other negroes think that after death they become white men [1]—a curious idea, which also occurs in Australia. Among the Tipperahs of Chittagong, if a man dies away from home, his relatives stretch a thread over all the intermediate streams, so that the spirit of the dead man may return to his own village; it being supposed that 'without assistance spirits are unable to cross running water; therefore the stream here had been bridged in the manner aforesaid.' [2]   We know that a somewhat similar idea existed in Europe, and it occurs also, as we shall see (p. 145), in the Fegee Islands.

Again, some modes of death are supposed to kill not only the body but the spirit also.   Thus a Bushman who was a magician, having put to death a woman, dashed the head of the corpse to pieces with large stones, buried her, and made a large fire over the grave, for fear, as he explained to Lichtenstein, lest she should rise again and 'trouble him.' [3]   Even the New Zealanders believed that a man who was eaten was destroyed both body and spirit. The same idea evidently influenced the Californian who, as recorded by Mr. Gibbs, did not dispute the immortality of the whites who buried their dead, but could not believe the same of his own people because they were in the habit of burning them. [4]

In these cases it will be observed that the existence of the ghost depends upon the manner of death.   This is no doubt absurd, but it is not illogical. The savage's idea of a spirit is something ethereal indeed, but not altogether immaterial, and consequently it may be injured by violence.

[1] *Loc. cit.* p 401.
[2] Lewin's Hill Tracts of Chittagong, p. 84.
[3] Lichenstein, vol. ii. p. 61.
[4] Schoolcraft's Indian Tribes, Pt. III. p. 107.

Some races believe in ghosts of the living as well as of the dead. For instance, the Fijians[1] believe 'that the spirit of a man who still lives will leave the body to trouble other people when asleep. When anyone faints or dies, their spirit, it is said, may sometimes be brought back by calling after it.

Even when the ideas of a soul and of future life are more developed, they are far from always taking the direction of our beliefs.

Thus the Caribs and Redskins believe that a man has more than one soul; to this they are probably led by the pulsation of the heart and the arteries, which they regard as evidences of independent life. Thus also they account for inconsistencies of behaviour.

The belief in ghosts, then, is essentially different from our notions of a future life. Ghosts are mortal, they haunt burial-grounds and hover round their own graves. Even when a higher stage has been gained, the place of departed souls is not a heaven, but merely a better earth.

Divination and sorcery are very widely distributed. Their characteristics are so well known and so similar all over the world, that I shall only give a few suggestive illustrations.

Whipple[2] thus describes a scene of divination among the Cherokees. The priest having concluded an eloquent address, took 'a curiously wrought bowl, alleged to be of great antiquity; he filled it with water and placed the black substance within, causing it to move from one side to the other, and from bottom to top, by a word. Alluding, then, to danger and foes, the enchanted mineral fled from the point of his knife; but as he began to speak of peace

[1] Fiji and the Fijians, vol. i. p. 242.   [2] Report on the Indian Tribes, p. 35.

and security, it turned toward and clung to it, till lifted entirely from the water. The priest finally interpreted the omen by informing the people that peace was in the ascendant, no enemy being near.'

In West Africa [1] they have a mode of divination with nuts, ' which they pretend to take up by guess, and let fall again; after which they tell them, and form their answers according as the numbers are even or odd.' The negroes of Egba[2] consult Shango by ' throwing sixteen pierced cowries: if eight fall upwards and eight downwards, it is peace; if all are upwards, it is also a good sign; and *vice versâ*, if all fall with their teeth to the ground, it is war.'

The Lapps have a curious mode of divination. They put a shoulder-blade in the fire, and then foretell the future by the arrangement of the cracks (figs. 15–17). The same custom exists among the Mongols[3] and Tunguses of Siberia,[4] and the Bedouins. The lines vary of course greatly, still there are certain principal cracks which usually occur. The following figures of Kalmuck specimens are copied from Klemm, who explains, after Pallas, the meaning of the various lines. The Chipewyans of North America also make their magic drawings on shoulder-blades, which they then throw into the fire.[5] Williams[6] describes various modes of divination practised in Fiji.

In New Zealand, before a warlike expedition is undertaken, sticks are sometimes stuck up in the ground in two rows, one of which denotes their own party, the other that of the enemy. If the wind blows the enemy's sticks

---

[1] Astley's Collection of Voyages, vol. ii. p. 674.

[2] Abbeokuta, vol. i. p. 188.

[3] Klemm, Cult. der Mens., vol. iii. p. 199.

[4] *Ibid.* p. 109.

[5] Tanner's Narrative, p. 192.

[6] Fiji and the Fijians, vol. i. p. 228. See also Mariner's Tonga Islands, vol. ii. p. 239.

backwards, they will be defeated ; if forwards, they will be victorious , if obliquely, the expedition will be indecisive. The same criterion is applied to their own sticks.[1]

This is a case of divination, but from it to sorcery is a short and obvious step. When once it is granted that the fall of a stick certainly preludes that of the person it

FIG. 15.

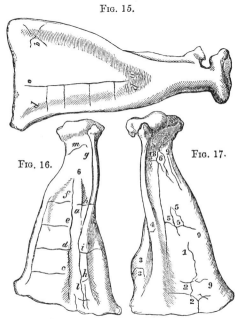

FIG. 16. FIG. 17.

SHOULDER-BLADES PREPARED FOR DIVINATION. (Klemm, Culturg. der Menscheit, vol. iii. p. 200)

represents, it follows that by upsetting the stick, his death can be caused.

We find a very similar idea in the western Highlands of Scotland. In the 'Sea Maiden' a mermaid appears to a fisherman, and gives him three seeds, which are to produce three trees, which 'will be a sign, when one of

[1] Yate's New Zealand, p. 91.

the sons dies, one of the trees will wither;' and this accordingly took place,[1]

A supposed prophet of the Shawneese (North America) sent word to Tanner that the fire in his lodge was intimately connected with his life. 'Henceforth,' said he, 'the fire must never be suffered to go out in your lodge. Summer and winter, day and night, in the storm, or when it is calm, you must remember that the life in your body and the fire in your lodge are the same. If you suffer your fire to be extinguished, at that moment your life will be at an end.'[2]

Father Merolla mentions a case in which a Congo (negro) witch tried to destroy him. With this object she dug a hole in the ground, and I resolved, says the worthy Father,[3] 'not to stand long in one place, thereby to avoid the design she had upon me to bewitch me to death, that having been the reason of her making a hole in the earth. It seems their custom is, that when they have a mind to bewitch anyone mortally, they put a certain herb or plant into the hole they have so dug; which, as it perishes or decays, so the vigour and spirits of the person they have a design upon will fail and decay.' In Fiji[4] 'one mode of operating is to bury a cocoa-nut, with the eye upwards, beneath the temple-hearth, on which a fire is kept constantly burning; and as the life of the nut is destroyed, so the health of the person it represents will fail, till death ensues. At Matuku there is a grove sacred to the god Tokalau, the wind. The priest promises the destruction of any hated person in four days if those who wish his death bring a portion of his hair, dress, or food which he has left. This priest keeps a fire burning, and approaches the place on his hands and knees.

[1] Campbell's Tales of the West Highlands, vol. i. p. 71.
[2] Tanner's Narrative, p. 156.
[3] Pinkerton, vol. xvi. p. 290.
[4] Fiji and the Fijians, vol. i. p. 248.

If the victim bathe before the fourth day, the spell is broken. The most common method, however, is the Vakadianikau, or compounding of certain leaves supposed to possess a magical power, and which are wrapped in other leaves, or put into a small bamboo case, and buried in the garden of the person to be bewitched, or hidden in the thatch of his house. The native imagination is so absolutely under the control of the fear of these charms, that persons, hearing that they were the objects of such spells, have lain down on their mats, and died through fear. Those who have reason to suspect others of plotting against them, avoid eating in their presence, or are careful to leave no fragment of food behind; they also dispose their garments so that no part can be removed. Most natives on cutting their hair hide what is cut off in the thatch of their own houses. Some build themselves a small house, and surround it with a moat, believing that a little water will neutralise the charms which are directed against them.' In North America, to ensure a successful war, courtship, or hunt, the Indians make a rude drawing, or a little image to represent the man, woman, or animal; then medicine is applied to it, or, if the design is to cause death, the heart is pierced.[1] In India also the magicians make small figures of mud, on the breasts of which they write the names of those whom they wish to annoy. They then 'pierce the images with thorns, or mutilate them,' so as to communicate a corresponding injury to the person represented.'[2]

In other cases, the possession of a person's name is sufficient, and indeed, all over the world we find more or less confusion between a thing or a person, and its or his name. Hence the importance attached among the North American

---

[1] Tanner's Narrative, p. 174.   [2] Dubois, The People of India, p. 347.

Indians and South Sea Islanders to an exchange of names. Hence, as already mentioned, we often find a person's real name concealed, lest a knowledge of it should give a power over the person.　Even the Romans when they besieged a town, had a curious ceremony founded on the same idea.　They invoked the tutelar deity of the city, and tempted him by the offer of rewards and sacrifices ' to betray his friends and votaries.　In that ceremony the name of the tutelar deity was thought of importance, and for that reason the tutelar deity of Rome was a profound secret.' [1]

Sumatra gives us a curious instance of long survival of this idea in a somewhat advanced community.　' A Sumatran[2] ever scrupulously abstains from pronouncing his own name ; not, as I understand, from any motive of superstition, but merely as a punctilio in manners.　It occasions him infinite embarrassment when a stranger, unacquainted with their customs, requires it of him.　As soon as he recovers from his confusion, he solicits the interposition of his neighbour.　He is never addressed, except in the case of a superior dictating to his dependant, in the second person, but always in the third ; using his name or title instead of the pronoun ; and when these are unknown, a general title of respect is substituted, and they say, for instance, " apa orang kaya punia suka," " what is his honour's pleasure," for " what is your, or your honour's pleasure."　When criminals or other ignominious persons are spoken to, use is made of the pronoun personal kau (a contraction of angkau), particularly expressive of contempt.'

Generally, however, it was considered indispensable that the sorcerer should possess ' something connected

[1] Lord Kames' History of Man, vol.　iv. p. 226.

[2] Marsden's History of Sumatra, p. 286.

with the body of the object of vengeance. The parings of the nails, a lock of the hair, the saliva from the mouth, or other secretions from the body, or else a portion of the food which the person was to eat. This was considered as the vehicle by which the demon entered the person, who afterwards became possessed. It was called the tubu, growing or causing to grow. When procured, the tara was performed; the sorcerer took the hair, saliva, or other substance that had belonged to his victim, to his house, or marae, performed his incantations over it, and offered his prayers; the demon was then supposed to enter the tubu, and through it the individual, who afterwards became possessed.'[1]

In New Zealand[2] also the sorcerers ' use the saliva of the people whom they intend to bewitch; and visitors carefully conceal their spittle, to give them no opportunity of working their evil.' Tylor[3] also says that a ' person who wished to bewitch another, sought to obtain something belonging to him—a lock of hair, a portion of his garment, or even some of his food; this being possessed, he uttered certain karakias over it, and then buried it; as the article decayed, the individual also was supposed to waste away. This was sure to be the case if the victim heard of it; fear quickly accomplishing his enemy's wish. The person who bewitched another, remained three days without eating; on the fourth he ate, and his victim died.'

So also Seemann[4] tells us that ' if a Fijian wishes to cause the destruction of an individual by other means than open violence or secret poison, the case is put in the hands of one of these sorcerers, care being taken to let this fact

[1] Williams' Polynesian Researches, vol. ii. p. 228.
[2] Dieffenbach, vol. ii. p. 59.
[3] New Zealand and its Inhabitants, pp. 89, 167.
[4] A Mission to Viti, p. 189.

be generally and widely known. The sorcerer now proceeds to obtain any article that has once been in the
possession of the person to be operated upon. These
articles are then burnt with certain leaves, and if the
reputation of the sorcerer be sufficiently powerful, in nine
cases out of ten the nervous fears of the individual to be
punished will bring on disease, if not death : a similar
process is applied to discover thieves.'

Sir G. Grey thus describes a scene of witchcraft in New
Zealand : ' The priests [1] then dug a long pit, termed the pit
of wrath, into which by their long enchantments they
might bring the spirits of their enemies, and hang them
and destroy them there ; and when they had dug the pit,
muttering the necessary incantations, they took large
shells in their hands to scrape the spirits of their enemies
into the pit with, whilst they muttered enchantments ;
and when they had done this they scraped the earth into
the pit again to cover them up, and beat down the earth
with their hands, and crossed the pit with enchanted
cloths, and wove baskets of flax-leaves to hold the spirits
of the foes which they had thus destroyed, and each of
these acts they accompanied with proper spells.'

In North America, also, ' a hair from the head of the
victim ' is supposed to increase greatly the efficacy of
charms.

We cannot wonder that savages believe in witchcraft,
since even the most civilised races have not long, nor
entirely, ceased to do so.

Like our spirit-rappers and table-turners, the Chinese
magicians,[2] ' though they have never seen the person who
consults them, they tell his name, and all the circumstances of his family; in what manner his house is situated,

[1] Polynesian Mythology, p. 168.
[2] Astley's Collection of Voyages, vol. iv. p. 205.

how many children he has, their names and age; with a hundred other particulars, which may be naturally enough supposed known to the demons, and are strangely surprising to weak and credulous minds among the vulgar.

'Some of these conjurers, after invoking the demons, cause the figures of the chief of their sect, and of their idols, to appear in the air. Formerly they could make a pencil write of itself, without anybody touching it, upon paper or sand, the answers to questions. They likewise cause all people of any house to pass in review in a large vessel of water; wherein they also show the changes that shall happen in the empire, and the imaginary dignities to which those shall be advanced who embrace their sect.'

In all parts of India, says De Faira,[1] 'there are prodigious wizards. When Vasco de Gama was sailing upon that discovery some of them at Kalekût showed people, in basins of water, the three ships he had with him. When Don Francisco de Almeyda, the first viceroy of India, was returning to Portugal, some witches of Kochîn told him he should not pass the Cape of Good Hope; and there he was buried. (This is strained a little; for he did pass the Cape, and was buried at the bay of Saldanna, some leagues beyond, as will be seen hereafter.) What follows is still more extraordinary. At Maskat there are such sorcerers that they eat the inside of a thing, only fixing their eyes upon it. With their sight they draw out the entrails of any human body, and so kill many people. One of these fascinators, fixing his eyes on a bateka, or water melon, sucked out the inside; for, being cut open to try the experiment, it was found empty; and the wizard, to satisfy the spectators, vomited it up again.'

Father Merolla,[2] a Capuchin 'missioner,' tells quite

---

[1] Quoted in Astley's Collection of Voyages, vol. i. p. 63.

[2] Voyage to Congo, Pinkerton, vol. xv. p. 229.

gravely the following story. The army of Sogno having captured a neighbouring town, found in it a large cock with a ring of iron round one leg. This they killed, cut in pieces, and put into a pot to boil; when, however, they thought to eat it, ' the boiled pieces of the cock, though sodden, and near dissolved, began to move about, and unite into the form they were in before, and being so united, the restored cock immediately raised himself up, and jumped out of the platter upon the ground, where he walked about as well as when he was first taken. Afterwards he leaped upon an adjoining wall, where he became new-feathered all of a sudden, and then took his flight to a tree hard by, where, fixing himself, he, after three claps of his wings, made a most hideous noise, and then disappeared. Everyone may easily imagine what a terrible fright the spectators were in at this sight, who, leaping with a thousand Ave-Marias in their mouths from the place where this had happened, were contented to observe most of the particulars at a distance.'

To doubt the reality of witchcraft, says Lafitau,[1] ' est une industrie des athées, et un effet de cet esprit d'irré-ligion qui fait aujourd'hui des progrès si sensibles dans le monde, d'avoir détruit en quelque sorte dans l'idée de ceux même qui se piquent d'avoir de la religion; qu'il se trouve des hommes, qui ayent commerce avec les démons par la voye des enchantemens et de la magie. On a attaché à cette opinion une certaine faiblesse d'esprit à la croire, qui fait qu'on ne la tolère plus, que dans les femmelettes et dans le bas peuple, ou dans les prêtres et dans les religieux, qu'on suppose avoir intérêt a entretenir ces visions populaires, qu'un homme de sens auroit honte d'avouer. Pour établir cependant cet esprit

---

[1] *Loc. cit.* vol. i. p. 374.

d'incrédulité, il faut que ces prétendus esprits forts veuil-
lent s'aveugler au milieu do la lumière, qu'ils renversent
l'Ancien et le Nouveau Testament; qu'ils contredisent
toute l'antiquité, l'histoire sacrée et la profane.   On
trouve partout des témoignages de ce commerce des
hommes avec les divinités du paganisme, ou pour mieux
dire avec les démons.'

He does not deny that some wizards were impostors,
but he maintains that ' ce seroit rendre le monde trop sot,
que de vouloir le supposer pendant plusieurs siècles, la
dupe de quelques misérables joureurs de gobelets.'   Nay,
he even maintained [1] that America was, for some mysterious reason, handed over to the devil, and accounted for
the remarkable similarity between some of the religious
ceremonies, &c., in the new and old worlds, by the hypothesis that ' le démon, jaloux de la gloire de Dieu, et
du bonheur de l'homme, a toujours été attentif à dérober
à l'un le culte qui lui est dû, et à perdre l'autre, en le
rendant son Adorateur.   Pour cela il a érigé Autel contre
Autel, et a affecté de maintenir le culte, qu'il vouloit se
faire rendre par les effets d'une puissance sur-humaine,
qui imposassent par le merveilleux, et qui fussent imités
et copiés d'après ceux, dont Dieu donnait à son peuple
des témoignages si autentiques, par l'évidence des miracles
qu'il faisoit en sa faveur.'

Labat [2] also, while admitting ' qu'on exagère souvent
dans ce qu'on en dit ; mais je croi qu'il faut convenir que
tout ce qu'on dit n'est pas entièrement faux, quoiqu'il ne
soit peut-être pas entièrement vrai.   Je suis aussi per-
suadé qu'il y a des faits d'une vérité très-constante ; '
and after mentioning four of these supposed facts, he
concludes, ' il me semble que ces quatre faits suffisent

[1] Vol. i. p. 355.
[2] Voyage aux Isles de l'Amérique, vol. ii. p. 57.

pour prouver qu'il y a véritablement des gens qui ont commerce avec le diable, et qui se servent de lui en bien des choses.'

Some, even of our recent missionaries, according to Williams, believed that the Polynesian wizards really possessed supernatural powers, and were 'agents of the infernal powers.' [1] Nay, Williams himself thought it 'not impossible.'

We may well be surprised that Europeans should believe in such things, and missionaries so credulous and ignorant ought, one might suppose, rather to learn than to teach; on the other hand, it is not surprising that savages should believe in witchcraft, nor even that the wizards should believe in themselves.

We must indeed by no means suppose that sorcerers were always, or indeed generally, impostors.

The Shamans of Siberia are, says Wrangel, [2] by no means 'ordinary deceivers, but a psychological phenomenon, well deserving of attention. Whenever I have seen them operate they have left with me a long-continued and gloomy impression. The wild look, the bloodshot eyes, the labouring breast and convulsive utterance, the seemingly involuntary distortion of the face and the whole body, the streaming hair, even the hollow sound of the drum, all contributed to the effect; and I can well understand that the whole should appear to the uncivilised spectator as the work of evil spirits.'

Speaking of the Ahts in North-west America, it is undoubtedly a fact, says Mr. Sproat, [3] 'that many of the sorcerers themselves thoroughly believe in their own supernatural powers, and are able, in their preparations

[1] Polynesian Researches, vol. ii. p. 226.
[2] Siberia, p. 124.
[3] Scenes and Studies of Savage Life, p. 170.

and practices, to endure excessive fatigue, want of food, and intense prolonged mental excitement.'

Dobritzhoffer also concludes that the sorcerers of the Abipones [1] themselves 'imagine that they are gifted with superior wisdom;' and Müller also is convinced that they honestly believe in themselves.[2]

We should, says Martius,[3] 'do them an injustice if we regarded the Brazilian sorcerers as mere impostors,' though, he adds, they do not scruple to cheat where they can.

Williams, also, who was by no means disposed to take a favourable view of the native sorcerers, admits that they believed in themselves, a fact which it is only fair to bear in mind.[4]

This self-deception was much facilitated by, if not mainly due to, the very general practice of fasting by those who aspired to the position of wizards. The Greenlander, says Cranz,[5] who would be an angekok, 'must retire from all mankind for a while into some solitary recess or hermitage, must spend the time in profound meditation, and call upon Torngarsuk to send him a torngak. At length, by abandoning the converse of men, by fasting and emaciating the body, and by a strenuous intenseness of thought, the man's imagination grows distracted, so that blended images of men, beasts, and monsters appear before him. He readily thinks these are real spirits, because his thoughts are full of spirits, and this throws his body into great irregularities and convulsions, which he labours to cherish and augment.'

Among the North American Indians,[6] when a boy reaches

[1] Loc. cit. vol. ii. p. 68.
[2] Ges. d. Am. Urr. p. 80.
[3] Von d. Rechtszus. unter den Ur. Brasiliens, p. 30.
[4] Polynesian Researches, vol. ii. p. 226.
[5] History of Greenland, vol. i. p. 210.
[6] Catlin's North American Indians, vol. i. p. 36.

maturity, he leaves home and absents himself for some days, during which he eats nothing, but lies on the ground thinking. When at length he falls asleep the first animal about which he dreams is, he thinks, ordained to be his special protector through life.[1] The dream itself he looks on as a revelation. Indeed the Redskins fast before any great expedition, thinking that during their dreams they receive indications as to the course of action which they should pursue.[2]

Among the Cherokees also fasting is very prevalent, 'and an abstinence of seven days renders the devotee famous.'[3]

The Flatheads of Oregon have a very similar custom. Here, however, a number of youths retire together. 'They spend three days and nights in the performance of these rites, without eating or drinking. By the languor of the body and the high excitement of the imagination produced during this time, their sleep must be broken and visited by visions adapted to their views.'[4] These, therefore, they not unnaturally look on as the visits of spirits.

Those who by continued fasts have thus purified and cleared their minds from gross ideas, are supposed to be capable of a clearer insight into the future than that which is accorded to ordinary men, and are called 'Saiotkatta' by the Hurons, and 'Agotsinnachen' by the Iroquois, terms which mean literally 'seers.'[5]

In Brazil, a young man who wishes to be a pajé dwells alone in some mountain, or in some lone place, and fasts for two years, after which he is admitted with certain

[1] Lafitau, *loc. cit.* vol. i. pp. 267, 290, 331, and especially pp. 336 and 370.

[2] Carver's Travels, p. 285.

[3] Whipple's Report on Indian Tribes, p. 36.

[4] Dunn's Oregon, p. 329.

[5] Lafitau, vol. i. p. 371.

ceremonies into the order of pajés.[1] Among the Abipones [2] and Caribs [3] those who aspire to be 'keebet' proceed in a similar manner. Among the South American Indians of the Rio de la Plata the Medicine-men were prepared for their office by a long fast.[4] Among the Lapps, also, would-be wizards prepare themselves by a strict fast.[5]

At first sight the introduction of the ' dance ' may seem out of place here. Among savages, however, it is no mere amusement. It is, says Robertson,[6] ' a serious and important occupation, which mingles in every occurrence of public or private life. If any intercourse be necessary between two American tribes the ambassadors of the one approach in a solemn dance and present the calumet or emblem of peace ; the sachems of the other receive it with the same ceremony. If war is denounced against an enemy, it is by a dance, expressive of the resentment which they feel, and of the vengeance which they meditate. If the wrath of their gods is to be appeased, or their beneficence to be celebrated—if they rejoice at the birth of a child, or mourn the death of a friend, they have dances appropriated to each of these situations, and suited to the different sentiments with which they are then animated. If a person is indisposed a dance is prescribed as the most effectual means to restore him to health ; and if he himself cannot endure the fatigue of such an exercise, the physician or conjurer performs it in his name, as if the virtue of his activity could be transferred to his patient.'

Among the Kols of Nagpore Colonel Dalton [7] describes

[1] Martius, Recht. unter d. Ur. Bras p. 30.
[2] Dobritzhoffer, vol. ii. p. 67.
[3] Du Tertre, History of the Caribby Islands, p. 342.
[4] Lafitau, vol. i. p. 335.
[5] Klemm, Cult. der Mens., vol. iii.
p. 85.
[6] Robertson's America, bk. iv. p. 133. See also Schoolcraft, loc. cit. vol. iii. p. 488, on the Sacred Dances of the Redskins.
[7] Trans. Ethn. Soc. vol. vi. p. 30.

FIG. 18.

A DANCE. (From Lafitau's 'Mœurs des Sauvages.')

several dances which, he says, ' are all more or less connected with some religious ceremony.'

The Ostyaks also perform sacred sword dances in honour
of their god Yelan.[1]

Fig. 18 represents a sacred dance as practised by the
natives of Virginia. It is very interesting to see here a
circle of upright stones, which, except that they are rudely
carved at the upper end into the form of a head, exactly
resemble our so-called Druidical temples.

The idea is by no means confined to mere savages.
Even Socrates [2] regarded the dance as a part of religion,
and David, we know, did so too.[3]

As sacrificial feasts so generally enter into religious cere-
monials, we need not wonder that smoking is throughout
America closely connected with all religious ceremonies,
just as incense is used for the same purpose in the Old
World.[4] Among the Sonthals also, one of the aboriginal
tribes of India, the whole of their religious observances
' are generally performed and attended to by the votaries
whilst in a state of intoxication; a custom which reminds
us of the worship of Bacchus among the Greeks and
Romans.' [5]

---

[1] Erman, vol. ii. p. 52.

[2] Soc. apud Athen. lib. 14, p. 628.
Quoted in Lafitau, vol. i. p. 200.

[3] 2 Sam. vi. 14, 22.

[4] Lafitau, vol. ii. p. 133.

[5] The People of India, by J. F.
Watson and J. W. Kaye, vol. i. p. 1.

CHAPTER V.

RELIGION (*continued*).

IN tracing up the gradual evolution of religious beliefs we may begin with the Australians, who possess merely certain vague ideas as to the existence of evil spirits, and a general dread of witchcraft. This belief cannot be said to influence them by day, but it renders them very unwilling to quit the camp fire by night, or to sleep near a grave. They have no idea of creation, nor do they use prayers; they have no religious forms, ceremonies, or worship. They do not believe in the existence of a Deity, nor is morality in any way connected with their religion, if it can be so called. The words ' good ' or ' bad ' had reference to taste or bodily comfort, and did not convey any idea of right or wrong.[1] Another curious notion of the Australians is that white men are blacks who have risen from the dead. This notion was found among the natives north of Sydney as early as 1795, and can scarcely, therefore, be of missionary origin.[2] It occurs also among the negroes of Guinea.[3] The ideas of the Australians on the subject, however, seem to have been very various and confused. They had certainly no general and definite view on the subject.

As regards the North Australians we have trustworthy accounts given by a Scotchwoman, Mrs. Thomson, who

[1] *Loc. cit.* pp. 354, 355, 356.

[2] Collins' English Colony in N.S. Wales, p. 303.

[3] Smith's Guinea, p. 215. Bosman, Pinkerton's Voyages, vol. xv. p. 40.

was wrecked on the Eastern Prince of Wales Island. Her husband and the rest of the crew were drowned, but she was saved by the natives, and lived with them nearly five years, until the visit of the ' Rattlesnake,' when she escaped with some difficulty. On the whole she was kindly treated by the men, though the women were long jealous of her, and behaved towards her with much cruelty. These people have no idea of a Supreme Being.[1] They do not believe in the immortality of the soul, but hold that they are ' after death changed into white people or Europeans, and as such pass the second and final period of their existence; nor is it any part of their creed that future rewards and punishments are awarded.'[2]

Mrs. Thomson was supposed to be the ghost of Giom, a daughter of a man named Piaquai, and when she was teased by children, the men would often tell them to leave her alone, saying, ' Poor thing! she is nothing—only a ghost.' This, however, did not prevent a man named Boroto making her his wife, which shows how little is actually implied in the statement the Australians believe in spirits. They really do no more than believe in the existence of men, somewhat different from, and a little more powerful than, themselves. The South Australians as described by Stephens had no religious rites, ceremonies, or worship; no idea of a Supreme Being; but a vague dread of evil spirits.[3]

The Veddahs of Ceylon, according to Davy, believe in evil beings, but ' have no idea of a supreme and beneficent God, or of a state of future existence, or of a system of rewards and punishments; and, in consequence, they are of opinion that it signifies little whether they do good or evil.'[4]

---

[1] Macgillivray's Voyage of the Rattlesnake, vol. ii. p. 29.
[2] Loc. cit. p. 29.
[3] Stephens' South Australia, p. 78.
[4] Davy's Ceylon, p. 118.

The Indians of California have been well described by Father Baegert, a Jesuit missionary, who lived among them no less than seventeen years.[1] As to government or religion, he says,[2] 'neither the one nor the other existed among them. They had no magistrates, no police, and no laws; idols, temples, religious worship or ceremonies were unknown to them, and they neither believed in the true and only God, nor adored false deities. They were all equals, and everyone did as he pleased, without asking his neighbour or caring for his opinion, and thus all vices and misdeeds remained unpunished, excepting such cases in which the offended individual or his relations took the law into their own hands and revenged themselves on the guilty party. The different tribes represented by no means communities of rational beings, who submit to laws and regulations and obey their superiors, but resembled far more herds of wild swine, which run about according to their own liking, being together to-day and scattered to-morrow, till they meet again by accident at some future time.

'In one word, the Californians lived, *salva venia*, as though they had been freethinkers and materialists.

'I made diligent enquiries, among those with whom I lived, to ascertain whether they had any conception of God, a future life, and their own souls, but I never could discover the slightest trace of such a knowledge. Their language has no words for " God " and " soul," for which reason the missionaries were compelled to use in their sermons and religious instructions the Spanish words Dios and alma. It could hardly be otherwise with people who thought of nothing but eating and merry-making and

---

[1] Nachrichten von der Amer. Halb. Californie, 1773. Translated in Smithsonian Reports, 1863-4.   [2] Smithsonian Reports, 1864, p. 390.

never reflected on serious matters, but dismissed everything that lay beyond the narrow compass of their conceptions with the phrase aipekériri, which means "who
knows that?" I often asked them whether they had
never put to themselves the question who might be the
Creator and Preserver of the sun, moon, stars, and other
objects of nature, but was always sent home with a vára,
which means "no" in their language.' They had, however, certain sorcerers, whom they believed to possess
power over diseases, to bring small-pox, famine, &c., and
of whom, therefore, they were in much fear.

Mr. Gibbs, speaking of the Indians living in the valleys
drained by the Sacramento and the San Joaquin, says:
' One of this tribe, who had been for three or four years
among the whites, and accompanied the expedition, on
being questioned as to his own belief in a Deity, acknowledged his entire ignorance on the subject. As
regarded a future state of any kind, he was equally unin-
formed and indifferent; in fact, did not believe in any for
himself. As a reason why his people did not go to another
country after death, while the whites might, he assigned
that the Indians burned their dead, and he supposed there
was an end of them.'[1]

The religion of the Bachapins, a Kaffir tribe, has been
described by Burchell. They had no outward worship,
nor, so far as he could learn, any private devotion; indeed,
they had no belief in a beneficent Deity, though they
feared an evil Being called 'Muleemo,' or 'Murimo.' They
had no idea of creation. Even when Burchell suggested it
to them, they did not attribute it to Muleemo, but ' asserted
that every thing made itself, and that trees and herbage
grew by their own will.'[2] They believed in sorcery, and
in the efficacy of amulets.

[1] Schoolcraft's Indian Tribes, vol. iii. p. 107.   [2] Travels, vol. ii. p. 550.

Dr. Vanderkemp, the first missionary to the Kaffirs, 'never could perceive that they had any religion, or any idea of the existence of God.' Mr. Moffat also, who lived in South Africa as a missionary for many years, says that they were utterly destitute of theological ideas;' and Dr. Gardner, in his 'Faiths of the World,' concludes as follows:[1] 'From all that can be ascertained on the religion of the Kaffirs, it seems that those of them who are still in their heathen state have no idea, (1) of a Supreme Intelligent Ruler of the universe; (2) of a Sabbath; (3) of a day of judgment; (4) of the guilt and pollution of sin; (5) of a Saviour to deliver them from the wrath to come.'

The Rev. Canon Callaway has recently published a very interesting memoir on 'The Religious System of the Amazulu,' who are somewhat more advanced in their religious conceptions. The first portion is entitled 'Unkulunkulu or the Tradition of Creation.' It does not, however, appear that Unkulunkulu is regarded as a Creator, or even as a Deity at all. It is simply the first man, the Zulu Adam. Some complication arises from the fact that not only the ancestor of all mankind, but also the first of each tribe, is called Unkulunkulu, so that there are many Onkulunkulu, or Unkulunkulus. None of them, however, have any of the characters of Deity; no prayers or sacrifices are offered to them;[2] indeed, they no longer exist, having been long dead.[3] Unkulunkulu was in no sense a Creator,[4] nor, indeed, is any special power attributed to him.[5] He, i.e. man, arose from 'Umklanga,' that is 'a bed of reeds,' but, how he did so, no one knew.[6] Mr. Callaway agrees with Casalis, that 'it never entered

---

[1] *Loc. cit.* p. 260.
[2] *Loc. cit.* pp. 9, 25, 34, 75.
[3] *Loc cit.* pp. 15, 33, 62.
[4] *Loc. cit.* p. 137.
[5] *Loc. cit.* p. 48.
[6] *Loc. cit.* pp. 9, 40.

the heads of the Zulus that the earth and sky might be the work of an invisible Being.' [1] One native thought the white men made the world. [2] They had, indeed, no idea of, or name for, God. [3] When Moffat endeavoured to explain to a chief about God, he exclaimed, ' Would that I could catch it! I would transfix it with my spear;' yet this was a man 'whose judgment on other subjects would command attention.' [4]

Yet they are not without a belief in invisible beings. This is founded partly on the shadow, but principally on the dream. They regard the shadow as in some way the spirit which accompanies the body (reminding us of the similar idea among the Greeks), and they have a curious notion that a dead body casts no shadow. [5]

Still more important has been the influence of dreams. When a dead father or brother appears to a man in his sleep, he does not doubt the reality of the occurrence, and hence concludes that they still live. Grandfathers, however, are by inverse reasoning regarded as generally dead. [6]

Diseases are regarded as being often caused by the spirits of discontented relatives. In other respects these spirits are not regarded as possessing any special powers ; though prayed to, it is not in such a manner as to indicate a belief that they have any supernatural influence, and they are clearly not regarded as immortal. In some cases departed relatives are regarded as reappearing in the form of snakes, [7] which may be known from ordinary snakes by certain signs, [8] such as their frequenting huts, not eating mice, and showing no fear of man. Sometimes a snake is recognised as the representative of a given man by some

[1] *Loc. cit.* pp. 54, 108.
[2] *Loc. cit.* p. 55.
[3] *Loc. cit.* pp. 107, 113, 136.
. [4] *Loc. cit.* p. 111.

[5] *Loc. cit.* p. 91.
[6] *Loc. cit.* p. 15.
[7] *Loc. cit.* p. 8.
[8] *Loc. cit.* pp. 198, 199.

peculiar mark or scar, the absence of an eye, or some other similar point of resemblance.

In such cases sacrifices are sometimes offered to the snake, and when a bullock is killed part is put away for the use of the dead or Amatongo, who are specially invited to the feast, whose assistance is requested, and whose wrath is deprecated. Yet this can hardly be called ' ancestor worship.' The dead have, it is true, the advantage of invisibility, but they are not regarded as omnipresent, omnipotent, or immortal. There are even means by which troublesome spirits may be destroyed or ' laid.' [1]

In such cases as these, then, we see religion in a very low phase; that in which it consists merely of belief in the existence of evil beings, less material than we are, but mortal like ourselves, and if more powerful than we are in some respects, even less so in others. The Fetichism of the negro is a decided step in advance. Religion, if it can be so called, is systematised, and greatly raised in importance. Nevertheless from another point of view Fetichism may almost be regarded as an anti-religion. For the negro believes that by means of the fetich he can coerce and control his deity. In fact Fetichism is mere witchcraft. We have already seen that magicians all over the world think that if they can obtain a part of an enemy the possession of it gives them a power over him. Even a bit of his clothing will answer the purpose, or, if this cannot be got, it seems to them natural that an injury even to an image would affect the original. That is to say, a man who can destroy or torture the image, thus inflicts pain on the original, and, this being magical, is independent of the power of that original. Even in Europe and in the eleventh century some unfortunate Jews were accused of having

---

[1] *Loc. cit.* p. 160.

murdered a certain Bishop Eberhard in this way. They made a wax image of him, had it baptised, and then burnt it, and so the bishop died.

Lord Kames says that at the time of Catherine de Medicis ' it was common to take the resemblance of enemies in wax, in order to torment them by roasting the figure at a slow fire, and pricking it with needles.' [1]

In India, says Dubois,[2] ' a quantity of mud is moulded into small figures, on the breasts of which they write the name of the persons whom they mean to annoy. . . They pierce the images with thorns, or mutilate them, so as to communicate a corresponding injury to the person represented.'

Now it seems to me that Fetichism is an extension of this belief. The negro supposes that the possession of a fetich representing a spirit, makes the spirit his servant. We know that the negroes beat their fetich if their prayers are unanswered, and I believe they seriously think they thus inflict suffering on the actual deity. Thus the fetich cannot fairly be called an idol. The same image or object may indeed be a fetich to one man and an idol to another; yet the two are essentially different in their nature. An idol is indeed an object of worship, while, on the contrary, a fetich is intended to bring the Deity within the control of man, an attempt which is less absurd than it at first sight appears, when considered in connection with their low religious ideas.

If then witchcraft be not confused with religion, as I think it ought not to be, Fetichism can hardly be called a religion; to the true spirit of which it is indeed entirely opposed.

Anything will do for a fetich; it need not represent the

---

[1] Lord Kames' History of Man, vol. iv. p. 261.   [2] *Loc. cit.* p. 347.

human figure, though it may do so.   Even an ear of maize will answer the purpose. If, said an intelligent negro to Bosman,[1] any of us is 'resolved to undertake anything of importance, we first of all search out a god to prosper our designed undertaking; and going out of doors with this design, take the first creature that presents itself to our eyes, whether dog, cat, or the most contemptible animal in the world, for our god: or perhaps, instead of that, any inanimate object that falls in our way, whether a stone, or piece of wood, or anything else of the same nature. This new-chosen god is immediately presented with an offering, which is accompanied with a solemn vow, that if he pleaseth to prosper our undertakings, for the future we will always worship and esteem him as a god. If our design prove successful, we have discovered a new and assisting god, which is daily presented with fresh offerings; but if the contrary happen, the new god is rejected as a useless tool, and consequently returns to his primitive estate.'   He went on in these following words, 'We make and break our gods daily, and consequently are the masters and inventors of what we sacrifice to.'

Even Europeans, extraordinary as it may seem, believed in these superstitions delusions.

The term Fetichism is generally connected with the negro race, but a corresponding state of mind exists in many other parts of the world.   In fact, it may almost be said to be universal, since it is nothing more nor less than witchcraft; and in the most advanced countries—even in our own—the belief in witchcraft has but recently been eradicated.

The Badagas (Hindostan), according to Metz, are still in a 'condition little above fetichism.   Anything

---

[1] Bosman's   Guinea, Pinkerton's   Loyer (1701), Astley's Collection, vol. Voyages, vol. xvi. p. 493. See also   ii. p. 440.

with them may become an object of adoration, if the head man or the village priest should take a fancy to deify it. As a necessary consequence, however, of this state of things, no real respect is entertained towards their deities, and it is not an uncommon thing to hear the people call them liars, and use opprobrious epithets respecting them.'[1] Again, speaking of the Chota Nagpore tribes of Central India, Colonel Dalton observes that certain 'peculiarities in the paganism of the Oraon, and only practised by Moondahs who live in the same village with them, appear to me to savour thoroughly of fetichism.'[2]

In Jeypore[3] the body of a small musk-rat is regarded as a powerful talisman. 'The body of this animal, dried, is inclosed in a case of brass, silver, or gold, according to the means of the individual, and is slung around the neck, or tied to the arm, to render the individual proof against all evil, not excepting sword and other cut, musket-shot, &c.'

In all these cases the tribes seem to me to be naturally in the state of Fetichism, disguised however and modified by fragments of the higher Hindoo religions, which they have adopted without understanding.

Though the Redskins of North America have reached a higher stage of religious development, they still retain fetiches in the form of 'medicine-bags.' 'Every Indian,' says Catlin,[4] 'in his primitive state, carries his medicine-bag in some form or other,' and to it he looks for protection and safety. The nature of the medicine-bag is thus determined. At fourteen or fifteen years of age the boy wanders away alone upon the Prairie, where he

---

[1] The Tribes of the Neilgherries, p. 60.

[2] Trans. Ethn. Soc. N.S. vol. vi. p. 33.

[3] Shortt, Trans. Ethn. Soc. vol. vi. p. 278.

[4] American Indians, vol. i. p. 36.

remains two, three, four, or even five days, lying on the
ground musing and fasting. He remains awake as long
as he can, but when he sleeps the first animal of which he
dreams becomes his 'medicine.' As soon as possible he
shoots an animal of the species in question, and makes a
medicine-bag of the skin. Unlike the fickle Negro, however, the Redskin never changes his fetich. To him it becomes an emblem of success, like the shield of the Greek,
or the more modern sword, and to lose it is disgrace. The
Columbian Indians have small figures in the form of a
quadruped, bird, or fish. These, though called idols, are
rather fetiches, because, as all disease is attributed to
them, when anyone is ill they are beaten together, and
the first which loses a tooth or claw is supposed to be the
culprit.[1]

In China,[2] also, 'if the people, after long praying to
their images, do not obtain what they desire, as it often
happens, they turn them off as impotent gods ; others use
them in a most reproachful manner, loading them with
hard names, and sometimes with blows. " How now, dog
of a spirit ! " say they to them ; " we give you a lodging in a
magnificent temple, we gild you handsomely, feed you well,
and offer incense to you ; yet, after all this care, you are so
ungrateful as to refuse us what we ask of you." Hereupon
they tie this image with cords, pluck him down, and drag
him along the streets, through all the mud and dunghills,
to punish him for the expense of perfume which they have
thrown away upon him. If in the meantime it happens
that they obtain their request, then, with a great deal of
ceremony, they wash him clean, carry him back, and
place him in his niche again ; where they fall down to
him, and make excuses for what they have done. " In a

[1] Dunn's Oregon, p. 125.
[2] Astley's Collection of Voyages, vol. iv. p. 218.

truth," say they, " we were a little too hasty, as well as you were somewhat too long in your grant. Why should you bring this beating on yourself? But what is done cannot be now undone; let us not therefore think of it any more. If you will forget what is past, we will gild you over again." '

Pallas, speaking of the Ostiaks, states that, ' Malgrè la vénération et le respect qu'ils ont pour leurs idoles, malheur à elles lorsqu'il arrive un malheur à l'Ostiak, et que l'idole n'y remédie pas. Il la jette alors par terre, la frappe, la maltraite, et la brise en morceaux. Cette correction arrive fréquemment. Cette colère est commune à tous les peuples idolâtres de la Siberie.' [1]

In Whydah (W. Africa), and I believe generally, the negroes will not eat the animal or plant which they have chosen for their fetich.[2]

In Issini, on the contrary, ' eating the fetich ' is a solemn ceremony on taking an oath, or as a token of friendship.[3]

Fetichism, strictly speaking, has no temples, idols, priests, sacrifices, or prayer. It involves no belief in creation or in a future life, and à fortiori none in a state of rewards and punishments. It is entirely independent of morality. In most, however, of the powerful negro monarchies religion has made some progress in organisation; but though we find both sacred buildings and priests, the religion itself shows little, if any, intellectual improvement.

The next stage in religious progress is that which may be called Totemism. The savage does not abandon his belief in fetichism, from which indeed no race of men has yet entirely freed itself, but he superinduces on it a belief

[1] Pallas's Voyages, vol. iv. p. 79.   p. 411.
[2] Phillips, 1693. Astley, vol. ii.   [3] Loyer, 1701, loc. cit. p. 436.

in beings of a higher and less material nature. In this stage everything may be worshipped—trees, stones, rivers, mountains, the heavenly bodies, plants, and animals.

How ready savages are to deify objects, both animate and inanimate, I shall presently bring forward abundant evidence; for the present, I will only quote the following story from Lander's ' Niger Expedition.'

In most African towns and villages, says Lander,[1] ' I was treated as a demigod.' On one occasion, having landed at a village which white men had never visited before, his party caused great terror. When they succeeded in establishing a communication with the natives, the chief gave the following account of what had taken place. ' A few minutes,'[2] he said, ' after you first landed, one of my people came to me and said, that a number of strange people had arrived at the market-place. I sent him back again to get as near to you as he could, to hear what you intended doing. He soon after returned to me and said that you spoke a language which he could not understand. Not doubting it was your intention to attack my village at night and carry off my people, I desired them to get ready to fight. We were all prepared and ready to kill you, and came down breathing vengeance and slaughter, supposing that you were my enemies, and had landed from the opposite side of the river. But when you came to meet us unarmed, and we saw your white faces, we were all so frightened that we could not pull our bows, nor move hand or foot; and when you drew near me, and extended your hands towards me, I felt my heart faint within me, and believed that you were " children of Heaven," and had dropped from the skies.'

The worship of animals is very prevalent among races

---

[1] R. and J. Lander's Niger Expedition, vol. iii. p. 198.
[2] *Loc. cit.* vol. iii. p. 78.

of men in a somewhat higher stage of civilisation than that characterised by Fetichism. Plutarch, long ago, suggested that it arose from the custom of representing animals upon standards; and it is possible that some few cases may be due to this cause, though it is manifestly inapplicable to the majority, because animal worship much precedes the use of standards in the scale of human development. Diodorus explains it by the myth that the gods, being at one time hard pressed by the giants, concealed themselves for a while under the form of animals, which in consequence became sacred, and were worshipped by men. This absurd theory needs no refutation.

Another ancient suggestion was that the Egyptian chiefs wore helmets in the form of animals' heads, and that hence these animals were worshipped. This theory, however, will not apply generally, because the other races which worship animals do not use such helmets, and even in Egypt there can be little doubt that the worship of animals preceded the use of helmets.

Plutarch, as already mentioned, supposed that the crocodile was worshipped because, having no tongue, it was a type of the Deity, who makes laws for nature by his mere will! This far-fetched explanation shows an entire misconception of savage nature.

The worship of animals is, however, susceptible of a very simple explanation, and has, I believe, really originated from the practice of naming, first individuals, and then their families, after particular animals. A family, for instance, which was called after the bear, would come to look on that animal first with interest, then with respect, and at length with a sort of awe.

The habit of calling children after some animal or plant is very common.

The Issinese of Guinea name their children 'after some

beast, tree, or fruit, according to their fancy. Sometimes
they call it after their fetich or some white, who is a
Mingo, that is friend to them.'[1]

The Hottentots also generally named their children after
some animal.[2] In Congo[3] 'some form of food is forbidden
to everyone : in some it is a fish, in others a bird, and so
on. This is not, however, expressly stated to be connected
with the totem.'

In China also the name is frequently 'that of a flower,
animal, or such like thing.'[4] In Australia we seem to find
the totem, or, as it is there called, kobong, almost in the
very moment of deification. Each family, says Sir G. Grey,[5]
'adopts some animal or vegetable, as their crest or sign,
or kobong as they call it. I imagine it more likely that
these have been named after the families, than that the
families have been named after them.

'A certain mysterious connection exists between the
family and its kobong, so that a member of the family will
never kill an animal of the species to which his kobong
belongs, should he find it asleep; indeed, he always kills it
reluctantly, and never without affording it a chance of
escape. This arises from the family belief, that some one
individual of the species is their nearest friend, to kill
whom would be a great crime, and to be carefully avoided.
Similarly a native who has a vegetable for his kobong, may
not gather it under certain circumstances, and at a
particular period of the year.'

Here we see a certain feeling for the kobong or totem,
though it does not amount to worship.[6] In America, on

[1] Astley's Collection of Voyages, vol.
ii. p. 436.
[2] *Ibid.* vol. iii. p. 357.
[3] *Ibid.* p. 282.
[4] *Ibid.* vol. iv. p. 91.
[5] Two Expeditions in Australia, vol.
ii. p. 228.
[6] See Eyre, vol. ii. p. 328.

the other hand, it has developed into a veritable religion.

The totem of the Redskins, says Schoolcraft,[1] 'is a symbol of the name of the progenitor,—generally some quadruped, or bird, or other object in the animal kingdom, which stands, if we may so express it, as the surname of the family. It is always some animated object, and seldom or never derived from the inanimate class of nature. Its significant importance is derived from the fact, that individuals unhesitatingly trace their lineage from it. By whatever names they may be called during their life-time, it is the totem, and not their personal name, that is recorded on the tomb, or adjedatig, that makes the place of burial. Families are thus traced when expanded into bands or tribes, the multiplication of which, in North America, has been very great, and has increased, in like ratio, the labours of the ethnologist. The turtle, the bear, and the wolf appear to have been primary and honoured totems in most of the tribes, and bear a significant rank to the traditions of the Iroquois and Lenapis, or Delawares ; and they are believed to have more or less prominency in the genealogies of all the tribes who are organised on the totemic principle.'

Thus again the Osages[2] believe themselves to be descended from a beaver, and consequently will not kill that animal.

So also among the Khonds of India, the different tribes 'take their designation from various animals, as the bear tribe, owl tribe, deer tribe,' &c. &c.

The Kols of Nagpore also are divided into ' keelis ' or clans, generally called after animals, which in consequence

---

[1] Schoolcraft's Indian Tribes, vol. ii. p. 49. See also Lafitau, vol. i. pp. 464, 467.

[2] Schoolcraft, vol. i. p. 320.

[3] Early Races of Scotland, vol. ii. p. 495.

they do not eat. Thus the eel, hawk, and heron tribe abstain respectively from the flesh of these animals,[1]

In Southern Africa the Bechuanas are subdivided into men of the crocodile, men of the fish, of the monkey, of the buffalo, of the elephant, porcupine, lion, vine, and so on. No one dares to eat the flesh, or wear the skin, of the animal to the tribe of which he belongs. In this case however, the totems are not worshipped.[2]

If, moreover, we bear in mind that the deity of a savage is merely a being of a slightly different nature from—and generally somewhat more powerful than—himself, we shall at once see that many animals, such as the bear or elephant, fulfil in a great measure his conception of a Deity.

This is still more completely the case with nocturnal animals, such as the lion and tiger, where the effect is heightened by a certain amount of mystery. As the savage crouching at night by his camp fire, listens to the cries and roars of the animals prowling round, or watches them stealing like shadows round and round among the trees, it would surely be difficult for him to resist the feeling that there is something mysterious about them; and if in his estimate of animals he errs in one direction, we perhaps have fallen into the opposite extreme.

As an object of worship, however, the serpent is pre-eminent among animals. Not only is it malevolent and mysterious, but its bite—so trifling in appearance and yet so deadly—producing fatal effects, rapidly, and apparently by no adequate means, suggests to the savage almost irresistibly the notion of something divine, according to his notions of divinity. There were also some

[1] Dalton, Trans. Ethn. Soc. N.S. vol. vi. p. 36.   [2] The Basutos, Rev. E. Casalis, p. 211.

lower, but powerful, considerations which tended greatly to the development of serpent-worship. The animal is long-lived and easily kept in captivity; hence the same individual might be preserved for a long time, and easily exhibited at intervals to the multitude. In other respects the serpent is a convenient god. Thus in Guinea, where the sea and the serpent were the principal deities, the priests, as Bosman expressly tells us, encouraged offerings to the serpent rather than to the sea, because, in the latter case, 'there happens no remainder to be left for them.'[1]

We are indebted to Mr. Fergusson for a special work on tree and serpent-worship. I cannot, however, agree with my friend in supposing that the beauty of the serpent, or the brilliancy of its eye, had any part among the causes of its original deification. Nor do I believe that serpent worship is to be traced up to any common local origin, but on the contrary, that it sprang up spontaneously in many places, and at very different times. In considering the wide distribution of serpent-worship, we must remember that in the case of the serpent we apply one name to a whole order of animals; and that serpents occur all over the world, except in very cold regions. On the contrary, the lion, the bear, the bull, have less extensive areas, and consequently their worship could never be so general. If, however, we compare, as we ought, serpent-worship with quadruped worship, or bird-worship, or sun-worship, we shall find that it has no exceptionally wide area.

Mr. Fergusson, like previous writers, is surprised to find that the serpent-god is frequently regarded as a beneficent Being. Müller, in his Scientific Mythology, has endeavoured to account for this by the statement that the serpent typified, not only barren, impure, nature, but also youth and health. This is not, I think, the true explanation.

[1] Pinkerton, vol. xvi. p. 500.

It may be the serpent-god commenced as a malevolent
being, who was flattered, as cruel rulers always are, and
that, in process of time, this flattery, which was at first the
mere expression of fear, came to be an article of faith.
If, moreover, the totemic origin of serpent-worship, as
above suggested, be the correct one, the serpent, like
other totemic deities, would, from its origin, have a benevolent character.

As mentioned in Mr. Fergusson's work, the serpent was
worshipped anciently in Egypt,[1] in India,[2] Phœnicia,[3]
Babylonia,[4] Greece,[5] as well as in Italy,[6] where, however,
it seems not to have prevailed much.

We may now pass on to those cases in which the serpent
is now worshipped, or was so until lately. Among the
Lithuanians 'every family entertained a real serpent as a
household god.'[7]

In Asia evidence of serpent-worship has been found in
Persia,[8] Cashmere,[9] Cambodia, Thibet,[10] India,[11] China,
(traces),[12] Ceylon,[13] and among the Kalmucks.[14]

In Africa the serpent was worshipped in some parts of
Upper Egypt,[15] and in Abyssinia.[16] Among the negroes on
the Guinea coast it used to be the principal deity.[17]

[1] Herodotus, Euterpe, 74.

[2] Tertullian, de Prescript. Heretico-
rum, c. xlvii. Epiphanius, lib. 1,
Heres, xxxvii. p. 267, et seq.

[3] Eusebius, Præ. Evan., vol. i. p. 9.
Maurice, Ind. Antiq., vol. vi. p. 273.

[4] Bel and the Dragon, v. 23.

[5] Pausanias, vol. ii. pp. 137, 175.
Ælian de Animal. xvi. 39. Herodotus, viii. p. 41.

[6] Ælian, Var. Hist., ix. p. 16. Pro-
pertius, Eleg. viii. p. 4.

[7] Lord Kames' History of Man, vol.
iv. p. 193.

[8] Mogruil, 156, Windischmann, 37,
Sháh Námeh, Atkinson's Translation,
p. 14.

[9] Asiatic Res. vol. xv. pp. 24, 25.
Ayeen Akbaree, Gladwin's Trans., p.
137.

[10] Hiouen-Thsang, vol. i. p. 4.

[11] Fergusson's Tree and Serpent
Worship, p. 56.

[12] Ibid. p. 51.

[13] History and Doctrine of Buddhism
in Ceylon, Upham.

[14] Klemm, Cult. der Mens., vol. iii.
p. 202.

[15] Pocock, Pinkerton's Voyages,
vol. xv. p. 269.

[16] Dillmann in Zeitsch. der Mor-
genlandischen Gesells. vol. vii. p. 338.
Ludolf. Comment. vol. iii. p. 284;
Bruce's Travels, vol. iv. p. 35.

[17] Astley's Voyages, vol. iii. p. 489;
Burton, vol. ii. p. 139; Smith, loc. cit.
p. 195.

Smith, in his Voyage to Guinea,[1] says that the natives 'are all Pagans, and worship three sorts of deities. The first is a large beautiful kind of snake, which is inoffensive in its nature. These are kept in fittish-houses, or churches, built for that purpose in a grove, to whom they sacrifice great store of hogs, sheep, fowls, and goats, &c., and if not devoured by the snake, are sure to be taken care of by the fetish-men or pagan priests.' From Liberia to Benzuela, if not farther, the serpent was the principal deity,[2] and, as elsewhere, is regarded as being on the whole beneficent. To it they resort in times of drought and sickness, or other calamities. No negro would intentionally injure a serpent, and anyone doing so by accident would assuredly be put to death. Some English sailors once having killed one which they found in their house, were furiously attacked by the natives, who killed them all, and burned the house. All over the country are small huts, built on purpose for the snakes,[3] which are attended and fed by old women. These snakes are frequently consulted as oracles.

In addition to these small huts were temples, which, judged by a negro standard, were of considerable magnificence,[4] with large courts, spacious apartments, and numerous attendants. Each of these temples had a special snake. That of Whydah was supposed to have appeared to the army during an attack on Ardra. It was regarded as a presage of victory, which so encouraged the soldiers that they were perfectly successful. Hence this fetich was reverenced beyond all others, and an annual pilgrimage was made to its temple with much ceremony. It is rather suspicious that any young women who may be

[1] Smith's Voyage to Guinea, p. 195. See also Bosman, Pinkerton's Voyages, vol. xvi. p. 494, *et seq.*

[2] Bosman, *loc. cit.* pp. 494–499.

Smith, *loc. cit.* p. 195.

[3] Astley, *loc. cit.* pp. 27, 32.

[4] *Ibid.* p. 29.

ill are taken off to the snake's house to be cured. For this questionable service the attendants charge a high price to the parents.

Fig. 19.

AGOYE, AN IDOL OF WHIDDAH. (Astley's Collection of Voyages.)

It is observable that the harmless snakes only are thus worshipped. 'Agoye,' the fetich of Whydah, which has serpents and lizards coming out of its head[1] (fig. 19), presents a remarkable similarity to some of the Hindoo idols.

The Kaffirs of South Africa have a general belief that the spirits of their ancestors appear to them in the form of serpents.[2]

Ellis mentions that in Madagascar the natives regard them 'with a sort of superstition.'[3]

In Feejee, 'the god[4] most generally known is Ndengei, who seems to be an impersonation of the abstract idea of eternal existence. He is the subject of no emotion or sensation, nor any appetite except hunger. The serpent—the world-wide symbol of eternity—is his adopted shrine. Some traditions represent him with the head and part of the body of that reptile, the rest of his form being stone, emblematic of everlasting and unchangeable duration. He passes a monotonous existence in a gloomy cavern; evincing no interest in anyone but his attendant, Uto, and giving no signs of life beyond eating, answering his priest, and changing his position from one side to the other.'

In the Friendly Islands the water snake was much respected.[5]

In America serpents were worshipped by the Aztecs,[6] Peruvians,[7] Natchez,[8] Caribs,[9] Monitarris,[10] Mandans,[11] &c.

Alvarez, during his attempt to reach Peru from Paraguay,

---

[1] Astley, *loc. cit.* vol. iii. p. 50.
[2] Casalis' Basutos, p. 246. Chapman's Travels, vol. i. p. 195. Callaway's Religious System of the Amazulu.
[3] Three Visits to Madagascar, p. 143.
[4] Fiji and the Fijians, vol. ii. p. 217.
[5] Mariner, vol. ii. p. 106.
[6] Squier's Serpent Symbol in America, p. 162. Gama, Descripcion Historica y Cronologica de las Pedras de Mexico, 1832, p. 39; Bernal Diaz, p. 125.
[7] Müller, Ges. d. Amer. Urreligionen, p. 366.
[8] *Ibid.* p. 62.
[9] *Ibid.* p. 221.
[10] Klemm, vol. ii. p. 162.
[11] *Ibid.* p. 163.

is reported[1] to have seen the 'temple and residence of a monstrous serpent, whom the inhabitants had chosen for their divinity, and fed with human flesh. He was as thick as an ox, and seven-and-twenty feet long, with a very large head, and very fierce though small eyes. His jaws, when extended, displayed two ranks of crooked fangs. The whole body, except the tail which was smooth, was covered with round scales of a great thickness. The Spaniards, though they could not be persuaded by the Indians that this monster delivered oracles, were exceedingly terrified at the first sight of him ; and their terror was greatly increased, when, on one of them having fired a blunderbuss at him, he gave a roar like that of a lion, and with a stroke of his tail shook the whole tower.'

The worship of serpents being so widely distributed, and presenting so many similar features, we cannot wonder that it has been regarded as something special, that attempts have been made to trace it up to one source, and that it has been regarded by some as the primitive religion of man.

I will now, however, proceed to mention other cases of zoolatry.

Animal worship was very prevalent in America.[2] The Redskins reverenced the bear,[3] the bison, the hare,[4] and the wolf,[5] and some species of birds.[6] The jaguar was worshipped in some parts of Brazil, and especially in La Plata.[7] In South America birds and jaguars seem to have been the specially sacred animals. The owl in Mexico was regarded as an evil spirit ;[8] in South America eagles

---

[1] Charlevoix's History of Paraguay, vol. i. p. 110.
[2] Müller, Am. Urr., p. 60, *et seq*.
[3] *Ibid*. p. 61.
[4] Schoolcraft, vol. i. p. 316.
[5] Müller, *loc. cit.* p. 257.
[6] Müller, Am. Urr., p. 134. Klemm, *loc. cit.* vol. ii. p. 164.
[7] *Loc. cit.* p. 256.
[8] Prescott, vol. i. p. 48.

and goatsuckers were much venerated.[1] The Abipones[2] think that certain little ducks 'which fly about at night, uttering a mournful hiss, are the souls of the departed.'

In Yucatan it was customary to leave an infant alone in a place sprinkled with ashes. Next morning the ashes were examined, and if the footprints of any animals were found on them, that animal was chosen as the deity of the infant.[3]

The semi-civilised races of Mexico[4] and Peru were more advanced in their religious conceptions. In the latter the sun was the great deity.[5] Yet in Peru,[6] even at the time of the conquest, many species of animals were still much reverenced, including the fox, dog, llama, condor, eagle, and puma, besides the serpent. Indeed, every species of animal was supposed to have a representative, or archetype, in heaven.[7] In Mexico a similar feeling prevailed, but neither here nor in Peru can it truly be said that animals at the time of the conquest were nationally regarded as actual deities.

The Polynesians, also, had generally advanced beyond the stage of Totemism. The heavenly bodies were not worshipped, and when animals were regarded with veneration, it was rather as representatives of the deities, than with idea that they were really deities. Still the Tahitians[8] had a superstitious reverence for various kinds of fish and birds; such as the heron, kingfisher, and woodpecker, the latter apparently because they frequented the temples.

The Sandwich Islanders[9] seem to have regarded the raven

[1] Müller, Amer. Urr., p. 237.
[2] Loc. cit. vol. ii. p. 74.
[3] De Brosses, Du Culte des Dieux Fetiches, p. 46.
[4] Müller, loc. cit. p. 481.
[5] Prescott's History of Peru, p. 88.
[6] Müller, p. 366.
[7] Prescott's History of Peru, p. 87.
[8] Polynesian Researches, vol. ii. p. 202.
[9] Cook's Third Voyage, vol. iii. p. 160.

as sacred, and the New Zealanders, according to Forster, regarded a species of tree-creeper as the 'bird of the divinity.'[1] The Tongans considered that the deities 'sometimes come into the living bodies of lizards, porpoises, and a species of water snake; hence these animals are much respected.'[2]

The Bishop of Wellington informs us that 'spiders were special objects of reverence to Maoris, and as the priests further told them that the souls of the faithful went to heaven on gossamer threads, they were very careful not to break any spiders' webs, or gossamers. Lizards were also supposed to be chosen by the Maori gods as favourite abodes.'[3]

In the Feejee[4] Islands, besides the serpent, 'certain birds, fish and plants, and some men, are supposed to have deities closely connected with or residing in them. At Lakemba, Tui Lakemba, and on Vanua Levu, Ravuravu, claim the hawk as their abode; Viavia, and other gods the shark. One is supposed to inhabit the eel, and another the common fowl, and so on, until nearly every animal becomes the shrine of some deity. He who worships the god dwelling in the eel must never eat of that fish, and thus of the rest; so that some are Tabu from eating human flesh, because the shrine of their god is a man.'

In Siberia Erman mentions that 'the Polar bear, as the strongest of God's creatures, and that which seems to come nearest to the human being, is as much venerated by the Samoyedes, as his black congener by the Ostyaks. They even swear by the throat of this strong animal, whom they kill and eat; but when it is once killed, they show their respect for it in various ways.'[5]

Each tribe of the Jakuts 'looks on some particular

[1] Voyage round the World, vol. i. p. 519.
[2] Mariner, *loc. cit.* vol. ii. p. 106.
[3] Trans. Ethn. Soc. 1870, p. 367.
[4] Williams' Fiji and the Fijians, vol. i. p. 219.
[5] Erman, vol. ii. p. 55.

creature as sacred, e.g., a swan, goose, raven, &c., and such is not eaten by that tribe, though the others may eat it.'[1] The same feeling extends even to plants, and in China, when the sacred apricot tree is broken to make the spirit pen, it is customary to write an apology on the bark.[2]

The Hindus, says Dubois,[3] 'in all things extravagant, pay honour and worship, less or more solemn, to almost every living creature, whether quadruped, bird, or reptile.' The cow, the ape, the eagle (known as garuda), and the serpent, receive the highest honours; but the tiger, elephant, horse, stag, sheep, hog, dog, cat, rat, peacock, cock, chameleon, lizard, tortoise, fish, and even insects, have been made objects of worship.

The ox is held especially sacred throughout most of India and Ceylon. Among the Todas[4] the 'buffaloes and bell are fused into an incomprehensible mystic whole, or unity, and constitute their prime object of adoration and worship.' . . . .

'Towards evening the herd is driven back to the tuel, when such of the male and female members of the family as are present assemble, and make obeisance to the animals.' The goose is worshipped in Ceylon,[5] and the alligator in the Philippines.

The ancient Egyptians were greatly addicted to animal worship, and even now Sir S. Baker states that on the White Nile the natives will not eat the ox.[6] The common fowl also is connected with superstitious ceremonies among the Obbo and other Nile tribes.[7]

The King of Ardra, on the Guinea Coast, had certain

[1] Strahlenberg, p. 383.
[2] Tylor, Roy. Inst. Journ., vol. v. p. 527.
[3] Loc. cit. p. 445.
[4] Trans. Ethn. Soc. N.S. vol. vii. pp. 250, 253. See also Ethn. Journ. 1869, p. 97.
[5] Tennent's Ceylon, vol. i. p. 484.
[6] Albert N'yanza, vol. i. p. 69.
[7] Baker, loc. cit. vol. i. p. 327.

black birds for his fetiches,[1] and the negroes of Benin also reverence several kinds of birds.

The negroes of Guinea regard [2] 'the sword-fish and the bonito as deities, and such is their veneration for them, that they never catch either sort designedly. If a sword-fish happen to be taken by chance, they will not eat it, till the sword be cut off, which, when dried, they regard as a *fetis-so*.' They also regard the crocodile as a deity. On the Guinea Coast, says Bosman, ' a great part of the negroes believe that man was made by Anansie, that is, a great spider.' [3]

In Madagascar, Ellis [4] tells us that the natives regard crocodiles ' as possessed of supernatural power, invoke their forbearance with prayers, or seek protection by charms, rather than attack them ; even the shaking of a spear over the waters would be regarded as an act of sacrilegious insult to the sovereign of the flood, imperilling the life of the offender the next time he should venture on the water.'

The nations of Southern Europe had for the most part advanced beyond animal worship even in the earliest historical times. The extraordinary sanctity attributed, in the Twelfth Odyssey, to the oxen of the sun, stands almost alone in Greek mythology, and is regarded by Mr. Gladstone as of Phœnician origin. It is true that the horse is spoken of with mysterious respect, and that deities on several occasions assumed the form of birds ; but this does not amount to actual worship.

The deification of animals explains probably the curious fact that various savage races habitually apologise to the animals which they kill in the chase ; thus, the Vogulitzi [5]

[1] Astley's Collection of Voyages, vol. iii. pp. 72, 99.
[2] Astley, vol. ii. p. 667.
[3] Pinkerton, *loc. cit.* vol. xvi. p. 396.
[4] Three Visits to Madagascar, p. 297.
[5] Strahlenberg's Voyage to Siberia, p. 97.

of Siberia, when they have killed a bear, address it
formally, and maintain ' that the blame is to be laid on
the arrows and iron, which were made and forged by the
Russians.' Pallas[1] narrates a similar action on the part of
an Ostyak.   Schoolcraft[2] mentions a case of an Indian on
the shores of Lake Superior begging pardon of a bear
which he had shot.

Before engaging in a hunt the Chippeways have a
' medicine ' dance in order to propitiate the spirits of the
bears or other game.[3]   So also in British Columbia,[4] when
the fishing season commences, and the fish begin coming
up the rivers, the Indians used to meet them, and ' speak
to them.   They paid court to them, and would address
them thus : " You fish, you fish ; you are all chiefs, you
are ; you are all chiefs." '

The Koussa Kaffirs[5] had a very similar custom.
' Before a party goes out hunting, a very odd ceremony
or sport takes place, which they consider as absolutely
necessary to ensure success to the undertaking. One of
them takes a handful of grass into his mouth, and crawls
about upon all-fours to represent some sort of game. The
rest advance as if they would run him through with their
spears, raising the hunting cry, till at length he falls upon
the ground as if dead. If this man afterwards kills a
head of game, he hangs a claw upon his arm as a trophy,
but the animal must be shared with the rest.' Lichtenstein
also mentions that ' if an elephant is killed after a very
long and wearisome chase, as is commonly the case, they
seek to exculpate themselves towards the dead animal,
by declaring to him solemnly, that the thing happened
entirely by accident, not by design.'[6] To make the

[1] Voyages, vol. iv. p. 85.
[2] Schoolcraft's Indian Tribes, vol.
iii. p. 229.
[3] Catlin's Amer. Ind. vol. ii. p. 248.
[4] Metlahkatlah, p. 96.
[5] Lichtenstein's Travels, vol. i. p.
269.
[6] *Ibid.* vol. i. p. 254.

apology more completely they cut off the trunk and bury it carefully with much flattery.

Speaking of a Mandingo who had killed a lion, Gray says: 'As[1] I was not a little surprised at seeing the man, whom I conceived ought to be rewarded for having first so disabled the animal as to prevent it from attacking us, thus treated, I requested an explanation; and was informed that being a subject only, he was guilty of a great crime in killing or shooting a sovereign, and must suffer this punishment until released by the chiefs of the village who, knowing the deceased to have been their enemy, would not only do so immediately, but commend the man for his good conduct. I endeavoured to no purpose to find out the origin of this extraordinary mock ceremony, but could only gain the answer, frequently given by an African, " that his forefathers had always done so." '

The Stiens of Cambodia[2] believe that 'animals also have souls which wander about after their death; thus, when they have killed one, fearing lest its soul should come and torment them, they ask pardon for the evil they have done to it, and offer sacrifices proportioned to the strength and size of the animal.'

The Sumatrans speak of tigers[3] 'with a degree of awe, and hesitate to call them by their common name (rimau or machang), terming them respectfully satwa (the wild animals), or even nenek (ancestors); as really believing them such, or by way of soothing and coaxing them. When an European procures traps to be set, by means of persons less superstitious, the inhabitants of the neighbourhood have been known to go at night to the place, and practise some forms, in order to persuade the animals that it was not laid by them, or with their consent.'

[1] Gray's Travels in Western Africa, p. 143
[2] Mouhot's Travels in the Central Parts of Indo-China, vol. i. p. 252.
[3] Marsden's Hist. of Sumatra, p. 292.

The deification of inanimate objects is perhaps somewhat more difficult to understand than that of animals.
The names of individuals, however, would be taken not
only from animals, but also from inanimate objects, and
would thus, as suggested at p. 171, lead to the worship of
the latter as well as of the former. Some of them, moreover,
are singularly lifelike.   No one, I think, can wonder that
rivers should have been regarded as alive.   The constant
movement, the ripples and eddies on their surface, the
vibrations of the reeds and other water plants growing in
them, the murmuring and gurgling sounds, the clearness
and transparency of the water, combine to produce a
singular effect on the mind even of civilised man.

The savage also is susceptible to such influences, and is
naturally prone to personify not only rivers but also other
inanimate objects.

Seneca long ago observed, that ' if you walk in a grove,
thick planted with ancient trees of unusual growth, the
interwoven boughs of which exclude the light of heaven ;
the vast height of the wood, the retired secrecy of the
place, the deep unbroken gloom of shade, impress your
mind with the conviction of a present deity.'

Again, who can wonder at that worship of the sun,
moon, and stars, which has been regarded as a special
form of religion, and is known as Sabæism ?   It does not
however, in its original form, essentially differ from
mountain or river worship.   To us with our knowledge
of the sun, it seems naturally a more sublime form
of religion, but we must remember that the lower races
who worship the heavenly bodies have no idea of their distance, nor consequently of their magnitude.   Hence the
curious ideas with reference to eclipses which I have
already mentioned (p. 136). Again, the New Zealanders
believed that Mawe, their ancestor, caught the sun in a

noose, and wounded it so severely that its movements have been slower, and the days consequently longer, ever since.[1]

According to another account, Mawe 'tied a string to the sun and fastened it to the moon, that as the former went down, the other, being pulled after it by the superior power of the sun, may rise and give light during his absence.'[2]

We must always bear in mind that the savage notion of a deity is essentially different from that entertained by higher races. Instead of being supernatural, he is merely a part of nature. This goes far to explain the tendency to deification which at first seems so strange.

A good illustration, and one which shows how easily deities are created by men in this frame of mind, is mentioned by Lichtenstein. The king of the Koussa Kaffirs having broken off a piece of a stranded anchor, died soon afterwards, upon which all the Kaffirs looked upon the anchor as alive, and saluted it respectfully whenever they passed near it.[3] Again, the natives near Sydney made it an invariable rule never to whistle when beneath a particular cliff, because on one occasion a rock fell from it and crushed some natives who were whistling underneath it.[4]

A very interesting case is recorded by Mr. Fergusson.[5] 'The following instance of tree-worship,' he says, 'which I myself witnessed, is amusing, even if not instructive. While residing in Tessore, I observed at one time considerable crowds passing near the factory I then had charge of. As it might be merely an ordinary fair they were going to attend, I took no notice; but as the

[1] Polynesian Mythology, p. 35.
[2] Yate, *loc. cit.* p. 143.
[3] Travels, vol. i. p. 254.
[4] Collins's English Colony in N.S. Wales, p. 382.
[5] Tree and Serpent Worship, p. 74.

crowd grew daily larger, and assumed a more religious
character, I enquired, and was told that a god had appeared
in a tree at a place about six miles off.   Next morning I
rode over, and found a large space cleared in a village I
knew well, in the centre of which stood an old decayed
date tree, hung with garlands and offerings.   Around it
houses were erected for the attendant Brahmins, and a
great deal of business was going on in offerings and Pûjâ.
On my enquiring how the god manifested his presence, I
was informed that soon after the sun rose in the morning
the tree raised its head to welcome him, and bowed it down
again when he departed.   As this was a miracle easily
tested, I returned at noon and found it was so!   After a
little study and investigation, the mystery did not seem
difficult of explanation.   The tree had originally grown
across the principal pathway through the village, but at
last hung so low, that in order to enable people to pass
under it, it had been turned aside and fastened parallel to
the road.   In the operation the bundle of fibres which
composed the root had become twisted like the strands of
a rope.   When the morning sun struck on the upper
surface of these, they contracted in drying, and hence a
tendency to untwist, which raised the head of the tree.
With the evening dews they relaxed, and the head of the
tree declined, thus proving to the man of science as to the
credulous Hindu, that it was due to the direct action of
the Sun God.'

The savage, indeed, accounts for all movement by life.
Hence the wind is a living being.   Nay, even motionless
objects are regarded in a particular stage of mental progress as possessing spirits.   The chief of Teah could
hardly be persuaded but that Lander's watch was alive and
had the power of moving.[1]   It is probably for this reason
that in most languages inanimate objects are distinguished

[1] Niger Expedition, vol. ii. p. 220.

by genders, being at first regarded as either male or female. Hence also the practice of breaking or burning the weapons, &c. buried with the dead. It has been generally supposed that this was merely to prevent them from being a temptation to robbers. This is not so, however; savages do not invade the sanctity of the tomb. Just, however, as they kill a man's wives and slaves, and favourite horse, that they may accompany him to the other world, so do they 'kill' the weapons, that the spirits of the bows, &c. may also go with their master, and that he may enter the other world armed and provided as a chief should be. Thus the Tahitians[1] believed 'that not only all other animals, but trees, fruit, and even stones, have souls which at death, or upon being consumed, or broken, ascend to the divinity, with whom they first mix, and afterwards pass into the mansion allotted to each.'

The Feejeeans[2] considered that 'if an animal or a plant die, its soul immediately goes to Bolotoo; if a stone or any other substance is broken, immortality is equally its reward; nay, artificial bodies have equal good luck with men and hogs, and yams. If an axe or a chisel is worn out or broken up, away flies its soul for the service of the gods. If a house is taken down, or any way destroyed, its immortal part will find a situation on the plains of Bolotoo.'

Sproat,[3] speaking of N. W. America, says, that 'when the dead are buried, the friends often burn blankets with them, for by destroying the blankets in this upper world, they send them also with the departed soul to the world below.'

In China,[4] 'if the dead man was a person of note, the Bonzes make great processions; the mourners following them with candles and perfumes burning in their hands.

---

[1] Cook's Third Voyage, vol. ii. p. 166.
[2] Mariner, *loc. cit.* vol. ii. p. 137.
[3] Sproat's Scenes and Studies of Savage Life, p. 213.
[4] Astley, vol. iv. p. 94.

They offer sacrifices at certain distances, and perform the obsequies; in which they burn statues of men, women, horses, saddles, and other things, and abundance of paper money : all which, they believe, in the next life, are converted into real ones, for the use of the party deceased.'

Thus then by man in this stage of progress everything was regarded as having life, and being more or less a Deity.

In India, says Dubois,[1] ' a woman adores the basket which serves to bring or to hold her necessaries, and offers sacrifices to it ; as well as to the rice-mill, and other implements that assist her in her household labours. A carpenter does the like homage to his hatchet, his adze, and other tools ; and likewise offers sacrifices to them. A Brahman does so to the style with which he is going to write ; a soldier to the arms he is to use in the field ; a mason to his trowel, and a labourer to his plough.'

Sir S. Baker[2] says, ' Should the present history of the country be written by an Arab scribe, the style of the description would be purely that of the Old Testament, and the various calamities or the good fortunes that have in the course of nature befallen both the tribes and the individuals, would be recounted either as special visitations of Divine wrath, or blessings for good deeds performed. If in a dream a particular course of action is suggested, the Arab believes that God has *spoken* and directed him. The Arab scribe or historian would describe the event as the " *voice* of the Lord " (Kallam el Allah) having spoken unto the person : or, that God appeared to him in a dream and " *said*, &c." Thus, much allowance would be necessary, on the part of a European reader, for the figurative ideas and expressions of the people.'

Mr. Fergusson, indeed, regards tree-worship, in associa-

[1] People of India, p. 373. See also   [2] The Nile Tributaries of Abyssinia,
pp. 383, 386.   by Sir S. W. Baker, p. 130.

tion with serpent-worship, as the primitive faith of mankind. Mr. Wake[1] also says, ' How are we to account for the
Polynesians also affixing a sacred character to a species of
the banyan, called by them the ava tree, and for the same
phenomenon being found among the African tribes on the
Zambesi and the Shire, among the negroes of Western
equatorial Africa, and even in Northern Australia? Such
a fact as this cannot be accounted for as a mere coincidence.'

Since, however, tree-worship equally prevails in America,
we cannot regard it as any ' evidence of the common origin
of the various races which practise ' it. It is, however, one
among many illustrations that the human mind, in its upward progress, everywhere passes through the same or very
similar phases.

Tree-worship formerly existed in Assyria, Greece,[2]
Poland,[3] France. In Persia the Homa or Soma worship
was perhaps a case in point; Tacitus[4] mentions the sacred
groves of Germany, and those of England are familiar to
everyone. In the eighth century, St. Boniface found it
necessary to cut down a sacred oak, and even recently an
oak copse at Loch Siant, in the Isle of Skye, was held so
sacred that no person would venture to cut the smallest
branch from it.[5]

At the present day tree-worship prevails throughout
Central Africa, south of Egypt and the Sahara. The
Shangallas in Bruce's[6] time worshipped ' trees, serpents
the moon, planets, and stars.'

The negroes of Guinea[7] worshipped three deities,

[1] Chapters on Man, p. 250.
[2] Baum cultus der Hellenen, Bot-
ticher. 1856.
[3] Olaus Magnus, bk. iii. Ch. I.
[4] Tacitus, Germania, ix.
[5] Early Races of Scotland, vol. i.
p. 171.

[6] Travels, vol. iv. p. 35. See also
vol. vi. p. 344.
[7] Voyage to Guinea, p. 195. Bosman, Pinkerton's Voyages, vol. xvi.
p. 494. Merolla, Pinkerton's Voyages,
vol. xvi. p. 236.

—serpents, trees, and the sea. Park[1] observed a tree on the confines of Bondou, hung with innumerable offerings, principally rags. 'It had,' he says 'a very singular appearance, being decorated with innumerable rags or strips of cloth, which persons travelling across the wilderness had tied to the branches.'

Chapman mentions a sacred tree among the Kaffirs, which was hung with numerous offerings.[2]

The negroes of Congo[3] adored a sacred tree called 'Mirrone.' One is generally planted near the houses, as if it were the tutular god of the dwelling, the Gentiles adoring it as one of their idols. They place calabashes of palm wine at the feet of these trees, in case they should be thirsty. Bosman also states that along the Guinea coast almost every village has its sacred grove.[4] At Addacoodah, Oldfield[5] saw a 'gigantic tree, twelve yards and eight inches in circumference. I soon found it was considered sacred, and had several arrows stuck in it, from which were suspended fowls, several sorts of birds, and many other things, which had been offered by the natives to it as a deity.'

The Bo tree is much worshipped in India[6] and Ceylon.[7] 'The planting of the Râjâyatana tree by Buddha,' says Fergusson, 'has already been alluded to, but the history of the transference of a branch of the Bo tree from the Buddh-gyâ to Anurâdhapura, is as authentic and as important as any event recorded in the Ceylonese annals. Sent by Asóka (250 B.C.), it was received with the utmost reverence by

[1] Travels, 1817, vol. i. pp. 64, 106. See also Caillié, vol. i. p. 156.

[2] Travels, vol. ii. p. 50. Klemm quotes also Villault, Rel. des Costes d'Afrique S., pp. 263, 267.

[3] Merolla's Voyage to Congo. Pinkerton, vol. xvi. p. 236. Astley's Collection of Voyages, vol. ii. pp. 95, 97.

[4] Loc. cit. p. 399. See also Astley's Collection of Voyages, vol. ii. p. 26.

[5] Expedition, vol. ii. p. 117.

[6] Tree and Serpent Worship, p. 56, et seq.

[7] Ibid. p. 56.

Devanampiyatisso, and planted in the most conspicuous spot in the centre of his capital. There it has been reverenced as the chief and most important "numen" of Ceylon for more than 2,000 years, and it, or its lineal descendant sprung at least from the old root, is there worshipped at this hour. The city is in ruins; its great dagobas have fallen to decay; its monasteries have disappeared; but the great Bo tree still flourishes according to the legend,—Ever green, never growing or decreasing, but living on for ever for the delight and worship of mankind. Annually thousands repair to the sacred precincts within which it stands, to do it honour, and to offer up those prayers for health and prosperity which are more likely to be answered if uttered in its presence. There is probably no older idol in the world, certainly none more venerated.'

Some of the Chittagong Hill Tribes worship the bamboo.[1] In Siberia the Jakuts have sacred trees on which they 'hang all manner of nicknacks, as iron, brass, copper, &c.'[2] The Ostyaks also, as Pallas informs us, used to worship trees.[3]

'There was pointed out to us,' says Erman,[4] 'as an important monument of an early epoch in the history of Beresov, a larch about fifty feet high, and now, through age, flourishing only at the top, which has been preserved in the churchyard. In former times, when the Ostyak rulers dwelt in Beresov, this tree was the particular object of their adoration. In this, as in many other instances, observed by the Russians, the peculiar sacredness of the tree was due to the singularity of its form and growth, for about six feet from the ground, the trunk separated into two equal parts; and again united. It was the custom of

[1] Lewin's Hill Tracts of Chittagong, p. 10.
[2] Strahlenberg, Travels in Siberia, p. 381.
[3] *Loc. cit.* vol. iv. p. 79.
[4] Erman's Travels in Siberia, vol. i. p. 464.

the superstitious natives to place costly offerings of every kind in the opening of the trunk; nor have they yet abandoned the usage; a fact well known to the enlightened Kosaks, who enrich themselves by carrying off secretly the sacrificial gifts.' 'Hanway,[1] in his Travels in Persia, mentions a tree to which were affixed a number of rags left there as health-offerings by persons afflicted with ague. This was beside a desolate caravanserai where the traveller found nothing but water.'

In some parts[2] of Sumatra ' likewise they superstitiously believe that certain trees, particularly those of venerable appearance (as an old jawi-jawi or banian tree), are the residence, or rather the material frame of spirits of the woods; an opinion which exactly answers to the idea entertained by the ancients of the dryades and hama-dryades. At Benkunat, in the Lampong country, there is a long stone, standing on a flat one, supposed by the people to possess extraordinary power of virtue. It is reported to have been once thrown down into the water, and to have raised itself again into its original position; agitating the elements at the same time with a prodigious storm. To approach it without respect, they believe to be the source of misfortune to the offender.'

Among the natives of the Philippines we also find the worship of trees.[3] They also ' believed that the world at first consisted only of sky and water, and between these two a glede; which, weary with flying about, and finding no place to rest, set the water at variance with the sky, which, in order to keep it in bounds, and that it should not get uppermost, loaded the water with a number of islands, in which the glede might settle and leave them at peace. Mankind, they said, sprang out of a large cane

---

[1] Quoted in the Early Races of Scotland, vol. i. p. 163. See also De Brosses, *loc. cit.* pp. 144, 145.

[2] Marsden's History of Sumatra, p. 301.

[3] *Ibid.* p. 303.

with two joints, that, floating about in the water, was at
length thrown by the waves against the feet of the glede,
as it stood on shore, which opened it with its bill, the man
came out of one joint, the woman out of the other.   These
were soon after married by consent of their god, Bathala
Meycapal, which caused the first trembling of the earth;
and from thence are descended the different nations of the
world.'

The Fijians also worshipped certain plants.[1]   Tree-
worship was less prevalent in America.   Trees and plants
were worshipped by the Mandans and Monitarees.[2]   A
large ash was venerated by the Indians of Lake Superior.[3]

In North America, Franklin[4] describes a sacred tree on
which the Crees 'had hung strips of buffalo flesh, and
pieces of cloth.'   They complained to him of some 'Stone
Indians, who, two nights before, had stripped their revered
tree of many of its offerings.'

In Mexico Mr. Tylor[5] observed an ancient cyprus of
remarkable size: 'all over its branches were fastened
votive offerings of the Indians, hundreds of locks of coarse
black hair, teeth, bits of coloured cloth, rags and morsels
of ribbon.   The tree was many centuries old, and had
probably had some mysterious influence ascribed to it,
and been decorated with such simple offerings long before
the discovery of America.'   In Nicaragua not only large
trees, but even maize and beans, were worshipped.[6]   Maize
was also worshipped in the Peruvian province of Huanca.[7]

In Patagonia Mr. Darwin[8] mentions a sacred tree

[1] Fiji and the Fijians, vol. i. p. 219.
[2] Müller, Amer. Urrel. p. 59.
[3] Müller, loc. cit. p. 125.
[4] Journeys to the Polar Sea, vol. i.
p. 221.
[5] Anahuac, p. 215.   He mentions
a second case of the same sort on
p. 265.
[6] Müller, loc. cit. p. 494.   See also
p. 491.
[7] Martius, loc. cit. p. 80.
[8] Researches in Geology and Natural History, p. 79.

' which the Indians reverence as the altar of Walleechu. It is situated on a high part of the plain, and hence is a landmark visible at a great distance. As soon as a tribe of Indians come in sight of it, they offer their adorations by loud shouts. . . . It stands by itself without any neighbour, and was indeed the first tree we saw; afterwards we met with a few others of the same kind, but they were far from common. Being winter the tree had no leaves, but in their place numberless threads, by which the various offerings, such as cigars, bread, meat, pieces of cloth, &c., had been suspended. Poor people not having anything better, only pulled a thread out of their ponchoo, and fastened it to the tree. The Indians, moreover, were accustomed to pour spirits and maté into a certain hole, and likewise to smoke upwards, thinking thus to afford all possible gratification to Walleechu. To complete the scene, the tree was surrounded by the bleached bones of the horses which had been slaughtered as sacrifices. All Indians, of every age and sex, made their offerings; they then thought that their horses would not tire, and that they themselves should be prosperous.

' The Gaucho who told me this, said that in the time of peace he had witnessed this scene, and that he and others used to wait till the Indians had passed by, for the sake of stealing their offerings from Walleechu. The Gauchos think that the Indians consider the tree as the god itself; but it seems far more probable that they regard it as the altar,'—a distinction, however, which a Patagonian Indian would hardly perceive.

The Abenaquis also had a sacred tree.[1]

Trees were worshipped by the ancient Celts, and De Brosses[2] even derives the word kirk, now softened into

---

[1] De Brosses, Du Culte des Dieux Fetiches, p. 51. Lafitau, vol. i. p. 146.   [2] *Loc. cit.* p. 175.

church, from quercus an oak, that species being peculiarly
sacred.

The Lapps also used to worship trees.[1]

Thus, then, this form of religion can be shown to be
general to most of the great races of men at a certain
stage of mental development.

We will now pass to the worship of lakes, rivers, and
springs, which we shall find to have been not less widely
distributed. It was at one time very prevalent in Western
Europe. According to Cicero, Justin, and Strabo, there
was a lake near Toulouse in which the neighbouring
tribes used to deposit offerings of gold and silver. Tacitus,
Pliny, and Virgil also allude to sacred lakes. In the
sixth century, Gregory of Tours mentions a sacred lake
on mount Helanus.

In Brittany there is the celebrated well of St. Anne of
Auray, and the sacred fountain at Lanmeur in the crypt
of the church of St. Melars to which crowds of pilgrims
still resort.[2]

In our own country traces of water-worship are also
abundant. It is expressly mentioned by Gildas,[3] and is
said to be denounced in a Saxon homily preserved in
Cambridge.[4] 'At St. Fillans[5] well at Comrie, in Perth-
shire, numbers of persons in search of health, so late as
1791, came or were brought to drink of the waters and
bathe in it. All these walked or were carried three
times deasil (sunwise) round the well. They also threw
each a white stone on an adjacent cairn, and left behind a
scrap of their clothing as an offering to the genius of the
place.' In the Scotch islands also are many sacred wells,
and I have myself seen the sacred well in one of the

---

[1] De Brosses, loc. cit. p. 169.

[2] Early Races of Scotland, vol. i.
p. 158.

[3] Mon. Hist. Brit. vii.

[4] Wright's Superstitions of England.

[5] Early Races of Scotland, vol. i.
p. 156.

islands of Loch Maree, surrounded by the little offerings of the peasantry, consisting principally of rags and half-pence.

Colonel Forbes Leslie even says that in Scotland 'there are few parishes without a holy well;' nor was it much less general in Ireland. The kelpie, or spirit of the waters, assumed various forms, those of a man, woman, horse, or bull being the most common. Scotland and Ireland are full of legends about this spirit, a firm belief in the existence of which was general in the last century, and is even now far from abandoned.[1]

Of river-worship we have many cases recorded in Greek history.[2] Peleus dedicated a lock of Achilles' hair to the river Spercheios. The Pulians sacrificed a bull to Alpheios; Themis summoned the rivers to the great Olympian assembly. Okeanos the Ocean, and various fountains, were regarded as divinities. Water-worship in the time of Homer was however gradually fading away; and belonged rather I think to an earlier stage in development, than to a different race as supposed by Mr. Gladstone.[3]

In Northern Asia the Tunguses worship various springs.[4] De Brosses mentions that the river Sogd was worshipped at Samarcand.[5] Whipple[6] states that 'in the tenth century a schism took place in Persia among the Armenians; one party being accused of despising the holy well of Vagars-chiebat.'

The Bouriats also, though Buddhists, have sacred lakes. Atkinson thus describes one. In an after-dinner ramble, he says,[7] 'I came upon the small and picturesque lake of Ikeougoun, which lies in the mountains to the north of

[1] See Forbes Leslie's Early Races of Scotland, vol. i. p. 145. Campbell's Tales of the West Highlands.
[2] Juventus Mundi, p. 190.
[3] Loc. cit. pp. 177, 187.
[4] Pallas, vol. iv. p. 641.
[5] Loc. cit. p. 146.
[6] Report on the Indian Tribes, p. 44.
[7] Siberia, p. 445.

San-ghin-dalai, and is held in veneration. They have
erected a small wooden temple on the shore, and here
they come to sacrifice, offering up milk, butter, and
the fat of the animals, which they burn on the little
altars. The large rock in the lake is with them a sacred
stone, on which some rude figures are traced ; and on the
bank opposite they place rods with small silk flags, having
inscriptions printed on them.' Lake Ahoosh also is
accounted sacred among the Bashkirs.[1]

The divinity of water, says Dubois, ' is recognised by all
the people of India.' Besides the well-known worship of
the holy Ganges, the tribes of the Neilgherry Hills[2]
worship rivers under the name of Gangamma, and in
crossing them it was usual to drop a coin into the water
as an offering, and the price of a safe passage. In the
Deccan and in Ceylon, trees and bushes near springs may
often be seen covered with votive offerings.[3] The Khonds
also worship rivers and fountains.[4] The people of Sumatra
' are said to pay a kind of adoration to the sea, and to
make it an offering of cakes and sweetmeats on their be-
holding it for the first time, deprecating its power of doing
them harm.'[5]

The negroes on the Guinea Coast worshipped the sea.[6]

Herodotus mentions the existence of sacred fountains
among the Libyans.[7] In the Ashantee country, Bosman
mentions ' the Chamascian river, or Rio de San Juan,
called by the Negroes Bossum Pra, which they adore as a
god, as the word Bossum signifies.'[8] The Eufrates, the
principal river of Whydah, is also looked on as sacred,

---

[1] Atkinson's Oriental and Western
Siberia, p. 141.
[2] The Tribes of the Neilgherry Hills,
p. 68.
[3] Early Races of Scotland, vol. i.
p. 163.
[4] Ibid. vol. ii. p. 497.

[5] Marsden, loc. cit. p. 301.
[6] Bosman, Pinkerton's Voyages, vol.
xvi. p. 494. Smith's Voyage to Guinea,
p. 197. Astley's Collection of Voyages,
vol. ii. p. 26.
[7] Melpomene, clviii., clxxxi.
[8] Loc. cit. p. 348.

and a yearly procession is made to it.[1] Phillips[2] mentions, that on one occasion in 1690, when the sea was unusually rough, the Kabosheers complained to the king, who ' desired them to be easy, and he would make the sea quiet next day. Accordingly he sent his *fetishman* with a jar of palm oil, a bag of rice and corn, a jar of *pitto*, a bottle of brandy, a piece of painted calico, and several other things to present to the sea. Being come to the seaside (as the author was informed by his men, who saw the ceremony), he made a speech to it, assuring it that his king was its friend, and loved the white men; that they were honest fellows, and came to trade with him for what he wanted; and that he requested the sea not to be angry, nor hinder them to land their goods; he told it, that if it wanted palm oil, his king had sent it some; and so threw the jar with the oil into the sea, as he did, with the same compliment, the rice, corn, *pitto*, brandy, calico, &c.' Again, Villault[3] mentions that ' lakes, rivers, and ponds come in also for their share of worship. The author was present at a singular ceremony paid to a pond not far from the Danish fort, near Akkra, to entreat rain of it, the season having been very dry. A great number of blacks assembled about the pond, bringing with them a sheep, whose throat the priests cut in the banks of the salt pond, so that the blood ran into it, and mingled with the water. Then they made a fire, while others cut the beast in pieces which they broiled on the coals, and eat as fast as it was ready. This being over, some of them threw a gallipot into the pond, muttering some words. A Dane who was present, and spoke their language fluently, informed the author, in the name of the blacks, that this lake, or pond, being one of their deities, and the common messenger of

[1] Astley, *loc. cit.* p. 26.   ii. p. 411.
[2] Astley's Collection of Voyages, vol.   [3] *Ibid.* p. 668.

all the rivers of their country, they threw in the gallipots with these ceremonies to implore his assistance; and to beg him to carry immediately that pot in their name, to the other rivers and lakes to buy water for them, and hoped, at his return, he would pour the pot-full on their corn, that they might have a good crop.'

Some of the Negroes on the Guinea Coast[1] 'looked on the Whites as the gods of the sea; that the mast was a divinity that made the ship walk, and the pump was a miracle, since it could make water rise up, whose natural property is to descend.'

In North America the Dacotahs[2] worship a god of the waters, under the name of Unktahe. They say that 'this god and its associates are seen in their dreams. It is the master-spirit of all their juggling and superstitious belief. From it the medicine-men obtain their supernatural powers, and a great part of their religion springs from this god.' Franklin[3] mentions that the wife of one of his Indian guides being ill, her husband 'made an offering to the water-spirits, whose wrath he apprehended to be the cause of her malady. It consisted of a knife, a piece of tobacco, and some other trifling articles, which were tied up in a small bundle, and committed to the rapid.' Carver[4] observes that when the Redskins 'arrive on the borders of Lake Superior, on the banks of the Mississippi, or any other great body of water, they present to the spirit who resides there some kind of offering, as the prince of the Winnebagoes did when he attended me to the Falls of St. Anthony.' Tanner also gives instances of this custom.[5] On one occasion a Redskin, addressing

---

[1] Astley, vol. ii. p. 105.
[2] Schoolcraft's Indian Tribes, pt. iii. p. 485.
[3] Journey to the Shores of the Polar Sea, 1819–22, vol. ii. p. 245.
[4] Carver's Travels, p. 383.
[5] Narrative of the Captivity of John Tanner, p. 46.

the spirit of the waters ' told him that he had come a long way to pay his adorations to him, and now would make him the best offerings in his power. He accordingly first threw his pipe into the stream; then the roll that contained his tobacco; after these, the bracelets he wore on his arms and wrists; next an ornament that encircled his neck, composed of beads and wires; and at last the earings from his ears; in short, he presented to his god every part of his dress that was valuable.'[1]

The Mandans also were in the habit of sacrificing to the spirit of the waters.[2]

In North Mexico, near the 35th Parallel, Lieutenant Whipple found a sacred spring which from time immemorial ' had been held sacred to the rain-god. No animal may drink of its waters. It must be annually cleansed with ancient vases, which, having been transmitted from generation to generation by the caciques, are then placed upon the walls, never to be removed. The frog, the tortoise, and the rattlesnake, represented upon them, are sacred to Montezuma, the patron of the place, who would consume by lightning any sacrilegious hand that should dare to take the relics away. In Nicaragua rain was worshipped under the name of Quiateot. The principal water-god of Mexico, however, was Tlaloc, who was worshipped by the Toltecs, Chichimecs, and Aztecs.[4] In New Mexico, not far from Zuni, Dr. Bell[5] describes a sacred spring ' about eight feet in diameter, walled round with stones, of which neither cattle nor men may drink: the animals sacred to water (frogs, tortoises, and snakes) alone must enter the pool. Once a year the cacique and his attendants perform certain religious rites at the spring:

[1] *Loc. cit.* p. 67.
[2] Catlin's North American Indians, vol. i. p. 160.
[3] Report on the Indian Tribes, p. 40.
[4] Müller, Amer. Urrel., p. 496.
[5] Ethn. Journ. 1869, p. 227.

it is thoroughly cleared out; water-pots are brought as an offering to the spirit of Montezuma, and are placed bottom upwards on the top of the wall of stones. Many of these have been removed; but some still remain, while the ground around is strewn with fragments of vases which have crumbled into decay from age.'

In Peru the sea, under the name of Mama Cocha, was the principal deity of the Chinchas;[1] one branch of the Collas deduced their origin from a river, the others from a spring : there was also a special rain-goddess.

In Paraguay[2] also the rivers are propitiated by offerings of tobacco.

We will now pass to the worship of stones and mountains, a form of religion as general as those already described.

M. Dulaure, in his 'Histoire Abrégée des Cultes,' explains the origin of Stone-worship as arising from the respect paid to boundary stones. I do not doubt that the worship of some particular stones may thus have originated. Hermes or Termes was evidently of this character, and hence we may perhaps explain the peculiar characteristics of Hermes or Mercury, whose symbol was an upright stone.

Mercury or Hermes, says Lemprière, 'was the messenger of the gods. He was the patron of travellers and shepherds; he conducted the souls of the dead into the infernal regions, and not only presided over orators, merchants, and declaimers, but he was also the god of thieves, pickpockets, and all dishonest persons.' He invented the letters and the lyre, and was the originator of arts and sciences.

It is difficult at first to see the connection between .

---

[1] Müller, Amer. Urrel., p. 368.   [2] *Loc. cit.* p. 258.

these various offices, characterised as they are by such opposite peculiarities. Yet they all follow from the custom of marking boundaries by upright stones. Hence the name Hermes, or Termes the boundary. In the troublous times of old it was usual, in order to avoid disputes, to leave a tract of neutral territory between the possessions of different nations. These are called marches; hence the title of Marquis, which means an officer appointed to watch the frontier or 'march.' These marches not being cultivated served as grazing grounds. To them came merchants in order to exchange on neutral ground the products of their respective countries; here also for the same reason treaties were negotiated. Here again international games and sports were held. Upright stones were used to indicate places of burial; and lastly on them were engraved laws and decrees, records of remarkable events, and the praises of the deceased.

Hence Mercury, represented by a plain upright stone, was the god of travellers because he was a landmark, of shepherds as presiding over the pastures; he conducted the souls of the dead into the infernal regions, because even in very early days upright stones were used as tombstones; he was the god of merchants because commerce was carried on principally at the frontiers; and of thieves out of sarcasm. He was the messenger of the gods, because ambassadors met at the frontiers; and of eloquence for the same reason. He invented the lyre and presided over games, because contests in music, &c. were held on neutral ground; and he invented letters, because inscriptions were engraved on upright pillars.

Stone-worship, however, in its simpler forms has, I think, a different origin from this, and is merely a form of that indiscriminate worship which characterises the human mind in a particular phase of development.

Pallas states that the Ostyaks[1] and Tunguses worship
mountains,' [2] and the Tatars stones.[3]   Near Lake Baikal[4]
is a sacred rock which is regarded as the special abode of
an evil spirit, and is consequently much feared by the
natives.   In India stone-worship is very prevalent.   The
Asagas of Mysore 'worship a god called Bhuma Devam,
who is represented by a shapeless stone.'[5]   ' One thing is
certain,' says Mr. Hislop, ' the worship (of stones) is spread
over all parts of the country, from Berar to the extreme
east of Bustar, and that not merely among the Hinduised
aborigines, who had begun to honour Khandova, &c., but
among the rudest and most savage tribes.   He is generally
adored in the form of an unshapely stone covered with
vermilion.'[6]   'Two rude slave castes in Tulava (Southern
India), the Bakadara and Betadára, worship a benevolent
deity named Buta, represented by a stone kept in every
house.'[7]   Indeed, ' in every part of Southern India, four or
five stones may often be seen in the ryots' field, placed in
a row and daubed with red paint, which they consider as
guardians of the field and call the five Pandus.'[8]   Colonel
Forbes Leslie supposes that this red paint is intended to
represent blood.[9]   The god of each Khond village is
represented by three stones.[10]   Pl. IV. represents a group
of sacred stones, near Delgaum in the Dekkan, from a
figure given by Colonel Forbes Leslie in his interesting
work.[11]   The three largest stood ' in front of the centre of
two straight lines, each of which consisted of thirteen
stones.   These lines were close together, and the edges of

[1] Voyages de Pallas, vol. iv. p. 79.
[2] *Ibid*. pp. 434, 648.
[3] *Ibid*. pp. 514, 598.
[4] Hill's Travels in Siberia, vol. ii.
p. 142.
[5] Buchanan's Journey, vol. i. p. 338.
Quoted in Ethnol. Journ. vol. viii. p. 96.
[6] Aboriginal Tribes, p. 16.   Quoted

in Ethnol. Journ. vol. viii. p. 96.
[7] Journ. Ethnol. Soc. vol. viii. p. 115.
[8] *Ibid*. vol. ix. p. 125.
[9] Early Races of Scotland, vol. ii.
p. 462.
[10] *Loc. cit*. vol. ii. p. 497.
[11] *Loc. cit*. vol. ii. p. 464.

INDIAN SACRED STONES.

Plate IV.

the stones were placed as near to each other as it was possible to do with slabs which, although selected, had never been artificially shaped. The stone in the centre of each line was nearly as high as the highest of the three that stood in front, but the others gradually decreased in size from the centre, until those at the ends were less than a foot above the ground, into which they were all secured. Three stones, not fixed, were placed in front of the centre of the group; they occupied the same position, and were intended for the same purposes, as those in the circular temple just described. All the stones had been selected of an angular shape, with somewhat of an obelisk form in general appearance. The central group and double lines faced nearly east, and on that side were whitewashed. On the white, near, although not reaching quite to the apex of each stone, nor extending altogether to the sides, was a large spot of red paint, two-thirds of which from the centre were blackened over, leaving only a circular external belt of red. This gave, as I believe it was intended to do, a good representation of a large spot of blood.'

In connection with these painted stones it is remarkable that in New Zealand red is a sacred colour, and 'the way of rendering anything tapu was by making it red. When a person died, his house was thus painted; when the tapu was laid on anything, the chief erected a post and painted it with the kura; wherever a corpse rested, some memorial was set up; oftentimes the nearest stone, rock, or tree served as a monument; but whatever object was selected, it was sure to be painted red. If the corpse was conveyed by water, wherever they landed a similar token was left; and when it reached its destination, the canoe was dragged on shore, painted red, and abandoned. When the hahunga took place, the scraped bones of the chief thus ornamented, and wrapped in a red-stained mat, were deposited in a box or bowl smeared with the sacred colour, and placed in a painted tomb. Near his final resting-place a lofty and elaborately carved monument was erected to his memory; this was called the tiki, which was also thus coloured.'[1] Red was also a sacred colour in Congo.[2]

Colonel Dalton describes[3] a ceremony which, as he truly observes, curiously resembles the well-known scene in the life of Elijah, when he recalled Israel to the old faith by producing rain when the priests of Baal had failed to do so. The Sonthals worship a conspicuous hill called 'Marang Boroo.' In times of drought they go to the top of the sacred mountain, and offer their sacrifices on a large flat stone, playing on drums and beseeching their god for rain. 'They shake their heads violently, till they work themselves into a phrensy, and the movement becomes involuntary. They go on thus wildly gesticulating, till a "little cloud like a man's hand" is seen. Then they arise, take up the drums, and dance the kurrun on the rock, till Marang Boroo's response to their prayer is heard in the distant rumbling of thunder, and they go home rejoicing. They must go "fasting to the mount," and stay there till "there is a sound of abundance of rain," when they get them down to eat and drink. My informant tells me it always comes before evening.'

The Arabians also down to the time of Mahomet worshipped a black stone. The Phœnicians also worshipped a deity under the form of an unshaped stone.[4] The god Heliogabalus was merely a black stone of a conical form. Upright stones were worshipped by the Romans and the Greeks under the name of Hermes or Mercury. The

---

[1] Taylor's New Zealand and the New Zealanders, p. 95.

[2] Merolla, Pinkerton, vol. xvi. p. 273.

[3] Trans. Ethn. Soc. N. S. vol. vi. p. 35.

[4] Kenrick's Phœnicia, p. 323.

Thespians had a rude stone which they regarded as a deity, and the Bœotians worshipped Hercules under the same form.[1] The Laplanders also had sacred mountains and rocks.[2]

In Western Europe during the middle ages we meet with several denunciations of stone-worship, proving its deep hold on the people. Thus ' the worship[3] of stones was condemned by Theodoric, Archbishop of Canterbury, in the seventh century, and is among the acts of heathenism forbidden by King Edgar in the tenth, and by Cnut in the eleventh century. In a council held at Tours in A.D. 567 priests were admonished to shut the doors of their churches against all persons worshipping upright stones, and Mahé states that a manuscript record of the proceedings of a council held at Nantes in the seventh century makes mention of the stone-worship of the Americans.'

' Les Français,' says Dulaure,[4] ' adorèrent des pierres plusieurs siècles après l'établissement du christianisme parmi eux. Diverses lois civiles et religieuses attestent l'existence de ce culte. Un capitulaire de Charlemagne, et le concile de Leptine, de l'an 743, défendent les cérémonies superstitieuses qui se pratiquent auprès des pierres et auprès des Fans consacrés à Mercure et Jupiter. Le concile de Nantes, cité par Réginon, fait la même défense. Il nous apprend que ces pierres étaient situées dans des lieux agrestes, et que le peuple, dupe des tromperies des démons, y apportait ses vœux et ses offrandes. Les conciles d'Arles, de Tours, le capitulaire d'Aix-la-Chapelle, de l'an 789, et plusieurs synodes, renouvellent ces prohibitions.'

In Ireland in the fifth century, King Laoghaire worshipped a stone pillar called the Crom-Cruach, which was

---

[1] See De Brosses, *loc. cit.* p. 155.
[2] Dulaure, *loc. cit.* p. 50.
[3] Forbes Leslie, *loc. cit.* vol. i. p. 256.
[4] Dulaure, *loc. cit.* vol. i. p. 304.

overthrown by St. Patrick.   Another stone at Clogher was
worshipped by the Irish under the name of Kermand-
Kelstach.[1]   There was a sacred stone in Jura[2] round
which the people used to move ' deasil,' i.e. sunwise.   ' In
some of the Hebrides[3] the people attributed oracular
power to a large black stone.'   In the island of Skye ' in
every district there is to be met with a rude stone consecrated to Gruagach or Apollo.   The Rev. Mr. McQueen of
Skye says that in almost every village the sun, called
Grugach or the Fair-haired, is represented by a rude stone ;
and he further states that libations of milk were poured
on the gruaich-stones.'

Passing to Africa, Caillié observed near the negro village
of N'pal a sacred stone, on which everyone as he passed
threw a thread out of his ' pagne ' or breech cloth, as a sort
of offering.   The natives firmly believe that when any
danger threatens the village, this stone leaves its place
and ' moves thrice round it in the preceding night, by
way of warning.'[4]

Bruce observes that the pagan Abyssinians ' worship a
tree, and likewise a stone.'[5]

The Tahitians believed in two principal gods ;   ' the
Supreme Deity, one of these two first beings, they call
Taroataihetoomoo, and the other, whom they suppose to
have been a rock, Tepapa.'[6]

In the Feejee[7] Islands ' rude consecrated stones (fig. 20)
are to be seen near Vuna, where offerings of food are
sometimes made.   Another stands on a reef near Naloa
to which the natives tama ; and one near Thokova, Na
Viti Levu, named Lovekaveka, is regarded as the abode of

[1] Dr. Todd's St. Patrick, p. 127.
[2] Martin's Western Isles, p. 241.
[3] Forbes Leslie, loc. cit. vol. i. p.
257.
[4] Caillié, vol. i. p. 25.

[5] Bruce's Travels, vol. vi. p. 343.
[6] Hawkesworth's Voyages, vol. ii.
p. 238.
[7] Williams' Fiji and the Fijians,
vol. i. p. 220.

a goddess, for whom food is provided. This, as seen in the engraving, is like a round black milestone, slightly inclined, and having a liku (girdle) tied round the middle. The shrine of O Rewau is a large stone, which, like the one near Naloa, hates mosquitoes, and keeps them from collecting near where he rules; he has also two large stones for his wives,

Fig. 20.

SACRED STONES. (Feejee Islands.)

one of whom came from Yandua, and the other from Yasawa. Although no one pretends to know the origin of Ndengei, it is said that his mother, in the form of two great stones, lies at the bottom of a moat. Stones are also used to denote the locality of some other gods, and the occasional resting places of others. On the southern beaches of Vanua Levu, a large stone is seen which has fallen upon a smaller one. These, it is said, represent the gods of two towns on that coast fighting, and their quarrel

has for years been adopted by those towns. The Sumatrans also, as already mentioned (*antè*, p. 195), had sacred
stones.

Prescott[1] says, that a Dacotah Indian ' will pick up a
round stone, of any kind, and paint it, and go a few rods
from his lodge, and clean away the grass, say from one to
two feet in diameter, and there place his stone, or god, as
he would term it, and make an offering of some tobacco
and some feathers, and pray to the stone to deliver him
from some danger that he has probably dreamed of, or
from imagination.'

The Monitarris also before any great undertaking were
in the habit of making offerings to a sacred stone named
Mih Choppenish.[2] In Florida a mountain called Olaimi
was worshipped, and the Natchez of Louisiana had a deity
which was a conical stone.[3]

Fire-worship is so widely distributed as to be almost
universal. Since the introduction of lucifer matches we
can hardly appreciate the difficulty which a savage has in
obtaining a light, especially in damp weather. It is said,
however, that some Australian tribes did not know how
to do so, and that others, if their fire went out, would
go many miles to borrow a spark from another tribe,
rather than attempt to produce a new one for themselves.
Hence in several very widely separated parts of the
world we find it has been customary to tell off some one
or more persons whose sole duty it should be to keep up
a continual fire. Hence, no doubt, the origin of the Vestal
virgins, and hence also the idea of the sacredness of fire
would naturally arise.

According to Lafitau,[4] M. Huet, in a work which I have

[1] Schoolcraft's Indian Tribes, vol.   p. 178.
ii. p. 229. Lafitau, vol. ii. p. 321.   [3] Lafitau, vol. i. p. 146.
[2] Klemm, Cultur. geschichte, vol. ii.   [4] *Loc. cit.* vol. i. p. 153.

not been able to see, 'fait une longue énumération des peuples qui entretenoient ce feu sacré, et il cite partout ses autorités, de sorte qu'il paroît qu'il n'y avoit point de partie du monde connu, où ce culte ne fût universellement répandu. Dans l'Asie, outre les Juifs et les Chaldéens dont nous venons de parler, outre les peuples de Phrygie, de Lycie, et de l'Asie-Mineure, il étoit encore chez les Perses, les Mèdes, les Scythes, les Sarmates, chez toutes les nations du Ponte et de la Cappadoce, chez toutes celles des Indes, où l'on se faisoit un devoir de se jeter dans les flammes, et de s'y consumer en holocauste, et chez toutes celles des deux Arabies, où chaque jour à certaines heures on faisoit un sacrifice au feu, dans lequel plusieurs personnes se dévouoient. Dans l'Afrique il étoit non-seulement chez les Égyptiens, qui entretenoient ce feu immortel dans chaque temple, ainsi que l'assure Porphyre, mais encore dans l'Éthiopie, dans la Lybie, dans le temple de Jupiter Ammon, et chez les Atlantiques, où Hiarbas, roy des Garamantes et des Getules, avoit dressé cent autels, et consacré autant de feux, que Virgile appelle des feux vigilans et les gardes éternelles des dieux. Dans l'Europe le culte de Vesta· étoit si bien établi, que, sans parler de Rome et de l'Italie, il n'y avoit point de ville de la Grèce qui n'eut un temple, un prytanée, et un feu éternel, ainsi que le remarque Casaubon dans ses " Notes sur Athénée." Les temples célèbres d'Hercule dans les Espagnes, et dans les Gaules, celui de Vulcain au Mont Ethna, de Venus Erycine, avoient tous leurs pyrèthes ou feux sacrés. On peut citer de semblables témoignages des nations les plus reculées dans le nord, qui étoient toutes originaires des Scythes et des Sarmates. Enfin M. Huet prétend qu'il n'y a pas encore long-temps que ce culte a été aboli dans l'Hybernie et dans la Moscovie, qu'il est encore aujourd'hui, non-seulement chez les Gaures, mais encore chez les Tartares, les Chinois, et dans l'Amérique chez les Mexiquains. Il pouvoit encore en ajouter d'autres.'

The Natchez had a temple in which they kept up a perpetual fire.[1] The Ojibwas[2] maintained ' a continual fire as a symbol of their nationality. They maintained also a civil polity, which, however, was much mixed up with their religious and medicinal beliefs.' In Mexico also we find the same idea of sacred fire. Colonel McLeod has seen the sacred fire still kept burning in some of the valleys of South Mexico.[3] At the great festival of Xiuh-molpia, the priests and people went in procession to the mountain of Huixachtecatl; then an unfortunate victim was stretched on the ' stone of sacrifice,' and killed by a priest with a knife of obsidian; the dish made use of to kindle the new fire was then placed on the wound, and fire was obtained by friction.[4]

In Peru[5] ' the sacred flame was entrusted to the care of the virgins of the sun; and if, by any neglect, it was suffered to go out in the course of the year, the event was regarded as a calamity that boded some strange disaster to the monarchy.'

Fire is also regarded as sacred in Congo.

No one can wonder that the worship of sun, moon, and stars is very widely distributed. It can, however, scarcely be regarded as of a higher character than the preceding forms of Totemism; it is unknown in Australia, and almost so in Africa.

In hot countries the sun is generally regarded as an evil, and in cold as a beneficent, being. It was the chief

[1] Lafitau, vol. i. p. 167.
[2] Warren in Schoolcraft's Indian Tribes, vol. ii. p. 138. See also Whipple's Report on Indian Tribes, p. 36.
[3] Jour. Ethn. Soc. 1869, p. 225. See also p. 246.
[4] Humboldt's Researches, London, 1824, vol. i. pp. 225, 382. Lafitau, vol. i. p. 170.
[5] Prescott, vol. i. p. 99.

object of religious worship among the Natchez,[1] and was also worshipped by the Navajos, and other allied tribes in N. America.[2] Among the Comanches of Texas 'the sun, moon, and earth are the principal objects of worship.'[3] Lafitau observes that the Americans did not worship the stars and planets, but only the sun.[4] The Ahts of North-west America worship both the sun and moon, but especially the latter. They regard the sun as feminine and the moon as masculine, being, moreover, the husband of the sun.[5] It has been said that the Esquimaux of Greenland used to worship the sun. This, however, seems more than doubtful, and Crantz[6] expressly denies the statement.

In South America the Coroados worship the sun and moon, the moon being the greatest.[7] The Abipones[8] thought that they were descended from the Pleiades, and 'as that constellation disappears at certain periods from the sky of South America, upon such occasions they suppose that their grandfather is sick, and are under a yearly apprehension that he is going to die: but as soon as those seven stars are again visible in the month of May, they welcome their grandfather, as if returned and re-stored from sickness, with joyful shouts, and the festive sound of pipes and trumpets, congratulating him on the recovery of his health.'

In Central India ' the worship of the sun as the Supreme Deity is the foundation of the religion of the Hos and

[1] Robertson's America, bk. iv. p. 126.
[2] Whipple's Report on Indian Tribes, p. 36. Lafitau, vol. ii. p. 189. Tertre's History of the Caribby Islands, p. 236.
[3] Neighbors in Schoolcraft's Indian Tribes, vol. ii. p. 127.
[4] Loc. cit. vol. i. p. 146.
[5] Sproat's Scenes and Studies of Savage Life, p. 206.
[6] Loc. cit. vol. i. p. 196. See also Graah's Voyage to Greenland, p. 124.
[7] Spix and Martius, vol. ii. p. 243.
[8] Loc. cit. vol. ii. p. 65.

Oraons as well as of the Moondahs. By the former he is
invoked as Dhurmi, the Holy One.   He is the Creator and
the Preserver, and with reference to his purity, white
animals are offered to him by his votaries.'[1] The sun and
moon are both regarded as deities by the Khonds, though
no ceremonial worship is addressed to them.[2]   In Northern
Asia the Samoyedes are said to have worshipped the sun
and moon.

As might naturally be expected from their habits, and
particularly from their partiality for nocturnal ceremonies,
we find traces of moon-worship among the Negroes.   In
Western Africa, according to Merolla,[3] ' at the appearance
of every new moon, these people fall on their knees, or else
cry out, standing and clapping their hands, " So may I
renew my life as thou art renewed." '   They do not, however, appear to venerate either the sun or the stars. Bruce
also mentions moon-worship as occurring among the
Shangallas.[4]

It is remarkable that the heavenly bodies do not appear
to be worshipped by the Polynesians.

According to Lord Kames, ' the inhabitants of Celebes
formerly acknowledged no gods but the sun and moon.'[5]
The people of Borneo also are said to have done the same.

Thus, then, I have attempted to show that animals and
plants, water, mountains and stones, fire and the heavenly
bodies, are, or have been, all very extensively worshipped.

These, indeed, are the principal deities of man in this
stage of his religious development.   They are, however,
by no means the only ones.   The Scythians worshipped
an iron scimetar as a symbol of Mars; ' to this scimetar

---

[1] Colonel Dalton, Trans. Ethn. Soc.,
vol. vi. p. 33.

[2] Forbes Leslie. Early Races of
Scotland, vol. ii. p. 496.

[3] Voyage to Congo, Pinkerton, vol.

xv. p. 273.

[4] Travels, vol. iv. p. 35, vol. vi. p.
344.

[5] History of Man, vol. iv. p. 252.

they bring yearly sacrifices of cattle and horses; and to these scimetars they offer more sacrifices than to the rest of their gods.'[1]   In the Sagas many of the swords have special names, and are treated with the greatest respect.   Similarly the Feejeeans regarded ' certain clubs with superstitious respect;'[2] and the Negroes of Irawo, a town in Western Yoruba, worshipped an iron bar with very expensive ceremonies.[3]   The New Zealanders and some of the Melanesians worshipped the rainbow.[4]

In Central India, as mentioned in p. 191, a great variety of inanimate objects are treated as deities.   The Todas are said to worship a buffalo-bell.[5]   The Kotas worship two silver plates, which they regard as husband and wife; 'they have no other deity.'[6]   The Kurumbas worship stones, trees, and anthills.   The Toreas, another Neilgherry Hill tribe, worship especially a ' gold nose-ring, which probably once belonged to one of their women.'[8]   Many other inanimate objects have also been worshipped.   De Brosses even mentions an instance of a king of hearts being made into a deity.[9]   According to Nonnius, the sacred lyre sang the victory of Jupiter over the Titans without being touched.[10]

According to some of the earlier travellers in America, even the rattle was regarded as a deity.[11]   ' Thévet, Hierôme Staad, et le Sieur de Léri, qui nous ont donné les premières relations des mœurs des Brésiliens, paroissent persuadée que ces peuples regardent ces Maraca ou Tamaraca comme une espèce de divinité; qu'ils les hono-

---

[1] Her. iv. 62. See also Klemm, Werkzeuge und Waffen, p. 225.
[2] Fiji and the Fijians, vol. i. p. 219.
[3] Burton's Abbeokuta, vol. i. p. 192.
[4] Trans. Ethn. Soc. 1870, p. 367.
[5] The Tribes of the Neilgherries, p. 15.
[6] Ibid. p. 114.
[7] Trans. Ethn. Soc. vol. vii. p. 278.
[8] The Tribes of the Neilgherries, p. 67.
[9] Loc. cit. p. 52.
[10] Lafitau, vol. i. p. 205.
[11] Ibid. p. 211.

rent d'un culte religieux ; qu'ils s'en servent dans toutes les occasions où la religion a quelque part ; que chaque ménage a le sien, à qui il offre constamment des offrandes; et surtout que leur usage est tellement consacré à la divination, que ces sauvages semblent croire que ces Maraca font le siége, le lieu de la résidence de l'esprit, qui les inspire, et qui de-là parle d'une manière claire, distincte, et leur fait savoir toutes ses volontés.'

CHAPTER VI.

RELIGION (*concluded*).

IN order to realise clearly the essential characteristics of the religions of different races, we must bear in mind that in the stage at which we have now arrived in the course of our enquiry, the modifications of which a religion is susceptible may be divided into two classes, viz., developmental and adaptational. I use the term 'developmental' to signify those changes which arise from the intellectual progress of the race. Thus a more elevated idea of the Deity is a developmental change. On the other hand, a northern people is apt to look on the sun as a beneficent deity, while to a tropical race he would suggest drought and destruction. Again, hunters tend to worship the moon, agriculturists the sun. These I call adaptational modifications. They are changes produced, not by difference of race or of civilisation, but by physical causes.

In some cases the character of the language has probably exercised much influence over that of religion. No one, for instance, can fail to be struck by the differences existing between the Aryan and Semitic religions. All Aryan races have a complicated mythology, which is not the case with the Semitic races. Moreover, the character of the gods is quite different. The latter have El, Strong; Bel or Baal, Lord; Adonis, Lord; Shet, Master; Moloch, King; Ram and Rimmon, the Exalted; and other similar names for their deities. The Aryans, on the contrary, Zeus, the sky; Phœbus Apollo, the sun; Neptune, the sea; Mars, war; Venus, beauty, &c. Max Müller[1] has very ingeniously endeavoured to explain this difference by the different character of the language in these two races.

In Semitic words the root remains always distinct and unmistakeable. In Aryan, on the contrary, it soon becomes altered and disguised. Hence Semitic dictionaries are mostly arranged according to the roots, a method which in Aryan languages would be most inconvenient, the root being often obscure, and in many cases doubtful. Now take such an expression as 'the sky thunders.' In any Semitic tongue the word 'sky' would remain unaltered, and so clear in its meaning, that it would with difficulty come to be thought of as a proper name. But among the Aryans the Sanskrit Dyaus, the sky, became the Greek Zeus, and when the Greek said $Z\varepsilon \dot{v}s \ \beta\rho o\nu\tau\tilde{q}$ his idea was not the sky thunders, but 'Zeus thunders.' When the Gods were thus once created, the mythology follows as a matter of course. Some of the statements may be obscure, but when we are told that Hupnos, the god of sleep, was the father of Morpheus, the god of dreams; or that Venus married to Vulcan, lost her heart to Mars, and that the intrigue was made known to Vulcan by Apollo, the sun, we can clearly see how such myths might have arisen.

The attitude of the ancients towards them is very interesting. Homer and Hesiod relate them, apparently without suspicion, and we may be sure that the uneducated public received them without a doubt. Socrates, however, explains the story that Boreas carried off Oreithyia from the Ilissos, to mean that Oreithyia was blown off the rocks by the north wind. Ovid also says

---

[1] See Müller's Chips from a German Workshop, vol. i. p. 363.

that under the name of Vesta, mere fire is to be understood. We can hardly doubt that many others also must
have clearly perceived the origin of at any rate a portion
of these myths, but they were probably restrained from
expressing their opinion by the dread of incurring the
odium of heterodoxy.

One great charm of this explanation is that we thus
remove some of the revolting features of ancient myths.
Thus as the sun destroys the darkness from which it
springs, and at evening disappears in the twilight; so
Œdipus was fabled to have killed his father, and then
married his mother. In this way the whole of that terrible
story may be explained as arising, not from the depravity
of the human heart, but from a mistaken application of
the statement that the sun destroys the darkness, and
ultimately marries, as it were, the twilight from which it
sprang.

But although Poetry may thus throw much light on the
origin of the myths which formed the religion of Greece
and Rome, it cannot explain the origin or character of
religion among the lower savages, because a mythology such
as that of Greece and Rome can only arise amongst a people
which have already made considerable progress. Tempting,
therefore, as it may be to seek in the nature of language
and the use of poetical expressions, an explanation of the
religious systems of the lower races, and fully admitting
the influence which these causes have exercised, we must
look deeper for the origin of religion, and can be satisfied
only by an explanation which is applicable to the lowest
races possessing any religious opinions. In the preceding
chapters I have attempted to do this, and to show how
certain phenomena, as for instance sleep and dreams, pain,
disease, and death, have naturally created in the savage
mind a belief in the existence of mysterious and invisible

Beings.   The last chapter was devoted to Totemism, and
we now pass to what may be most conveniently termed
'Shamanism.'

SHAMANISM.

As Totemism overlies Fetichism so does Shamanism
overlie Totemism.   The word is derived from the name
used in Siberia, where the 'Shamans' work themselves up
into a fury, supposing or pretending that in this condition
they are inspired by the Spirit in whose name they speak,
and through whose inspiration they are enabled to answer
questions and to foretell the future.   In the phases of
religion hitherto considered (the deities, if indeed they
deserve the name), are regarded as visible to all, and
present amongst us.   Shamanism is a considerable advance,
inasmuch as it presents us with a higher conception of
religion.   Although the name is Siberian, the phase of
thought is widely distributed, and seems to be a necessary
stage in the progress of religious development.   Those
who are disposed to adopt the view advocated in this work
will not be surprised to find that 'Shamanism' is no
definite system of theology.   Wrangel, however, regarding
Shamanism as religion in the ordinary sense, was astonished
at this : 'it is remarkable,' he says, 'that Shamanism has
no dogmas of any kind; it is not a system taught or
handed down from one to another; though it is so widely
spread, it seems to originate with each individual separately, as the fruit of a highly excited imagination, acted
upon by external impressions, which closely resemble each
other throughout the deserts of Northern Siberia.'[1]

It is far from easy in practice always to distinguish
Shamanism from Totemism on the one hand, and Idolatry

---

[1] Siberia and Polar Sea, p. 123.

on the other. The main difference lies in the conception
of the Deity. In Totemism the deities inhabit our earth,
in Shamanism they live generally in a world of their own,
and trouble themselves little about what is passing here.
The Shaman is occasionally honoured by the presence
of Deity, or is allowed to visit the heavenly regions.
Among the Esquimaux the 'Angekok' answers precisely
to the Shaman. Graah thus describes a scene in Greenland.

The Angekok came in the evening, and, 'the lamps [1]
being extinguished, and skins hung before the windows
(for such arts, for evident reasons, are best practised in
the dark), took his station on the floor, close by a well-
dried seal-skin there suspended, and commenced rattling
it, beating the tambourine and singing, in which last he
was seconded by all present. From time to time his chant
was interrupted by a cry of " Goie, Goie, Goie, Goie, Goie,
Goie !" the meaning of which I did not comprehend,
coming first from one corner of the hut, and then from
the other. Presently all was quiet, nothing being heard
but the angekok puffing and blowing as if struggling with
something superior to him in strength, and then again a
sound resembling somewhat that of castanets, whereupon
commenced once more the same song as before, and the
same cry of " Goie, Goie, Goie !" In this way a whole
hour elapsed before the wizard could make the torngak,
or spirit, obey his summons. Come he did, however, at
last, and his approach was announced by a strange rushing
sound, very like the sound of a large bird flying beneath
the roof. The angekok still chanting, now proposed his
questions, which were replied to in a voice quite strange
to my ears, but which seemed to me to proceed from the
entrance passage, near which the angekok had taken

[1] Graah's Voyage to Greenland, p. 123. See also Egede's Greenland, p. 183.

his station. These responses, however, were somewhat oracular, insomuch that Ernenek's wives were obliged to request some more explicit answer, whereupon they received the comfortable assurance that he was alive and well, and would shortly make his appearance.'

The account given by Crantz agrees with the above in all essential particulars.[1]

Williams gives the following very similar account of a scene in Fiji:—'Unbroken silence follows; the priest becomes absorbed in thought and all eyes watch him with unblinking steadiness. In a few minutes he trembles; slight distortions are seen in his face, and twitching movements in his limbs. These increase to a violent muscular action, which spreads until the whole frame is strongly convulsed, and the man shivers as with a strong ague fit. In some instances this is accompanied with murmurs and sobs, the veins are greatly enlarged and the circulation of the blood quickened. The priest is now possessed by his god, and all his words and actions are considered as no longer his own, but those of the deity who has entered into him. Shrill cries of "Koi au, Koi au!" "It is I, It is I!" fill the air, and the god is supposed thus to notify his approach. While giving the answer, the priest's eyes stand out and roll as in a frenzy; his voice is unnatural, has face pale, his lips livid, his breathing depressed, and his entire appearance like that of a furious madman; the sweat runs from every pore, and tears start from his strained eyes; after which the symptoms gradually disappear. The priest looks round with a vacant stare, and, as the god says, "I depart," announces his actual departure by violently flinging himself down on the mat, or by suddenly striking the ground with his club, when

[1] History of Greenland, vol. i. p. 210.   [2] Fiji and the Fijians, vol. i. p. 224.

those at a distance are informed by blasts on the conch, or the firing of a musket, that the deity has returned into the world of spirits. The convulsive movements do not entirely disappear for some time.' The process described by Dobritzhoffer [1] as occurring among the Abipones is also somewhat similar.

Among the Negroes of W. Africa Brue [2] mentions a 'prophet' who pretended 'to be inspired by the Deity in such a manner as to know the most hidden secrets; and go invisible wherever he pleased, as well as to make his voice be heard at the greatest distance. His disciples and accomplices attested the truth of what he said by a thousand fabulous relations; so that the common people, always credulous and fond of novelty, readily gave in to the cheat.'

Colonel Dalton states that 'the paganism of the Ho and Moondah in all essential features is shamanistic.'[3]

IDOLATRY.

The worship of Idols characterises a somewhat higher stage of human development. We find no traces of it among the lowest races of men; and Lafitau [4] says truly, ' On peut dire en général que le grand nombre des peuples sauvages n'a point d'idoles.' The error of regarding Idolatry as the general religion of low races, has no doubt mainly arisen from confusing the Idol and the Fetich. Fetichism, however, is an attack on the Deity, Idolatry is an act of submission to him; rude, no doubt, but yet humble. Hence Fetichism and Idolatry are not only different, but opposite, so that the one could not be developed directly out of the other. We must therefore

[1] History of the Abipones, vol. ii. p. 73.
[2] Astley's Collection of Voyages, vol. ii. p. 83.
[3] Trans. Ethn. Soc. 1868, p. 32.
[4] Mœurs des Sauvages Américains, vol. i. p. 151.

expect to find between them, as indeed we do, a stage of religion without either the one or the other.

Neither among the Esquimaux nor the Tinne,' says Richardson, 'did I observe any image or visible object of worship.'[1] Carver states that the Canadian Indians had no idols;[2] and this seems to have been true of the North American Indians generally. Lafitau mentions as an exception the existence of an idol named Oki in Virginia.[3]

In Eastern Africa Burton states that he knows ' but one people, the Wanyika, who have certain statuettes called Kisukas.' Nor do the West African negroes worship idols.[4] It is true that some writers mention idols, but the context almost always shows that fetiches are really meant. In the kingdom of Whydah ' Agoye' was represented under the form of a deformed black man from whose head proceed lizards and snakes,[5] offering a striking similarity to some of the Indian idols. This is, however, an exceptional case. Battel only mentions particularly two idols;[6] and Bosman[7] expressly says that ' on the Gold Coast the natives are not in the least acquainted with image-worship ; adding, ' but at Ardra there are thousands of idols,' i.e. fetiches. At Loango there was a small black image named Chikokke, which was placed in a little house close to the port.[8] These, however, were merely fetiches in human form. Thus we are told by the same author that in Kakongo, the kingdom which lies to the south of Loango, the natives during the plague ' burnt their idols, saying, *If they will not help us in such a misfortune as this, when can we expect they should?'*[9] Thus, apparently, doubting not so much their power as their will. Again, in Congo, the

[1] Boat Journey, vol. ii. p. 44.

[2] Travels, p. 387.

[3] Vol. i. p. 168.

[4] Astley's Collection of Voyages, vol. ii. p. 240 for Futa, and for Guinea as far as Ardrah, p. 666.

[5] Astley's Collection of Voyages, pp. 26 and 50.

[6] Adventures of A. Battel. Pinkerton, vol. xvi. p. 331.

[7] Bosman's Guinea. Pinkerton, *loc. cit.* p. 403.

[8] Astley, *loc. cit.* p. 216.

[9] Astley, *loc. cit.* p. 217.

so-called idols are placed in fields to protect the growing crops.[1] This is clearly the function of a fetich, not of a true idol.

Idolatry, says Williams of the Fijian, ' he seems never to have known; for he makes no attempt to fashion material representations of his gods.'[2] As regards the New Zealanders, Yate[3] says, that 'though remarkably superstitious, they have no gods that they worship; nor have they anything to represent a being which they call God.' Dieffenbach also observes that in New Zealand ' there is no worship of idols, or of bodily representations of the Atoua.'[4]

Speaking of the Singè Dyaks,[5] Sir James Brooke says, ' Religion they have none; and although they know the name for a god' (which is probably taken from the Hindoos), ' they have no priests nor idols, say no prayers, offer no offerings.' He subsequently modified this opinion on some points, but as regards the absence of idols it seems to be correct.

The Kols of Central India worship the sun, ' material idol worship they have none.'[6] Originally, says Dubois, the Hindoos did not resort ' to images of stone or other materials. . . . but when the people of India had deified their heroes or other mortals, they began then, and not before, to have recourse to statues and images.'[7] In China ' it is observable[8] that there is not to be found, in the canonical books, the least footstep of idolatrous worship till the image of Fo was brought into China, several ages, after Confucius.'

The Ostyaks never made an image of their god

[1] Astley, *loc. cit.* vol. iii. p. 229.
[2] Fiji and the Fijians, vol. i. p. 216.
[3] *Loc. cit.* p. 141.
[4] *Loc. cit.* vol. ii. p. 118.
[5] Keppel's Expedition to Borneo, vol. i. p. 231.
[6] Dalton, Trans. Ethn. Soc., N. S., vol. vi. p. 32.
[7] Dubois, The People of India, p. 370
[8] Astley, vol. iv. p. 203.

'Toruim.'[1] In fact, idols do not occur until we arrive at the stage of the highest Polynesian Islanders. Even then they are often, as Ellis expressly tells us,[2] mere shapeless pieces of wood; thus leaving much to the imagination. It may, I think, be laid down almost as a constant rule, that mankind arrives at the stage of monarchy in government before he reaches idolatry in religion.

The idol usually assumes the human form, and idolatry is closely connected with that form of religion which consists in the worship of ancestors. We have already seen how imperfectly uncivilised man realises the conception of death; and we cannot wonder that death and sleep should long have been intimately connected together in the human mind. The savage, however, knows well that in sleep the spirit lives, even though the body appears to be dead. Morning after morning he rouses himself, and sees others rise, from sleep. Naturally therefore he endeavours to rouse the dead. Nor can we wonder at the very general custom of providing food and other necessaries for the use of the dead. Among races leading a settled and quiet life this habit would tend to continue longer and longer. Prayers to the dead would reasonably follow from such customs, for even without attributing a greater power to the dead than to the living, they might yet, from their different sphere and nature, exercise a considerable power whether for good or evil. But it is impossible to distinguish a request to an invisible being from prayer; or a powerful spirit from a demi-god.

The nations of Mysore at the new moon 'observe a feast in honour of deceased parents.'[3] The Kurumbars of the Deccan also 'sacrifice to the spirits of ancestors,' and the

[1] Erman, *loc. cit.* vol. ii. p. 50.
[2] Polynesian Researches, vol. ii. p. 220.
[3] Buchanan, quoted in Trans. Ethn. Soc., N.S., vol. viii. p. 96.

same is the case with the Santals.[1] Indeed, the worship of ancestors appears to be more or less prevalent among all the aboriginal tribes of Central India.

Burton[2] considers that some of the Egba deities are 'palpably men and women of note in their day.'

The Kaffirs also sacrifice and pray to their deceased relatives, although 'it would perhaps be asserting too much to say absolutely that they believe in the existence and the immortality of the soul.'[3] In fact, their belief seems to go no further than this, that the ghosts of the dead haunt for a certain time their previous dwelling-places, and either assist or plague the living. No special powers are attributed to them, and it would be a misnomer to call them ' Deities.'

Other races endeavour to preserve the memory of the dead by rude statues. Thus Pallas[4] mentions that the Ostyaks of Siberia ' rendent aussi un culte à leurs morts. Ils sculptent des figures de bois pour représenter les Ostiaks célèbres. Dans les repas de commémoration on place devant ces figures une partie des mets. Les femmes qui ont chéri leurs maris ont de pareilles figures, les couchent avec elles, les parent, et ne mangent point sans leur présenter une partie de leur portion.' Erman[5] also mentions that when a man dies ' the relatives form a rude wooden image representing, and in honour of, the deceased, which is set up in their yurt, and receives divine honours ' for a certain time. ' At every meal they set an offering of food before the image ; and should this represent a deceased husband, the widow embraces it from time to time and lavishes on it every sign of attachment.' In ordinary

---

[1] Elliott, Trans. Ethn. Soc., N.S., vol. viii. pp. 104, 106.

[2] Abbeokuta, vol. i. p. 191.

[3] The Basutos ; Casalis, p. 243. See also Callaway's Religious System of the Amazulu.

[4] Pallas' Voyages, vol. iv. p. 79.

[5] Erman, loc. cit. vol. ii. p. 51.

cases this semi-worship only lasts a few years, after which the image is buried. 'But when a Shaman dies, this custom changes, in his favour, into a complete and decided canonisation; for it is not thought enough that, in this case, the dressed block of wood which represents the deceased should receive homage for a limited period, but the priest's descendants do their best to keep him in vogue from generation to generation; and by well-contrived oracles and other arts, they manage to procure offerings for these their families' penates, as abundant as those laid on the altars of the universally acknowledged gods. But that these latter also have an historical origin, that they were originally monuments of distinguished men, to which prescription and the interest of the Shamans gave by degrees an arbitrary meaning and importance, seems to me not liable to doubt; and this is, furthermore, corroborated by the circumstance that of all the sacred yurts dedicated to these saints, which have been numerous from the earliest times in the vicinity of the river, only one has been seen (near Samarovo) containing the image of a woman.'

It seems to me that in other countries also, statues have in this manner come to be worshipped as Deities.

Solomon,[1] long ago, observed truly of idols that

' 13. Neither were they from the beginning, neither shall they be for ever.

' 14. For by the vain glory of men they entered into the world, and therefore shall they come shortly to an end.

' 15. For a father afflicted with untimely mourning, when he hath made an image of his child soon taken away, now honoured him as a god, which was then a dead man, and delivered to those that were under him ceremonies and sacrifices.

---

[1] Wisdom, ch. xiv. p. 12.

'16. Thus, in process of time, an ungodly custom grown strong was kept as a law, and graven images were worshipped by the commandments of kings :

'17. Whom men could not honour in presence, because they dwelt far off, they took the counterfeit of the visage from far, and made an express image of a king whom they honoured, to the end that by this their forwardness, they might flatter him that was absent, as if he were present.

'18. Also the singular diligence of the artificer did help to set forward the ignorant to more superstition.

'19. For he, peradventure willing to please one in authority, forced all his skill to make the resemblance of the best fashion.

'20. And so the multitude, allured by the grace of the work, took him now for a god, which a little before was but honoured as a man.'

The idol is by no means regarded as a mere emblem. In India,[1] when the offerings of the people have been less profuse than usual, the Brahmans sometimes 'put the idols in irons, chaining their hands and feet. They exhibit them to the people in this humiliating state, into which they tell them they have been brought by rigorous creditors, from whom their gods had been obliged, in times of trouble, to borrow money to supply their wants. They declare that the inexorable creditors refuse to set the god at liberty, until the whole sum, with interest, shall have been paid. The people come forward, alarmed at the sight of their divinity in irons ; and thinking it the most meritorious of all good works to contribute to his deliverance, they raise the sum required by the Brahmans for that purpose.'

'A statue of Hercules[2] was worshipped at Tyre, not as a

[1] Dubois, The People of India, p. 407. [2] History of Man, vol. iv. p. 316.

representative of the Deity but as the Deity himself; and
accordingly when Tyre was besieged by Alexander, the
Deity was fast bound in chains, to prevent him from
deserting to the enemy.'

It is hard for us to appreciate the difficulty which an
undeveloped mind finds in raising itself to any elevated
conception.   Thus Campbell mentions that a Highlander
wishing to describe a castle of the utmost possible magnificence, ended with this climax : ' That was the beautiful
castle !   There was not a shadow of a thing that was
for the use of a castle that was not in it, even to a herd
for the geese.' As, however, civilisation progresses, and
the chiefs, becoming more despotic, exact more and more
respect, the people are introduced to conceptions of power
and magnificence higher than any which they had previously entertained.   In many of the cases above quoted
the religion is merely in the stage of Totemism, but as
men advanced in civilisation they became more and more
impressed by the mystery of existence, and gradually
acquired more elevated conceptions of Deity.

Hence, though the worship of ancestors occurs among
races in the stage of Totemism, it long survives, and may
be regarded as characterising Idolatry, which is really a
higher religion; and generally, though not always, indicates
a higher mental condition than the worship of animals or
even of the heavenly bodies.   At first sight the reverse
would appear to be the case : most would regard the sun
as a far grander deity than any in human form.   As a
matter of fact, however, this is not so, and sun-worship is
generally, though not invariably, associated with a lower
idea of the Deity than is the case with Idolatry.   This
arises partly from the fact that the gradually increasing
power of chiefs and kings has familiarised the mind with
the existence of a power greater than any which had been

previously conceived. Thus in Western Africa, the slave trade having added considerably to the wealth and consequently to the power of the chiefs or kings, they maintained much state, and insisted upon being treated with servile homage. No man was allowed to eat with them, nor to approach them excepting on his knees with an appearance of fear, which no doubt was in many cases sufficiently well-founded.

These marks of respect so much resembled adoration, that ' the individuals[1] of the lower classes are persuaded that his (the king's) power is not confined to the earth, and that he has credit enough to make rain fall from heaven: hence they fail not, when a continuance of drought makes them fearful about the harvest, to represent to him that if he does not take care to water the lands of his kingdom, they will die of hunger, and will find it impossible to make him the usual presents.'

Battel also mentions that the king of Loango ' is honoured among them as though he were a god; and is called Sambee and Pango, which means God. They believe he can let them have rain when he likes.'[2] He is so holy that no one is allowed to see him eat or drink. The tyrants of Natal, says Casalis, ' exacted almost divine homage.'[3]

The king and queen of Tahiti were regarded as so sacred that nothing once used by them, not even the sounds forming their names, could be used for any ordinary purpose.[4] The language of the court was characterised by the most ridiculous adulation. The king's ' houses were called the aarai, the clouds of heaven; anuanua, the rain-

[1] Proyart's History of Loango, Pinkerton, vol. xvi. p. 577. See also Bosman, *loc. cit.* pp. 488, 491. Astley's Collection of Voyages, vol. iii. pp. 70, 223, 226.

[2] Pinkerton's Travels, vol. xvi. p. 330.

[3] The Basutos, p. 219.

[4] Ellis' Polynesian Researches, vol. ii. pp. 348, 360.

bow was the name of the canoe in which he voyaged ; his
voice was called thunder ; the glare of the torches in his
dwelling was denominated lightning ; and when the people
saw them in the evening, as they passed near his abode,
instead of saying the torches were burning in the palace,
they would observe that the lightning was flashing in the
clouds of heaven.'

Man-worship would not, indeed, be long confined to the
dead.   In many cases it extends to the living also.
Indeed, the savage who worships an animal or a tree, would
see no absurdity in worshipping a man.   His chief is, in
his eyes, almost as powerful, if not more so, than his
Deity.   Yet man-worship does not prevail in altogether
uncivilised communities, because the chiefs, associating
constantly with their followers, lack that mystery which
religion requires, and which nocturnal animals so eminently possess.   As, however, civilisation progresses, and
the chiefs separate themselves more and more from their
subjects, this ceases to be the case and man-worship
becomes an important element of religion.

The worship of a great chief seems quite as natural as
that of an idol.   'Why,' said a Mongol[1] to Friar Ascelin,
'since you Christians make no scruple to adore sticks and
stones, why do you refuse to do the same honour to Bayoth
Noy, whom the Khân hath ordered to be adored in the
same manner as he is himself?'   This worship is, however,
almost always accompanied by a belief in higher beings.
We have already seen that the New Zealanders and some
other nations have entirely abandoned the worship of
animals, &c., without as yet realising the higher stage of
Idolatry, owing probably in great measure to their political
condition.   In other cases where Shamanism has not so

---

[1] Astley, vol. iv. p. 551.

effectually replaced Totemism, the establishment of monarchical government with its usual pomp and ceremonial,
led to a much more organised worship of the old gods.
Of this the serpent-worship in Western Africa, and the
sun-worship in Peru, are striking examples.

I do not therefore wonder that white men should have
been so often taken for deities. This was the case with
Captain Cook in the Pacific, with Lander in Western
Africa, and, as already mentioned, Mrs. Thomson was
regarded by the North Australians as a spirit, though
she lived with them for some years.

'Tuikilakila,[1] the chief of Somosomo, offered Mr. Hunt
a preferment of the same sort. " If you die first," said he,
" I shall make you my god." In fact there appears to be
no certain line of demarcation between departed spirits and
gods, nor between gods and living men, for many of the
priests and old chiefs are considered as sacred persons, and
not a few of them will also claim to themselves the right
of divinity. " I am a god," Tuikilakila would sometimes
say; and he believed it too. They were not merely the
words of his lips; he believed he was something above a
mere man.'

It seems at first sight hard to understand how men can
be regarded immortal. Yet even this belief has been
entertained in various countries.

Merolla tells us[2] that in his time the wizards of Congo
were called Scinghili, that is to say Gods of the Earth.
The head of them is styled ' Ganga Chitorne, being reputed
God of all the Earth.' ' He further asserts that his body
is not capable of suffering a natural death; and, therefore,
to confirm his adorers in that opinion, whenever he finds
his end approaching, either through age or disease, he calls

[1] Erskine's Western Pacific, p. 246.   [2] Pinkerton, vol. xvi. p. 226, *et seq.*

for such a one of his disciples as he designs to succeed him, and pretends to communicate to him his great powers : and afterwards in public (where this tragedy is always acted) he commands him to tie a halter about his neck and to strangle him therewith, or else to take a club, and knock him down dead.   This command being once pronounced, is soon executed, and the wizard thereby sent a martyr to the devil.   The reason that this is done in public, is to make known the successor ordained by the last breath of the predecessor, and to show that it has the same power of producing rain, and the like.   If this office were not thus continually filled, the inhabitants say that the earth would soon become barren, and mankind consequently perish.   In my time, one of these magicians was cast into the sea, another into a river, a mother and her son put to death, and many others banished by our order, as has been said.'

So also the Great Lama of Thibet is regarded as immortal; though his spirit occasionally passes from one earthly tenement to another.

These, then, are the lowest intellectual stages through which religion has passed.   It is no part of my plan to describe the various religious beliefs of the higher races. I have, however, stopped short sooner perhaps than I should otherwise have done, because the worship of personified principles, such as Fear, Love, Hope, &c., could not have been treated apart from that of the Phallus or Lingam with which it was so intimately associated in Greece, India, Mexico, and elsewhere ; and which, though at first modest and pure, as all religions are in their origin, led to such abominable practices, that it is one of the most painful chapters in human history.

I will now therefore pass on to some points intimately

connected with religion, but which could not be conveniently treated in the earlier part of this work.

There is no difficulty in understanding that when once the idea of Spiritual Beings had become habitual—when once man had come to regard them as exercising an important influence, whether for good or evil—he would endeavour to secure their assistance and support. Before a war he would try to propitiate them by promising a share of the spoil after victory; and fear, even if no higher motive, would ensure the performance of his promise.

We, no doubt, regard, and justly regard, sacrifices as unnecessary. 'I will take no bullock,' says David,[1] ' out of thine house, nor he-goat out of thy folds.' This sentiment, however, was far in advance of its time, and even Solomon felt that sacrifices, in the then condition of the Jews, were necessary. They are, indeed, a stage through which, in any natural process of development, religion must pass. At first it is supposed that the Spirits actually eat the food offered to them. Soon, however, it would be observed that animals sacrificed did not disappear; and the natural explanation would be that the Spirit ate the spiritual part of the victim, leaving the grosser portion to his devout worshipper. Thus the Limboos near Darjeeling eat their sacrifices, dedicating, as they forcibly express it, 'the life-breath, to the gods, the flesh to ourselves.'[2]

So also, as Sir G. Grey tells us, the New Zealand fairies, when Te Kanawa gave them his jewels, carried off the shadows only, not caring for the earthly substance.[3] In Guinea, according to Bosman, 'the idol hath only the blood, because they like the flesh very well themselves.'[4]

---

[1] Psalm l.

[2] Campbell, in Trans. Ethn. Soc., N.S., vol. vii. p. 153.

[3] Polynesian Mythology, p. 294.

[4] Bosman. Pinkerton's Voyages, vol. xvi. p. 531. Astley's Collection of Voyages, vol. ii. p. 97.

In other cases the idols were smeared with the blood, while the devotees feasted on the flesh. The Ostyaks when they kill an animal rub some of the blood on the mouths of their idols. Even this seems at length to be replaced in some cases, as Mr. Tylor has suggested, by red paint. Thus the sacred stones in India, as Colonel Forbes Leslie has shown, are frequently ornamented with red.[1] So also in Congo it is customary to daub the fetiches with red every new moon.[2] Atkinson[3] thus describes a Kirghiz sacrifice :—'A ram was led up by the owner, who wished for a large increase of his flocks and herds. It was handed to an assistant of the priest, who killed it in the usual manner. His superior stood near, looking towards the east, and began chanting a prayer, and beating on his large tambourine to rouse up his god, and then made his request for multitudes of sheep and cattle. The ram was being flayed ; and when the operation was completed, the skin was put on a pole as shown in the accompanying sketch, raised above the framework, and placed with its head towards the east. The tambourine thundered forth its sound, and the performer continued his wild chant. The flesh was cooked in the large cauldron, and the tribe held a great festival.'

Of the great offerings of food among the Fijians, says Williams,[4] 'native belief apportions merely the soul thereof to the gods, who are described as being enormous eaters ; the substance is consumed by the worshippers.'

Ellis[5] mentions an indication of this in Tahiti, when human sacrifices prevailed but cannibalism was abandoned. The priest handed a portion of the victim to the king,

---

[1] See, for instance, Early Races of Scotland, vol. ii. p. 464.

[2] See *antè*, p. 208.

[3] Siberia, p. 383.

[4] Fiji and the Fijians, vol. i. p. 231. See also p. 223.

[5] Polynesian Researches, vol. ii. p. 214.

'who raised it to his mouth as if desirous to eat it,' but then handed it to an attendant.

In many cases, indeed, it seems to be a necessary portion of the ceremony that the victim should be eaten by those present. Thus, in India,[1] when the sacrifice ' is over, the priest comes out, and distributes part of the articles which had been offered to the idols. This is received as holy, and is eaten immediately.'

Among the Redskins,[2] at the feast held when the hunting season begins, the victim 'must be all eaten and nothing left.' It is remarkable that among the Algonkins, another rule at the same feast is that not a bone of the victim must be broken.[3]

In many cases a curious confusion arises between the victim and the Deity, and the former is worshipped before it is sacrificed and eaten. Thus in ancient Egypt, Apis the victim was also regarded as the God,[4] and Iphigenia was supposed by some to be the same as Artemis.[5]

In Mexico[6] at a certain period of the year the priest of Quetzalcoatl made an image of the Deity of meal mixed with infants' blood, and then, after many impressive ceremonies, killed the image by shooting it with an arrow, and tore out the heart, which was eaten by the king, while the rest of the body was distributed among the people, every one of whom was most anxious to procure a piece to eat, however small.[7]

[1] Dubois, The people of India, p. 401.

[2] Schoolcraft's Indian Tribes, vol. iii. p. 61. Tanner's Narrative, p. 287.

[3] Tanner's Narrative, p. 195.

[4] Cox's Manual of Mythology, p. 213.

[5] Ibid., p. 158.

[6] See Müller, Ges. d. Amer. Urr. p. 605.

[7] Die Priester verfertigen nämlich sein Bild von allerlei Samen, die mit dem Blute geopferter Kinder zusammengebacken wurden. Mancherlei religiöse Reinigungen und Sühnungen, Waschungen mit Wasser, Aderlassen, Fasten, Prozessionen, Räucherungen, Wachtelopfer, Menschenopfer bereiteten zur Feier vor. Alsdann schoss ein Priester Quetzalcoatls einen Pfeil gegen jenes Bild Huitzilopochtlis, und

The great yearly sacrifice in honour of Tezcatlipoca was also very remarkable. Some beautiful youth, usually a war captive, was chosen as the victim. For a whole year he was treated and worshipped as a god. When he went out he was attended by a numerous train of pages, and the crowd as he passed prostrated themselves before him, and did him homage as the impersonation of the good Deity. Everything he could wish was provided for him, and at the commencement of the last month, four beautiful girls were allotted to him as wives. Finally, when the fatal day arrived, he was placed at the head of a solemn procession, taken to the temple, and after being sacrificed with much ceremony and every token of respect, he was eaten by the priests and chiefs.

Again, among the Khonds[2] of Central India human sacrifices prevailed until quite lately. 'A stout stake is driven into the soil, and to it the victim is fastened, seated, and anointed with ghee, oil, and turmeric, decorated with flowers, and *worshipped* during the day by the assembly. At nightfall the licentious revelry is resumed, and on the third morning the victim gets some milk to drink, when the presiding priest implores the goddess to shower her blessings on the people, that they may increase and multiply, prosperity attend their cattle and poultry, fertility their fields, and happiness to the people generally. The priest recounts the origin and advantage of the rite, as previously detailed, and concludes by stating that the goddess has been obeyed and the people assembled.

.   .   .   .

durchschoss den Gott. So galt dieser nun für todt, es wurde ihm wie den Menschenopfern vom Priester das Herz ausgeschnitten, und vom Könige, dem Stellvertreter des Gottes auf Erden, gegessen. Den Leib aber vertheilten sie für die verschiedenen Quartiere der Stadt so, dass jeder Mann ein Stückchen erhielt.'

[1] Müller, *loc. cit.* p. 617. Prescott, *loc. cit.* vol. i. p. 5.

[2] Dr. Shortt, Trans. Ethn. Soc., N.S., vol. vi. p. 273.

' Other softening expressions are recited to excite the
compassion of the multitude. After the mock ceremony,
nevertheless, the victim is taken to the grove where the
sacrifice is to be carried out; and, to prevent resistance,
the bones of the arms and legs are broken, or the victim
drugged with opium or datura, when the janni wounds his
victim with his axe. This act is followed up by the crowd ;
a number now press forward to obtain a piece of his
flesh, and in a moment he is stripped to the bones.'

So also in some parts of Africa ' eating the fetich ' is a
solemn ceremony, by which women swear fidelity to their
husbands, men to their friends. On a marriage in Issini,
the parties ' eat the fetish together, in token of friendship,
and as an assurance of the woman's fidelity to her husband.'[1]
In taking an oath also the same ceremony is observed. To
know, says Loyer, ' the truth from any negro, you need only
mix something in a little water, and steeping a bit of bread,
bid him eat or drink that fetish as a sign of the truth. If
the thing be so, he will do it freely ; but if otherwise, he
will not touch it, believing he should die on the spot if he
swore falsely. Their way is to rasp or grate a little of
their fetish in water, or on any edible, and so put it in
their mouth without swallowing it.'

The sacrifices, however, were as a general rule not eaten
by all indiscriminately. In Feejee they were confined to
the old men and priests; women and young men being
excluded from any share.

Gradually the priests established their claim to the
whole, a result which could not fail to act as a considerable stimulus to the practice of sacrifice. It also affected
the character of the worship. Thus, as Bosman tells us,

---

[1] Loyer, in Astley's Collection of Voyages, vol. ii. pp. 436, 441.

the priests encouraged offerings to the Serpent rather than to the Sea, because, in the latter case, as he expresses it, ' there happens no remainder to be left for them.'

As already mentioned, the feeling which has led to the sacrifice of animals would naturally culminate in that of men. So natural, indeed, does the idea of human sacrifice appear to the human mind in this stage, that we meet it in various nations all over the world.

Human sacrifices occurred in Guinea,[1] and Burton[2] saw ' at Benin city a young woman lashed to a scaffolding upon the summit of a tall blasted tree, and being devoured by the turkey buzzards. The people declared it to be a " fetish " or charm for bringing rain.'

Our early navigators describe them as taking place occasionally in the Pacific Islands. War captives were frequently sacrificed in Brazil.

Various nations in India, besides the Khonds who have been already mentioned, used to offer up human sacrifices on extraordinary occasions ; and even now in some places, though the actual sacrifice is no longer permitted, they make human figures of flour, paste, or clay, and then cut off the heads in honour of their gods.[3]

Many cases of human sacrifice are mentioned in ancient history. The Carthaginians after their defeat of Agathocles burnt some of their captives as a sacrifice ; the Assyrians offered human sacrifices to the god Nergal. Many cases are on record in Greek history, and among the Romans even down to the time of the emperors. In Rome a statue of Jupiter was sprinkled every year with human blood, down to the second or third century after Christ, and in Northern Europe human sacrifices continued to a much later period. In Mexico and Peru they seem to have been peculiarly

[1] Astley s Collection of Voyages, vol. iii. p. 113.
[2] Abbeokuta, vol. i. p. 19.
[3] Dubois, *loc. cit.* p. 490.

numerous. Müller[1] has suggested that this may have partly arisen from the fact that these races were not softened by the possession of domestic animals. Various estimates have been made of the number of human victims annually sacrificed in the Mexican temples. Müller thinks 2,500 is a moderate estimate; but in one year it appears to have exceeded 100,000.

Among the Jews we find a system of animal sacrifices on a great scale, and symbols of human sacrifices, which can, I think, only be understood on the hypothesis that they were once usual. The case of Jephtha's daughter is generally looked upon as quite exceptional, but the twenty-eighth and twenty-ninth verses of the twenty-seventh chapter of Leviticus appear to indicate that human sacrifices were at one time habitual among the Jews.[2]

The lower savages have no Temples or sacred buildings. Throughout the New World there was no such thing as a temple, excepting among the semi-civilised races of Central America and Peru.

The Stiens of Cambodia 'have neither priest nor temples.'[3] We should seek in vain, says Casalis,[4] 'from the extremity of the southern promontory of Africa to the country far beyond the banks of the Zambesi, for anything like the pagodas of India, the maraes of Polynesia, or the fetish huts of Nigritia.' The people of Madagascar, as we are informed by Drury,[5] who resided fifteen years among them, although they have settled abodes, keep large herds of cattle, and are diligent agriculturists, 'have no temples, no tabernacles, or groves for the public performance of their divine worship; neither have they solemn fasts, or

[1] Geschichte der Americanishen Urreligionem, p. 23.
[2] But see Kalisch, Commentary on the Old Testament, Lev. Pt. I. p. 409.
[3] Mouhot's Travels in the Central Parts of Indo-China, vol. i. p. 250.
[4] The Basutos, p. 237.
[5] Adventures of Robert Drury, p. x.

festivals, or set days or times, nor priests to do it for them.'

Professor Nillson was, I believe, the first to point out that certain races buried the dead in their houses, and that the chambered tumuli of Northern Europe are probably copies of the dwellings then used, sometimes perhaps the actual dwellings themselves. We know that as the power of chiefs increased, their tombs became larger and more magnificent, and Mr. Fergusson has well shown how in India the tumulus has developed into the temple.

In some cases, as for instance in India, it is far from easy to distinguish between a group of stone gods and a sacred fane. In fact, we may be sure that the very same stones are by some supposed to be actual deities, while others more advanced regard them as sacred only because devoted to religious purposes. Some of the ruder Hindostan tribes actually worship upright stones; but Colonel Forbes Leslie regards the sacred stones represented in Pl. IV. as a place of worship, rather than as actual deities; and this is at any rate the case with another group (*Frontispiece*) similarly painted, which he observed near Andlee, also in the Dekhan, and which is peculiarly interesting from its resemblance to the stone circles of our own country.

Fig. 18, p. 156, represents, after Lafitau,[1] a religious dance as practised by the Redskins of Virginia. Here, also, as already mentioned, we see a sacred circle of stones, differing from those of our own country and of India only in having a human head rudely carved on each stone.

The lower races of men have no Priests properly so called. Many passages, indeed, may be quoted which, at first sight, appear to negative this assertion. If, however, we examine more closely the true functions of these so-called 'priests,' we shall easily satisfy ourselves that the term is a misno-

---

[1] Mœurs des Sauv. Amer., vol. ii. p. 136.

mer, and that wizards only are intended. Without temples
and sacrifices there cannot be priests.

Even the New Zealanders[1] had ' no regular priesthood.'
Mr. Gladstone[2] observes that the priest was not, ' as such
a significant personage in Greece at any period, nor had
the priest of any one place or deity, so far as we know,
any organic connection with the priest of any other ; so
that if there were priests, yet there was not a priesthood.'

I have already pointed out (ante, p. 138) the great difference between the belief in ghosts and in the existence
of a soul. Even, however, those races which have so far
advanced as to believe in the latter, yet differ from us very
much in their views ; and in fact the belief in an universal,
independent, and endless existence is confined to the very
highest races of men. The New Zealanders believe that
a man who is eaten as well as killed, is thus destroyed
both soul and body.[3] Even, however, those who have
proper interment are far from secure of reaching the
happier regions in the land of spirits. The road to them
is long and dangerous, and many a soul perishes by the
way. In the Tonga Islands the chiefs are regarded as
immortal, the Tooas or common people as mortal ; with
reference to the intermediate class or Mooas there is a
difference of opinion.

A friend of Mr. Lang's [4] ' tried long and patiently to
make a very intelligent docile Australian black understand
his existence without a body, but the black never could
keep his countenance and generally made an excuse to get
away. One day the teacher watched and found that he
went to have a hearty fit of laughter at the absurdity of
the idea of a man living and going about without arms,
legs, or mouth to eat ; for a long time he could not believe

[1] Yate, p. 146.   [2] Juventus Mundi, p. 181.
[3] Taylor, New Zealand and its Inhabitants, p. 101.
[4] The Aborigines of Australia, p. 31.

that the gentleman was serious, and when he did realise it, the more serious the teacher was the more ludicrous the whole affair appeared to the black.'

The resurrection of the body as preached by the missionaries,[1] appeared to the Tahitians 'astounding' and 'incredible;' and 'as the subject was more frequently brought under their notice in public discourse, or in reading the Scriptures, and their minds were more attentively exercised upon it in connection with their ancestry, themselves, and their descendants, it appeared invested with more than ordinary difficulty, bordering, to their apprehension, on impossibility.'

Although the Feejeeans believe that almost everything has a spirit, few spirits are immortal: the road to Mbulu is long, and beset with so many difficulties, that after all 'few attain to immortality.'[2] As regards Central India, Colonel Dalton says,[3] 'I do not think that the present generation of Kols have any notion of a heaven or a hell that may not be traced to Brahminical or Christian teaching. The old idea is that the souls of the dead become "bhoots," spirits, but no thought of reward or punishment is connected with the change. When a Ho swears, the oath has no reference whatever to a future state. He prays that if he speak not the truth he may be afflicted in this world with the loss of all—health, wealth, wife, children; that he may sow without reaping, and finally may be devoured by a tiger; but he swears not by any happiness beyond the grave. He has in his primitive state no such hope; and I believe that most Indian aborigines, though they may have some vague ideas of continuous existence, will be found equally devoid of original notions in regard to the judgment to come.'

[1] Ellis' Polynesian Researches, vol. ii. p. 165.

[2] Fiji and the Fijians, vol. i. p. 247.
[3] Trans. Ethn. Soc. 1867, p. 38.

Even when the spirit is supposed to survive the body, the condition of souls after death is not at first considered to differ materially from that during life.   Heaven is merely a distant part of earth.   Thus the 'seats of happiness are represented by some Hindu writers to be vast mountains on the north of India.'[1]   Again, in Tonga the souls are supposed to go to Bolotoo, a large island to the north-west, well stocked[2] with all kinds of useful and ornamental plants, ' always bearing the richest fruits and the most beautiful flowers according to their respective natures; that when these fruits or flowers are plucked, others immediately occupy their place . . . the island is also well stocked with the most beautiful birds of all imaginable kinds, as well as with abundance of hogs, all of which are immortal, unless they are killed to provide food for the hotooas or gods, but the moment a hog or bird is killed, another hog or bird immediately comes into existence to supply its place, the same as with the fruits and flowers; and this, as far as they know or suppose, is the only mode of propagation of plants and animals.   The island of Bolotoo is supposed to be so far off as to render it dangerous for their canoes to attempt going there ; and it is supposed, moreover, that even if they were to succeed in reaching so far, unless it happened to be the particular will of the gods, they would be sure to miss it.'

They believe, however, that on one occasion a canoe actually reached Bolotoo.   The crew landed, but when they attempted to touch anything, ' they could no more lay hold of it than if it had been a shadow.'   Consequently hunger soon overtook them, and forced them to return, which they fortunately succeeded in doing.

A curious notion, already referred to, is the belief that each man has several souls.   It is common to various

---

[1] Dubois, *loc. cit.* p. 485.   [2] Mariner, *loc. cit.* vol. ii. p. 108.

parts of America,[1] and exists also in Madagascar. It apparently arises from the idea that each pulse is the seat of a different life. It also derives an appearance of probability from the inconsistencies of behaviour to which savages are so prone. The Feejeeans also believed that each man has two spirits.[2] Among the ancient Greeks and Romans there are some indications of the existence of a similar belief.[3]

The belief in a future state, if less elevated than our own, is singularly vivid among some barbarous races. Thus Cæsar assures us that among the ancient Britons money was habitually lent on what may strictly be termed 'postobits'—promises to pay in another world.

The Feejeeans believe that 'as they die, such will be their condition in another world; hence their desire to escape extreme infirmity.'[4] The way to Mbulu, as already mentioned, is long and difficult; many always perish, and no diseased or infirm person could possibly succeed in surmounting all the dangers of the road. Hence as soon as a man feels the approach of old age, he notifies to his children that it is time for him to die. If he neglects to do so, the children after a while take the matter into their own hands. A family consultation is held, a day appointed, and the grave dug. The aged person has his choice of being strangled or buried alive. Mr. Hunt gives the following striking description of such a ceremony once witnessed by him. A young man came to him and invited him to attend his mother's funeral, which was just going to take place. Mr. Hunt accepted the invitation, and joined the procession, but, surprised to see no corpse,

---

[1] Tertre's History of the Caribby Islands, p. 288. It prevails also in Greenland. Müller, Ges. der Am. Urreligionem, p. 66.

[2] Fiji and the Fijians, vol. i. p. 241.
[3] Lafitau, vol. ii. p. 424.
[4] Fiji and the Fijians, vol. i. p. 183.

he made enquiries, when the young man ' pointed out his
mother, who was walking along with them, as gay and
lively as any of those present, and apparently as much
pleased. Mr. Hunt expressed his surprise to the young
man, and asked how he could deceive him so much by
saying his mother was dead, when she was alive and well.
He said, in reply, that they had made her death-feast, and
were now going to bury her; that she was old, that his
brother and himself had thought she had lived long
enough, and it was time to bury her, to which she had
willingly assented, and they were about it now. He had
come to Mr. Hunt to ask his prayers, as they did those of
the priest.

' He added, that it was from love for his mother that he
had done so; that, in consequence of the same love, they
were now going to bury her, and that none but themselves
could or ought to do such a sacred office! Mr. Hunt did
all in his power to prevent so diabolical an act; but the
only reply he received was that she was their mother, and
they were her children, and they ought to put her to death.
On reaching the grave, the mother sat down, when they
all, including children, grandchildren, relations and friends,
took an affectionate leave of her; a rope, made of twisted
tapa, was then passed twice around her neck by her sons,
who took hold of it and strangled her; after which she
was put in her grave, with the usual ceremonies.'[1]

So general was this custom that in one town containing
several hundred inhabitants Captain Wilkes did not see
one man over forty years of age, all the old people having
been buried.

In Dahomey the king sends constant messages to his
deceased father, by messengers who are killed for the

[1] Wilkes' Exploring Expedition. Condensed edition, p. 211.

purpose. The same firm belief which leads to this reconciles
the messengers to their fate. They are well treated beforehand, and their death being instantaneous is attended
with little pain. Hence we are assured that they are quite
cheerful and contented, and scarcely seem to look on their
death as a misfortune.

The North American Indian, as Schoolcraft tells us, has
little dread of death. ' He does not fear to go to a land
which, all his life long, he has heard abounds in rewards
without punishments.'[1]

We know that the Japanese commit suicide for the
most trifling causes ; and it is said that in China, if a rich
man is condemned to death, he can always purchase a
willing substitute at a very small expense.

The lower races have no idea of Creation, and even among
those somewhat more advanced, it is at first very incomplete. Their deities are part of, not the makers of, the
world ; and even when the idea of creation dawns upon the
mind, it is not strictly a creation, but merely the raising
of land already existing at the bottom of the original sea.

The Abipones had no theory on the subject; when
questioned by Dobritzhoffer,[2] ' my father, replied Yehoalay
readily and frankly, our grandfathers, and great-grandfa-
thers, were wont to contemplate the earth alone, solicitous
only to see whether the plain afforded grass and water for
their horses. They never troubled themselves about what
went on in the heavens, and who was the creator and
governor of the stars.'

Father Baegert,[3] in his account of the Californian
Indians, says, ' I often asked them whether they had never
put to themselves the question who might be the Creator
and Preserver of the sun, moon, stars, and other objects of

[1] Schoolcraft's Indian Tribes, vol.
ii. p. 68.
[2] *Loc. cit.* vol. ii. p. 59.
[3] *Loc. cit.* p. 390.

nature, but was always sent home with a "vara," which means " no " in their language.'

The Chipewyans [1] thought that the world existed at first in the form of a globe of water, out of which the Great Spirit raised the land. The Lenni Lenape [2] say that Manitu at the beginning swam on the water, and made the earth out of a grain of sand. He then made a man and woman out of a tree. The Mingos and Ottawwaws believe that a rat brought up a grain of sand from the bottom of the water, and thus produced the land. The Crees [3] had no ideas at all as to the origin of the world.

Stuhr, who was, as Müller says, a good observer of such matters, tells us that the Siberians had no idea of a Creator. When Burchell suggested the idea of Creation to the Bachapin Kaffirs, they 'asserted that everything made itself, and that trees and herbage grew by their own will.' [4] It also appears from Canon Callaway's researches that the Zulu Kaffirs have no notion of Creation. Casalis makes the same statement: all the natives, he says, ' whom we questioned on the subject have assured us that it never entered their heads that the earth and sky might be the work of an Invisible Being.' [5] The same is also the case with the Hottentots.

The Australians, again, had no idea of Creation. According to Polynesian mythology, heaven and earth existed from the beginning. [6] The latter, however, was at first covered by water, until Mawe drew up New Zealand by means of an enchanted fish-hook. [7] This fish-hook was made from the jawbone of Muri-ranga-whenna, and is now the cape forming the southern extremity of Hawkes' Bay. The

[1] Dunn's Oregon, p. 102.

[2] Müller, Ges. d. Amer. Urr., p. 107.

[3] Franklin's Journey to the Polar Sea, vol. i. p. 143.

[4] *Loc. cit.* vol. ii. p. 550.

[5] The Basutos, p. 238.

[6] Polynesian Mythology, p. 1.

[7] *Ibid.* p. 45.

Tongans[1] have a very similar tale. Here the islands were drawn up by Tangaloa, ' but the line accidentally breaking, the act was incomplete, and matters were left as they now are. They show a hole in the rock, about two feet in diameter, which quite perforates it, and in which Tangoloa's hook got fixed. It is moreover said that Tooitonga had, till within a few years, this very hook in his possession.'

As regards Tahiti, Williams[2] observes that the ' origin of the Gods, and their priority of existence in comparison with the formation of the earth, being a matter of uncertainty even among the native priests, involves the whole in the greatest obscurity.' Even in Sanskrit there is no word for creation, nor does any such idea appear in the Rigveda, in the Zendavesta, or in Homer.

When the Capuchin missionary Merolla[3] asked the queen of Singa, in Western Africa, who made the world, she ' without the least hesitation, readily answered, "My ancestors." "Then," replied the Capuchin, " does your majesty enjoy the whole power of your ancestors?" " Yes," answered she, " and much more, for over and above what they had, I am absolute mistress of the kingdom of Matamba!" A remark which shows how little she realised the meaning of the term "Creation."' The negroes in Guinea thought that man was created by a great black spider.[4] Other negroes, however, have more just ideas on the subject, probably derived from the missionaries.

The Kumis of Chittagong believe that a certain Deity made the world and the trees and the creeping things, and lastly ' he set to work to make one man and one woman, forming their bodies of clay; but each night, on the com-

---

[1] Mariner, loc. cit. vol. i. p. 284.
[2] Polynesian Researches, vol. ii. p. 191.
[3] Pinkerton's Voyages, vol. xvi. p. 305.
[4] Loc. cit. p. 469.

pletion of his work, there came a great snake, which, while God was sleeping, devoured the two images.'[1] At length the Deity created a dog, which drove away the snake, and thus the creation of man was accomplished.

We cannot fail also to be struck with the fact that the lower forms of religion are almost independent of prayer. To us prayer seems almost a necessary part of religion. But it evidently involves a belief in the goodness of God, a truth which, as we have seen, is not early recognised.

Of the Hottentots Kolben says, ' It is most certain they neither pray to any one of their deities nor utter a word to any mortal concerning the condition of their souls or a future life. . . . Preparation for death, in a spiritual sense, is a thing they never appeared to me to have any notion of.'[2] And again : ' It does not appear that they have any institution of worship directly regarding the supreme God. I never saw, nor could I hear, that any one of them paid any act of devotion immediately to him.'[3] Even those negroes, says Bosman, who have a faint conception of a higher Deity ' do not pray to him, or offer any sacrifices to him ; for which they give the following reasons : " God," say they, "is too high exalted above us, and too great to condescend so much as to trouble himself, or think of mankind." '[4]

The Mandingoes, according to Park, regard the Deity as ' so remote, and of so exalted a nature, that it is idle to imagine the feeble supplications of wretched mortals can reverse the decrees, and change the purposes, of unerring Wisdom.'[5] They seem, however, to have little confidence in their own views, and generally assured Park, in answer to his enquiries about religion and the immortality of the soul, that ' no man knows anything about it.' ' Neither

[1] Lewin's Hill Tracts of Chittagong, p. 90.
[2] *Loc. cit.* p. 315.
[3] *Loc. cit.* p. 95.
[4] Bosman, *loc. cit.* p. 493.
[5] Park's Travels, vol. i. p. 267.

among the Eskimos nor Tinne,' says Richardson, ' could I
ascertain that prayer was ever made to the "*Kitche Manito*,"
the Great Spirit or " Master of Life." ' [1]   Mr. Prescott, in
Schoolcraft's Indian Tribes, also states that the North
American Indians do not pray to the Great Spirit.[2]   The
Caribs considered that the Good Spirit ' is endued with so
great goodness, that it does not take any revenge even of
its enemies : whence it comes that they render it neither
honour nor adoration.' [3]

According to Metz, the Todas (Neilgherry Hills) never
pray.   Even among the priests, he says, ' the only sign of
adoration that I have ever seen them perform is lifting the
right hand to the forehead, covering the nose with the
thumb, when entering the sacred dairy : and the words,
" May all be well," are all that I have ever heard them utter
in the form of a prayer.' [4]

The connection between morality and religion will be
considered in a later chapter.   Here, I will only observe
that the deities of the lower races being subject to the same
passions as man, and in many cases, indeed, themselves
monsters of iniquity, regarded crime with indifference, so
long as the religious ceremonies and sacrifices in their
honour were not neglected.   Hence it follows that through
all these lower races there is no idea of any being corresponding to Satan.   So far, indeed, as their deities are evil
they may be so called ; but the essential character of
Satan is that of the Tempter ; hence in the order of succession this idea cannot arise until morality has become
connected with religion.

Thus, then, I have endeavoured to trace the gradual
development of religion among the lower races of man.

[1] Richardson's Boat Journey, vol. ii.
p. 44.
[2] Prescott.   Schoolcraft's   Indian
Tribes, vol. iii. p. 226.
[3] Tertre's History of the Caribby
Islands, p. 278.
[4] Tribes of the Neilgherries, p. 27.

The higher faiths, however, merely superimposed themselves on, and did not eradicate, the lower superstitions.
How low these were, is not perhaps generally realised.
Thus even Lord Kames lays it down as a self-evident
proposition that 'the ancient Egyptians were not idiots,
to pay divine honours to a bull or a cat as such : the
divine honours were paid to a deity as residing in these
animals.'[1] Yet the very same author tells us that
Augustus, having twice lost his fleet by storm, forbade
Neptune to be carried in procession along with the other
gods; imagining he had avenged himself of Neptune by
neglecting his favourite statue.[2] And again, as I have
already mentioned (antè, p. 231), he quotes the fact that
during a siege the Tyrians chained up a statue of Hercules,
in the idea that they would thus prevent their deity from
deserting to the enemy.[3]

Nay, in the absence of education, not even Christianity
prevents mankind from falling into these errors. Thus,
'when we were in Portugal,'[4] says Captain Brydone,
'the people of Castelbranco were so enraged at St. An-
tonio for suffering the Spaniards to plunder their town,
contrary, as they affirmed, to his express agreement
with them, that they broke many of his statues to pieces;
and one that had been more revered than the rest, they
took the head off, and in its stead placed one of St. Francis.
The great St. Januarius himself was in imminent danger
during the last famine at Naples. They loaded him with
abuse and invectives, and declared point-blank that if he
did not procure them corn by such a time, he should be
no longer their saint.' Here we have the grossest fetichism, and indeed we know that a belief in witchcraft was

---

[1] *Loc. cit.* vol. iv. p. 193. iv. p. 325.
[2] History of Man, vol. iv. p. 320. [4] *Loc. cit.* p. 329.
[3] Lord Kames' History of Man, vol.

all but universal until recently even in our own country.[1]
This dark superstition has indeed flourished for centuries
in Christian countries, and has only been expelled at
length by the light of science.   It still survives wherever
science has not penetrated.

The immense service which Science has thus rendered
to the cause of religion and of humanity, has not hitherto
received the recognition which it deserves.   Science is still
regarded by many excellent, but narrow-minded, persons as
hostile to religious truth, while in fact she is only opposed
to religious error.   No doubt her influence has always been
exercised in opposition to those who present contradictory
assertions under the excuse of mystery, and to all but the
highest conceptions of Divine power.   The time, however,
is approaching when it will be generally perceived that
so far from science being opposed to religion, true religion
is, without science, impossible; and if we consider the
various aspects of Christianity as understood by different
nations, we can hardly fail to perceive that the dignity,
and therefore the truth, of their religious beliefs is in
direct relation to the knowledge of science and of the
great physical laws by which our universe is governed.

[1] See Lecky's History of Rationalism, *loc. cit.* pp. 8, 9, 67, 134, &c.

CHAPTER VII.

CHARACTER AND MORALS.

THE accounts which we possess of the character of savage races are both conflicting and unsatisfactory. In some cases travellers have expressed strong opinions for which they had obviously no sufficient foundation. Thus the unfortunate La Perouse, who spent only one day on Easter Island, states his belief that the inhabitants ' are as corrupt as the circumstances in which they are placed will permit them to be.'[1] On the other hand, the Friendly Islanders were so called by Captain Cook on account of the apparent kindness and hospitality with which they received him. Yet, as we now know, this appearance of friendship was entirely hypocritical. The natives endeavoured to lull him into security, with the intention of seizing his ship and massacring the crew, which design a fortunate accident alone prevented them from carrying into effect; yet Captain Cook never had the slightest suspicion of their treachery, or of the danger which he so narrowly escaped.

In some cases the same writer gives accounts at variance with one another. Thus Mr. Ellis,[2] the excellent missionary of the Pacific, speaking of the Tahitians, states that their moral character was ' awfully dark, and notwithstanding the apparent mildness of their disposition, and the cheerful vivacity of their conversation, no portion

[1] Perouse's Voyage, English edition, vol. ii. p. 327.
[2] Polynesian Researches, vol. ii. p. 25.

of the human race was ever, perhaps, sunk lower in brutal licentiousness and moral degradation.' Yet, speaking of this same people, and in the very same volume, he states that they were most anxious to obtain Bibles : on the day when they were to be distributed, the natives came from considerable distances, and 'the place was actually thronged until the copies were expended. In their application at our own houses, we found it impossible to restrain the people, so great was their anxiety.' Under these circumstances we cannot wonder that Captain Cook and other navigators found in them much to admire as well as to condemn.

The Kalmouks, again, have been very differently described by different travellers. Pallas, speaking of their character, says, ' Il m'a paru infiniment meilleur que ne l'ont dépeint plusieurs de nos historiens voyageurs. Il est infiniment préférable à celui des autres peuples nomades. Les Kalmouks sont affables, hospitaliers et francs ; ils aiment à rendre service ; ils sont toujours gais et enjoués, ce qui les distingue des Kirguis, qui sont beaucoup plus flegmatiques. Telles sont leurs bonnes qualités ; voici les mauvaises. Ils sont sales, paresseux et fort rusés ; ils abusent très-souvent de ce dernier défaut.'[1] So also the aboriginal tribes of India, as pointed out by M. Hunter,[2] have been painted in the blackest colours by some, and highly praised by others.

Mariner gives an excellent account of the state of manners among the Tongans, and one which well illustrates the difficulty of arriving at correct ideas on such a subject, especially among a people of a different race from ourselves and in a different state of civilisation. He describes them as loyal[3] and pious,[4] obedient children,[5] affectionate

[1] Voyages, vol. i. p. 499.
[2] Comparative Dictionary of the Non-Aryan Languages of India and High Asia, pp. 5, 9.
[3] *Loc. cit.* vol. ii. p. 155.
[4] P. 154.
[5] P. 155.

parents,[1] kind husbands,[2] modest and faithful wives,[3] and true friends.[4]

On the other hand, they seem to have little feeling of morality. They have no words for justice or injustice, for cruelty or humanity.[5] 'Theft, revenge, rape, and murder under many circumstances are not held to be crimes.' They have no idea of future rewards and punishments. They saw no harm in seizing ships by treachery and murdering the crew. The men were cruel, treacherous, and revengeful. Marriages were terminable at the whim of the husband,[6] and excepting in married women chastity was not regarded as a virtue, though it was thought improper for a woman frequently to change her lover. Yet we are told that on the whole,[7] this system, although so opposed to our feelings, had 'not the least appearance of any bad effect. The women were tender kind mothers, the children well cared for.' Both sexes appeared to be contented and happy in their relations to each other, and 'as to domestic quarrels they were seldom known.' We must not judge them too hardly for their proposed treachery to Captain Cook. Even in Northern Europe shipwrecks were long considered fair spoil, the strangers being connected with the natives by no civil or family ties, and the idea of natural right not being highly developed.[8]

Lastly, if in addition to the other sources of difficulty, we remember that of language, we cannot wonder that the characters of savage races have been so differently described by different travellers. We all know how difficult it is to judge an individual, and it must be much more so to judge a nation. In fact, whether any given writer

[1] P. 179.
[2] P. 179.
[3] P. 170.
[4] P. 152.
[5] P. 148.

[6] P. 167.
[7] *Loc. cit.* vol. ii. p. 177.
[8] See Montesquieu, Esprit des Lois, vol. ii. p. 119.

praises or blames a particular race, depends at least as much on the character of the writer as on that of the people.

On the whole, however, I think we may assume that life and property are far less secure in savage than in civilised communities; and though the guilt of a murder or a theft may be very different under different circumstances, to the sufferer the result is much the same.

Mr. Galbraith, who lived for many years, as Indian agent, among the Sioux (North America), thus describes them:[1] They are 'bigoted, barbarous, and exceedingly superstitious. They regard most of the vices as virtues. Theft, arson, rape, and murder are among them regarded as the means of distinction; and the young Indian from childhood is taught to regard killing as the highest of virtues. In their dances, and at their feasts, the warriors recite their deeds of theft, pillage, and slaughter as precious things; and the highest, indeed the only, ambition of a young brave is to secure "the feather," which is but a record of his having murdered or participated in the murder of some human being—whether man, woman, or child, it is immaterial; and, after he has secured his first "feather," appetite is whetted to increase the number in his cap, as an Indian brave is estimated by the number of his feathers.'

In Tahiti the missionaries considered that 'not less than two-thirds of the children were murdered by their parents.'[2] Mr. Ellis adds, 'I do not recollect having met with a female in the islands during the whole period of my residence there, who had been a mother while idolatry prevailed, who had not imbrued her hands in the blood of her offspring.' Mr. Nott also makes the same assertion.

---

[1] Ethn. Journal, 1869, p. 304.
[2] Polynesian Researches, vol. i. pp. 334, 340.

Girls were more often killed than boys, because they were of less use in fishing and in war.

Mr. Wallace maintains that savages act up to their simple moral code at least as well as we do ; but if a man's simple moral code permits him to rob or murder, that may be some excuse for him, but it is little consolation to the sufferer.

As a philosophical question, however, the relative character of different races is less interesting than their moral condition.

Mr. Wallace, in the concluding chapter of his interesting work on the Malay Archipelago, has expressed the opinion that while civilised communities ' have progressed vastly beyond the savage state in intellectual achievements, we have not advanced equally in morals.'   Nay, he even goes further : in a perfect social state, he says, ' every man would have a sufficiently well-balanced intellectual organisation to understand the moral law in all its details, and would require no other motive but the free impulses of his own nature to obey that law.   Now, it is very remarkable that among people in a very low stage of civilisation, we find some approach to such a perfect social state ;' and he adds, ' it is not too much to say that the mass of our populations have not at all advanced beyond the savage code of morals, and have in many cases sunk below it.'

Far from thinking this true, I should rather be disposed to say that Man has, perhaps, made more progress in moral than in either material or intellectual advancement ; for while even the lowest savages have many material and intellectual attainments, they are, it seems to me, almost entirely wanting in moral feeling, though I am aware that the contrary opinion has been expressed by many eminent authorities.

Thus Lord Kames[1] assumes as an undoubted fact 'that every individual is endued with a sense of right and wrong, more or less distinct;' and after admitting that very different views as to morals are held by different people and different races, he remarks, 'these facts tend not to disprove the reality of a common sense in morals: they only prove that the moral sense has not been equally perfect at all times, nòr in all countries.'

Hume expresses the same opinion in very decided language. 'Let a man's insensibility,' he says, 'be ever so great, he must often be touched with the images of right and wrong; and let his prejudices be ever so obstinate, he must observe that others are susceptible of like impressions.'[2] Nay he even maintains that 'those who have denied the reality of moral distinctions, may be ranked among the disingenuous disputants; nor is it conceivable that any human creature could ever seriously believe that all characters and actions were alike entitled to the affection and regard of every one.'

Mr. Wallace draws a charming picture of some small savage communities which he has visited. Each man, he says, 'scrupulously respects the rights of his fellow, and any infraction of those rights rarely or never takes place. In such a community all are nearly equal. There are none of those wide distinctions of education and ignorance, wealth and poverty, master and servant, which are the product of our civilisation; there is none of that widespread division of labour, which, while it increases wealth, produces also conflicting interests; there is not that severe competition and struggle for existence, or for wealth, which the population of civilised countries inevitably creates.'

[1] History of Man, vol. ii. p. 9, vol. iv. p. 18. [2] Hume's Essays, vol. ii. p. 203.

But does this prove that they are in a high moral condition? does it prove even that they have any moral sense at all? Surely not. For if it does, we must equally credit rooks and bees, and most other gregarious animals, with a moral state higher than that of civilised man. I would not indeed venture to assert that the ant or the bee is not possessed of moral feelings, but we are surely not in a position to affirm it. In the very passage quoted, Mr. Wallace has pointed out that the inducements to crime are in small communities much less than in populous countries. The absence of crime, however, does not constitute virtue, and, without temptation, mere innocence has no merit.

Moreover, in small communities almost all the members are related to one another, and family affection puts on the appearance of virtue. But though parental and filial affection possesses a very moral aspect, they have a totally different origin and a distinct character.

We do not generally attribute moral feelings to quadrupeds and birds, yet there is perhaps no stronger feeling than that of the mother for her offspring. She will submit to any sacrifices for their welfare, and fight against almost any odds for their protection. No follower of Mr. Darwin will be surprised at this; because for generation after generation, those mothers in whom this feeling was most strong have had the best chance of rearing their young. It is not, however, moral feeling in the strict sense of the term; and she would indeed be a cold-hearted mother who cherished and protected her infant only because it was right to do so.

Family affection and moral feeling have indeed been very generally confused together by travellers, yet there is some direct testimony which appears to show that the moral condition of savages is really much lower than has been generally supposed.

Thus, Mr. Dove, speaking of the Tasmanians, asserts that they were entirely without any 'moral views and impressions.'

Governor Eyre says of the Australians that 'having no moral sense of what is just and equitable in the abstract, their only test of propriety must in such cases be, whether they are numerically or physically strong enough to brave the vengeance of those whom they may have provoked, or injured.'[1]

'Conscience,' says Burton, does not exist in Eastern Africa, and 'repentance' expresses regret for missed opportunities of mortal crime. Robbery constitutes an honourable man; murder—the more atrocious the midnight crime the better—makes the hero.[2]

The Yoruba negroes, on the west coast of Africa, according to the same author,[3] 'are covetous, cruel, and wholly deficient in what the civilised man calls conscience;' though it is right to add that some of his other statements with reference to this tribe seem opposed to this view.

Mr. Neighbors states, that among the Comanches of Texas 'no individual action is considered a crime, but every man acts for himself according to his own judgment, unless some superior power, for instance, that of a popular chief, should exercise authority over him. They believe that when they were created, the Great Spirit gave them the privilege of a free and unconstrained use of their individual faculties.'[4]

Speaking of the Kaffirs, Mr. Casalis, who lived for twenty-three years in South Africa, says[5] that 'morality among these people depends so entirely upon social order,

[1] Discoveries in Central Australia, vol. ii. p. 384.
[2] Burton's First Footsteps in East Africa, p. 176.
[3] Abbeokuta, vol. i. p. 303. See
also vol. ii. p. 218.
[4] Schoolcraft's Indian Tribes, vol. ii. p. 131.
[5] The Basutos, p. 300.

that all political disorganisation is immediately followed by a state of degeneracy, which the re-establishment of order alone can rectify.' Thus then, although their language contained words signifying most of the virtues, as well as the vices, it would appear from the above passages that their moral quality was not clearly recognised; it must be confessed, however, that the evidence is not very conclusive, as Mr. Casalis, even in the same chapter, expresses an opinion on the point scarcely consistent with that quoted above.

The Tongans, or Friendly Islanders, had in many respects made great advances, yet Mariner[1] states that, ' on a strict examination of their language, we discover no words essentially expressive of some of the higher qualities of human merit: as virtue, justice, humanity, nor of the contrary, as vice, injustice, cruelty, &c. They have, indeed, expressions for these ideas, but they are equally applicable to other things. To express a virtuous or good man, they would say " tangata lillé," a good man, or " tangata loto lillé," a man with a good mind; but the word lillé, good (unlike our virtuous) is equally applicable to an axe, canoe, or anything else; again, they have no word to express humanity, mercy, &c., but afa, which rather means friendship, and is a word of cordial salutation.'

Mr. Campbell observes that the Soors (one of the aboriginal tribes of India), ' while described as small, mean, and very black, and like the Santals naturally harmless, peaceable, and industrious, are also said to be without moral sense.' [2]

Indeed, I do not remember a single instance in which a savage is recorded as having shown any symptoms of remorse; and almost the only case I can at this moment

[1] Tonga Islands, vol. ii. p. 147.
[2] G. Campbell. The Ethnology of India, p. 37.

call to mind, in which a man belonging to one of the lower races has accounted for an act, by saying explicitly that it was right, was when Mr. Hunt asked a young Feejeean why he had killed his mother.[1]

It is very clear that religion, except in very advanced races, has no moral aspect or influence. The deities are almost invariably evil.

In Feejee[2] 'the names of the gods indicate their characters. Thus, Tunambanga is the adulterer. Ndauthina steals women of rank and beauty by night or torch-light. Kumbunavanua is the rioter; Mbatimona, the brain-eater; Ravuravu, the murderer; Mainatavasara, fresh from the cutting-up or slaughter; and a host besides of the same sort.'

The character of the Greek gods is familiar to us, and was anything but moral. Such Beings would certainly not reward the good, or punish the evil. Hence, it is not surprising that Socrates saw little connection between ethics and religion, or that Aristotle altogether separated morality from theology. Hence also we cannot be surprised to find that, even when a belief in a future state has dawned on the uncivilised mind, it is not at first associated with reward or punishment.

The Australians, though they had a vague belief in ghosts, and supposed that after death they become white-men; that, as they say 'Fall down blackman, jump up whiteman,' have no idea of retribution.[3] The Guinea negroes 'have no idea of future rewards or punishments, for the good or ill actions of their past life.'[4] Other negro races, however, have more advanced ideas on the subject.

'The Tahitians believe the immortality of the soul, at least its existence in a separate state, and that there are

[1] Wilkes' Voyage, p. 95.
[2] Fiji and the Fijians, vol. i. p. 218.
[3] Voyage of the 'Fly,' vol. ii. p. 29.
[4] Bosman, *loc. cit.* p. 401.

two situations of different degrees of happiness, somewhat analogous to our heaven and hell: the superior situation they call " Tavirua l'erai," the other " Tiahoboo." They do not, however, consider them as places of reward and punishment, but as receptacles for different classes; the first for their chiefs and principal people, the other for those of inferior rank ; for they do not suppose that their actions here in the least influence their future state, or indeed that they come under the cognizance of their deities at all. Their religion, therefore, if it has no influence upon their morals, is at least disinterested : and their expressions of adoration and reverence, whether by words or actions, arise only from a humble sense of their own inferiority, and the ineffable excellence of divine perfection.'[1]

In Tonga and at Nukahiva the natives believe that their chiefs are immortal, but not the common people.[2] The Tonga people, says Mariner, ' do not indeed believe in any future state of rewards and punishments.'[3]

Williams [4] tells us that ' offences, in Fijian estimation, are light or grave according to the rank of the offender. Murder by a chief is less heinous than a petty larceny committed by a man of low rank. Only a few crimes are regarded as serious ; e.g., theft, adultery, abduction, witchcraft, infringement of a tabu, disrespect to a chief, incendiarism, and treason ;' and he elsewhere mentions that the Fijians,[5] though believing in a future existence, ' shut out from it the idea of any moral retribution in the shape either of reward or punishment.' The Sumatrans, according to Marsden, ' had some idea of a future life, but not as a state of retribution ; conceiving immortality to be the lot of a rich rather than of a good man. I recollect that an

[1] See Cook's Voyage round the World in Hawkesworth's Voyages, vol. ii. p. 239.
[2] Klemm, vol. iv. p. 351.
[3] Tonga Islands, vol. ii. pp. 147, 148.
[4] Fiji and the Fijians, vol. i. p. 28.
[5] Ibid. p. 243.

inhabitant of one of the islands farther eastward observed to me, with great simplicity, that only great men went to the skies; how should poor men find admittance there ?'[1]

In the Island of Bintang,[2] 'the people having an idea of predestination, always conceived present possession to constitute right, however that possession might have been acquired; but yet they made no scruple of deposing and murdering their sovereigns, and justified their acts by this argument; that the fate of concerns so important as the lives of kings was in the hands of God, whose vicegerents they were, and that if it was not agreeable to him, and the consequence of his will, that they should perish by the daggers of their subjects, it could not so happen. Thus it appears that their religious ideas were just strong enough to banish from their minds every moral sentiment.'

The Kookies of Chittagong 'have no idea of hell or heaven, or of any punishment for evil deeds, or rewards for good actions.'[3] According to Bailey, again, the Veddahs of Ceylon 'have no idea of a future state of rewards and punishments.'[4]

The Hos in Central India 'believe that the souls of the dead become " bhoots," spirits, but no thought of reward or punishment is connected with the change.'[5]

Speaking of South Africa Kolben[6] says, 'that the Hottentots believe the immortality of the soul has been shown in a foregoing chapter. But they have no notion, that ever I could gather, of rewards and punishments after death.'

Among the Mexicans[7] and Peruvians,[8] again, the religion

[1] Marsden's History of Sumatra, p. 289.

[2] Ibid. p. 412.

[3] Rennel, quoted in Lewin's Hill Tracts of Chittagong, p. 110.

[4] Trans. Ethn. Soc. N.S., vol. ii. p. 300.

[5] Dalton, Trans. Ethn. Soc., 1868, p. 38.

[6] History of the Cape of Good Hope, vol. i. p. 314.

[7] Müller, Ges. der Amer. Urreligion., p. 565.

[8] Ibid. p. 410. But see Prescott, vol. i. p. 83.

was entirely independent of moral considerations, and in some other parts of America the future condition is supposed to depend not on conduct, but on rank.[1] In North America 'it is rare,' says Tanner, 'to observe among the Indians any ideas which would lead to the belief that they look upon a future state as one of retribution.'[2]

The Arabs conceive that a broken oath brings misfortune on the place where it was uttered.[3]

In fact, I believe that the lower races of men may be said to be deficient in any idea of right, though quite familiar with that of law. This leads to some curious, though not illogical results. Thus at Jenna,[4] and in the surrounding districts, 'whenever a town is deprived of its chief, the inhabitants acknowledge no law—anarchy, troubles, and confusion immediately prevail, and till a successor is appointed all labour is at an end. The stronger oppress the weak, and consummate every species of crime, without being amenable to any tribunal for their actions. Private property is no longer respected; and thus before a person arrives to curb its licentiousness, a town is not unfrequently reduced from a flourishing state of prosperity and of happiness to all the horrors of desolation.'

That there should be any races of men so deficient in moral feeling, was altogether opposed to the preconceived ideas with which I commenced the study of savage life, and I have arrived at the conviction by slow degrees, and even with reluctance. I have, however, been forced to this conclusion, not only by the direct statements of travellers, but also by the general tenor of their remarks,

---

[1] Müller, Ges. des Amer. Urreligion., p. 139. See also pp. 289, 565.
[2] Tanner's Narrative, p. 369.
[3] Klemm, Culturgeschichte, vol. iv.
[4] R. and J. Lander's Niger Expedition, vol. i. p. 96.
p. 190.

and especially by the remarkable absence of repentance and remorse among the lower races of men.

On the whole, then, it appears to me that the moral feelings deepen with the gradual growth of a race.

External circumstances, no doubt, exercise much influence on character. We very often see, however, that the possession of one virtue is counterbalanced by some corresponding defect. Thus the North American Indians are brave and generous, but they are also cruel and reckless of life. Moreover, in the early stages of law, motive is never considered; a fact which shows how little hold morality once had even on communities which have made considerable progress. Some cases which have been quoted as illustrating the contrast between the ideas of virtue entertained by different races seem to prove the absence, rather than the perversity, of sentiment on the subject. I cannot believe, for instance, that theft and murder have ever been really regarded as virtues. In a barbarous state they were, no doubt, means of distinction, and in the absence of moral feelings were regarded with no reprobation. I cannot, however, suppose that they could be considered as 'right,' though they might give rise to a feeling of respect, and even of admiration. So also the Greeks regarded the duplicity of Ulysses as an element in his greatness, but surely not as a virtue in itself.

What, then, is the origin of moral feeling? Some regard it as intuitive, as an original instinct implanted in the human mind. Herbert Spencer,[1] on the contrary, maintains that 'moral intuitions are the results of accumulated experiences of utility; gradually organised and inherited, they have come to be quite independent of conscious experience. Just in the same way that I believe the intuition of space, possessed by any living individual, to

[1] Bain's Mental and Moral Science, p. 722.

have arisen from organised and consolidated experiences of all antecedent individuals, who bequeathed to him their slowly-developed nervous organisation; just as I believe that this intuition, requiring only to be made definite and complete by personal experiences, has practically become a form of thought apparently quite independent of experience; so do I believe that the experiences of utility, organised and consolidated through all past generations of the human race, have been producing corresponding nervous modifications, which, by continued transmission and accumulation, have become in us certain faculties of moral intuition—certain emotions responding to right and wrong conduct, which have no apparent basis in the individual experiences of utility.'

I cannot entirely subscribe to either of these views. The moral feelings are now, no doubt, intuitive, but if the lower races of savages have none, they evidently cannot have been so originally nor can they be regarded as natural to man. Neither can I accept the opposite theory; while entirely agreeing with Mr. Spencer that 'there have been, and still are, developing in the race, certain fundamental moral intuitions,' I feel, with Mr. Hutton, much difficulty in conceiving that, in Mr. Spencer's words, 'these moral intuitions are the results of the accumulated experiences of Utility,' that is to say, of Utility to the individual. It is evident, indeed, that feelings acting on generation after generation might produce a continually deepening conviction, but I fail to perceive how this explains the difference between 'right' and 'utility.' Yet utility in one sense *has*, I think, been naturally and yet unconsciously selected as the basis of morals. Mr. Hutton, if I understand him correctly, doubts this.

Honesty, for instance, he says,[1] 'must certainly have

[1] Macmillan's Magazine, 1869, p. 271.

been associated by our ancestors with many unhappy as
well as many happy consequences, and we know that in
ancient Greece dishonesty was openly and actually associated with happy consequences, in the admiration for
the guile and craft of Ulysses. Hence the moral associations slowly formed, according to Mr. Spencer, in favour
of honesty, must have been, in fact, a mere predominance
of association with a balance on one side.'

This seems to me a good crucial case. Honesty, on their
own part, may, indeed, have been, and no doubt was, 'associated by our ancestors with many unhappy, as well as
many happy consequences;' but honesty on the part of
others could surely have nothing but happy consequences.
Thus, while the perception that 'Honesty is the best policy'
was, no doubt, as Mr. Hutton observes, 'long subsequent
to the most imperious enunciation of its sacredness as a
duty,' honesty would be recognised as a virtue so soon as
men perceived the sacredness of any duty. As soon as
contracts were entered into between individuals or states,
it became manifestly the interest of each that the other
should be honest. Any failure in this respect would
naturally be condemned by the sufferer. It is precisely
because honesty is sometimes associated with unhappy consequences, that it is regarded as a virtue. If it had always
been directly advantageous to all parties, it would have
been classed as useful, not as right; it would have lacked
the essential element which renders it a virtue.

Or take respect for Age. We find, even in Australia,
laws, if I may so term them, appropriating the best of
everything to the old men. Naturally the old men lose no
opportunity of impressing these injunctions on the young;
they praise those who conform, and condemn those who
resist. Hence the custom is strictly adhered to. I do
not say, that to the Australian mind, this presents

itself as a sacred duty, but it would I think in the course of time have come to be so considered.

For when a race had made some progress in intellectual development, a difference would certainly be felt between those acts which a man was taught to do as conducive to his own direct advantage, and those which were not so, and yet which were enjoined for any other reason. Hence would arise the idea of *right* and *duty*, as distinct from mere utility.

How much more our notions of right depend on the lessons we receive when young than on hereditary ideas, becomes evident if we consider the different moral codes existing in our own country. Nay, even in the very same individual two contradictory systems may often be seen side by side in incongruous association. Thus the Christian code and the ordinary code of honour seem to be opposed in some respects, yet the great majority of men hold, or suppose that they hold, them both.

Lastly it may be observed that in our own case religion and morality are closely connected together. Yet the sacred character, which forms an integral part in our conception of duty, could not arise until Religion became moral. Nor would this take place until the Deities were conceived to be beneficent beings. As soon, however, as this was the case, they would naturally be supposed to regard with approbation all that tended to benefit their worshippers, and to condemn all actions of the opposite character. This step was an immense benefit to mankind, since that dread of the unseen powers which had previously been wasted on the production of mere ceremonies and sacrifices, at once invested the moral feelings with a sacredness, and consequently with a force, which they had not until then possessed.

Authority, then, seems to me the origin, and utility,

though not in the manner suggested by Mr. Spencer, the
criterion, of virtue.   Mr. Hutton, however, in the conclud
ing paragraph of his interesting paper, urges that surely
by this time 'some *one* elementary moral law should be as
deeply ingrained in human practice as the geometrical
law that a straight line is the shortest way between two
points.   Which of them is it?'   I see no such necessity.
A child whose parents belong to different nations, with
different moral codes, would, I suppose, have the moral
feeling deep, and yet might be without any settled ideas
as to particular moral duties.   And this is in reality our
own case.   Our ancestors have, now for many generations,
had a feeling that some actions were right and some were
wrong, but at different times they have had very different
codes of morality.   Hence we have a deeply-seated moral
feeling, and yet, as anyone who has children may satisfy
himself, no such decided moral code.   Children have a
deep feeling of right and wrong, but no such decided or
intuitive conviction which actions are right and which are
wrong.

CHAPTER VIII.

LANGUAGE.

ALTHOUGH it has been at various times stated that certain savage tribes are entirely without language, none of these accounts appear to be well authenticated, and they are *à priori* extremely improbable.

At any rate, even the lowest races of which we have any satisfactory account possess a language, imperfect though it may be, and eked out to a great extent by signs. I do not suppose, however, that this custom has arisen from the absence of words to represent their ideas, but rather because in all countries inhabited by savages the number of languages is very great, and hence there is a great advantage in being able to communicate by signs.

Thus James, in his expedition to the Rocky Mountains, speaking of the Kiawa-Kaskaia Indians, says, 'These nations, although constantly associating together and united under the influence of the Bear-Tooth, are yet totally ignorant of each other's language, insomuch that it was no uncommon occurrence to see two individuals of different nations sitting upon the ground, and conversing freely by means of the language of signs. In the art of thus conveying their ideas they were thorough adepts; and their manual display was only interrupted at remote intervals by a smile, or by the auxiliary of an articulated word of the language of the Crow Indians, which to a very limited extent passes current among them.'[1] Fisher,[2] also, speaking of the Comanches and various surrounding tribes, says that they have 'a language of signs, however, by which all Indians and traders can understand one another; and they always make these signs when communicating among themselves. The men, when conversing together, in their lodges, sit upon skins, cross-legged like a Turk, and speak and make signs in corroboration of what they say, with their hands, so that either a blind or a deaf man could understand them. For instance, I meet an Indian, and wish to ask him if he saw six waggons drawn by horned cattle, with three Mexican and three American teamsters, and a man mounted on horseback. I make these signs:—I point "you," then to his eyes, meaning " see; " then hold up all my fingers on the right hand and the fore finger on the left, meaning " six; " then I make two circles by bringing the ends of my thumbs and forefingers together, and, holding my two hands out, move my wrists in such a way as to indicate waggon wheels revolving, meaning " waggons; " then, by making an upward motion with each hand from both sides of my head, I indicate " horns," signifying horned cattle; then by first holding up three fingers, and then by placing my extended right hand below my lower lip and moving it downward stopping in midway down the chest, I indicate " beard," meaning Mexican; and with three fingers again, and passing my right hand from left to right in front of my forehead, I indicate " white brow " or " pale face." I then hold up my fore finger, meaning one man, and by placing the fore finger of my left hand between the fore and second finger of my right hand, representing a man astride of a horse, and by moving my hands up and down give the motion of a horse gallop-

[1] See James's Expedition to the Rocky Mountains, vol. iii. p. 52.   [2] Trans. Ethn. Soc. 1869, vol. i. p. 283.

ing with a man on his back. I in this way ask the Indian, "You see six waggons, horned cattle, three Mexicans, three Americans, one man on horse-back?" If he holds up his fore finger and lowers it quickly, as if he was pointing at some object on the ground, he means "Yes;" if he moves it from side to side, upon the principle that people sometimes move their head from side to side, he means "No." The time required to make these signs would be about the same as if you asked the question verbally.' The Bushmen also are said to intersperse their language with so many signs that they are unintelligible in the dark, and when they want to converse at night, are compelled to collect round their camp fires. So also Burton tells us that the Arapahos of North America, 'who possess a very scanty vocabulary, can hardly converse with one another in the dark; to make a stranger understand them they must always repair to the camp fire for pow wow.'[1]

A very interesting account of the sign-language, especially with reference to that used by the deaf and dumb, is contained in Tylor's 'Early History of Man.' But although signs may serve to convey ideas in a manner which would probably surprise those who have not studied this question; still it must be admitted that they are far inferior to the sounds of the voice; which, as already mentioned, are used for this purpose by all the races of men with whom we are acquainted.

Language, as it exists among all but the lowest races, although far from perfect, is yet so rich in terms, and possesses in its grammar so complex an organisation, that we cannot wonder at those who have attributed to it a divine and miraculous origin. Nay, their view may be admitted as correct, but only in that sense in which a ship

---

[1] City of the Saints, p. 151.

or a palace may be so termed : they are human insofar as they have been worked out by man ; divine, inasmuch as in doing so he has availed himself of the powers which Providence has given him.[1]

M. Renan[2] draws a distinction between the origin of words and that of language, and as regards the latter, says : 'Je persiste donc, après dix ans de nouvelles études, à envisager le langage comme formé d'un seul coup, et comme sorti instantanément du génie de chaque race,' a theory which involves that of the plurality of human species. No doubt the complexity and apparent perfection of the grammar among very low races, is at first sight very surprising, but we must remember that the language of children is more regular than ours. A child says, 'I goed,' 'I comed,' badder, baddest, &c. Moreover the preservation of a complicated system of grammar among savage tribes shows that such a system is natural to them, and not merely a survival from more civilised times. Indeed, we know that the tendency of civilisation is towards the simplification of grammatical forms.

Nor must it by any means be supposed that complexity implies excellence, or even completeness, in a language. On the contrary, it often arises from a cumbersome mode of·supplying some radical defect. Adam Smith long ago pointed out that the verb ' to be ' is ' the most abstract and metaphysical of all verbs ; and consequently could by no means be a word of early invention.' And he suggests that

---

[1] Lord Monboddo in combating those who regard language as a revelation, expresses a hope that he will not, on that account, be supposed to ' pay no respect to the account given in our sacred books of the origin of our species ; but it does not belong to me,' he adds, ' as a philosopher or grammarian, to enquire whether such account is to be understood allegorically, according to the opinions of some divines.' He forgets, however, that those who regard language as a revelation, do so in the teeth of the express statement in Genesis that God brought the animals ' unto Adam to see what he would call them : and whatsoever Adam called every living creature, that was the name thereof.'

[2] De l'Origine du Langage, p. 16.

the absence of this verb probably led to the intricacy of conjugations. 'When' he adds, 'it came to be invented, however, as it had all the tenses and modes of any other verb,
by being joined with the passive participle, it was capable
of supplying the place of the whole passive voice, and of
rendering this part of their conjugations as simple and
uniform, as the use of prepositions had rendered their de-
clensions.'[1] He goes on to point out that the same remarks apply also to the possessive verb 'I have,' which
affected the active voice, as profoundly as 'I am' influenced
the passive; thus these two verbs between them, when
once suggested, enabled mankind to relieve their memories,
and thus unconsciously, but most effectually, to simplify
their grammar.

In English we carry the same principle much further,
and not only use the auxiliary verbs 'to have' and 'to be,'
but also several others—as do, did; will, would; shall,
should; can, could; may, might.[2] Adam Smith was,
however, mistaken in supposing that the verb 'to be'
exists 'in every language;'[3] on the contrary, the complexity
of the North American languages is in a great measure
due to its absence. The auxiliary verb 'to be' is entirely absent in most American languages, and the consequence is that they turn almost all their adjectives and
nouns into verbs, and conjugate them, through all the
tenses, persons, and moods.[4]

Again, the Esquimaux, instead of using adverbs, conjugate the verb; they have special terminations implying ill,
better, rarely, hardly, faithfully, &c.; hence such a word
as aglekkigiartorasuarniarpok, 'he goes away hastily and
exerts himself to write.'[5]

---

[1] Smith's Moral Sentiments, vol. ii.
p. 426.

[2] Smith, *loc. cit.* p. 432.

[3] *Loc. cit.* p. 426.

[4] See Gallatin, Trans. Amer. Antiq.
Soc., vol. ii. p. 176.

[5] Crantz, His. of Greenland, vol. i.
p. 224.

The number of words in the languages of civilised races is no doubt immense. Chinese, for instance, contains 40,000; Todd's edition of Johnson, 58,000; Webster's Dictionary, 70,000; and Flugel's more than 65,000.[1] The great majority of these, however, can be derived from certain original words, or roots, which are very few in number. In Chinese there are about 450, Hebrew has been reduced to 500, and Müller doubts whether there are more in Sanskrit. M. D'Orsey even assures us that an ordinary agricultural labourer has not 300 words in his vocabulary.

Professor Max Müller[2] observes, that 'this fact simplifies immensely the problem of the origin of language. It has taken away all excuse for those rapturous descriptions of language which invariably preceded the argument that language must have a divine origin. We shall hear no more of that wonderful instrument which can express all we see, and hear, and taste, and touch, and smell; which is the breathing image of the whole world; which gives form to the airy feelings of our souls, and body to the loftiest dreams of our imagination; which can arrange in accurate perspective the past, the present, and the future, and throw over everything the varying hues of certainty, of doubt, of contingency.'

This, indeed, is no new view, but was that generally adopted by the philologists of the last century, and is fully borne out by more recent researches.

In considering the origin of these root-words, we must remember that most of them are very ancient, and much worn by use. This greatly enhances the difficulty of the problem.

Nevertheless, there are several large classes of words with reference to the origin of which there can be no doubt.

[1] Saturday Review, November 2, 1861. Lectures on Language, p. 268.
[2] *Loc. cit.* p. 359.

Many names of animals, such as cuckoo, crow, peewit, &c., are evidently derived from the sounds made by those birds. Everyone admits that such words as bang, crack, purr, whizz, hum, &c., have arisen from the attempt to represent sounds characteristic of the object it is intended to designate.[1] Take, again, the inarticulate human sounds —sob, sigh, moan, groan, laugh, cough, weep, whoop, shriek, yawn: or of animals; as cackle, chuckle, gobble, quack, twitter, chirp, coo, hoot, caw, croak, chatter, neigh, whinny, mew, purr, bark, yelp, roar, bellow: the collision of hard bodies; clap, rap, tap, knap, snap, trap, flap, slap, crack, smack, whack, thwack, pat, bat, batter, beat, butt; and again, clash, flash, plash, splash, smash, dash, crash, bang, clang, twang, ring, ding, din, bump, thump, plump, boom, hum, drum, hiss, rustle, bustle, whistle, whisper, murmur, babble, &c. So also sounds denoting certain motions and actions; whirr, whizz, puff, fizz, fly, flit, flow, flutter, patter, clatter, crackle, rattle, bubble, guggle, dabble, grapple, draggle, rush, shoot, shot, shut, &c. Many words for cutting, and the objects cut, or used for cutting &c., are obviously of similar origin. Thus we have the sound sh—r with each of the vowels; share, a part cut off; shear, an instrument for cutting; shire, a division of a country; shore, the division between land and sea, or as we use it in Kent, between two fields; a shower, a number of separate particles; again scissors, scythe, shread, scrape, shard, scale, shale, shell, shield, skull, shaist, shatter, scatter, scar, scoop, score, scrape, scratch, scum, scour, scurf, surf, scuttle, sect, shape, sharp, shave, sheaf, shed, shoal, shred, split, splinter, splutter, &c. Another important class of words is evidently founded on the sounds by which we naturally express our feelings. Thus from Oh!

---

[1] Wedgwood, Introduction to Dic. of English Etymology. Farrar, Origin of Language, p. 89.

Ah! the instinctive cry of pain, we get woe, væ, Latin, wail, ache, αχος Gr.

From the deep guttural sound ugh, we have ugly, huge, and hug.

From pr, or prut, indicating contempt or self-conceit, comes proud, pride, &c.

From fie, we have fiend, foe, feud, foul, Latin putris, Fr. puer, filth, fulsome, fear. In addition I will only remark that,

From that of smacking the lips we get γλυκυς, dulcis, lick, like.

Under these circumstances I cannot but think that we may look upon the words above mentioned as the still recognisable descendants of roots which were onomatopœic in their origin; and I am glad to see that Professor Max Müller in his second series of lectures on language,[1] wishes to be understood as offering no opposition to this theory, although for the present ' satisfied with considering roots as phonetic types.'

It may be said, and said truly, that other classes of ideas are not so easily or naturally expressible by corresponding sounds; and that abstract terms seldom have any such obvious derivation. We must remember, however, firstly, that abstract terms are wanting in the lowest languages, and secondly, that most words are greatly worn by use, and altered by the difference of pronunciation. Even among the most advanced races a few centuries suffice to produce a great change; how then can we expect that any roots (excepting those which are preserved from material alteration by the constant suggestion of an obvious fitness) should have retained their original sound throughout the immense period which has elapsed since the origin

[1] *Loc. cit.* p. 92.

of language? Moreover everyone who has paid any attention to children, or schoolboys, must have observed how nicknames, often derived from slight and even fanciful characteristics, are seized on and soon adopted by general consent. Hence even if root-words had remained with little alteration, we should still be often puzzled to account for their origin.

Without, then, supposing with Farrar that all our root-words have originated from onomatopœia, I believe that they arose in the same way as the nicknames and new slang terms of our own day. These we know are often selected from some similarity of sound, or connection of ideas, often so quaint, fanciful, or far-fetched, that we are unable to recall the true origin even of words which have arisen in our own time. How then can we wonder that the derivations of root-words which are thousands of years old should be in so many cases lost, or at least undeterminable with certainty.

Again, the words most frequently required, and especially those used by children, are generally represented by the simplest and easiest sounds, merely because they are the simplest. Thus in Europe we have papa and daddy, mamma, and baby; poupee for a doll; amme for a nurse, &c. Some authorities, indeed, have derived Pater and Papa from a root Pa to cherish, and Mater, Mother, from Ma to make; this derivation is accepted by writers representing the most opposite theories, as for instance by Renan, Müller, and even apparently by Farrar.

Professor Max Müller says that ' the name father was coined at that early period, shows that the father acknowledged the offspring of his wife as his own, for thus only had he a right to claim the title of father. Father is derived from a root Pa, which means, not to beget but to protect, to support, to nourish. The father, as genitor, was called in Sanskrit ganitár, but as protector and supporter of his offspring he was called pitar ; hence, in the Veda, these two names are used together, in order to express the full idea of father. Thus the poet says :—

> Dyaús me petâ ganitâ
> Jovis mei pater genitor
> Ζεὺς ἐμοῦ πατὴρ γενετήρ.

In a similar manner mâtar, mother, is joined with ganitû, genitrix, which shows that the word mâtar must soon have lost its etymological meaning, and have become an expression of respect and endearment. For among the early Arians, mâtar had the sense of maker, from Ma, to fashion.'[1]

Now let us see what are the names for father and mother among some other races, omitting all languages derived from Sanskrit.

AFRICA.

Language.	Father.	Mother.
Bola (N. W. Africa)	Papa	Ni
Sarar	Paba	Ne
Pepel	Papa	Nana
Biafada	Baba	Na
Baga	Bapa	Mana
Timne	Pa	Kara
Mandenga	Fa	Na
Kabunga	,,	,,
Toronka	,,	,,
Dsalunka	,,	,,
Kankanka	,,	,,
Bambara	,,	Ba
Kono	,,	Ndé
Vei	,,	Ba
Soso	Fafe	Nga
Kisekise	,,	,,

[1] Comparative Mythology. Oxford Essays, 1856, p. 14.

Language.	Father.	Mother.
Tono	Fafa	Nga
Dewoi (Guinea)	Ba	Ma
Basa	,,	Ne
Gbe	,,	De
Dahome	Da	Noc
Mahi	,, also Dadye	,,
Ota	Baba	Iya
Egba	,,	,,
Idsesa	,,	,,
Yoruba	,,	,,
Yagba	,,	,,
Eki	,,	,,
Dsumu	,,	,,
Oworo	,,	,,
Dsebu	,,	,,
Ife	,,	Yeye
Ondo	,,	Ye
Mose (High Sudan)	Ba	Ma
Gurma	,,	Na
Sobo (Niger District)	Wawa	Nene
Udso	Dada	Ayo
Nupe	Nda	Nna
Kupa	Dada	Mo
Esitako	Da	Na
Musu	Nda	Meya
Basa	Ba	Nno
Opanda	Ada	Onyi
Igu	,,	Onya
Egbira	,,	,,
Buduma (Central Africa)	Bawa	Ya
Bornu	Aba	,,
Munio	Bawa	,,
Nguru	,,	Iya
Kanem	Mba	,,
Karehare	Baba	Nana
Ngodsin	,,	,,
Doai	,,	Aye
Basa	Ada	Am
Kamuku	Baba	Bina
Songo (S. W. Africa)	Papa	Mama

Language.	Father.	Mother.
Kiriman (S. E. Africa)	Baba	Mma
Bidsogo (Unclassified languages)	,,	Ondsunei
Wun	,,	Omsion
Gadsaga	,,	Ma
Gura	Da	Nye
Banyun	Aba	Aai
Nalu	Baba	Nya
Bulanda	,,	Ni
Limba	Papa	Na
Landoma	,,	Mama
Barba	Baba	Inya
Timbuktu	,,	Nya
Bagrmi	Babi	Kunyun
Kadzina	Baba	Ua
Timbo	,,	Nene
Salum	,,	Yuma
Goburu	,,	Inna
Kano	,,	Ina
Yala	Ada	Ene
Dsarawa	Tada	Nga
Koro	Oda	Ma
Yasgua	Ada	Ama
Kambali	Dada	Omo
Soa (Arabic group)	Aba	Aye
Wadai	Abba	Omma

NON-ARYAN NATIONS OF EUROPE AND ASIA.

Turkish	Baba	Ana
Georgian	Mama	Deda
Mantshu	Ama	Eme
Javanese	Bapa	Ibu
Malay	Bapa	Ibu
Syami (Thibet)	Dhada	Ma
Thibetan	Pha	Ama
Serpa (Nepal)	Aba	Ama
Murmi ,,	Apa	Amma
Pakhya ,,	Babai	Ama
Lepcha (Sikkim)	Abo	Amo
Bhutani	Appa	Ai

Language.	Father.	Mother.
Dhimal (N. E. Bengal)	Aba	Ama
Kocch ,,	Bap	Ma
Garo ,,	Aba	Ama
Burman (Burmah)	Ahpa	Ami
Mru ,,	Pa	Au
Sak	Aba	Anu
Talain (Siam)	Ma	Ya
Ho (Central India)	Appu	Enga
Santhali	Baba	Ayo
Uraon ,,	Babe	Ayyo
Gayeti ,,	Baba	Dai
Khond	Abba	Ayya
Tuluva (Southern India)	Amme	Appe
Badaga ,,	Appa	Avve
Irula ,,	Amma	Avve
Cinghalese	Appa	Amma
Chinese	Fu	Mu

ISLANDERS.

New Zealand	Pa-Matuatana	Matua wahina
Tonga Islands	Tamny	Fae
Erroob (N. Australia)	Bab	Ama
Lewis' Murray Island	Baab	Hammah

AUSTRALIA.

Jajowrong (N. W. Australia)	Marmook	Barbook
Knenkorenwurro ,,	Marmak	Barpanorook
Burapper ,,	Marmook	Barbook
Taungurong ,,	Warredoo	Barbanook
Boraipar (S. Australia)	Marmme	Parppe
Murrumbidgee	Kunny	Mamma
Western Australia	Mammun	Ngangan
Port Lincoln	Pappi	Maitya

ESQUIMAUX.

Esquimaux (Hudson's Bay)	Atata	Amama
Tshuktchi (Asia)	Atta	?

The American languages seem at first sight opposed to the view here suggested; on close examination, however, this is not the case, since the pronunciation of the labials is very difficult to many American races. Thus, La Hontan informs us that the Hurons do not use the labials, and that he spent four days in attempting without success to teach a Huron to pronounce b, p, and m. Garcilasso de la Vega tells us that the Peruvian language wanted the letters b, d, f, g, s, and x, and the Indians of Port au Français, according to M. Lamanon, made no use of the consonants b, d, f, j, p, v, or x.[1] Still even in America we find some cases in which the sounds for father resemble those so general elsewhere; thus

Language.	Father.	Mother.
Costanos (N. W. America)	Ah Pah	Ah nah
Tahkali ,,	Apa	,,
Tlatskanai ,,	Mama	Naa
Nasqually ,,	Baa	Sogo
Nootka ,,	Api	Una
Athapascans (Canada)	Appa	Unnungcool
Omahas (Missouri)	Dadai	Eehong
Minnetarees ,,	Tantai	Eeka
Choctas (Mississippi)	Aunkke	Iskeh
Caribs	Baba	Bibi
Uainamben (Amazons)	Pai	Ami
Cobeu ,,	Ipaki	Ipako
Tucano ,,	Pagui	Maou
Tariana ,,	Paica	Naca
Baniwa	Padjo	Nadjo
Barre	Mbaba	Memi

Finding, then, that the easiest sounds which a child can produce denote father and mother almost all over the world; remembering that the root ba or pa indicates baby as well as father; and observing that in some cases the

---

[1] See also Gallatin, in Trans. Am. Antiq. Soc. vol. i. p. 63.

usual sounds are reversed; as for instance in Georgian, where mama stands for father, and dada for mother; or in Tuluva, where amme is father, and appe mother; or some of the Australian tribes, in which combinations of the sound mar stands for father, and bar for mother; we must surely admit that the Sanskrit verb Pa, to protect, comes from pa, father, and not *vice versâ*.

There are few more interesting studies than the steps by which our present language has been derived from these original roots. This subject has been admirably dealt with by my friend Professor Max Müller in his ' Lectures on Language,' and, tempting as it would be to do so, I do not propose to follow him into that part of the science. As regards the formation of the original roots, however, he declines to express any opinion. Rejecting what he calls the pooh-pooh and bow-wow theories[1] (though they are in reality but one), he observes that ' the theory which is suggested to us by an analysis of language carried out according to the principles of comparative philology is the very opposite. We arrive in the end at roots, and every one of these expresses a general, not an individual idea.' But the whole question is how were these roots chosen? How did particular sounds come to be allotted to particular things?

Here, however, Professor Max Müller stops. Nothing, he admits,[2] ' would be more interesting than to know from historical documents the exact process by which the first man began to lisp his first words, and thus to be rid for ever of all the theories on the origin of speech. But this knowledge is denied us; and, if it had been otherwise, we should probably be quite unable to understand those primitive events in the history of the human mind.'

[1] Science of Language, p. 373.   [2] *Loc. cit.* p. 346.

Yet in his last chapter he says,[1] 'and now I am afraid I have but a few minutes left to explain the last question of all in our science, namely—How can sound express thought? How did roots become the signs of general ideas? How was the abstract idea of measuring expressed by mâ, the idea of thinking by man? How did gâ come to mean going, sthâ standing, sad sitting, dâ giving, mar dying, char walking, kar doing? I shall try to answer as briefly as possible. The 400 or 500 roots which remain as the constituent elements in different families of language are not interjections, nor are they imitations. They are phonetic types produced by a power inherent in human nature. They exist, as Plato would say, by nature; though with Plato we should add that, when we say by nature, we mean by the hand of God. There is a law which runs through nearly the whole of nature, that everything which is struck rings.

.   .   .   .

'Man, in his primitive and perfect state, was not only endowed, like the brute, with the power of expressing his sensations by interjections, and his perceptions by onomatopœia. He possessed likewise the faculty of giving more articulate expression to the natural conceptions of his mind. That faculty was not of his making. It was an instinct, an instinct of the mind as irresistible as any other instinct. So far as language is the production of that instinct, it belongs to the realm of nature.'

This answer, though expressed with Professor Max Müller's usual eloquence, does not carry to my mind any definite conception. On the other hand, it appears to me that at any rate as regards some roots, we have, as already pointed out, a satisfactory explanation. Professor Max Müller,[2] indeed, admits that 'there are some names,

---

[1] *Loc. cit.* p. 386.   [2] Science of Language, p. 363.

such as cuckoo, which are clearly formed by an imitation of sound. But,' he adds, 'words of this kind are, like artificial flowers, without a root. They are sterile, and are unfit to express anything beyond the one object which they imitate. If you remember the variety of derivatives that could be formed from the root spac, to see, you will at once perceive the difference between the fabrication of such a word as cuckoo, and the true natural growth of words.'

It has, however, been already shown that such roots, far from being sterile, are on the contrary very fruitful, and we must remember that savage languages are very poor in abstract terms. Indeed the vocabularies of the various races are most interesting from the indications which they afford with reference to the condition of those by whom they are used. Thus we get a melancholy idea of the moral state and family life of tribes which are deficient in terms of endearment. Colonel Dalton [1] tells us that the Hos of Central India have no 'endearing epithets.' The Algonquin language, one of the richest in North America, contained no verb ' to love,' and when Elliot translated the Bible into it in 1661, he was obliged to coin a word for the purpose. The Tinné Indians on the other side of the Rocky Mountains had no equivalent for ' dear ' or ' beloved.' ' I endeavoured,' says General Lefroy, ' to put this intelligibly to Nanette, by supposing such an expression as ma chère femme ; ma chère fille. When at length she understood it, her reply was (with great emphasis), " I' disent jamais ca; i' disent ma femme, ma fille." ' The Kalmucks and some of the South Sea Islanders are said to have had no word for ' thanks.' Lichtenstein,[2] speaking of the Bushmen, mentions it as a remarkable instance of the total absence of civilisation among them that ' they have

[1] Trans. Ethn. Soc. N.S., vol. vi. p. 27.   [2] Vol. i. p. 119 ; vol. ii. p. 49.

no names, and seem not to feel the want of such a means of distinguishing one individual from another.' Pliny[1] makes a similar statement concerning a race in Northern Africa. Freycinet[2] also asserts that some of the Australian tribes did not name their women. I confess that I am inclined to doubt these statements, and to refer the supposed absence of names to the curious superstitions already referred to (antè, p. 145), and which make savages so reluctant to communicate their true names to strangers. The Brazilian tribes, according to Spix and Martius, had separate names for the different parts of the body, and for all the different animals and plants with which they were acquainted, but were entirely deficient in such terms as ' color,' ' tone,' ' sex,' ' genus,' ' spirit,' &c.

Bailey[3] mentions that the language of the Veddahs (Ceylon) ' is very limited. It only contains such phrases as are required to describe the most striking objects of nature, and those which enter into the daily life of the people themselves. So rude and primitive is their dialect that the most ordinary objects and actions of life are described by quaint periphrases.'

According to missionaries the Fuegians had ' no abstract terms.' In the North American languages a term ' sufficiently general to denote an oak-tree is exceptional.' Thus the Choctaw language has names for the black oak, white oak, and red oak, but none for an oak ; still less for a tree.

The Tasmanians, again, had no general term for a tree, though they had names for each particular kind ; nor could they express ' qualities such as hard, soft, warm, cold, long, short, round,' &c.

Speaking of the Coroados (Brazil), Martius observes that ' it would be in vain to seek among them words for

---

[1] Nat. His., l. v. s. viii.　　　　[3] Trans. Ethn. Soc. N.S., vol. ii. p.
[2] Vol. ii. p. 749.　　　　　　　　298; see also p. 300.

the abstract ideas of plant, animal, and the still more abstract notions colour, tone, sex, species, &c.; such a generalisation of ideas is found among them only in the frequently used infinitive of the verbs to walk, to eat, to drink, to dance, to see, to hear, &c. They have no conception of the general powers and laws of nature, and therefore cannot express them in words.'[1]

There is perhaps no more interesting part of the study of language than that which concerns the system of numeration, nor any more striking proof of the low mental condition of many savage races than the undoubted fact that they are unable to count their own fingers, even of one hand.

According to Lichtenstein the Bushmen could not count beyond two; Spix and Martius make the same statement about the Brazilian Wood-Indians. The Cape Yorkers of Australia count as follows :—

One	Netat.
Two	Naes.
Three	Naes-netat.
Four	Naes-naes.
Five	Naes-naes-netat.
Six	Naes-naes-naes.

Speaking of the Lower Murray nations Mr. Beveridge says, ' their numerals are confined to two alone, viz. ryup, politi, the first signifying " one " and the second " two." To express five, thay say ryup murnangin, or one hand, and to express ten, politi murnangin, or two hands.' [2] Indeed, no Australian can go beyond four, their term for five simply implying a large number. The Dammaras, according to Galton, used no term beyond three. He gives so admirable and at the same time so amusing an account of Dammara

---

[1] Spix and Martius, Travels in Brazil, vol. ii. p. 253.

[2] Trans. of the R. S. of Victoria, vol. vi. p. 151.

difficulties in language and arithmetic that I cannot resist quoting it in full. ' We had,' he says,[1] ' to trust to our Dammara guides, whose ideas of time and distance were most provokingly indistinct; besides this they have no comparative in their language, so that you cannot say to them, " which is the longer of the two, the next stage or the last one?" but you must say, " the last is little; the next is it great?" The reply is not, it is a " little longer," or "very much longer," but simply, "it is so," or "it is not so." They have a very poor notion of time. If you say "suppose we start at sunrise, where will the sun be when we arrive?" they make the wildest points in the sky, though they are something of astronomers, and give names to several stars. They have no way of distinguishing days, but reckon by the rainy season, or the pig-nut season. When inquiries are made about how many days' journey off a place may be, their ignorance of all numerical ideas is very annoying. In practice, whatever they may possess in their language, they certainly use no numeral greater than three. When they wish to express four, they take to their fingers, which are to them as formidable instruments of calculation as a sliding rule is to an English school-boy. They puzzle very much after five, because no spare hand remains to grasp and secure the fingers that are required for units. Yet they seldom lose oxen; the way in which they discover the loss of one is not by the number of the herd being diminished, but by the absence of a face they know. When bartering is going on, each sheep must be paid for separately. Thus, suppose two sticks of tobacco to be the rate of exchange for one sheep, it would sorely puzzle a Dammara to take two sheep and give him four sticks. I have done so, and seen a man put two of the

---

[1] Galton, Tropical South Africa, p. 132.

sticks apart, and take a sight over them at one of the
sheep he was about to sell   Having satisfied himself that
that one was honestly paid for and finding to his surprise
that exactly two sticks remained in hand to settle the
account for the other sheep, he would be afflicted with
doubts ; the transaction seemed to come out too " pat " to
be correct, and he would refer back to the first couple of
sticks ; and then his mind got hazy and confused, and
wandered from one sheep to the other, and he broke off
the transaction until two sticks were put into his hand,
and one sheep driven away, and then the other two sticks
given him, and the second sheep driven away.   When a
Dammara's mind is bent upon number, it is too much
occupied to dwell upon quantity ; thus a heifer is bought
from a man for ten sticks of tobacco, his large hands
being both spread out upon the ground, and a stick placed
upon each finger.   He gathers up the tobacco, the size of
the mass pleases him, and the bargain is struck. You then
want to buy a second heifer ; the same process is gone
through, but half sticks instead of whole sticks are put
upon his fingers ; the man is equally satisfied at the time,
but occasionally finds it out, and complains the next day.

' Once while I watched a Dammara floundering hopelessly in a calculation on one side of me, I observed Dinah,
my spaniel, equally embarrassed on the other. She was
overlooking half-a-dozen of her new-born puppies, which
had been removed two or three times from her, and her
anxiety was excessive, as she tried to find out if they were
all present, or if any were still missing. She kept puzzling
and running her eyes over them, backwards and forwards,
but could not satisfy herself.   She evidently had a vague
notion of counting, but the figure was too large for her
brain.   Taking the two as they stood, dog and Dammara,
the comparison reflected no great honour on the man.'

All over the world the fingers are used as counters, and although the numerals of most races are so worn down by use that we can no longer detect their original meaning, there are many savage tribes in which the words used are merely the verbal expressions of the signs used in counting with the fingers.

Of this I have just given one instance. In Labrador 'Tallek,' a hand, means also 'five,' and the term for twenty means hands and feet together. Speaking of the Ahts, Mr. Sproat[1] says, 'it may be noticed that their word for one occurs again in that for six and nine, and the word for two in that for seven and eight. The Aht Indians count upon their fingers. They always count, except where they have learnt differently from their contact with civilisation, by raising the hands with the palms upwards, and extending all the fingers, and bending down each finger as it is used for enumeration. They begin with the little finger. This little finger, then, is one. Now six is five (that is, one whole hand) and one more. We can easily see then, why their word for six comprehends the word for one. Again, seven is five (one whole hand) and two more—thus their word for seven comprehends the word for two. Again, when they have bent down the eighth finger, the most noticeable feature of the hand is that two fingers, that is, a finger and a thumb, remain extended. Now the Aht word for eight comprehends atlah, the word for two. The reason for this I imagine to be as follows:—Eight is ten (or the whole hands) wanting two. Again, when the ninth finger is down, only one finger is left extended. Their word for nine comprehends tsow-wauk, the word for one. Nine is ten (or two whole hands) wanting one.'[2]

---

[1] Scenes and Studies of Savage Life, p. 121.

[2] Scenes and Studies of Savage Life, p. 121–122.

The Zamuca and Muysca Indians[1] have a cumbrous, but very interesting system of numeration.   For five they say, 'hand finished.'   For six, 'one of the other hand,' that is to say take a finger of the other hand; for ten they say, 'two hands finished,' or sometimes more simply 'quicha,' that is 'foot.'   Eleven is foot-one; twelve, foot-two, thirteen, foot-three, and so on : twenty is the feet finished; or in other cases 'Man,' because a man has ten fingers and ten toes, thus making twenty.

Among the Jaruroes the word for forty is 'noenipume,' *i.e.* two men, from noeni, two, and canipune, men.   Hence, no doubt, the prevalence of the decimal system in arithmetic; it has no particular advantage; indeed, either eight or twelve would, in some respects have been more convenient; eight, because you can divide it by two, and then divide the result again by two; and twelve because it is divisible by six, four, three, and two.   Ten, however, has naturally been selected, because we have ten fingers.

Speaking of the Guiana natives, Mr. Brett observes[2] that, 'Another point in which the different nations agree is their method of numeration. The first four numbers are represented by simple words, as in the table above given. Five is "my one hand," *abar-dakabo* in Arawâk. Then comes a repetition, *abar timen, biam timen,* &c., up to nine. *Biam-dakabo,* "my two hands," is ten. From ten to twenty they use the toes (*kuti* or *okuti*), as *abar-kuti-bana,* "eleven," *biam-kuti-bana,* "twelve," &c. They call twenty *abar-loko,* one *loko* or man.   They then proceed by *men* or scores; thus forty-five is laboriously expressed by *biam-loko-abardakabo tajeago,* "two men and one hand upon it." For higher numbers they have now recourse to our words, *hundred* and *thousand.*' So also among the Caribs, the word

<hr/>

[1] Humboldt's Personal Researches, vol. ii. p. 117.   [2] Brett's Indian Tribes of Guiana, p. 417.

for 'ten,' Chonnoucabo raim, meant literally 'the fingers of both hands,' and that for 'twenty' was Chonnougonoi raim, *i.e.* the fingers and toes.[1]

The Coroados[2] generally count only by the joints of the fingers, consequently only to three. Every greater number they express by the word 'mony.'

According to Dobritzhoffer 'the Guaranies when questioned respecting a thing exceeding four, immediately reply ndipapahabi, or ndipapahai, innumerable.'[3] So also 'the Abipones[4] can only express three numbers in proper words. *Iñitára*, one, *Iñoaka*, two, *Iñoaka yekaini*, three. They make up for the other numbers by various arts; thus, *geyenk ñatè*, the fingers of an emu, which, as it has three in front and one turned back, are four, serves to express that number: *neènhalek*, a beautiful skin spotted with five different colours, is used to signify the number five.' '*Hanámbegem*, the fingers of one hand, means five: *lanám rihegem*, the fingers of both hands, ten; *lanám rihegem, cat gracherhaka anamichirihegem*, the fingers of both hands and both feet, twenty.'

Among the Malays and throughout Polynesia the word for five is ima, lima, or rima. In Bali, lima also means a hand; this is also the case in the Bugis, Mandhar, and Endé languages; in the Makasar dialect it is liman; in Sasak it is ima; in Bima it is rima; in Sembawa it is limang.[5]

In the Mpongwe language 'tyani' or 'tani' is five, 'ntyame' is 'hand.'[6] The Koossa Caffres make little use of numerals. Lichtenstein could never discover that

[1] Tertre's History of the Caribby Islands.

[2] Spix and Martius, Travels in Brazil, vol. ii. p. 255.

[3] History of the Abipones, vol. ii. p. 171.

[4] *Loc. cit.* p. 169.

[5] Raffles's History of Java, Appendix F.

[6] Grammar of the Mpongwe Language. New York, Snowden and Prall, 1847.

they had any word for eight, few could reckon beyond ten, and many did not know the names of any numerals. Yet if a single animal was missing out of a herd of several hundred, they observed it immediately.[1] This, however, as Mr. Galton explains, is merely because they miss a face they know. Among the Zulu 'talitisupa' six, means literally 'take the thumb,' *i.e.* having used the finger of one hand, take the thumb of the next. 'The numbers,' says Lichtenstein, 'are commonly expressed among the Beetjuans by fingers held up, so that the word is rarely spoken; many are even unacquainted with these numerals and never employ anything but the sign. It therefore occasioned me no small trouble to learn the numerals, and I could by no means arrive at any denomination for the numbers five and nine. Beyond ten even the most learned could not reckon, nor could I make out by what signs they ever designated these higher numbers.'[2]

Even in our own language the word 'five' has a similar origin, since it comes from the Greek πέντε, which again is evidently connected with the Persian pendji; now in Persian 'pentcha,' means a hand, as Humboldt has already pointed out.[3]

These examples appear to me very instructive; we seem as it were to trace up the formation of the numerals; we perceive the true cause of the decimal system of notation; and we obtain interesting if melancholy, evidence of the extent to which the faculty of thought lies dormant among the lower races of man.

---

[1] Lichtenstein, vol. i. p. 280. See also App.

[2] *Loc. cit.* vol. ii. App.

[3] Personal Researches, London, 1814, vol. ii. p. 116.

CHAPTER IX.

LAWS.

THE customs and laws of the lower races, so far as religious and family relations are concerned, have already been discussed. There are, however, some other points of view with reference to which it seems desirable to make some remarks. The progress and development of law is indeed one of the most interesting as well as important sections of human history. It is far less essential, as Goguet[1] truly observes, 'de savoir le nombre des dynasties et les noms des souverains qui les composoient; mais il est essentiel de connoître les loix, les arts, les sciences et les usages d'une nation que toute l'antiquité a regardée comme un modèle de sagesse et de vertu. Voilà les objets que je me suis proposés, et que je vais traiter avec le plus d'exactitude qu'il me sera possible.' It is, however, impossible thoroughly to understand the laws of the most advanced nations, unless we take into consideration those customs of ruder communities from which they took their origin, by which they are so profoundly influenced.

The subject is, moreover, of peculiar importance to us, forming as we do part of a great and composite empire.

It is, therefore, very much to be regretted that we are not more thoroughly acquainted with the laws and customs of savage races. At the time Goguet published his cele-

[1] De l'Origine des Loix, des Arts et des Sciences, vol. i. p. 45.

brated work, our knowledge was even more defective than is now the case.

Still I am surprised that with the evidence which was before him, and especially as he was one of the first to point out that much light is thrown by the condition of modern savages on that of our ancestors in times now long gone by,[1] he should have regarded the monarchical form of government as the most ancient and most universally established.[2] 'C'est, sans contredit,' he says, 'le plus anciennement et le plus universellement établi.'

A more careful consideration of the evidence afforded by the lower races of man would probably have modified his views on some other points. For instance,[3] he observes that 'il n'est pas difficile de faire sentir par quelles raisons le gouvernement monarchique est le premier dont l'idée a dû se présenter. Il étoit plus aisé aux peuples, lorsqu'ils ont pensé à établir l'ordre dans la société, de se rassembler sous un seul chef, que sous plusieurs : la royauté est d'ailleurs une image de l'autorité que les pères avoient originairement sur leurs enfants : ils étoient dans ces premiers tems les chefs et les législateurs de leur famille.'

Whereas it has been already shown in the earlier chapters of this work that the family is by no means so perfectly organised among the lowest races.

[1] M. Goguet remarks that some races, being ignorant of the art of writing, even now, 'pour constater leurs ventes, leurs achats, leurs emprunts, etc., emploient certains morceaux de bois entaillés diversement. On les coupe en deux : le créancier en garde une moitié, et le débiteur retient l'autre. Quand la dette ou la promesse est acquittée, chacun remet le morceau qu'il avoit par devers lui' (p. 26). This method of keeping accounts is not confined to savage races. It was practised by the English Government down to the commencement of the present century, and I myself possess such a receipt given by the English Government to the East India Company in the year 1770, and duly preserved in the India House, until within the last ten years. It represents 24,000l., represented by twenty-four equal notches in a rod of wood.

[2] *Loc. cit.* vol. i. p. 9.

[3] *Loc. cit.* p. 10.

Sir G. Grey,[1] speaking of the Australians, truly says that the 'laws of this people are unfitted for the government of a single isolated family, some of them being only adapted for the regulation of an assemblage of families; they could, therefore, not have been a series of rules given by the first father to his children: again, they could not have been rules given by an assembly of the first fathers to their children, for there are these remarkable features about them, that some are of such a nature as to compel those subject to them to remain in a state of barbarism.'

Again Goguet[2] states that 'les loix du mariage ont mis un frein à une passion qui n'en voudroit reconnoître aucun. Elles ont fait plus: en déterminant les degrés de consanguinité qui rendent les alliances illégitimes, elles ont appris aux hommes à connoître et à respecter les droits de la nature. Ce sont ces loix enfin qui, en constatant la condition des enfans, ont assuré des citoyens à l'État, et donné aux sociétés une forme fixe et assurée,' which is very far from being the case. I have already observed (antè, p. 2) that even Mr. Maine would doubtless have modified in some points the views expressed in his excellent work,[3] if he had paid more attention to the manners, customs, and laws of savages. But, although the progress and development of law belong, for the most part, to a more advanced stage of human society than that which is the subject of this work, still, in one sense, as already mentioned, even the lowest races of savages have laws. Nay, every action of their lives is regulated by numerous rules, none the less stringent because unwritten. Thus Mr. Lang, speaking of the Australians,[4] tells us that 'instead of enjoying perfect personal freedom, as it would at first appear, they are

[1] Grey's Australia, vol. ii. p. 222.
[2] *Loc. cit.* p. 20.
[3] Ancient Law.
[4] Aborigines of Australia, p. 7. Eyre, *loc. cit.* vol. ii. p. 385.

governed by a code of rules and a set of customs which form one of the most cruel tyrannies that has ever, perhaps, existed on the face of the earth, subjecting not only the will, but the property and life of the weak to the dominion of the strong. The whole tendency of the system is to give everything to the strong and old, to the prejudice of the weak and young, and more particularly to the detriment of the women. They have rules by which the best food, the best pieces, the best animals, &c., are prohibited to the women and young men, and reserved for the old. The women are generally appropriated to the old and powerful, some of whom possess from four to seven wives; while wives are altogether denied to young men, unless they have sisters to give in exchange, and are strong and courageous enough to prevent their sisters from being taken without exchange.'

This is no peculiar case. No savage is free. All over the world his daily life is regulated by a complicated and apparently most inconvenient set of customs (as forcible as laws), of quaint prohibitions and privileges; the prohibitions as a general rule applying to the women, and the privileges to the men.

'To believe,' says Sir G. Grey,[1] 'that man in a savage state is endowed with freedom, either of thought or action, is erroneous in the highest degree.'

In Tahiti,[2] 'the men were allowed to eat the flesh of the pig, and of fowls, and a variety of fish, cocoa-nuts, and plantains, and whatever was presented as an offering to the gods, which the females, on pain of death, were forbidden to touch, as it was supposed they would pollute them. The fires on which the men's food was cooked, were also sacred, and were forbidden to be used by the females.

[1] Grey's Australia, vol. ii. p. 217.   [2] Polynesian Researches, vol. i. p. 222.

The baskets in which their provisions were kept, and the house in which the men ate, were also sacred, and prohibited to the females under the same cruel penalty ; hence the inferior food, both for wives, daughters, &c., was cooked at separate fires, deposited in distinct baskets, and eaten in lonely solitude by the females, in little huts erected for the purpose.'

'Nothing,' says the Bishop of Wellington, 'can be more mistaken than to represent the New Zealanders as a people without law and order. They are, and were, the slaves of law, rule, and precedent.'[1]

If savages pass unnoticed many actions which we should consider as highly criminal, on the other hand they strictly forbid others which we should consider altogether immaterial.

The natives of Russian America, near the Yukon river, 'have certain superstitions with regard to the bones of animals, which they will neither throw on the fire nor to the dogs, but save them in their houses or *caches*. When they saw us careless in such matters, they said it would prevent them from catching or shooting successfully. Also, they will not throw away their hair or nails just cut short, but save them, hanging them frequently in packages on the trees.'

The Mongols[3] think it a fault with a knife to touch the fire, or take flesh out of the pot; or to cleave wood with a hatchet near the hearth, imagining it takes away the fire's power. It is no less faulty to lean on a whip, or touch arrows with it; to kill young birds; or pour liquor on the ground: to strike a horse with the bridle; or break one bone against another. Mr. Tylor has already pointed out[4] that almost exactly the same prohibitions occur in America.

[1] Trans. Ethn. Soc. 1870, p. 367.   [3] Astley's Coll., vol. iv. p. 548.
[2] Whymper, Trans. Ethn. Soc., N.S.   [4] Early History of Man, p. 136.
vol. vii. p. 174.

Some of these rules are very sensible. Thus Tanner states that the Algonkin Indians, when on a war-path, must not sit upon the naked ground ; but must, at least, have some grass or bushes under them. They must, if possible, avoid wetting their feet ; but if they are compelled to wade through a swamp, or to cross a stream, they must keep their clothes dry, and whip their legs with bushes or grass, when they come out of the water.'[1] For others the reason is not so obvious. Thus the small bowls out of which they drink are marked across the middle, in going out they must place one side to their mouth ; in returning, the other. The vessels must also on their return be thrown away, or hung up in a tree.

Hunting tribes generally have rules, well understood, with reference to game. Thus among the Greenlanders, should a seal escape with a hunter's javelin in it, and be killed by another man afterwards, it belongs to the former. But if the seal is struck with the harpoon and bladder, and the string breaks, the hunter loses his right. If a man finds a seal dead with a harpoon in it, he keeps the seal but returns the harpoon. In reindeer hunting, if several hunters strike a deer together, it belongs to the one whose arrow is nearest the heart. The arrows are all marked, so that no dispute can arise, but since guns have been introduced, many quarrels have taken place. Any man who finds a piece of drift wood (which in the far North is extremely valuable), can appropriate it by placing a stone on it, as a sign that some one has taken possession of it. No other Greenlander will then touch it.

Again, far from being informal or extemporary, the salutations, ceremonies, treaties, and contracts of savages are characterised by the very opposite qualities.

Eyre mentions that in Australia ' in their intercourse

---

[1] Tanner's Narrative, p. 123.

with each other, natives of different tribes are exceedingly punctilious.' [1]

Mariner gives a long account of the elaborate ceremonies practised by the Tongans, and of their regard for rank.' [2]

Thus the king [3] was by no means of the highest rank. The Tooitonga, Veachi, and several others preceded him. Indeed the name Tooitonga means King of Tonga; the office, however, was wholly of a religious character: the Tooitonga being regarded as descended from the gods, if not a deity himself. He was so sacred that some words were retained for his exclusive use.

Below Tooitonga and Veachi came the priests, while civil society was divided into five ranks, the king, the nobles, the Matabooles, the Mooas, and the Tooas. The child took the rank of the mother among the nobles, but the Matabooles were succeeded by the eldest son.

It is curious that the use of the third person in token of respect occurs in Tonga, as well as some other countries. 'Thus the King of Tonga addressing the Tooitonga says, "Ho egi Tooitonga," that is, literally, thy Lord Tooitonga, in which the possessive pronoun thy, or your, is used instead of my: or, if the word egi be translated lordship, or chiefship, the term of address will be more consistent and similar to ours, your lordship, your grace, your majesty. The title, ho egi, is never used but in addressing a superior chief, or speaking of a god, or in a public speech. Ho egi! also means chiefs, as in the commencement of Finow's speech.' [4]

The Egbas, a negro race of West Africa, who are, says Burton,[5] 'gifted with uncommon loquacity and spare time, have invented a variety of salutations and counter-saluta-

---

[1] Discoveries in Australia, vol. ii. p. 214.

[2] Tonga Islands, vol. ii. pp. 185, 199, 207.

[3] *Loc. cit.* vol. ii. p. 79.

[4] Mariner, vol. ii. p. 142.

[5] Burton, Abbeokuta, vol. i. p. 113.

tions applicable to every possible occasion.   For instance,
Oji re, did you wake well ?   Akwaro, good morning !
Akuasan, good day ! Akwale, good evening ! Akware, to
one tired.   Akushe, to one at work.   Akurin (from rin,
to walk), to a traveller.   Akule, to one in the house.
Akwatijo, after a long absence. Akwalejo, to a stranger.
Akurajo, to one in distress.   Akujiko, to one sitting.
Akudaro to one standing.   Akuta, to one selling.   Wolebe
(be careful) to one met, and so forth.   The servile *shash-
tanga* or postration of the Hindus is also a universal custom.
It is performed in different ways ; the most general is,
after depositing the burden, and clapping hands once,
twice, or thrice, to go on all-fours, touch the ground with
the belly and breast, the forehead, and both sides of the
face successively ; kiss the earth, half rise up, then pass
the left over the right forearm, and *vice versâ*, and finally,
after again saluting mother Hertha, to stand erect.   The
inferior prostrates to the superior, the son to the mother,
the younger to the elder brother, and I have been obliged
to correct a Moslem boy of the evil practice of assuming a
position in which man should address none but his Maker.
The performance usually takes place once a day on first
meeting, but meetings are so numerous that at least one
hour out of the twenty-four must thus be spent by a man
about town.   Equals kneel, or rather squat, before one-
another, and snap the fingers in the peculiarly West
African way, which seems to differ in every tribe.'

In the religious customs of Tahiti,[1] 'however large or
costly the sacrifices that had been offered, and however near
its close the most protracted ceremony might be, if the
priest omitted or misplaced any word in the prayers with
which it was always accompanied, or if his attention was
diverted by any means, so that the prayer was hai, or broken,

[1] Ellis' Polynesian Researches, vol. ii. p. 157.

the whole was rendered unavailable, he must prepare other victims, and repeat his prayers over from the commencement.'

In Feegee [1] 'public business is conducted with tedious formality. Old forms are strictly observed, and innovations opposed. An abundance of measured clapping of hands, and subdued exclamations, characterise these occasions. Whales' teeth and other property are never exchanged or presented without the following or similar form : "A ! woi ! woi ! woi ! A ! woi ! woi ! woi !! A tabua levu ! woi ! woi ! A mudua, mudua, mudua !" (clapping).' But little consideration is required to show that this is quite natural. In the absence of writing, evidence of contracts must depend on the testimony of witnesses, and it is necessary therefore to avoid all haste which might lead to forgetfulness, and to imprint the ceremony as much as possible on the minds of those present.

Passing on to the question of property, ' La première loi,' says Goguet,[2] ' qu'on aura établie, aura été pour assigner et assurer à chaque habitant une certaine quantité de terrein. Dans les tems où le labourage n'étoit point encore connu, les terres étoient en commun. Il n'y avoit ni bornes ni limites qui en réglassent le partage, chacun prenoit sa subsistance où il jugeoit à-propos. On abandonnoit, on reprenoit successivement les mêmes cantons, suivant qu'ils étoient plus ou moins épuisés : cette manière de vivre n'a plus été praticable quand l'agriculture a été introduite. Il fallut alors distinguer les possessions et prendre les mesures nécessaires pour faire jouir chaque citoyen du fruit de ses travaux. Il étoit dans l'ordre que celui qui avoit semé du grain fût sûr de le recueillir, et ne vît pas les autres profiter des peines et des soins qu'ils s'étoit donnés.

[1] Williams' Fiji and the Fijians, vol. i. p. 28.   [2] Loc. cit.

De-là sont émanées les loix sur la propriété des terres, sur la manière de les partager et d'en jouir.'

The same view has been taken by other writers. It does not, however, appear that property in land implies, or necessarily arose from, agriculture. On the contrary, it exists even in hunting communities. Usually, indeed, during the hunting stage, property in land is tribal, not individual. The North American Indians seem, as a general rule, to have had no individual property in land. It appears, therefore, at first sight remarkable, that among the Australians,[1] who are in most respects so much lower in the scale, ' every male has some portion of land, of which he can always point out the exact boundaries. These properties are subdivided by a father among his sons during his own lifetime, and descend in almost hereditary succession. A man can dispose of or barter his lands to others, but a female never inherits, nor has primogeniture among the sons any peculiar rights or advantages.' Nay, more than this, there are some tracts of land, peculiarly rich in gum, &c., and over which, at the period when the gum is in season, numerous families have an acknowledged right, although they are not allowed to come there at other times.[2] Even the water of the rivers is claimed as property by some of the Australian tribes. ' Trespass for the purpose of hunting' is in Australia regarded as a capital offence, and is, when possible, punished with death.[3]

The explanation seems to be that the Redskins depended mainly on the larger game, while the Australians fed on opossums, reptiles, insects, roots, &c. The Redskin, therefore, if land had been divided into individual allotments, might have been starved in the vicinity of abundance;

[1] Eyre, Discoveries in Australia, vol. ii. p. 297. See also Lang in Grey's Australia, vol. ii. p. 232.
[2] Grey's Australia, vol. ii. p. 298.
[3] *Loc. cit.* p. 236.

while the Australian could generally obtain food on his own property.

In Polynesia,[1] where cultivation was carefully attended to, as in Tahiti, ' every portion of land has its respective owner; and even the distinct trees on the land had sometimes different proprietors, and a tree, and the land it grew on, different owners.'

Even, however, an agricultural condition does not necessarily require *individual* property in land; in the Russian ' Mirs,' or communal villages, moveable property alone was individual; the land was common.[2]

In other parts of Russia, ' after the expiration of a given, but not in all cases of the same, period, separate ownerships are extinguished, the land of the village is thrown into a mass, and then it is re-distributed among the families composing the community, according to their number. This repartition having been effected, the rights of families and of individuals are again allowed to branch out into various lines, which they continue to follow till another period of division comes round.'[3]

It is stated to have been a principle of the earliest Sclavonian laws that the property of families could not be divided for a perpetuity. Even now in parts of Servia, Croatia, and Austrian Sclavonia, the entire land is cultivated by the villagers, and the produce is annually divided.

Diodorus Siculus states that the Celtiberians divided their land annually among individuals, to be laboured for the use of the public; and that the product was stored up, and distributed from time to time among the necessitous.[4]

In New Zealand there were three distinct tenures of land:[5] viz., by the tribe, by the family, and by the indi-

---

[1] Ellis' Polynesian Researches, vol. ii. p. 362. Dieffenbach, vol. ii. p. 114.

[2] Fancher, in Systems of Land Tenure, p. 362, *et seq.*

[3] Maine's Ancient Law, p. 267.

[4] Lord Kames' History of Man, vol. i. p. 93.

[5] Taylor, New Zealand and its Inhabitants, p. 384.

vidual. The common rights of a tribe were often very extensive, and complicated by intermarriages. The eel cuts, also, are strictly preserved as private property. Children, as soon as they were born, had a right to a share of the family property.

It does not, however, necessarily follow that property in land involves the power of sale. 'We are too apt,' says Campbell,[1] ' to forget that property in land, as a transferable mercantile commodity absolutely owned and passing from hand to hand like any chattel, is not an ancient institution, but a modern development, reached only in a few very advanced countries.' 'It may be said,' he adds,[2] 'of all landed tenures in India previous to our rule, that they were practically not transferable by sale; and that only certain classes of the better-defined claims were to some extent transferable by mortgage. The seizure and sale of land for private debt was wholly and utterly unknown,—such an idea had never entered into the native imagination.'

Still less does the possession of land necessarily imply the power of testamentary disposition, and we find as a matter of fact that the will is a legal process of very late origin.

I have already mentioned the state of entire lawlessness which exists in Africa, between the death of one ruler and the election of his successors.

It is stated that formerly, when a Greenlander died, if he had no grown-up children, his property was regarded as having no longer an owner, and every one took what he chose, or at least what he could get, without the slightest regard to the wretched widow or children.[3]

There is, indeed, no more interesting chapter in Mr. Maine's work than that on the early history of testa-

---

[1] Systems of Land Tenure, p. 151.
[2] Ibid. p. 171.
[3] Crantz, History of Greenland, vol. i. p. 192.

mentary succession. He points out that the essence of a will, as now understood, is, firstly, that it should take effect at death; secondly, that it may be preserved secret; and thirdly, that it is revocable. Yet in Roman law wills acquired these characteristics but slowly and gradually, and in the earlier stages of civilisation wills were entirely unknown.

In Athens the power of willing was introduced by Solon, only, however, in cases when a person died childless. The barbarians on the north of the Roman Empire were, says Maine,[1] 'confessedly strangers to any such conception as that of a Will. The best authorities agree that there is no trace of it in those parts of their written codes which comprise the customs practised by them in their original seats and in their subsequent settlement on the edge of the Roman Empire.'

And again in studying the ancient German laws, 'one result has invariably disclosed itself—that the ancient nucleus of the code contains no trace of a will.'[2]

The Hindoos also were entire strangers to the will.[3]

It is therefore remarkable in Australia, 'a father divides his land during his lifetime, fairly apportioning it amongst his several sons, and at as early an age as fourteen or fifteen they can point out the portion which they are eventually to inherit. If the males of a family become extinct, the male children of the daughters inherit their grandfather's land.'[4]

Again, in Tahiti, the system of willing was (I presume when there were no children), in full force,[5] 'not only with reference to land, but to any other kind of property. Unacquainted with letters, they could not leave a written

---

[1] *Loc. cit.* p. 172.

[2] *Loc. cit.* p. 196.

[3] Maine's Ancient Law, p. 193. Campbell in Systems of Land Tenure,

p. 177.

[4] Eyre's Australia, vol. ii. p. 236.

[5] Ellis' Polynesian Researches, vol. ii. p. 362.

will, but during a season of illness, those possessing property frequently called together the members of the family,
or confidential friends, and to them gave directions for the
disposal of their effects after their decease. This was
considered a kind of sacred charge, and was usually
executed with fidelity.'

For the modern will, however, we are mainly indebted to
the Romans. At first, indeed, even Roman wills, if so
they may be called, were neither secret, deferred, nor
revocable. On the contrary, they were made in public,
before not less than five witnesses, they took effect at once,
and were irrevocable. Hence it is probable that they were
only made just before death.

It seems probable that the power of willing was confined to those who had no natural heirs; such was certainly the case in Athens. So also in Rome, the will
does not seem to have been used as a means of disinheriting,
or of effecting an unequal distribution of the property.

Under these circumstances it appears at first sight
remarkable that the Romans should have regarded for-
feiture of testamentary privileges as one of the greatest
misfortunes, and should have regarded as a bitter curse
the wish that a man might die intestate. The explanation
of this seems to lie in the ideas of family relationship.
Children being slaves, and as such incapable of holding
property,[1] it would naturally be the wish of the father to
emancipate his favourite sons; but as soon as this was
effected they ceased to belong to the family, and could not
consequently inherit as heirs at law. On the death of a
Roman citizen, in the absence of a will, the property descended to the unemancipated children, and after them to
the nearest grade of the agnatic kindred. Hence the same
feeling which induced a Roman to emancipate his sons,

[1] Maine's Ancient Law, p. 180.

impelled him also to make a will, for if he did not do so, emancipation involved disinheritance.

The turning point in the history of the Roman will appears to have been the period at which the presence of the true heir was dispensed with when the will was made. When this was first permitted does not seem to be exactly known, but it was sanctioned in the time of Gaius, who lived during the reigns of the Antonines; at this period also wills had become revocable,[1] and even in the time of Hadrian a testament was rendered invalid when a 'posthumus suus' arose, i.e. when a child was born after the will was made.[2]

In the absence of wills, the interests of the children were in some cases secured by customs resembling those of the Russian village communities, or 'Mirs,' in which children have a right to their share as soon as they are born. Nor are such rights confined to communal properties. In some countries the children have a vested right to a portion of their father's estate. Here therefore, in the absence of children, the will is replaced by adoption, the importance attached to which is, as I have already mentioned, one of the reasons for the inaccuracy of thought among the lower races on the subject of relationship.

Among the Hindoos, 'the instant a son is born[3] he acquires a vested right in his father's property, which cannot be sold without recognition of his joint-ownership. On the son's attaining full age, he can sometimes compel a partition of the estate even against the consent of the parent; and, should the parent acquiesce, one son can always have a partition even against the will of the others. On such partition taking place, the father has no advantage over his children, except that he has two of the shares

---

[1] Tomkin's and Lemon's Commentaries of Gaius, com. 11, sec. cxliv.

[2] loc. cit. com. 11, sec. cxliii.

[3] Maine's Ancient Law, p. 228.

instead of one. The ancient law of the German tribes was exceedingly similar. The Allod or domain of the family was the joint property of the father and his sons.' According to ancient German law, also, children were co-proprietors with their father, and the family endowment could not be parted with except by general consent.

This probably explains the remarkable custom that in Tahiti the king abdicated as soon as a son was born to him ; and landowners under similar circumstances lost the fee-simple of their land, and became mere trustees for the infant possessors.[1]

The Basutos have a strict system of primogeniture, and, even during the father's life, the eldest son has considerable power both over the property and the younger children.[2]

The same system, in combination with inheritance through females, is also in full force in Feejee, where it is known as Vasu. The word means a nephew or niece, ' but becomes a title of office in the case of the male, who, in some localities, has the extraordinary privilege of appropriating whatever he chooses belonging to his uncle, or those under his uncle's power.'[3] This is one of the most remarkable parts of Feejee despotism. ' However high a chief may be, if he has a nephew he has a master,' and resistance is rarely thought of. Thakonauto, while at war with his uncle, actually supplied himself with ammunition from his enemies' stores.

Perhaps also the curious custom of naming the father after the child, may have originated from some such regulation. Thus in Australia,[4] when a man's eldest child is named, the father takes ' the name of the child, Kadlit-

---

[1] Ellis' Polynesian Researches, vol. ii. pp. 346, 347.

[2] Casalis' Basutos, p. 179.

[3] Fiji and the Fijians, vol. i. p. 34.

[4] Eyre, *loc. cit.* vol. ii. p. 325.

pinna, the father of Kadli; the mother is called Kadling-angki, or mother of Kadli, from ngangki, a female or woman.' This custom seems very general throughout the continent.

In America we find the same habit.[1] Thus 'with the Kutchin the father takes his name from his son or daughter, not the son from the father as with us. The father's name is formed by the addition of the word tee to the end of the son's name; for instance, Que-ech-et may have a son and call him Sah-neu. The father is now called Sah-neu-tee, and the former name of Que-ech-et is forgotten.'

In Sumatra, ' the father,[2] in many parts of the country, particularly in Passum-mah, is distinguished by the name of his first child, as "Pa-Ladin," or "Pa-Rindu," (Pa for bapa, signifying "the father of") and loses, in this acquired, his own proper name. This is a singular custom, and surely less conformable to the order of nature than that which names the son after the father. There, it is not usual to give them a galar on their marriage, as with the Rejangs, among whom the filionymic is not so common, though sometimes adopted, and occasionally joined with the galar; as Radin-pa-Chirano. The women never change the name given them at the time of their birth; yet frequently they are called through courtesy, from their eldest child, " Ma si ano," the mother of such an one; but rather as a polite description than a name.'

As a general rule property decends to the eldest son, if any, but Duhalde mentions that among the Tartars the youngest son inherited the property, because the elder ones as they reach manhood leave the paternal tent, and take with them the quantity of cattle which their father chooses to give them. A similar custom existed

[1] Smithsonian Report, 1866, p. 326.   [2] Marsden's History of Sumatra, p. 286.

among the Mrus of the Arrawak hills also,[1] and even in some districts of our own country, during ante-Norman times, under the name of Borough English.[2]

There are also cases, as for instance among the Hindoos, in which the rule of primogeniture is followed as regards office or power, politically, but not with reference to property.

Among the lower races of men, the chiefs scarcely take any cognisance of offences, unless they relate to such things as directly concern, or are supposed to concern, the interests of the community generally. As regards private injuries, every one must protect or avenge himself. The administration of justice, says Du Tertre,[3] 'among the Caribbians is not exercised by the captain, nor by any magistrate; but, as it is among the Tapinambous, he who thinks himself injured gets such satisfaction of his adversary as he thinks fit, according as his passion dictates to him, or his strength permits him: the public does not concern itself at all in the punishment of criminals, and if any one among them suffers an injury or affront, without endeavouring to revenge himself, he is slighted by all the rest, and accounted a coward, and a person of no esteem.'

Among the North American Indians,[4] if a man was murdered, 'the family of the deceased only have the right of taking satisfaction; they collect, consult, and decree. The rulers of a town or of the nation have nothing to do or say in the business.' Indeed, it would seem that the object of legal regulations was at first not so much to punish the offender, as to restrain and mitigate the vengeance inflicted by the aggrieved party.

[1] Lewin's Hill Tracts of Chittagong, p. 194.
[2] Wren Hoskyns in Customs of Land Tenure, p. 104.
[3] History of the Caribby Islands, p. 316. Labat also makes a very similar statement. Voyage aux Isles d'Amérique, vol. ii. p. 83.
[4] Trans. Amer. Antiq. Soc. vol. i. p. 251.

The amount of legal revenge, if I may so call it, is often strictly regulated, even where we should least expect to find such limitations. Thus in Australia,[1] crimes 'may be compounded for by the criminal appearing and submitting himself to the ordeal of having spears thrown at him by all such persons as conceive themselves to have been aggrieved, or by permitting spears to be thrust through certain parts of his body; such as through the thigh, or the calf of the leg, or under the arm. The part which is to be pierced by a spear, is fixed for all common crimes, and a native who has incurred this penalty sometimes quietly holds out his leg for the injured party to thrust his spear through.' So strictly is the amount of punishment limited, that if in inflicting such spear wounds, a man, either through carelessness or from any other cause, exceeded the recognised limits—if, for instance, he wounded the femoral artery—he would in his turn become liable to punishment.

Such cases as these seem to me to throw great light on the origin of the idea of property. Possession de facto needs of course no explanation. When, however, any rules were laid down regulating the amount or mode of vengeance which might be taken in revenge for disturbance; or when the chief thought it worth while himself to settle disputes about possession, and thus, while increasing his own dignity, to check quarrels which might be injurious to the general interests of the tribe; the natural effect would be to develop the idea of mere possession into that of property.

Since, then, crimes were at first regarded merely as personal matters, in which the aggressor and the victim alone were interested, and with which society was not concerned, any crime, even murder, might be atoned for by the pay-

[1] Sir G. Grey's Australia, vol. ii. p. 243.

ment of such a sum of money as satisfied the representatives of the murdered man. This payment was proportioned to the injury done, and had no relation to the crime as a crime. Hence, as the injury was the same whether the death was accidental or designed, so also was the penalty. Hence our word 'pay,' which comes from the Latin 'pacare,' to appease or pacify.

The Romans, on the contrary, based any claim for compensation on the existence of a 'culpa;' and hence laid down that where there had been no 'culpa,' no action for reparation could lie. This led to very inconvenient consequences. Thus, as Lord Kames[1] has pointed out, 'Labeo scribit, si cum vi ventorum navis impulsa esset in funes anchorarum alterius, et nautæ funes præcidissent; si, nullo alio modo, nisi præcisis funibus, explicare se potuit, nullam actionem dandam;' b. 29, § 3, *ad leg. Aquil.* 'Quod dicitur damnum injuria datum Aquilia persequi sic erit accipiendum, ut videatur damnum injuria datum quod cum damno injuriam attulerit; nisi magna vi cogente, fuerit factum. Ut Celsus scribit circa eum, qui incendii arcendi gratia vicinas ædes intercidit: et sive pervenit ignis, sive antea extinctus est, extimat legis Aquiliæ actionem cessare.' b. 49, § 1, eod. In English thus: In the opinion of Labeo, if a ship is driven by the violence of a tempest among the anchor-ropes of another ship and the sailors cut the ropes, having no other means of getting free, there is no action competent. The Aquilian law must be understood to apply only to such damage as carries the idea of an injury along with it, unless such injury has not been wilfully done, but from necessity. 'Thus Celsus puts the case of a person who, to stop the progress of a fire, pulls down his neighbour's house; and whether the fire had reached that house which is pulled down, or was extinguished before it got

---

[1] History of Man, vol. iv. p. 34.

to it, in neither case, he thinks, will an action be competent from the Aquilian law.'

It would however appear that, even in Roman law, the opposite and more usual principle originally prevailed. This is indicated, for instance, by the great difference in the penalties imposed by ancient laws on offenders caught in the act, and those only detected after considerable delay. In the old Roman law, as in that of some other countries, thieves were divided into manifest, and non-manifest. The manifest thief who was caught in the act, or at any rate with the stolen goods still in his possession, became, according to the law of the twelve tables, the slave of the person robbed, or if he was already a slave, was put to death. The non-manifest thief, on the other hand, was only liable to return double the value of the goods he had stolen. Subsequently, the very severe punishment in the case of the manifest thief was mitigated, but he was still forced to pay four times the value of what he had stolen, or twice as much as the non-manifest thief.

The same principle was followed by the North American Indians.[1] Again, in the German and Anglo-Saxon codes, a thief caught in the act might be killed on the spot. Thus the law followed the old principles of private vengeance, and in settling the amount of punishment, took as a guide the measure of revenge likely to be taken by an aggrieved person under the circumstances of the case.[2]

In the South Sea Islands, according to Williams,[3] cases of theft were seldom brought before the king or chiefs, but the people avenged their own injuries. The rights of retaliation, however, had almost a legal force, for ' although

---

[1] Trans. Amer. Antiq. Soc. vol. i. p. 285.

[2] See Maine, *loc. cit.* p. 378.

[3] Polynesian Researches, vol. ii. pp. 369, 372.

the party thus plundered them, they would not attempt to prevent the seizure: had they done so, the population of the district would have assisted those, who, according to the established custom, were thus punishing the aggressors. Such was the usual method resorted to for punishing the petty thefts committed among themselves.'

So also as regards personal injuries. Among the Anglo-Saxons the ' wergild,' or fine for injuries, was evidently a substitute for personal vengeance. Every part of the body had a recognised value, even the teeth, nails, and hair. Nay, the value assigned to the latter was proportionately very high; the loss of the beard being estimated at twenty shillings, while the breaking of a thigh was only fixed at twelve. In other cases also the effect on personal appearance seems to have carried great weight, for the loss of a front tooth was estimated at six shillings, while the fracture of a rib was only fixed at three. In the case of a slave the fine was paid to the owner.

The amount varied according to the rank of the person injured. All society below the royal family and the Ealdorman was divided into three classes; the Tywhind man, or Ceorl, was estimated at 200 shillings according to the laws of Mercia; the Sixhind man at 600 shillings, while the death of a royal thane was estimated at 1,200 shillings.[1]

The severity of early codes, and the uniformity in the amounts of punishment which characterises them, is probably due to the same cause. An individual who felt himself aggrieved would not weigh very philosophically the amount of punishment which he was entitled to inflict; and no doubt when in any community some chief, in advance of his time, endeavoured to substitute public law for private

[1] Student. Hum. p. 74. Hallam, vol. i. p. 272.

vengeance, his object would be to induce those who had cause of complaint to apply to the law for redress, rather than to avenge themselves; which of course would not be the case if the penalty allotted by the law was much less than that which custom would allow them to inflict for themselves.

Subsequently, when punishment was substituted for pecuniary compensation, the same rule was at first applied, and the distinction of intention was overlooked. Nay, so long had the importance of intention been disregarded, that although it is now recognised in our criminal courts, yet, as Mr. Bain points out,[1] 'a moral stigma is still attached to intellectual error by many people, and even by men of cultivation.'

In this, as in so many of our other ideas and tastes, we are still influenced by the condition of our ancestors in bygone ages. What that condition was I have in this work attempted to indicate, believing as I do that the earlier mental stages through which the human race has passed, are illustrated by the condition of existing, or recent, savages. The history of the human race has, I feel satisfied, on the whole been one of progress. I do not of course mean to say that every race is necessarily advancing: on the contrary, most of the lower ones are almost stationary; and there are, no doubt, cases in which nations have fallen back; but it seems an almost invariable rule that such races are dying out, while those which are stationary in condition, are stationary in numbers also; on the other hand, improving nations increase in numbers, so that they always encroach on less progressive races.

In conclusion then, while I do not mean for a moment to

[1] Mental and Moral Science, p. 718.

deny that there are cases in which nations have retrograded, I regard these as exceptional instances. The facts and arguments mentioned in this work afford, I think, strong grounds for the following conclusions; namely,—

That existing savages are not the descendants of civilised ancestors.

That the primitive condition of man was one of utter barbarism.

That from this condition several races have independently raised themselves.

These views follow, I think, from strictly scientific considerations. We shall not be the less inclined to adopt them, on account of the cheering prospects which they hold out for the future.

In the closing chapter of 'Prehistoric Times,' while fully admitting the charms of savage life, I have endeavoured to point out the immense advantages which we enjoy. Here I will only add that if the past history of man has been one of deterioration, we have but a groundless expectation of future improvement: on the other hand, if the past has been one of progress, we may fairly hope that the future will be so also; that the blessings of civilisation will not only be extended to other countries and to other nations, but that even in our own land they will be rendered more general and more equable; so that we shall not see before us always, as now, countrymen of our own living in our very midst a life worse than that of a savage; neither enjoying the rough advantages and real, though coarse, pleasures of savage life, nor yet availing themselves of the far higher and more noble opportunities which lie within the reach of civilised Man.

APPENDIX.

———◆◇◆———

ON THE PRIMITIVE CONDITION OF MAN.

PART I.

BEING THE SUBSTANCE OF A PAPER READ BEFORE THE BRITISH ASSOCIATION
AT DUNDEE.

SIDE by side with the different opinions as to the origin of man, there are two opposite views with reference to the primitive condition of the first men, or first beings worthy to be so called. Many writers have considered that man was at first a mere savage, and that the course of history has on the whole been a progress towards civilisation, though at times—and at some times for centuries—some races have been stationary, or even have retrograded. Other authors, of no less eminence, have taken a diametrically opposite view. According to them, man was, from the commencement, pretty much what he is at present; if possible, even more ignorant of the arts and sciences than now, but with mental qualities not inferior to our own. Savages they consider to be the degenerate descendants of far superior ancestors. Of the recent supporters of this theory, the late Archbishop of Dublin was amongst the most eminent.

Dr. Whately enunciates his opinions in the following words :[1]—

'We have no reason to believe that any community ever did, or ever can emerge, unassisted by external helps, from a state of utter barbarism unto anything that can be called civilisation.' 'Man has not emerged from the savage state ; the progress of any community in civilisation, by its own internal means, must always have begun from a condition removed from that of complete barbarism, out of which it does not appear that men ever did or can raise themselves.'

Thus, he adds, ' the ancient Germans, who cultivated corn—though

---

[1] Whately.   Political Economy, p. 68.

their agriculture was probably in a very rude state—who not only had numerous herds of cattle, but employed the labour of brutes, and even made use of cavalry in their wars, . . . these cannot with propriety be reckoned savages; or if they are to be so called (for it is not worth while to dispute about a word), then I would admit that, in this sense, men may advance, and in fact have advanced, by their own unassisted efforts, from the savage to the civilised state.' This limitation of the term 'savage' to the very lowest representatives of the human race no doubt renders Dr. Whately's theory more tenable by increasing the difficulty of bringing forward conclusive evidence against it. The Archbishop, indeed, expresses himself throughout his argument, as if it would be easy to produce the required evidence in opposition to his theory, supposing that any race of savages ever had raised themselves to a state of civilisation. The manner, however, in which he has treated the case of the Mandans—a tribe of North American Indians—effectually disposes of this hypothesis. This unfortunate people is described as having been decidedly more civilised than those by which they were surrounded. Having, then, no neighbours more advanced than themselves, they were quoted as furnishing an instance of savages who had civilised themselves without external aid. In answer to this, Archbishop Whately asks,—

' 1st. How do we know that these Mandans were of the same race as their neighbours?'

' 2ndly. How do we know that theirs is not the original level from which the other tribes have fallen?'

' 3rdly and lastly. Supposing that the Mandans did emerge from the savage state, how do we know that this may not have been through the aid of some strangers coming among them—like the Manco-Capac of Peru—from some more civilised country, perhaps long before the days of Columbus?'

Supposing, however, for a moment, and for the sake of argument, that the Mandans, or any other race, were originally savages, and had civilised themselves, it would still be manifestly—from the very nature of the case—impossible to bring forward the kind of evidence demanded by Dr. Whately. No doubt he 'may confidently affirm that we find no one *recorded* instance of a tribe of savages, properly so styled, rising into a civilised state without instruction and assistance from a people already civilised.' Starting with the proviso that savages, properly so styled, are ignorant of letters, and laying it down as a condition that no civilised example should be placed before them, the existence of any such record is an impossibility : its very presence would destroy its value. In another passage, Archbishop Whately says, indeed, 'If man generally, or some particular race, be capable of self-civilisation, in either case it may be expected that some record, or tradition, or monument of the actual occurrence of such an event should be found.' So far from this, the existence of any such record would, according to the very hypothesis itself, be impossible. Traditions are short-lived and untrustworthy. A 'monument' which could prove the actual occurrence of a race capable of self-civilisation, I confess myself unable to conceive. What kind of a monument would the Archbishop accept as proving that the people by whom it was made had been originally savage? that they had raised themselves, and had never been influenced by strangers of a superior race?

But, says Archbishop Whately, 'We have accounts of various savage tribes, in different parts of the globe, who have been visited from time to time at considerable intervals, but have had no settled intercourse with civilised people, and who appear to continue, as far as can be ascertained, in the same uncultivated condition ; ' and he adduces one case, that of the New Zealanders, who 'seem to have been in quite as advanced a state when Tasman discovered the country in 1642, as they were when Cook visited it one hundred and twenty-seven years after.' We have been accustomed to see around us an improvement so rapid that we forget how short a period a century is in the history of the human race. Even taking the ordinary chronology, it is evident that if in 6,000 years a given race has only progressed from a state of utter savagery to the condition of the Australian, we could not expect to find much change in one more century. Many a fishing village, even on our own coast, is in very nearly the same condition as it was one hundred and twenty-seven years ago. Moreover, I might fairly answer that, according to Whately's own definition of a savage state, the New Zealanders would certainly be excluded. They cultivated the ground, they had domestic animals, they constructed elaborate fortifications and made excellent canoes, and were certainly not in a state of utter barbarism. Or I might argue that a short visit, like that of Tasman, could give little insight into the true condition of a people. I am, however, the less disposed to question the statement made by Archbishop Whately, because the fact that many races are now practically stationary is in reality an argument against the theory of degradation, and not against that of progress. Civilised races are the descendants of races which, I believe, were once in a state of barbarism. On the contrary, argue our opponents, savages are the descendants of civilised races, and have sunk to their present condition. But Archbishop Whately admits that the civilised races are still rising, while the savages are stationary; and, oddly enough, seems to regard this as an argument in support of the very untenable proposition, that the difference between the two is due, not to the progress of the one set of races—a progress which every one admits—but to the degradation of those whom he himself maintains to be stationary. The delusion is natural, and like that which every one must have sometimes experienced in looking out of a train in motion, when the woods and fields seem to be flying from us, whereas we know that in reality we are moving and they are stationary.

But it is argued, 'If man, when first created, was left, like the brutes, to the unaided exercise of those natural powers of body and mind which are common to the European and to the New Hollander, how comes it that the European is not now in the condition of the New Hollander?' The answer to this is, I think, the following:—In the first place, Australia possesses neither cereals nor any animals which can be domesticated with advantage; and in the second, we find even in the same family—among children of the same parents— the most opposite dispositions; in the same nation, there are families of high character, and others in which every member is more or less criminal. But in this case, as in the last, the Archbishop's argument, if good at all, is good against his own view. It is like an Australian boomerang, which recoils upon its owner. The Archbishop believed in the unity of the human race, and argued that man was originally civilised (in a certain sense). 'How comes it, then,' I might ask him, 'that the New Hollander is not now in the condition of the European?' In another passage, Archbishop Whately quotes, with approbation, a passage from President Smith, of the college of New Jersey, who says that man, 'cast out an orphan of nature, naked and helpless into the savage forest, must have perished before he could have learned how to supply his most immediate and urgent wants. Suppose him to have been created, or to have started into being, one knows not how, in the full strength of his bodily powers, how long must it have been before he could have known the proper use of his limbs, or how to apply them to climb the tree!' &c. &c. Exactly the same, however, might be said of the gorilla or the chimpanzee, which certainly are not the degraded descendants of civilised ancestors.

Having thus very briefly considered the arguments brought forward by Archbishop Whately, I will proceed to state, also very briefly, some facts which seem to militate against the view advocated by him.

Firstly, I will endeavour to show that there are indications of progress even among savages.

Secondly, That among the most civilised nations there are traces of original barbarism.

The Archbishop supposes that men were, from the beginning, herdsmen and cultivators. We know, however, that the Australians, North and South Americans, and several other more or less savage races, living in countries eminently suited to our domestic animals, and to the cultivation of cereals, were yet entirely ignorant both of the one and the other. It is, I think, improbable that any race of men who had once been agriculturists and herdsmen should entirely abandon pursuits so easy and advantageous; and it is still more improbable that, if we accept Usher's very limited chronology, all tradition of such a change should be lost. Moreover, even if in the course of time the descendants of the present colonists in (say) America or Australia were to fall into such a state of barbarism, still herds of wild cattle, descended from those imported, would probably continue to live in those countries; and even if these were exterminated, their skeletons would testify to their previous existence; whereas, we know that not a single bone of the ox or of the domestic sheep has been found either in Australia or in America. The same argument applies to the horse, since the fossil horse of South America did not belong to the same species as our domestic race. So, again, in the case of plants. We do not know that any of our cultivated cereals would survive in a wild state, though it is highly probable that, perhaps in a modified form, they would do so. But there are many other plants which follow in the train of man, and by which the botany of South America, Australia, and New Zealand, has been almost as profoundly modified as their ethnology has been by the arrival of the white man. The Maoris have a melancholy proverb, that the Maoris disappear before the white man, just as the white man's rat destroys the native rat, the European fly drives away the Maori fly, and the clover kills the New Zealand fern.

A very interesting paper on this subject, by Dr. Hooker, whose authority no one will question, is contained in the ' Natural History Review ' for 1864 :—' In Australia and New Zealand,' he says, ' for instance, the noisy train of English emigration is not more surely doing its work, than the stealthy tide of English weeds, which are creeping over the surface of the waste, cultivated, and virgin soil, in annually increasing numbers of genera, species, and individuals. Apropos of this subject, a correspondent, W. T. Locke Travers, Esq., F.L.S., a most active New Zealand botanist, writing from Canter- bury, says, " You would be surprised at the rapid spread of European and foreign plants in this country.   All along the sides ot the main lines of road through the plains, a *Polygonum* (*aviculare*), called cow-grass, grows most luxuriantly, the roots sometimes two feet in depth, and the plants spreading over an area from four to five feet in diameter.   The dock (*Rumex obtusifolius* or *R. crispus*) is to be found in every river-bed, extending into the valleys of the mountain- rivers, until these become mere torrents.   The sow-thistle is spread all over the country, growing luxuriantly nearly up to 6,000 feet. The watercress increases in our still rivers to such an extent as to threaten to choke them altogether." '   The cardoon of the Argentine Republics is another remarkable instance of the same fact.   We may therefore safely assume that if Australia, New Zealand, or South America had ever been peopled by a race of herdsmen and agri- culturists, the fauna and flora of those countries would almost inevitably have given evidence of the fact, and differed much from the condition in which they were discovered.   We may also assert, as a general proposition, that no weapons or implements of metal have ever been found in any country inhabited by savages wholly ignorant of metallurgy.   A still stronger case is afforded by pot- tery.   Pottery is very indestructible; when used at all, it is always abundant, and it possesses two qualities—those, namely, of being easy to break and yet difficult to destroy, which render it very valuable in an archæological point of view.   Moreover it is, in most cases, associated with burials.   It is therefore a very significant fact, that no fragment of pottery has ever been found in Australia, New Zealand, or the Polynesian Islands.   It seems to me extremely improbable that an art so easy and so useful should ever have been lost by any race of men.   Moreover, this argument applies to several other arts and instruments.   I will mention only two, though several others might be brought forward.   The art of spinning and the use of the bow are quite unknown to many races of savages, and yet would hardly be likely to have been abandoned when once known.   The absence of architectural remains in these countries is another argument.   Archbishop Whately, indeed, claims this as being in his favour; but the absence of monuments in a country is surely indicative of barbarism, and not of civilisation.

The mental condition of savages also seems to me to speak strongly against the 'degrading' theory.   Not only do the religions of the low races appear to be indigenous, but, as already shown[1]— according to many trustworthy witnesses, merchants, philosophers, naval men, and missionaries alike—there are many races of men who are altogether destitute of a religion.   The cases are, perhaps, less numerous than they are asserted to be; but some of them rest on good evidence.   Yet I feel it difficult to believe that any people who once possessed a religion would ever entirely lose it.   Religion appeals so strongly to the hopes and fears of men, it takes so deep a hold on most minds, in its higher forms it is so great a consolation in times of sorrow and sickness, that I can hardly think any nation would ever abandon it altogether.   Moreover, it produces a race of men who are interested in maintaining its influence and authority.   Where, therefore, we find a race which is now ignorant of religion, I cannot but assume that it has always been so.

I will now proceed to mention a few cases in which some improvement does appear to have taken place, though, as a general rule, it may be observed that the contact of two races tends to depress rather than to raise the lower one.   According to Mac-Gillivray, the Australians of port Essington, who, like all their fellow-countrymen, had formerly bark-canoes only, have now completely abandoned them for others hollowed out of the trunk of a tree, which they buy from the Malays.   The inhabitants of the Andaman Islands have recently introduced outriggers.   The Bachapins, when visited by Burchell, had just commenced working iron.   According to Burton, the Wajiji negroes have recently learned to make brass.   In Tahiti, when visited by Captain Cook, the largest morai, or burial-place, was that erected for the then reigning queen.   The Tahitians, also, had then very recently

---

[1] *Antè*, p. 121 ; and Prehistoric Times, 2nd ed. p. 564.

abandoned the habit of cannibalism. Sha-gwaw-koo-sink, an Ottawwaw, who lived at the beginning of this century, first intro-duced the cultivation of corn among the Ojibbeways.[1] Moreover, there are certain facts which speak for themselves. Some of the American races cultivated the potato. Now, the potato is an American plant, and we have here, therefore, clear evidence of a step in advance made by these tribes. Again, the Peruvians had domesticated the llama. Those who believe in the diversity of species of men may endeavour to maintain that the Peruvians had domestic llamas from the beginning. Archbishop Whately, however, would not take this line. He would, I am sure, admit that the first settlers in Peru had no llamas, nor, indeed, any other domestic animal, excepting, probably, the dog. The bark-cloth of the Polynesians is another case in point. Another very strong case is the boomerang of the Australians. This weapon is known to no other race of men.[2] We cannot look on it as a relic of primeval civilisation, or it would not now be confined to one race only. The Australians cannot have learnt it from any civilised visitors, for the same reason. It is, therefore, as it seems to me, exactly the case we want, and a clear proof of a step in advance—a small one, in-deed, but still a step made by a people whom Archbishop Whately would certainly admit to be true savages. The Cherokees afford a remarkable instance of progress, and indeed—alone among the North American hunting races—have really become agriculturists. As long ago as 1825, with a population of 14,000, they possessed 2,923 ploughs, 7,683 horses, 22,500 black cattle, 46,700 pigs, and 2,566 sheep. They had 49 mills, 69 blacksmiths' shops, 762 looms, and 2,486 spinning-wheels. They kept slaves, having captured several hundred negroes in Carolina. Nay, one of them, a man of the name of Sequoyah, invented a system of letters, which, as far as the Cherokee language is concerned, is better than ours. Cherokee contains twelve consonants and five vowels, with a nasal sound 'ung.' Multiplying, then, the twelve consonants by the six vowels, and adding the vowels which occur singly, but omitting any sign for 'mung,' as that sound does not occur in Cherokee, he acquired seventy-seven cha-racters, to which he added eight—representing the sounds s, ka, hna, nah, ta, te, ti, tla—making, altogether, eighty-five characters. This alphabet, as already mentioned, is superior to ours. The characters are indeed more numerous, but, when once learnt, the pupil can read

[1] Tanner's Narrative, p. 180.   [2] With one doubtful exception.

at once. It is said that a boy can learn to read Cherokee, when thus expressed, in a few weeks; while, if ordinary letters were used, two years would be required. Obviously, however, this alphabet is not applicable to other languages. Again, the rude substitutes for writing found among various tribes—the wampum of the North American Indians, the picture-writing and quippu of Central America—must be regarded as of native origin. In the case of the system of letters invented by Mohammed Doalu, a negro of the Vei country, in West Africa, the idea was no doubt borrowed from the missionaries, although it was worked out independently. In other cases, however, I think this cannot be. Take the case of the Mexicans. Even if we suppose that they are descended from a primitively civilised race, and had gradually and completely lost both the use and tradition of letters—to my mind, a most improbable hypothesis—still we must look on their system of picture-writing as being of American origin. Even if a system of writing by letters could ever be altogether lost, which I doubt, it certainly could not be abandoned for that of picture-writing, which is inferior in every point of view. If the Mexicans had owed their civilisation, not to their own gradual improvement, but to the influence of some European visitors, driven by stress of weather or the pursuit of adventure on to their coasts, we should have found in their system of writing, and in other respects, unmistakable proofs of such an influence. Although, therefore, we have no historical proof that the civilisation of America was indigenous, we have in its very character evidence, perhaps more satisfactory, than any historical statements would be. The same argument may be derived from the names used for numbers by savages. I feel great difficulty in supposing that any race which had learned to count up to ten would ever unlearn a piece of knowledge so easy and yet so useful. Yet, as has been already pointed out, few, perhaps none, of those whom Archbishop Whately would call savages can count so far.

In many cases, where the system of numeration is at present somewhat more advanced, it bears on it the stamp of native and recent origin. Among civilised nations, the derivations of the numerals have long since been obscured by the gradual modification which time effects in all words—especially those in frequent use, and before the invention of printing. And if the numerals of savages were relics of a former civilisation, the waifs and strays saved out of the general wreck, they would certainly have suffered so much from the wear and tear of constant use, that their derivations would be obscured or wholly undiscoverable, instead of which they are often perfectly clear and obvious, especially among races whose arithmetical attain-ments are lowest.   These numerals, then, are recent, because they are uncorrupted; and they are indigenous, because they have an evi-dent meaning in the language of the tribes by whom they are used.[1]

Again, as I have already pointed out,[2] many savage languages are entirely deficient in such words as 'colour,' 'tone,' 'tree,' &c., having names for each kind of colour, every species of tree, but not for the general idea.   I can hardly imagine a nation losing such words, if it had once possessed them.

Other similar evidence might be extracted from the language of savages; and arguments of this nature are entitled to more weight than statements of travellers, as to the objects found in use among savages.   Suppose, for instance, that an early traveller mentioned the absence of some art or knowledge among a race visited by him, and that later ones found the natives in possession of it.   Most people would hesitate to receive this as a clear evidence of progress, and rather be disposed to suspect that later travellers, with perhaps better opportunities, had seen what their predecessors had overlooked. This is no hypothetical case.   The early Spanish writers assert that the inhabitants of the Ladrone Islands were ignorant of the use of fire.   Later travellers, on the contrary, find them perfectly well acquainted with it.   They have, therefore, almost unanimously assumed, not that the natives had made a step in advance, but that the Spaniards had made a mistake; and I have not brought this case forward in opposition to the assertions of Whately, because I am inclined to be of this opinion myself.   I refer to it here, however, as showing how difficult it would be to obtain satisfactory evidence of material progress among savages, even admitting that such exists. The arguments derived from language, however, are liable to no such suspicions, but tell their own tale, and leave us at liberty to draw our conclusions.

I will now very briefly refer to certain considerations which seem to show that even the most civilised races were once in a state of bar-barism.   Not only throughout Europe—not only in Italy and Greece —but even in the so-called cradle of civilisation itself, in Palestine, and Syria, in Egypt, and in India, the traces of a stone age have been

[1] See Chapter VIII. This argument would be conclusive were it not that new words are coined from time to time in all languages.   [2] Ch. VIII.

discovered.   It may, indeed, be said that these were only the fragments of those stone knives, &c., which we know were used in
religious ceremonies long after metal was in general use for secular
purposes.   This, indeed, resembles the attempt to account for the
presence of elephants' bones in England by supposing that they
were the remains of elephants which might have been brought over
by the Romans.   But why were stone knives used by the Egyptian
and Jewish priests? evidently because they had been at one time in
general use, and there was a feeling of respect which made them
reluctant to use the new substance in religious ceremonies.

There are, moreover, other considerations; for instance, the gradual
improvement in the relation between the sexes, and the development
of correct ideas on the subject of relationship, seem to me strongly
to point to the same conclusion.

In the publications of the Nova Scotian 'Institute of Natural
Science' is an interesting paper, by Mr. Haliburton, on 'The Unity
of the Human Race, proved by the universality of certain superstitions connected with sneezing.'   'Once establish,' he says, 'that
a large number of arbitrary customs—such as could not have
naturally suggested themselves to all men at all times—are universally observed, and we arrive at the conclusion that they are
primitive customs which have been inherited from a common source,
and, if inherited, that they owe their origin to an era anterior to the
dispersion of the human race.'   To justify such a conclusion, the
custom must be demonstrably arbitrary.   The belief that two and
two make four, the decimal system of numeration, and similar coincidences of course prove nothing; but I very much doubt the existence of any universal, or even general, custom of a clearly arbitrary
character.   The fact is, that many things appear to us arbitrary and
strange because we live in a condition so different from that in which
they originated.   Many things seem natural to a savage which to us
appear absurd and unaccountable.

Mr. Haliburton brings forward, as his strongest case, the habit of
saying 'God bless you!' or some equivalent expression, when a
person sneezes.   He shows that this custom, which, I admit, appears
to us at first sight both odd and arbitrary, is ancient and widely extended.   It is mentioned by Homer, Aristotle, Apuleius, Pliny, and
the Jewish rabbis, and has been observed in Koordistan, in Florida,
in Otaheite, and in the Tonga Islands.   It is not arbitrary, however,
and it does not, therefore, come under his rule.

A belief in invisible beings is very general among savages; and while they think it unnecessary to account for blessings, they attribute any misfortune to the ill-will of these mysterious beings. Many savages regard disease as a case of possession. In cases of illness, they do not suppose that the organs are themselves affected, but that they are being devoured by a god; hence their medicine-men do not try to cure the disease, but to extract the demon. Some tribes have a distinct deity for every ailment. The Australians do not believe in natural death. When a man dies, they take it for granted that he has been destroyed by witchcraft, and the only doubt is, who is.the culprit? Now, a people in this state of mind—and we know that almost every race of men is passing, or has passed, through this stage of development—seeing a man sneeze, would naturally, and almost inevitably, suppose that he was attacked and shaken by some invisible being; equally natural is the impulse to appeal for aid to some other invisible being more powerful than the first.

Mr. Haliburton admits that a sneeze is ' an omen of impending evil;' but it is more—it is evidence, which to the savage mind would seem conclusive, that the sneezer was possessed by some evil-disposed spirit; evidently, therefore, this case, on which Mr. Haliburton so much relies, is by no means an ' arbitrary custom,' and does not, therefore, fulfil the conditions which he himself laid down. He has incidentally brought forward some other instances, most of which labour under the disadvantage of proving too much. Thus, he instances the existence of a festival in honour of the dead, ' at or near the beginning of November.' Such a feast is very general; and as there are many more races holding such a festival than there are months in the year, it is evident that, in several cases, they must be held together. But Mr. Haliburton goes on to say : ' The Spaniards were very naturally surprised at finding that, while they were cele-brating a solemn mass for All Souls, on November 22, the heathen Peruvians were also holding their annual commemoration of the dead.' This curious coincidence would, however, not only prove the existence of such a festival, as he says, ' before the dispersion ' (which Mr. Haliburton evidently looks on as a definite event rather than as a gradual process), but also the ancestors of the Peruvians were at that epoch sufficiently advanced to form a calendar, and that their descendants were able to keep it unchanged down to the present time. This, however, we know was not the case. Again Mr. Haliburton says: ' The belief in Scotland and equatorial

Africa is found to be almost precisely identical respecting there being ghosts, even of the living, who are exceedingly troublesome and pugnacious, and can be sometimes killed by a silver bullet.' Here we certainly have what seems at first sight to be an arbitrary belief; but if it proves that there was a belief in ghosts of the living before the dispersion, it also proves that silver bullets were then in use. This illustration is, I think, a very interesting one; because it shows that similar ideas in distant countries owe their origin, not ' to an era before the dispersion of the human race,' but to the fundamental similarity of the human mind. While I do not believe that similar customs in different nations are ' inherited from a common source,' or are necessarily primitive, I certainly do see in them an argument for the unity of the human race, which, however (be it remarked), is not necessarily the same thing as the descent from a single pair.

On the other hand, I have attempted to show that ideas, which might at first sight appear arbitrary and unaccountable, arise naturally in very distinct nations as they arrive at a similar stage of progress; and it is necessary, therefore, to be extremely cautious in using such customs or ideas as implying any special connection between different races of men.

PART II.[1]

AT the Dundee Meeting of the British Association, I had the honour of reading a Paper ' On the Origin of Civilisation and the Primitive Condition of Man,' in answer to certain opinions and arguments brought forward by the late Archbishop of Dublin. The views therein advocated met with little opposition at the time. The then Presidents of the Ethnological and Anthropological Societies both expressed their concurrence in the conclusions to which I arrived; and the Memoir was printed *in extenso* by the Association. It has, however, subsequently been attacked at some length by the Duke of Argyll;[2] and as the Duke has in some cases strangely

[1] The substance of this was read before the British Association, during their meeting at Exeter in 1869.

[2] Good Words: March, April, May, and June, 1868. Also since republished in a separate form.

misunderstood me, and in others (I am sure unintentionally) misrepresented my views—as, moreover, the subject is one of great interest and importance—I am anxious to make some remarks in reply to his Grace's criticisms. The Duke has divided his work into four chapters:—I. Introduction; II. The Origin of Man; III. and IV. His Primitive Condition.

I did not in my first Memoir, nor do I now propose to, discuss the subjects dealt with in the first half of the Duke's ' Speculations.' I will only observe that in attacking Prof. Huxley for proposing to unite the Bimana and Quadrumana in one Order, ' Primates,' the Duke uses a dangerous argument; for if, on account of his great mental superiority over the Quadrumana, Man forms an Order or even Class by himself, it will be impossible any longer to regard all men as belonging to one species or even genus. The Duke is in error when he supposes that ' mental powers and instincts ' afford tests of easy application in other parts of the animal kingdom. On the contrary, genera with the most different mental powers and instincts are placed, not only in the same Order, but even in the same family. Thus our most learned hymenopterologist (Mr. Frederick Smith) classes the Hive-bee, the Humble-bee, and the parasitic Apathus, in the same subfamily of Apidæ. It seems to me, therefore, illogical to separate man zoologically from the other primates on the ground of his mental superiority, and yet to maintain the specific unity of the human race, notwithstanding the mental differences between different races of men.

I do not, however, propose to discuss the origin of man, and pass on therefore at once to the Duke's third chapter; and here I congratulate myself at the outset that the result of my paper has been to satisfy him that ' Whately's argument,[1] though strong at some points, is at others open to assault, and that, as a whole, the subject now requires to be differently handled, and regarded from a different point of view.' ' I do not, therefore,' he adds in a subsequent page,[2] ' agree with the late Archbishop of Dublin, that we are entitled to assume it as a fact that, as regards the mechanical arts, no savage race has ever raised itself.' And again: [3] 'The aid which man had from his Creator may possibly have been nothing more than the aid of a body and of a mind, so marvellously endowed, that thought was an instinct, and contrivance a necessity.'

---

[1] Good Words, 1868, p. 156.   [2] *Ibid*. June, p. 386.   [3] P. 392.

I feel, however, less satisfaction on this account than would otherwise have been the case, because it seems to me that, though the
Duke acknowledges the Archbishop's argument to be untenable,
he practically reproduces it with but a slight alteration and somewhat protected by obscurity. What Whately called 'instruction'
the Duke terms 'instinct;' and he considers that man had instincts
which afforded all that was necessary as a starting ground. He
admits, however, that monkeys use stones to break nuts; he might
have added that they throw sticks at intruders. But he says,
'between these rudiments of intellectual perception and the next
step (that of adapting and fashioning an instrument for a particular
purpose) there is a gulf in which lies the whole immeasurable distance between man and brutes.' I cannot agree with the Duke in
this opinion, nor indeed does he agree with himself, for he adds,
in the very same page, that—'The wielding of a stick is, in all
probability, an act equally of primitive intuition, and from this to
throwing of a stick, and the use of javelins, is an easy and natural
transition.'

He continues as follows:—'Simple as these acts are, they involve
both physical and mental powers which are capable of all the
developments which we see in the most advanced industrial arts.
These acts involve the instinctive idea of the constancy of natural
causes and the capacity of thought, which gives men the conviction
that what has happened under given conditions will, under the same
conditions, always occur again.' On these, he says, 'as well as on
other grounds, I have never attached much importance to Whately's
argument.' These are indeed important admissions, and amount to
a virtual abandonment of Whately's argument.

The Duke blames the Archbishop of Dublin for not having
defined the terms 'civilisation' and 'barbarism.' It seems to me
that Whately illustrated his meaning better by examples than he
could have done by any definition. The Duke does not seem to have
felt any practical difficulty from the omission; and it is remarkable that, after all, he himself omits to define the terms, thus being
himself guilty of the very omission for which he blames Whately. In
truth, it would be impossible in a few words to define the complex
organisation which we call civilisation, or to state in a few words
how a civilised differs from a barbarous people. Indeed, to define
civilisation as it should be, is surely as yet impossible, since
we are far indeed from having solved the problem how we may

best avail ourselves of our opportunities, and enjoy the beautiful world in which we live.

As regards barbarism, the Duke observes, ' All I desire to point out here is, that there is no necessary connection between a state of mere childhood in respect to knowledge and a state of utter barbarism, words which, if they have any definite meaning at all, imply the lowest moral as well as the lowest intellectual condition.' To every proposition in this remarkable sentence I entirely demur. There is, I think, a very intimate connection between knowledge and civilisation. Knowledge and barbarism cannot coexist—knowledge and civilisation are inseparable.

Again, the words ' utter barbarism ' have certainly a very definite signification, but as certainly, I think, not that which the Duke attributes to them. The lowest moral and the lowest intellectual condition are not only, in my opinion, not inseparable, they are not even compatible. Morality implies responsibility, and consequently intelligence. The lower animals are neither moral nor immoral. The lower races of men may be, and are, vicious; but allowances must be made for them. On the contrary (*corruptio optimi, pessima est*), the higher the mental power, the more splendid the intellectual endowment, the deeper is the moral degradation of him who wastes the one and abuses the other.

On the whole, the fair inference seems to be that savages are more innocent, and yet more criminal, than civilised races; they are by no means in the lowest possible moral condition, nor are they capable of the higher virtues.

In the first part of this paper I laid much stress on the fact that even in the most civilised nations we find traces of early barbarism. The Duke maintains, on the contrary, that these traces afford no proof, or even presumption, that barbarism was the primeval condition of man. He urges that all such customs may have been not primeval, but medieval ; and he continues: ' Yet this assumption runs through all Sir J. Lubbock's arguments. Wherever a brutal or savage custom prevails, it is regarded as a sample of the original condition of mankind. And this in the teeth of facts which prove that many of such customs, not only may have been, but must have been, the result of corruption.'

Fortunately, it is unnecessary for me to defend myself against this criticism, because in the very next sentence the Duke directly contradicts himself, and shows that I have not done that of which he accuses me. He continues his argument thus :—'Take cannibalism as one of these. Sir J. Lubbock seems to admit that this loathsome practice was not primeval.' Thus, by way of proof that I regard all brutal customs as primeval, he states, and correctly states, that I do not regard cannibalism as primeval. It would be difficult, I think, to find a more curious case of self-contradiction.

The Duke refers particularly to the practice of Bride-catching, which he states ' cannot possibly have been primeval.' He omits, however, to explain why not ; and of course, assuming the word ' primeval' to cover a period of some length, I am of opinion, in opposition to his Grace, that capture was the early form of marriage in our sense of the term. As the Duke correctly observes, I laid some stress on this custom, and am sorry that his Grace here meets me with a mere contradiction, instead of an argument. It may perhaps, however, be as well to state emphatically that all brutal customs are not, in my opinion, primeval. Human sacrifices, for instance, were, I think, certainly not so.

My argument, however, was that there is a definite sequence of habits and ideas; that certain customs (some brutal, others not so), which we find lingering on in civilised communities, are a page of past history, and tell a tale of former barbarism, rather on account of their simplicity than of their brutality, though many of them are brutal enough. Again, no one would go back from letter-writing to the use of the quippu or hieroglyphics ; no one would abandon the fire-drill and obtain fire by hand-friction.

Believing, as he does, that the primitive condition of man was one of civilisation, the Duke accounts for the existence of savages by the remark that they are ' mere outcasts of the human race,' descendants of weak tribes which were ' driven to the woods and rocks.' But until the historical period these ' mere outcasts' occupied almost the whole of North and South America, all Northern Europe, the greater part of Africa, the great continent of Australia, a large part of Asia, and the beautiful islands of the Pacific. Moreover, until modified by man the great continents were either in the condition of open plains, such as heaths, downs, prairies, and tundras, or they were mere ' woods and rocks.' Now everything tends to show that mere woods and rocks exercised on the whole a favourable influence. Inhabitants of great plains rarely rose beyond the pastoral stage. In America the most advanced civilisation was attained, not by the occupants of the fertile valleys, not along the banks of the Missis-

sippi or the Amazon, but among the rocks and woods of Mexico and
Peru.   Scotland itself is a brilliant proof that woods and rocks are
compatible with a high state of civilisation.

My idea of the manner in which, and the causes owing to which,
man spread over the earth, is very different from that of the Duke.
He evidently supposes that new countries have been occupied by
weaker races, driven there by more powerful tribes.   This I believe
to be an entirely erroneous notion.   Take for instance our own
island.   We are sometimes told that the Celts were driven by the
Saxons into Wales and Cornwall.   On the contrary, however, we
know that Wales and Cornwall were both occupied long before the
Saxons landed on our shores.   Even as regards the rest of the
country, it would not be correct to say that the Celts were driven
away ; they were either destroyed or absorbed.

The gradual extension of the human race has not in my opinion
been effected by force acting on any given race from without, but by
internal necessity, and the pressure of population; by peaceful, not
by hostile force; by prosperity, not by misfortune.   I believe that
of old, as now, founders of new colonies were men of energy and
enterprise; animated by hope and courage, not by fear and despair;
that they were, in short, anything but mere outcasts of the human
race.

The Duke relies a good deal on the case of America.   ' Is it not
true,' he asks, ' that the lowest and rudest tribes in the population of
the globe have been found at the furthest extremities of its great
continents, and in the distant islands which would be the last refuge
of the victims of violence and misfortune ?   " The New World" is
the continent which presents the most uninterrupted stretch of habi-
table land from the highest northern to the lowest southern latitude.
On the extreme north we have the Esquimaux, or Inuit race, maintaining human life under conditions of extremest hardship, even
amid the perpetual ice of the Polar Seas.   And what a life it is !
Watching at the blow-hole of a seal for many hours, in a tempera-
ture of 75° below freezing point, is the constant work of the Inuit
hunter.   And when at last his prey is struck, it is his luxury to feast
upon the raw blood and blubber.   To civilised man it is hardly
possible to conceive a life so wretched, and in many respects so
brutal as the life led by this race during the long lasting night of
the arctic winter.'

To this question, I confidently reply, No, it is not true ; it is not
true as a general proposition that the lowest races are found furthest

from the centres of continents; it is not true in the particular case of America. The natives of Brazil, possessing a country of almost unrivalled fertility, surrounded by the most luxuriant vegetation, watered by magnificent rivers, and abounding in animal life, were yet unquestionably lower than the Esquimaux,[1] whom the Duke pities and despises so much.[2] More, indeed, I think than the case requires. Our own sportsmen willingly undergo great hardships in pursuit of game; and hunting in reality possesses a keen zest which it can never attain when it is a mere sport.

'When we rise,' says Mr. Hill,[3] 'twice or thrice a day from a full meal, we cannot be in a right frame either of body or mind for the proper enjoyments of the chase. Our sluggish spirits then want the true incentive to action, which should be hunger, with the hope before us of filling a craving stomach. I could remember once before being for a long time dependent upon the gun for food, and feeling a touch of the charm of a savage life (for every condition of humanity has its good as well as its evil), but never till now did I fully comprehend the attachment of the sensitive, not drowsy Indian.'

Esquimaux life, indeed, as painted by our Arctic voyagers, is by no means so miserable as the Duke supposes. Capt. Parry, for instance, gives the following picture of an Esquimaux hut. ' In the few opportunities we had in putting their hospitality to the test we had every reason to be pleased with them. Both as to food and accommodation, the best they had were always at our service; and their attention both in kind and degree, was everything that hospitality and even good breeding could dictate. The kindly offices of drying and mending our clothes, cooking our provisions and thawing snow for our drink, were performed by the women with an obliging cheerfulness which we shall not easily forget, and which demanded its due share of our admiration and esteem. While thus their guest I have passed an evening not only with comfort, but with extreme gratification; for with the women working and singing, their husbands quietly mending their lines, the children playing before the door, and the pot boiling over the blaze of a cheerful lamp, one might

---

[1] See Martius, p. 77. Dr. Rae ranks the Esquimaux above the Red Indians, Trans. Ethn. Soc. 1866.

[2] When the Duke states that 'neither an agricultural nor pastoral life is possible on the borders of a frozen sea,' he forgot for the moment the inhabitants of Lapland and of Siberia.

[3] Travels in Siberia. vol. ii. p. 288.

well forget for the time that an Esquimaux hut was the scene of this
domestic comfort and tranquillity ; and I can safely affirm with Cart-
wright that, while thus lodged beneath their roof, I know no people
whom I would more confidently trust, as respects either my person
or my property, than the Esquimaux.'   Dr. Rae,[1] who had ample
means of judging, tells us that the Eastern Esquimaux 'are sober,
steady, and faithful. . . . . Provident of their own property and
careful of that of others when under their charge. . . . . Socially
they are a lively, cheerful, and chatty people, fond of associating with
each other and with strangers, with whom they soon become on
friendly terms, if kindly treated. . . . . In their domestic relations
they are exemplary.   The man is an obedient son, a good husband,
and a kind father. . . . . The children when young are docile. . .
The girls have their dolls, in making dresses and shoes for which
they amuse and employ themselves.   The boys have miniature
bows, arrows, and spears. . . . . When grown up they are dutiful
to their parents. . . . . Orphan children are readily adopted and
well cared for until they are able to provide for themselves.'   He
concludes by saying, ' the more I saw of the Esquimaux the higher
was the opinion I formed of them.'

Again, Hooper[2] thus describes a visit to an Asiatic Esquimaux
belonging to the Tuski race : ' Upon reaching Mooldooyah's habita-
tion, we found Captain Moore installed at his ease, with every pro-
vision made for comfort and convenience.   Water and venison were
suspended over the lamps in preparation for dinner ; skins nicely
arranged for couches, and the hangings raised to admit the cool air ;
our baggage was bestowed around us with care and in quiet, and we
were free to take our own way of enjoying such unobtrusive hospitality without a crowd of eager gazers watching us like lions at
feed ; nor were we troubled by importunate begging such as de-
tracted from the dignity of Metra's station, which was undoubtedly
high in the tribe.'

I know no sufficient reason for supposing that the Esquimaux were
ever more advanced than they are now.   The Duke indeed considers
that before they were ' driven by wars and migrations ' (a somewhat
curious expression) they 'may have been nomads living on their
flocks and herds ;' and he states broadly that ' the rigours of the
region they now inhabit have reduced this people to the condition in

---

[1] Trans. Eth. Soc. 1866, p. 138.   [2] The Tents of the Tuski, p. 102.

which we now see them ;' a conclusion for which I know no reason, particularly as the Tinné and other Indians living to the south of the Esquimaux are ruder and more barbarous.

It is my belief that the great continents were already occupied by a widespread, though sparse population, when man was no more advanced than the lowest savages of to-day ; and although I am far from believing that the various degrees of civilisation which now occur can be altogether accounted for by the external circumstances as they at present exist, still these circumstances seem to me to throw much light on the very different amount of progress which has been attained by different races.

In referring to the backwardness of the aboriginal Australians, I had observed that New Holland contained 'neither cereals nor any animals which could be domesticated with advantage,' upon which the Duke remarks that ' Sir John Lubbock urges in reply to Whately that the low condition of Australian savages affords no proof whatever that they could not raise themselves, because the materials of improvement are wanting in that country which affords no cereals, nor animals capable of useful domestication. But Sir J. Lubbock does not perceive that the same argument which shows how improvement could not possibly be attained, shows also how degradation could not possibly be avoided. If with the few resources of the country it was impossible for savages to rise, it follows that with those same resources it would be impossible for a half-civilised race not to fall. And as in this case again, unless we are to suppose a separate Adam and Eve for Van Diemen's Land, its natives must originally have come from countries where both corn and cattle were to be had, it follows that the low condition of these natives is much more likely to have been the result of degradation than of primeval barbarism.'

But my argument was that a half-civilised race would have brought other resources with them. The dog was, I think, certainly introduced into that country by man, who would have brought with him other animals also if he had possessed any. The same argument applies to plants ; the Polynesians carried the sweet potato and the yam, as well as the dog, with them from island to island ; and even if the first settlers in Australia happened to have been without them, and without the means of acquiring them, they would certainly have found some native plants which would have been worth the trouble of cultivation, if they had attained to the agricultural stage.

This argument applies with even more force to pottery; if the first settlers in Australia were acquainted with this art, I can see no reason why they should suddenly and completely have lost it.

The Duke, indeed, appears to maintain that though the natives of Van Diemen's Land (whom he evidently regards as belonging to the same race as the Australians and Polynesians, from both of which they are entirely distinct) ' must originally have come from countries where both corn and cattle were to be had,' still ' degradation could not possibly be avoided.' This seems to be the natural inference from the Duke's language, and suggests a very gloomy feature for our Australian fellow-countrymen. The position is, however, so manifestly untenable, when once put into plain language, that I think it unnecessary to dwell longer on this part of the subject. Even the Duke himself will hardly maintain that our colonists must fall back because the natives did not improve. Yet he extends and generalises this argument in a subsequent paragraph, saying, ' there is hardly a single fact quoted by Sir J. Lubbock in favour of his own theory, which when viewed in connection with the same indisputable principles, does not tell against that theory rather than in its favour.' So far from being 'indisputable,' the principle that when savages remained savages, civilised settlers must descend to the same level, appears to me entirely erroneous. On reading the above passage, however, I passed on with much interest to see which of my facts I had so strangely misread.

The great majority of facts connected with savage life have no perceptible bearing on the question, and I must therefore have been not only very stupid, but also singularly unfortunate, if of all those quoted by me in support of my argument there was ' hardly a single one,' which read aright was not merely irrelevant, but actually told against me. In support of his statement the Duke gives three illustrations, but it is remarkable that not one of these three cases was referred to by me in the present discussion, or in favour of my theory. If all the facts on which I relied told against me, it is curious that the Duke should not give an instance. The three illustrations which he quotes from my 'Prehistoric Times' seem to me irrelevant, but as the Duke thinks otherwise, and many may agree with him, it will be worth while to see how he uses them, and to enquire whether they give any real support to his argument.   As already mentioned, they are three in number.

' Sir J. Lubbock,' he says, ' reminds us that in a cave on the north-west coast (of Australia), tolerable figures of sharks, porpoises, turtles, lizards, canoes, and some quadrupeds, &c. were found, and yet that the present natives of the country where they were found were utterly incapable of realising the most artistic vivid representations, and ascribe the drawings in the cave to diabolical agency.'   This does not prove much, because the Australian tribes differ much in their artistic condition ; some of them still make rude drawings like those above described.

Secondly, he says, ' Sir J. Lubbock quotes the testimony of Cook, in respect to the Tasmanians, that they had no canoes.   Yet their ancestors could not have reached the island by walking on the sea.' This argument would equally prove that the kangaroo and the Echidna must have had civilised ancestors ; they inhabit both Australia and Tasmania, and it would have been impossible for *their* ancestors to have passed from the one to the other, ' by walking on the sea.'   The Duke, though admitting the antiquity of man, does not I think appreciate the geological changes which have taken place during the human period.

The only other case which he quotes is that of the highland Esquimaux who had no weapons nor any idea of war.   The Duke's comment is as follows.   ' No wonder, poor people ! They had been driven into regions where no stronger race could desire to follow them.   But that the fathers had once known what war and violence meant, there is no more conclusive proof than the dwelling place of their children.'   It is perhaps natural that the head of a great High-land Clan should regard with pity a people who having ' once known what war and violence meant,' have no longer any neighbours to pillage or to fight, but a lowlander can hardly be expected seriously to regard such a change as one calculated to excite pity, or as any evidence of degradation.

In my first paper I deduced an argument from the condition of reli-gion among the different races of man, a part of the subject which has since been admirably dealt with by Mr. Tylor in a lecture at the Royal Institution.   The use of flint for sacrificial purposes long after the introduction of metal, seemed to me a good case of what Mr. Tylor has aptly called ' Survival.'   So also is the method of obtaining fire. The brahman will not use ordinary fire for sacred purposes, he does not even obtain a fresh spark from flint and steel, but reverts to, or rather continues the old way of obtaining it by friction with a wooden drill, one brahman pulling the thong backwards and forwards while another watches to catch the sacred spark.

I also referred to the non-existence of religion among certain savage races, and as the Duke correctly observes, I argued that this was probably their primitive condition, because it is difficult to believe that a people which had once possessed a religion would ever entirely lose it.[1]

This argument filled the Duke with ' astonishment.' Surely, he says, ' if there is one fact more certain than another in respect to the nature of Man, it is that he is capable of losing religious knowledge, of ceasing to believe in religious truth, and of falling away from religious duty. If by " religion " is meant the existence merely of some impressions of powers invisible and supernatural, even this, we know, can not only be lost, but be scornfully disavowed by men who are highly civilised.' Yet in the very same page, the Duke goes on to say, ' the most cruel and savage customs in the world are the direct effect of its " religions." And if men could drop religions when they would, or if they could even form the wish to get rid of those which sit like a nightmare on their life, there would be many more nations without a " religion " than there are found to be. But religions can neither be put on nor cast off like garments, according to their utility, or according to their beauty, or according to their power of comforting.'

With this I entirely agree. Man can no more voluntarily abandon or change the articles of his religious creed than he can make one hair black or white, or add one cubit to his stature. I do not deny that there may be exceptional cases of intellectual men entirely devoid of religion ; but if the Duke means to say that men who are highly civilised, habitually or frequently lose, and scornfully disavow religion, I can only say that I should adopt such an opinion with difficulty and regret. There is, so far as I know, no evidence on record which would justify such an opinion, and as far as my private experience goes, I at least have met with no such tendency. It is indeed true that from the times of Socrates downwards, men in advance of their age have disavowed particular dogmas, and particular myths ; but the Duke of Argyll would, I am sure, not con-

---

[1] It is hardly necessary to explain to anyone that I did not intend to question the possibility of a change in, but a total loss of religion.

fuse a desire for reformation with the scornful disavowal of religion as a whole. Some philosophers may object to prayers for rain, but they are foremost in denouncing the folly of witchcraft; they may regard matter as aboriginal, but they would never suppose with the Redskin that land was created while water existed from the beginning; nor would anyone now suppose with the South-Sea Islanders that the Peerage were immortal, but not commoners. If, indeed, there is 'one fact more certain than another in respect to the nature of man,' I should have considered it to be the gradual diffusion of religious light, and of nobler conceptions as to the nature of God.

The lowest savages have no idea of a deity at all. Those slightly more advanced regard him as an enemy to be dreaded, but who may be resisted with a fair prospect of success, who may be cheated by the cunning and defied by the strong. Thus the natives of the Nicobar islands endeavour to terrify their deity by scarecrows, and the Negro beats his fetish if his prayers are not granted. As tribes advance in civilisation, their deities advance in dignity, but their power is still limited; one governs the sea, another the land; one reigns over the plains, another among the mountains. The most powerful are vindictive, cruel, and unjust. They require humiliating ceremonies and bloody sacrifices. But few races have arrived at the conception of an omnipotent and beneficent Deity.

Perhaps the lowest form of religion may be considered to be that presented by the Australians, which consists of a mere unreasoning belief in the existence of mysterious beings. The native who has in his sleep a nightmare, or a dream, does not doubt the reality of that which passes, and as the beings by whom he is visited in his sleep are unseen by his friends and relations, he regards them as invisible.

In Fetichism this feeling is more methodized. The Negro, by means of witchcraft, endeavours to make a slave of his deity. Thus Fetichism is almost the opposite of Religion; it stands towards it in the same relation as Alchemy to Chemistry, or Astrology to Astronomy; and shows how fundamentally our idea of a deity differs from that which presents itself to the savage. The Negro does not hesitate to punish a refractory Fetish, and hides it in his waistcloth if he does not wish it to know what is going on. Aladdin's lamp is, in fact, a well-known illustration of a Fetish.

A further stage, and the superiority of the higher deities is more fully recognised. Everything is worshipped indiscriminately—

animals, plants, and even inanimate objects.   In endeavouring to
account for the worship of animals, we must remember that names
are very frequently taken from them.   The children and followers
of a man called the Bear or the Lion would make that a tribal
name.   Hence the animal itself would be first respected, at last
worshipped.   This form of religion can be shown to have existed,
at one time or another, almost all over the world.

'The Totem,' says Schoolcraft, ' is a symbol of the name of the
progenitor,—generally some quadruped, or bird, or other object in
the animal kingdom, which stands, if we may so express it, as the
surname of the family. . It is always some animated object, and
seldom or never derived from the inanimate class of nature.   Its
significant importance is derived from the fact that individuals unhesitatingly trace their lineage from it.   By whatever names they
may be called during their life-time, it is the totem, and not their
personal name, that is recorded on the tomb or " adjedating " that
marks the place of burial.   Families are thus traced when expanded
into bands or tribes, the multiplication of which, in North America,
has been very great, and has decreased, in like ratio, the labours of
the ethnologist.'   Totemism, however, is by no means confined to
America.   In Central India ' the Moondah " Enidhi," or Oraon
" Minijrar," or Eel tribe, will not kill or eat that fish.   The Hawk,
Crow, or Heron tribes will not kill or eat those birds.   Livingstone,
quoted in Latham, tells us that the subtribes of Bitshaunas (or
Bechuanas) are similarly named after certain animals, and a tribe
never eats the animal from which it is named, using the term " ila,"
hate or dread, in reference to killing it.' [1]

Traces, indeed, of Totemism, more or less distinct, are widely
distributed, and often connected with marriage prohibitions.

As regards inanimate objects, we must remember that the savage
accounts for all action and movement by life ; hence a watch is to
him alive.   This being taken in conjunction with the feeling that
anything unusual is ' great medicine,' leads to the worship of any remarkable inanimate object.   Mr. Fergusson has recently attempted to
show the special prevalence of Tree and Serpent worship. He might,
I believe, have made out as strong a case for many other objects.
It seems clear that the objects worshipped in this stage are neither
to be regarded as emblems, nor are they personified.   Inanimate

---

[1] Trans. Ethnological Soc. N. S., vol. vi. p. 36.

objects have spirits as well as men; hence when the wives and slaves are sacrificed, the weapons also are broken in the grave, so that the spirits of the latter, as well as of the former, may accompany their master to the other world.

The gradually increasing power of chiefs and priests led to Anthropomorphism, with its sacrifices, temples, and priests, &c. To this stage belongs idolatry, which must by no means be regarded as the lowest state of religion. Solomon,[1] indeed, long ago pointed out how it was connected with monarchical power.

'Whom men could not honour in presence, because they dwelt far off, they took the counterfeit of his visage from far, and made an express image of a king, whom they honoured, to the end that by this, their forwardness, they might flatter him that was absent, as if he were present.

' Also the singular diligence of the artificer did help to set forward the ignorant to more superstition.

' For he, peradventure willing to please one in authority, forced all his skill to make the resemblance of the best fashion.

' And so the multitude, allured by the grace of the work, took him now for a God, which a little before was but honoured as a man.'

The worship of principles may be regarded as a still further stage in the natural development of religion.

It is important to observe that each stage of religion is superimposed on the preceding, and that bygone beliefs linger on among the children and the ignorant. Thus witchcraft is still believed in by the ignorant, and fairy tales flourish in the nursery.

It certainly appears to me that the gradual development of religious ideas among the lower races of men is a fair argument in opposition to the view that savages are degenerate descendants of civilised ancestors. Archbishop Whately would admit the connexion between these different phases of religious belief but I think he would find it very difficult to show any process of natural degradation and decay which could explain the quaint errors and opinions of the lower races of men, or to account for the lingering belief in witchcraft, and other absurdities, &c., in civilised races, excepting by some such train of reasoning as that which I have endeavoured to sketch.

[1] Wisdom, xiv. 17.

There is another case in this memoir wherein the Duke, although generally a fair opponent, brings forward an unsupportable accusation. He criticises severely the 'Four Ages,' generally admitted by archæologists, especially referring to the terms 'Palæolithic' and 'Neolithic,' which are used to denote the two earlier.

I have no wish to take to myself in particular the blame which the Duke impartially extends to archæologists in general, but having suggested the two terms in question, I will simply place side by side the passage in which they first appeared, and the Duke's criticism, and confidently ask whether there is any foundation for the sweeping accusation made by the noble Duke.

The Duke says: 'For here I must observe that Archæologists are using language on this subject which, if not positively erroneous, requires, at least, more rigorous definitions and limitations of meaning than they are disposed to attend to. They talk of an Old Stone Age (Palæolithic), and of a Newer Stone Age (Neolithic), and of a Bronze Age, and of an Iron Age. Now, there is no proof whatever that such Ages ever existed in the world. It may be true, and it probably is true, that most nations in the progress of the Arts have passed through the stages of using stone for implements before they were acquainted with the use of metals. Even this, however, may not be true of all nations. In Africa there appear to be no traces of any time when the natives were not acquainted with the use of iron, and I am informed by Sir Samuel Baker that iron ore is so common in Africa, and of a

My words, in proposing the terms, were as follows:—

'From the careful study of the remains which have come down to us, it would appear that the prehistoric archæology may be divided into four great epochs.

'Firstly, that of Drift, when man shared the possession of Europe with the Mammoth, the cave-bear, the woolly-haired rhinoceros and other extinct animals. This we may call the "Palæolithic" period.

'Secondly, the later or polished Stone Age; a period characterized by beautiful weapons and instruments made of flint and other kinds of stone, in which, however, we find no trace of the knowledge of any metal, excepting gold, which seems to have been sometimes used for ornaments. This we may call the Neolithic period.

'Thirdly, the Bronze Age, in which bronze was used for arms and cutting instruments of all kinds.

kind so easily reducible by heat, and its use might well be discovered by the rudest tribes, who were in the habit of lighting fires. Then again it is to be remembered that there are some countries in the world where stone is as rare and difficult to get as metals.

'The great alluvial plains of Mesopotamia are a case in point. Accordingly we know from the remains of the first Chaldean monarchy that a very high civilisation in the arts of agriculture and of commerce coexisted with the use of stone implements of a very rude character. This fact proves that rude stone implements are not necessarily any proof whatever of a really barbarous condition. And even if it were true that the use of stone has in all cases preceded the use of metals, it is quite certain that the same age which was an Age of Stone in one part of the world was an Age of Metal in the other. As regards the Eskimo and the South Sea islanders, we are now, or were very recently, living in a Stone Age.'

'Fourthly, the Iron Age, in which that metal had superseded bronze for arms, axes, knives, &c.; bronze, however, still being in common use for ornaments, and frequently also for the handles of swords and other arms, but never for the blades.

'Stone weapons, however, of many kinds were still in use during the Age of Bronze, and even during that of Iron. So that the mere presence of a few stone implements is not in itself sufficient evidence that any given "find" belongs to the Stone Age.

'In order to prevent misapprehension, it may be as well to state at once, that I only apply this classification to Europe, though in all probability it might also be extended to the neighbouring parts of Asia and Africa. As regards other civilised countries, China and Japan for instance, we, as yet, know nothing of their prehistoric archæology. It is evident, also, that some nations, such as the Fuegians, Andamaners, &c., are even now only in an Age of Stone.'

I cannot, of course, on this occasion repeat the arguments adduced in my first memoir. I will, however, now bring forward one or two additional reasons in support of my view. There is a considerable body of evidence tending to show that the offspring produced by crossing different varieties tends to revert to the type from which these varieties are descended. Thus Tegetmeier states that 'a cross between two non-sitting varieties (of the common fowl) almost invariably produces a mongrel that becomes broody, and sits with remarkable steadiness.' Mr. Darwin gives several cases in which such hybrids or mongrels are singularly wild and untameable, the mule being a familiar instance. Messrs. Boitard and Corbié state that, when they crossed certain breeds of pigeons, they invariably get some young ones coloured like the wild *C. livia.* Mr. Darwin repeated these experiments, and found the statement fully confirmed.

So again the same is the case with fowls. Tens of thousands of the Black Spanish and the white silk fowls might be bred without a single red feather appearing, yet Mr. Darwin found that on crossing them he immediately obtained specimens with red feathers. Similar results have been obtained with ducks, rabbits, and cattle. Mules also have not unfrequently barred legs. It is unnecessary to give these cases in detail, because Mr. Darwin's work on ' Animals and Plants under Domestication ' is in the hands of every naturalist.

Applying the same test to man, Mr. Darwin observes that crossed races of men are singularly savage and degraded. ' Many years ago,' he says, ' I was struck by the fact that in South America men of complicated descent between Negroes, Indians, and Spaniards, seldom had, whatever the cause might be, a good expression. Livingstone remarks that " it is unaccountable why half-castes are so much more cruel than the Portuguese, but such is undoubtedly the case." A native remarked to Livingstone " God made white men, and God made black men, but the devil made half-castes !" When two races, both low in the scale, are crossed, the progeny seems to be eminently bad. Thus the noble-hearted Humboldt, who felt none of that prejudice against the inferior races now so current in England, speaks in strong terms of the bad and savage disposition of Zambas, or half-castes between Indians and Negroes, and this conclusion has been arrived at by various observers. From these facts we may perhaps infer that the degraded state of so many half-castes is in part due to reversion to a primitive and savage condition, induced by the act of crossing, as well as to the unfavourable moral conditions under which they generally exist.'

I confess, however, that I am not sure how far this may not he accounted for by the unfortunate circumstances in which half-breeds are generally placed. The half-breeds between the Hudson's Bay Company's servants and the native women, being well treated and looked after, appear to be a creditable and well-behaved set.[1]

---

[1] Dunn's ' Oregon Territory,' p. 147.

I would also call particular attention to the remarkable similarity between the mental characteristics of savages and those of children. 'The Abipones,' says Dobritzhoffer,[1] ' when they are unable to com prehend anything at first sight, soon grow weary of examining it, and cry ' orqueenàm ?' what is it after all ? Sometimes the Guaranies, when completely puzzled, knit their brows and cry " tupâ oiquaà," God knows what it is. Since they possess such small reasoning powers, and have so little inclination to exert them, it is no wonder that they are neither able nor willing to argue one thing from another.'

Richardson says of the Dogrib Indians, ' that however high the reward they expected to receive on reaching their destination, they could not be depended on to carry letters. A slight difficulty, the prospect of a banquet on venison, or a sudden impulse to visit some friend, were sufficient to turn them aside for an indefinite length of time.'[2] Le Vaillant[3] also observes of the Namaquas, that they closely resembled children in their great curiosity.

M. Bourien,[4] speaking of the wild tribes in the Malayan Peninsula, says that an ' inconstant humour, fickle and erratic, together with a mixture of fear, timidity, and diffidence, lies at the bottom of their character, they seem always to think that they would be better in any other place than in the one they occupy at the time. Like children, their actions seem to be rarely guided by reflection, and they almost always act impulsively.' The tears of the South-Sea Islanders, ' like those of children, were always ready to express any passion that was strongly excited, and, like those of children, they also appeared to be forgotten as soon as shed.'[5]

At Tahiti Captain Cook mentions that Oberea, the Queen, and Tootahah, one of the principal chiefs, amused themselves with two large dolls. D'Urville tells us that a New Zealand chief, Tauvarya by name, ' cried like a child because the sailors spoilt his favourite cloak by powdering it with flour.'[6] Williams[7] mentions that in Feejee not only the women, but even the men give vent to their feelings by crying. Burton even says that among East Africans the men cried more frequently than the women.[8]

Not only do savages closely resemble children in their general

[1] His. of the Abipones, vol. ii. p. 59.
[2] Arctic Expedition, vol. ii. p. 23.
[3] Travels in Africa, 1776, vol. iii. p. 12.
[4] Trans, Ethn. Soc. N. S. vol. iii. p. 78.
[5] Cook's first Voyage, p. 103.
[6] Vol. ii. p. 398. See also ' Yate's New Zealand,' p. 101.
[7] Fiji and the Fijians, vol. ii. p. 121.
[8] Lake Regions, p. 332.

character, but a curious similarity exists between them in many small points. For instance, the tendency to reduplication, which is so characteristic of children, prevails remarkably also amongst savages. The first 1000 words in Richardson's dictionary (down to allege), contain only three, namely, adscititious, adventitious, agitator, and even in these it is reduced to a minimum. There is not a single word like *ahi ahi*, evening; *ake ake*, eternal; *aki aki*, a bird; *aniwaniwa*, the rainbow; *anga anga*, agreement; *angi angi*, aboard; *aro aro*, in front; *aruaru*, to woo; *ati ati*, to drive out; *awa awa*, a valley; or *awanga wanga*, hope, words of a class which abound in savage languages.

The first 1000 words in a French dictionary I found to contain only two reduplications, namely, anana and assassin, both of which are derived from a lower race, and cannot, strictly speaking, be regarded as French.

Again 1000 German words, taking for variety the letters C and D, contain six cases, namely, *Cacadu* (Cockatoo), *cacao, cocon* (cocoon), *cocosbaum*, a cocao tree, *cocosnuss*, cocao nut, and *dagegen*, of which again all but the last are foreign.

Lastly, the first 1000 Greek words contained only two reduplications, one of which is ἀβαρβαρος.

For comparison with the above I have examined the vocabularies of seventeen savage tribes, and the results are given in the following Table :—

Languages	Number of words	Number of redu- plications	Propor- tion per mil.	
Europe.				
English . . .	1000	3	3	
French . . .	1000	2	2	Both foreign.
German . . .	1000	6	6	All but one foreign.
Greek . . .	1000	2	2	One being ἀβαρβαρος.
Africa.				
Beetjuan . .	188	7	37	Lichtenstein.
Bosjesman . .	129	5	38	,,
Namaqua Hottentot	1000	75	75	H. Tindall.
Mpongwe . .	1264	70	60	Snowden and Prall.
Fulup . . .	204	28	137	Koelle.
Mbofon . .	267	27	100	,,
America.				
Darien Indians .	184	13	70	Trans. Eth. Soc. vol. vi.
Ojibwa . . .	283	21	74	Schoolcraft.
Tupy (Brazil) . .	1000	66	66	Gonsalvez Dias.
Negroid.				
Brumer Island .	214	37	170	M'Gillivray.
Redscar Bay . .	125	10	80	,,
Louisiade . .	138	22	160	,,
Erroob . . .	513	23	45	Jukes.
Lewis Murray Island	506	19	38	,,
Australia.				
Kowrarega . .	720	26	36	M'Gillivray.
Polynesia.				
Tonga . . .	1000	166	166	Mariner.
New Zealand . .	1300	220	169	Dieffenbach.

For African languages I have examined the Beetjuan and Bos-jesman dialects, given by Lichtenstein in his 'Travels in Southern Africa;' the Namaqua Hottentot, as given by Tindall in his 'Grammar and Vocabulary of the Namaqua Hottentot;' the Me-pongwe of the Gaboon, from the Grammar of the Mpongwe language published by Snowden and Prall of New York; and lastly the Fulup and Mbofon languages from Koelle's 'Polyglotta Africana.' For America, the Ojibwa vocabulary, given in Schoolcraft's 'Indian Tribes;' the Darien vocabulary, from the 6th vol. N. S. of the Ethnological Society's Transactions; and the Tupy vocabulary, given in A. Gonsalves Dias's 'Diccionaria da Lingua Tupy chamada lingua geral dos indigenas do Brazil.' To these I have added the languages spoke on Brumer Island, at Redscar Bay, Kowrarega, and at the Louisiade, as collected by M'Gillivray in the 'Voyage of the Rattlesnake;' and the dialects of Erroob and Lewis Murray Island, from Jukes's 'Voyage of the Fly.' Lastly, for Polynesia, the

Tongan dictionary given by Mariner, and that of New Zealand by Dieffenbach.

The result is, that while in the four European languages we get about two reduplications in 1000 words, in the savage ones the number varies from thirty-eight to 170, being from twenty to eighty times as many in proportion.

In the Polynesian and Feejee Islands they are particularly numerous; thus, in Feejee, such names as Somosomo, Raki raki, Raviravi, Luma-luma are numerous. Perhaps the most familiar New Zealand words are meremere, patoo patoo, and kivi kivi. So generally, however, is reduplication a characteristic of savage tongues that it even gave rise to the term 'barbarous.'

The love of pets is very strongly developed among savages. Many instances have been given by Mr. Galton in his Memoir on the 'Domestication of Animals.' [1]

Among minor indications may be mentioned the use of the rattle. Originally a sacred and mysterious instrument, as it is still among some of the Siberian Red-skin and Brazilian [2] tribes, it has with us degenerated into a child's toy. Thus Dobritzhoffer tells us, the Abipones at a certain season of the year worshipped the Pleiads. The ceremony consisted in a feast accompanied with dancing and music, accompanied with praises of the stars, during which the principal priestess ' who conducts the festive ceremonies, dances at intervals, rattling a gourd full of hardish fruit-seeds to musical time, and whirling round to the right with one foot, and to the left with another, without ever removing from one spot, or in the least varying her motions.' [3] Spix and Martius [4] thus describe a Coroado chief : —' In the middle of the assembly, and nearest to the pot, stood the chief, who, by his strength, cunning, and courage, had obtained some command over them, and had received from Marlier the title of Captain. In his right hand he held the maracá, the above-mentioned castanet, which they call gringerina, and rattled with it, beating time with his right foot.' ' The Congo Negroes had a great wooden rattle, upon which they took their oaths.' [5] The rattle also

[1] Trans. Ethn. Soc. vol. iii. p. 122.

[2] Martius, Von dem Rectszustand. Ur. Brasiliens, p. 34.

[3] Dobritzhoffer, vol. ii. p. 65. See also p. 72.

[4] Travels in Brazil. London, 1824, vol. ii. p. 234.

[5] Astley's Coll. of Voyages, vol. iii. p. 233.

is very important among the Indians of North America.[1] When any person is sick, the sorcerer or medicine-man brings his sacred rattle and shakes it over him. This, says Prescott, ' is the principal catholicon for all diseases.' Catlin [2] also describes the 'rattle' as being of great importance. Some tribes have a sacred drum, closely resembling that of the Lapps.[3] When an Indian is ill, the magician, says Carver,[4] 'sits by the patient day and night, rattling in his ears a gourd-shell filled with dried beans, called a chichiconé.'

Klemm [5] also remarks on the great significance attached to the rattle throughout America, and Staad even thought that it was worshipped as a divinity.[6]

Schoolcraft [7] also gives a figure of Oshkabaiwis, the Redskin medical chief, ' holding in his hand the magic rattle,' which is indeed the usual emblem of authority in the American pictographs. I know no case of a savage infant using the rattle as a plaything.

Tossing halfpence, as dice, again, which used to be a sacred and solemn mode of consulting the oracles, is now a mere game for children.

So again the doll is a hybrid between the baby and the fetish, and exhibiting the contradictory characters of its parents, becomes singularly unintelligible to grown-up people. Mr. Tylor has pointed out other illustrations of this argument, and I would refer those who feel interested in this part of the subject to his excellent work.

Dancing is another case in point. With us it is a mere amusement. Among savages it is an important and, in some cases, religious ceremony. 'If,' says Robertson, [8] ' any intercourse be necessary between two American tribes, the ambassadors of the one approach in a solemn dance, and present the calumet or emblem of peace ; the sachems of the other receive it with the same ceremony. If war is denounced against an enemy, it is by a dance, expressive of the resentment which they feel, and of the vengeance which they meditate. If the wrath of their gods is to be appeased, or their beneficence to be celebrated, if they rejoice at the birth of a child, or mourn the death of a friend, they have dances appropriated to each

---

[1] Prescott in Schoolcraft's 'Indian Tribes,' vol. ii. pp. 179, 180.

[2] American Indians, vol. i. pp. 39, 40, 163, &c.

[3] Catlin, l. c. p. 40.

[4] Travels, p. 385.

[5] Culturgéchichte, vol. ii. p. 172.

[6] Mœurs des Sauvages Américains, vol. ii. p. 297.

[7] Indian Tribes, pt. iii. pp. 490-492.

[8] Robertson's America, bk. iv. p. 133.

of these situations, and suited to the different sentiments with which they are then animated. If a person is indisposed, a dance is prescribed as the most effectual means of restoring him to health : and if he himself cannot endure the fatigue of such an exercise, the physician or conjuror performs it in his name, as if the virtue of his activity could be transferred to his patient.'

But it is unnecessary to multiply illustrations. Every one who has read much on the subject will admit the truth of the statement. It explains the capricious treatment which so many white men have received from savage potentates; how they have been alternately petted and illtreated, at one time loaded with the best of everything, at another neglected or put to death.

The close resemblance existing in ideas, language, habits, and character between savages and children, though generally admitted, has usually been disposed of in a passing sentence, and regarded rather as a curious accident than as an important truth. Yet from several points of view it possesses a high interest. Better understood, it might have saved us many national misfortunes, from the loss of Captain Cook down to the Abyssinian war. It has also a direct bearing on the present discussion.

The opinion is rapidly gaining ground among naturalists, that the development of the individual is an epitome of that of the species, a conclusion which, if fully borne out, will evidently prove most instructive. Already many facts are on record which render it, to say the least, highly probable. Birds of the same genus, or of closely allied genera, which, when mature, differ much in colour, are often very similar when young. The young of the Lion and the Puma are often striped, and fœtal whales have teeth. Leidy has shown that the milk-teeth of the genus *Equus* resemble the permanent teeth of *Anchitherium*, while the milk-teeth of *Anchitherium* again approximate to the dental system of *Merychippus*.[1] Rutimeyer, while calling attention to this interesting observation, adds that the milk-teeth of *Equus caballus* in the same way, and still more those of *E. fossilis*, resemble the permanent teeth of *Hipparion*.[2]

Agassiz, according to Darwin, regards it as a 'law of nature,' that the young states of each species and group resemble older forms of the same group; and Darwin himself says,[3] that ' in two or more

[1] Proc. Acad. Nat. Soc. Philadelphia, 1858, p. 26.
[2] Beitrage zur kenntniss der fossilen
Pferde. Basle, 1863.
[3] Origin of Species, 4th edition
p. 532.

groups of animals, however much they may at first differ from each other in structure and habits, if they pass through closely similar embryonic stages, we may feel almost assured that they have descended from the same parent form, and are therefore closely related.' So also Mr. Herbert Spencer says,[1] 'Each organism exhibits within a short space of time, a series of changes which, when supposed to occupy a period indefinitely great, and to go on in various ways instead of one way, gives us a tolerably clear conception of organic evolution in general.'

It may be said that this argument involves the acceptance of the Darwinian hypothesis ; this would, however, be a mistake; the objection might indeed be tenable if men belonged to different species, but it cannot fairly be urged by those who regard all mankind as descended from common ancestors; and, in fact, it is strongly held by Agassiz, one of Mr. Darwin's most uncompromising opponents. Regarded from this point of view, the similarity existing between savages and children assumes a singular importance and becomes almost conclusive as regards the question now at issue.

The Duke ends his work with the expression of a belief that man, 'even in his most civilised condition, is capable of degradation, that his knowledge may decay, and that his religion may be lost.' That this is true of individuals, I do not of course deny ; that it holds good with the human race, I cannot believe.[2] Far more true, far more noble, as it seems to me, are the concluding passages of Lord Dunraven's opening address to the Cambrian Archæological Association, 'that if we look back through the entire period of the past history of man, as exhibited in the result of archæological investigation, we can scarcely fail to perceive that the whole exhibits one grand scheme of progression, which, notwithstanding partial periods of decline, has for its end the ever-increasing civilisation of man, and the gradual development of his higher faculties, and for its

---

[1] Principles of Biology, vol. i. p. 349.

[2] The Duke appears to consider that the first men, though deficient in knowledge of the mechanical arts, were morally and intellectually superior, or at least equal, to those of the present day ; and it is remarkable that supporting such a view he should regard himself as a champion of orthodoxy. Adam is represented to us in Genesis not only as naked, and subsequently clothed with leaves, but as unable to resist the most trivial temptation, and as entertaining very gross and anthropomorphic conceptions of the Deity. In fact in all three characteristics—in his mode of life, in his moral condition, and in his intellectual conceptions—Adam was a typical Savage.

object the continual manipulation of the design, the power, the wisdom, and the goodness of Almighty God.'

I confess therefore that, after giving the arguments of the Duke of Argyll my most attentive and candid consideration, I see no reason to adopt his melancholy conclusion, but I remain persuaded that the past history of man has, on the whole, been one of progress, and that, in looking forward to the future, we are justified in doing so with confidence and with hope.

NOTES.

Page 52.

Position of Women in Australia.[1]

' Fœminæ sese per totam pene vitam prostituunt. Apud plurimas tribus juventutem utriusque sexus sine discrimine concumbere in usus est. Si juvenis forte indigenorum cœtum quendam in castris manentem adveniat, ubi quævis sit puella innupta, mos est: nocte veniente et cubantibus omnibus, illam ex loco exsurgere et juvenem accidentem cum illo per noctem manere unde in sedem propriam ante diem redit. Cui fœmina sit, eam amicis libenter præbet; si in itinere sit, uxori in castris manenti aliquis supplet illi vires. Advenis ex longinquo accedentibus fœminas ad tempus dare hospitis esse boni judicatur. Viduis et fœminis jam senescentibus sæpe in id traditis, quandoque etiam invitis et insciis cognatis, adolescentes utuntur. Puellæ teneræ a decimo primùm anno, et pueri a decimo tertio vel quarto, inter se miscentur. Senioribus mos est, si forte gentium plurium castra appropinquant, viros noctu hinc inde transeuntes, uxoribus alienis uti et in sua castra ex utraque parte mane redire.

' Temporibus quinetiam certis, machina quædam ex ligno ad formam ovi facta, sacra et mystica, nam fœminas aspicere haud licitum, decem plus minus uncias longa et circa quatuor lata, insculpta ac figuris diversis ornata, et ultimam perforata partem ad longam (plerumque e crinibus humanis textam) inserendam chordam cui nomen " Moo yumkarr," extra castra in gyrum versata, stridore magno e percusso ære facto, libertatem coeundi juventuti esse tum concessam omnibus indicat. Parentes sæpe infantum, viri uxorum quæstum corporum faciunt. In urbe Adelaide panis præmio parvi aut paucorum denariorum meretrices fieri eas libenter cogunt. Facile potest

---

[1] Eyre's *Discoveries*, &c., ii. 320.

intelligi, amorem inter nuptos vix posse esse grandem, quum omnia
quæ ad fœminas attinent, hominum arbitrio ordinentur et tanta
sexuum societati laxitas, et adolescentes quibus ita multæ ardoris
explendi dantur occasiones, haud magnopere uxores, nisi ut servos
desideraturos.'

PAGE 66.

Adoption.

' Adjiciendum et hoc, quod post evectionem ad Deos, Juno, Jovis
suasu, filium sibi Herculem adoptavit, et omne deinceps tempus
materna ipsum benevolentia complexa fuerit. Illam adoptionem
hoc modo factam perhibent: Juno lectum ingressa, Herculem
corpori suo admotum, ut verum imitaretur partum, subter vestes
ad terram demisit. Quem in hoc usque tempus adoptionis ritum
barbari observant.'[1]

PAGE 87.

Expiation for Marriage.

Mela[2] tells us that among the Auziles, another Æthiopian tribe,
' Feminis solemne est, nocte, qua nubunt, omnium stupro patere,
qui cum munere advenerint: et tum, cum plurimis concubuisse,
maximum decus ; in reliquum pudicitia insignis est.'

Speaking of the Nasamonians, Herodotus observes :

πρῶτον δὲ γαμέοντος Νασαμῶνος ἀνδρὸς, νόμος ἐστὶ τὴν νύμφην
νυκτὶ τῇ πρώτῃ διὰ πάντων διεξελθεῖν τῶν δαιτυμόνων μισγομένην· τῶν
δὲ ὡς ἕκαστός οἱ μιχθῇ, διδοῖ δῶρον τὸ ἂν ἔχῃ φερόμενος ἐξ οἴκου.[3]

Diodorus[4] also gives a very similar account of marriage in the
Balearic Islands.

The passage in St. Augustin is as follows :

' Sed quid hoc dicam, cum ibi sit et Priapus nimius masculus,
super cujus immanissimum et turpissimum fascinum sedere nova
nupta jubeatur, more honestissimo et religiosissimo matronarum.'[5]

Lastly, in his description of Babylonian customs, Herodotus says :[6]

Ο δὲ δὴ αἴσχιστος τῶν νόμων ἐστὶ τοῖσι Βαβυλωνίοισι ὅδε· δεῖ

---

[1] Diodorus, iv. 39.   [2] Mela, i. 8.   [3] Melpomene, iv. 172.
[4] Diodorus, v. 18.   [5] Civit. Dei, vi. 9.   [6] Clio, 1. 199.

πᾶσαν γυναῖκα ἐπιχωρίην ἰζομένην ἐς ἱρὸν Ἀφροδίτης, ἅπαξ ἐν τῇ ζόῃ
μιχθῆναι ἀνδρὶ ξείνῳ. Πολλαὶ δὲ καὶ οὐκ ἀξιεύμεναι ἀναμίσγεσθαι
τῇσι ἄλλῃσι, οἷα πλούτῳ ὑπερφρονέουσαι, ἐπὶ ζευγέων ἐν καμάρῃσι
ἐλάσασαι, πρὸς τὸ ἱρὸν ἑστᾶσι· θεραπηΐη δέ σφι ὄπισθεν ἕπεται πολλή.
αἱ δὲ πλεῦνες ποιεῦσι ὧδε· ἐν τεμένεϊ Ἀφροδίτης κατέαται στέφανον
περὶ τῇσι κεφαλῇσι ἔχουσαι θώμιγγος, πολλαὶ γυναῖκες· αἱ μὲν γὰρ
προσέρχονται, αἱ δὲ ἀπέρχονται· σχοινοτενέες δὲ διέξοδοι πάντα τρόπον
ὁσαιῶν ἔχουσι διὰ τῶν γυναικῶν, δι᾽ ὧν οἱ ξεῖνοι διεξιόντες ἐκλέγονται.
ἔνθα ἐπεὰν ἵζηται γυνή, οὐ πρότερον ἀπαλλάσσεται ἐς τὰ οἰκία, ἤ τίς
οἱ ξείνων ἀργύριον ἐμβαλὼν ἐς τὰ γούνατα μιχθῇ ἔξω τοῦ ἱροῦ·
ἐμβαλόντα δὲ δεῖ εἰπεῖν τοσόνδε· ‘ἐπικαλέω τοι τὴν θεὸν Μύλιττα·’
Μύλιττα δὲ καλέουσι τὴν Ἀφροδίτην Ἀσσύριοι· τὸ δὲ ἀργύριον μέγαθός
ἐστι ὁσονῶν· οὐ γὰρ μὴ ἀπώσηται· οὐ γάρ οἱ θέμις ἐστί· γίνεται γὰρ
ἱρὸν τοῦτο τὸ ἀργύριον· τῷ δὲ πρώτῳ ἐμβαλόντι ἕπεται, οὐδὲ ἀποδο-
κιμᾷ οὐδένα· ἐπεὰν δὲ μιχθῇ, ἀποσιωσαμένη τῇ θεῷ ἀπαλλάσσεται ἐς
τὰ οἰκία, καὶ τὠπὸ τούτου οὐκ οὕτω μέγα τί οἱ δώσεις· ὥς μιν λάμψεαι.
ὅσαι μέν νυν εἴδεός τε ἐπαμμέναι εἰσὶ καὶ μεγάθεος, ταχὺ ἀπαλλάσ-
σονται· ὅσαι δὲ ἄμορφοι αὐτέων εἰσί, χρόνον πολλὸν προσμένουσι
οὐ δυνάμεναι τὸν νόμον ἐκπλῆσαι· καὶ γὰρ τριέτεα καὶ τετραέτεα
μετεξέτεραι χρόνον μένουσι. ἐνιαχῇ δὲ καὶ τῆς Κύπρου ἐστὶ παραπλήσιος
τούτῳ νόμος.

INDEX.